D1499470

SUPERFILMS

An International Guide
to Award-Winning
Educational Films

by

Salvatore J. Parlato, Jr.

The Scarecrow Press, Inc.
Metuchen, N.J.   1976

Library of Congress Cataloging in Publication Data

Parlato, Salvatore J   1931-
  Superfilms.

  Includes index.
  1. Moving-picture--Catalogs. 2. Moving-pictures in
education. I. Title.
LB1044.Z9P35   011   76-10801
ISBN 0-8108-0953-2

Dedicated to

the movers and the makers

TABLE OF CONTENTS

PREFACE

The purpose of this book is to provide a starting point for the selection of better than average films. As such, this directory is quality-oriented--the only known attempt to identify superior films on a large scale. Elsewhere are found lists of films rated "best" for certain clientele, or within specific age groups, or about definite subjects. Such lists, however, have two limiting characteristics: 1) they are too narrow in scope, rarely exceeding 100-200 titles; and 2) the criteria for selection are totally subjective, usually the opinion of one person or (at best) a local or similarly inbred claque of self-ordained authorities. By contrast, Superfilms encompasses almost 1,500 productions on every imaginable subject. And each film described in Superfilms has been rated by evaluators who, however uneven in expertise, are strengthened in their credibility by the very diversity of their composition, by the public nature of the festivals, and by the on-going (usually annual) nature of their operations. By providing this data, by offering this support, Superfilms hopes to prove itself a pivotal, new, and indispensable force in the programming and utilization of educational films.

The structure of this guide is designed to be as functional as possible. For example, Section III is a straight alphabetical list of descriptions of all films entered. There is no duplication of titles, and all descriptions are based on or originate from producers' notes, edited down for brevity and clarity.

Section II, the heart of this book, is the topical or subject index. Its range, while not encyclopedic, is more comprehensive than may at first appear, for, in the interest of streamlining the process of browsing and of pinpoint-searches, the broadest possible categories were used. Most of those categories are fairly familiar ones; those that aren't, are self-explanatory, e.g., Women's Studies, Crime and Punishment, The Generation Gap.

Section IV alphabetically itemizes each of the festivals, events, and competitions, along with the name or level of awards, the full name or initials of the festival, and the location (if known).

Section VI lists the sales and rental sources of the distributors of these films, giving exact addresses for zip-coded ease of correspondence and ordering.

For those who are interested in figures, the number of festivals listed totals 255. For others who are curious about comparative statistics most of these festivals are American, as might be expected. Still, because locales range all the way from Ann Arbor to Zagreb, the scope of the awards is international. Of interest is the fact that after the USA, the runner-up host to film exhibits is Italy. Next in line are the British Isles, Spain and Canada. Other frequent festival sites are France, Argentina, West Germany, Australia, the Netherlands, and Japan. Japan is the only one of the non-Western nations to whose scrutiny Western materials are regularly subjected, which prevents the media field from claiming truly international perspective. Iran, with its annual Tehran convocation, may well prove to be the bridge to inter-cultural communication between East and West. After all, how universal can films claim to be unless they enjoy frequent, formal, and full display within India and the People's Republic of China? Those geographic giants alone account for one-third of the earth's population and, besides, are proportionately ahead of us in their film viewing habits and film-making activities. Although the Asian wall remains to be cracked, a curtain has been lifted in Eastern Europe, as evidenced by broad participation in screenings sponsored by the Communist states of Czechoslovakia, Yugoslavia, East Germany, Poland, Bulgaria, and the U.S.S.R. itself. Film-sharing is idea-sharing, and such exchanges are welcome signs of a trend in the direction of better political understanding among economic systems, among governments, and ... more important ... among people.

INTRODUCTION

"No artist--however objective--can accept any criticism (no matter how gentle) without feeling some resentment ... regardless how little." With that paraphrase as our premise, is the inverse also true? In other words, creative people crave praise and, in all but the most transparently flattering amounts, they'll accept compliments without too much question or suspicion. That's what made the compilation of Superfilms such a pleasure: every film here is a winner. Every entry listed is here because of honors received, quality proclaimed, or prizes conferred. And, what makes these selections easier to accept: they are the result of impartial group decisions. These entries are not drawn from my (or anyone else's) personal list of favorites. Nor are they the projection of some "authority's" judgment or interpretation of what makes good films good. Individual opinion--anyone's opinion--is too unreliable as a yardstick for quality.

I've been on just enough film juries to know, first hand, how violently people can differ on any given film or even any scene of a film. How can film viewing change us so? Colleagues we respected as sharers of our own high taste, perception, and sophistication suddenly turn out, under the light of the projector, to be sadly unobservant, incredibly old-fashioned, or surprisingly naive. Are we talking about the same film? Were we looking at the same film? Well, friendships somehow survive such tests and contests but, unfortunately, some good films don't. Even when subjected to the process of "groupthink," good films can undeservingly fail to make the honor roll, for want of unanimous approval. These same films often go on to reap huge rewards (if not awards) in the form of commercial acceptance and critical praise where it counts--with film users and film buyers. Equally ironic is the fate of the gem of a film that runs away with festival honors ... straight into a stone wall of buyer boycott long after the novelty has worn thin or after being shown, under normal conditions, to more practical audiences than critics. In short, there is no predictable way to measure intrinsic quality or to guarantee acceptability of any commodity--especially such a dynamic and subjective product, whose very essence is based on movement and change at the rate of 24 scenes per second.

So, where are we in our quest for the best? Doesn't the above reasoning bring us right back to where we started? In our search for better films, in other words, can we trust neither individuals nor groups? My answer is this: without personally seeing a film for ourselves, we have no choice but to trust group decisions more than any other single judgment. We have no alternative. Outside of personal previews, what other basis do we have for ranking a film, sight unseen? Consider the options:

Advertisements: the best of any advertising is, by definition and by its very nature, biased;

Evaluations: a film critic or reviewer is just that: one individual person whose tastes or preferences are no more reliable than yours;

Colleagues: the same limitation applies to trusted colleagues: even they represent only a relatively narrow-gauge spectrum of personal insights, and have biases of their own.

In the long haul ahead, with the great quantities of films growing larger every day, and in the face of conflicting claims for and clamor against specific materials, how else can film programmers start to select better films from the embarrassment of riches already available? I stress the word "start," because this directory is just that--a starting point, not the last word. Let me also emphasize the quantities involved or, better yet, let's work with a measurable set of numbers. Based on my own fairly meticulous tabulations, there are about 21,000 to 24,000 non-theatrical 16mm films currently on the market. (That 3,000-film difference may depend on the semantics behind the terms "non-theatrical" or "educational".) Even the lower of these two figures--even half of either figure--would be enough to intimidate many film bookers from further inquiry. Faced with such a myriad of materials, potential 16mm users are likely to give up altogether. Even veteran film buyers and film buffs have guessed wrong when ordering blind. Or they've confused similar-sounding titles. Or they've forgotten production data. Or overlooked age-level limitations.

What about the film companies themselves as criteria of quality? Aren't there real differences in quality between producers? The answer is, of course, yes; there are substantial differences in quality and style and price and service and personalities. And that's exactly where that criterion fails us. We all have our partialities toward people as well as productions, but none of us could survive professionally if we depended on a few favorites. Besides, we know how widely product quality can vary, even within subject areas within a company. And what about the new, small, or specialized film-makers we haven't been exposed to? Relying on the tried and true can bury us in programs that are trite and true ... which is the unforgivable sin of film selection: needless repetition of popular themes or films. There are many good film sources at our disposal now; to draw on only a few is self-defeating. Some of the smaller distributors have surprisingly large numbers of award-winning productions--too many to ignore.

There's another reason for choosing from award-winners: just entering a film into competitive showing is a vote of confidence on the part of the film-maker who (don't forget) is also a business person. Though entry fees are relatively low, producer/business-person types don't practice the exercise of wasting money, even for the sake of vanity or the pride of ownership. Then, too, there's professional ego. Film-makers want to put their "best footage forward," especially before an audience of prospective customers and fellow photographers. Better not to enter into comparative screenings, if your product is obviously inferior. If it is inferior, better to withhold your film from public comparison; nobody welcomes criticism. Faith is one thing; naiveté is another. And if festival entry suggests confidence in one's craft, then recognition reflects justification. Winning is achievement. This line of reasoning has its qualifications, though, because just as there are differences in film-makers, there are differences in film festivals. Festivals differ in professionalism, criteria, fees, and the number and level of honors offered. Some events are easier than others, and try to accommodate as many entrants as possible so that candidates will have something to show for their time, trouble, and fee. Then, there are other festivals that, because of their prestige and standards, are almost too selective and, in their process of elimination, unavoidably reject or overlook many excellent candidates.

Just as there are differences in companies, in colleges, in libraries, and in schools, there are differences in film festivals, too. Then how distinguish good festivals from bad? Answer: in the same way we distinguish good from bad in our choice of schools, libraries, colleges, and companies: by comparison. Compare the films you know are good. Compare them in relation to festivals that honor them. Do the same with motion pictures you feel aren't so good. Do they show up as winners at the same, old, friendly film fairs year after year? If so, then that fact becomes part of your input for decision--and suspicion. The main points hold up, though: by combining your own standards with those of an outside group, you <u>can</u> arrive at valid conclusions about what's right for your program, for your audience, and for you. Is there any other way? Yes, there is another way of personally endorsing every film you schedule for others' usage: you can view each and every one of the 21,000-24,000 films mentioned above. At an average of 17-1/2 minutes each (not counting rewind time), that little task would consume 3-3 1/2 years. The only trouble is that within that period, there'd be another 5,400-6,300 new films released that you'd somehow have to: 1) disregard; 2) pay someone else to evaluate; or 3) check for in the next edition of <u>Superfilms</u>.

PART I

SUBJECT INDEX CATEGORIES

ACUPUNCTURE
ADOLESCENCE
AERONAUTICS
AFRICA
AGRICULTURE
ALCOHOLISM
ANIMALS
ANTHROPOLOGY
ARCHITECTURE
ART
ASIA
AUSTRALIA
BIOGRAPHY
BIOLOGY
BIRDS
BLACK STUDIES
CANADA
CAREERS
CHEMISTRY
CHILDREN'S STORIES
COMMUNICATION
CONFORMITY
CONSUMERISM
CRAFTS
CREATIVITY
CRIME & PUNISHMENT
DANCE
DISCOVERY & EXPLORATION

DISCUSSION
DRUGS
EARTH SCIENCE
ECONOMICS
ENERGY
ESKIMO LIFE
EUROPE
EVOLUTION
EXPRESSION
FAMILY LIFE
FILM TECHNIQUES
FISHING
FUTURE STUDIES
GARDENING
GENERATION GAP
GOVERNMENT
HANDICAPPED
HEALTH
HISTORY - UNITED STATES
HISTORY - WORLD
HOLIDAYS
HUMAN RELATIONS
HUMOR
INDIA
ISLANDS
ISRAEL
LABOR RELATIONS
LATIN AMERICA

1

LIFE & DEATH
LITERATURE
MAN & WOMAN
MANAGEMENT
MATHEMATICS
MENTAL HEALTH
MEXICO
MIDDLE EAST
MINORITIES
MUSIC
NATURE
NON-VERBAL FILMS
NUTRITION
OCEANOGRAPHY
OLD AGE
PANTOMIME
PHOTOGRAPHY
PHYSICS
POETRY
POLITICS
POLLUTION
PSYCHOLOGY
QUALITY OF LIFE
RACE RELATIONS
READING AND LANGUAGE
  DEVELOPMENT
RELIGION
RIVERS
RUSSIA
SAFETY
SCIENCE (GENERAL)
SCIENTIFIC METHOD
SCULPTURE
SEASONS
SEX EDUCATION
SOCIAL PROTEST

SOLAR SYSTEM
SPIRITUALISM
SPORTS & RECREATION
TEACHING
THEATRE
TRANSPORTATION
TV PROGRAMMING
THE UNREAL
URBAN LIVING
VALUES
VENEREAL DISEASE
VISUAL LITERACY
WAR & PEACE
WOMEN'S STUDIES

PART II

TOPICAL INDEX OF FILM TITLES

ACUPUNCTURE

Acupuncture: An Exploration
Report on Acupuncture

ADOLESCENCE

Adolescence
Cry Help!
Day That Sang & Cried
Frank Film
Genevieve
Girls at 12
Nobody Waved Goodbye
Place In The Sun
Sixteen in Webster Groves
Skater Dater
Summerplay
Teen Scene
This Child Is Rated X

AERONAUTICS

Acceleration
Bird of Prey
First Aid for Air Crew
Flight
Freedom in Flight
Monument to the Dream
Perception of Orientation

AFRICA

Africa Is My Home
African Elephant
African Girl ... Malobi
Aurum
Cheetah

Come Back, Africa
Dr. Leakey and the Dawn of Man
Ethiopia: Hidden Empire
Golden Transvaal
Katutura
Kifaru: Black Rhinoceros
Lake Wilderness
Miss Goodall & the Wild Chim-
    panzees
Nigeria ... Problems of Nation
    Building
Nzuri: East Africa
River People of Chad
Rivers of Sand
Sahara - La Caravane du Sel
South Africa's Animal Kingdom

AGRICULTURE

And Who Shall Feed This Land
Country Vet
Decision at Delano
Farm Boy of Hungary
Farm Village of India
Hindu Village Boy
India and Her Food Problem
Indian Summer
Japanese Farmers
Maple Sugar Farmer
Navajo Girl
New Life for a Spanish Farmer
Rice Farmers in Thailand
Scarecrow

ALCOHOLISM

Alcoholism: Model of Drug De-
    pendency
America on the Rocks

3

4 / Superfilms

Fifth Street
On the Bowery
To Your Health
Us

ANIMALS

African Elephant
Ali and his Baby Camel
Animal Movie
Apryl and Her Baby Lamb
Bighorn (10 Min.)
Bighorn! (26 min.)
Birth of the Red Kangaroo
Buffalo: Ecological Success
   Story
Caterpillar and the Wild Animals
Cheetah
Corral
Country Vet
Cow
Death of a Legend
Dogs, Cats & Rabbits
Farmyard Babies
Forest Fisherman: Story of an
   Otter
Grizzly!
Grizzly Bear
Horses
How Beaver Stole Fire
Jacky Visits the Zoo
Kangaroos - Part One, Biography
Kangaroos - Part Two, Varieties
Kifaru: Black Rhinoceros
Me and You, Kangaroo
Miguelin
Miss Goodall & and Wild Chim-
   panzees
Perils of Priscilla
Poetry for Fun: Poems about
   Animals
Ponies
Shepherd
South Africa's Animal Kingdom
Spotty: Story of a Fawn
Thoroughbred
What Is a Cat?
Where Should a Squirrel Live?
White Mane
World of the Beaver
Zebras

ANTHROPOLOGY

Ancient Egyptian
Ancient Peruvian
Angotee
At the Time of Whaling
Bali Today
Bayanihan
Cajititlan
Children of Fogo Island
Desert People
Digging for the History of Man
Dr. Leakey and the Dawn of
   Man
Island Observed
Journey to Chinale
Land Divers of Melanesia
Land of the Long Day, Part II
Man Hunters
Primitive Man in a Modern
   World
Tassili N'Ajjer
Winds of Fogo

ARCHITECTURE

Antonio Gaudi
Capitol: Chronicle of Freedom
City Out of Time
Cosmopolis/Big City 2000 A.D.
Future for the Past
Gallery Down Under
Hectorologie
It Couldn't Be Done
Jefferson's Monticello
Mathematics of the Honeycomb
Monument to the Dream
Nubia 64
Of Picks, Shovels & Words
Opus
Peru: Inca Heritage
Sydney Opera House
Time and Place
Venice Be Damned

ART

Ancient Egyptian
Animation Pie
Art Is ...

ASIA

Report on Acupuncture
Rice Farmers in Thailand
Seacoast Villages of Japan
Southern Asia - Problems of
    Transition
Stones of Eden
Tibetan Traders (revised)
Tokyo - The 51st Volcano
Vesak

AUSTRALIA

Bullocky
Country Jazz
Desert People
Eighteen Footer
Everything Under the Sun
Gallery Down Under
I'm Going to School Today
Kangaroos - Part I, Biography
Kangaroos - Part II, Varieties
The Line Across Australia
Paddington Lace
Question of Attitude
Shades of Puffing Billy
Sheltered Workshops
Sports Medicine
Story of the Southern Cross
Style of Champions
Swimmer
Sydney Opera House
Tempo - Australia in the
    Seventies
Time and Place
Where the Pelican Builds Her
    Nest

BIOGRAPHY

Abraham Lincoln: Background
Angry Prophet: Frederick Douglass
Antonia
Autumn: Frost Country
Balzac
Beethoven and His Music
Beethoven: Ordeal & Triumph
Benjamin Franklin
Bethune
Boyhood of Abraham Lincoln
Boyhood of George Washington
Boyhood of Thomas Edison

Christ Is Born
Cortez and the Legend
D. H. Lawrence in Taos
Dancing Prophet
Days of Dylan Thomas
The Dreamer That Remains
e. e. cummings: The Making
    of a Poet
Edgar Allan Poe: Background
    for his Works
El Greco
Eleanor Roosevelt Story
Frederick Douglass: House on
    Cedar Hill
George Washington
Golda Meir
Helen Keller
Hurdler
Imogen Cunningham, Photogra-
    pher
James Dickey: Poet
James Monroe
James Weldon Johnson
Jefferson's Monticello
John Paul Jones
Journey of Robert F. Kennedy
Kennedy: What Is Remembered
    is Never Lost
Legacy of a Dream
Leo Beuerman
Leonardo da Vinci: Man of
    Mystery
Lonely Boy
Lover's Quarrel with the World
Meet George Washington
My Childhood
Picasso Is 90
Robert E. Lee: Background
    Study
Saul Alinsky Went to War
Story of Dr. Lister
Story of My Life: Hans Chris-
    tian Andersen
This is Edward Steichen
Thomas Jefferson
The Titan, Story of Michelangelo
Walt Whitman: Poet For a New
    Age
World of Carl Sandburg
World of Enrico Fermi

BIOLOGY

Adaptation of Insects
Adaptations of Plants & Animals
Aggregation of Dissociated
  Sponge Cells
Alone in the Midst of the Land
Beginning of Life
Bighorn! (26 min.)
Biography of a Bee
Birth of the Red Kangaroo
Buffalo: Ecological Success
  Story
CBW: Secrets of Secrecy
Carnivorous Plants
Cave Ecology
Cell: A Functioning Structure,
  Part I
Darwin's Galapagos Today
Development of the Chick Em-
  bryo
Drop of Water
Ecology of a Hot Spring
Egg Into Animal - Sea Horse
Embryonic Development of the
  Chick
Embryonic Development of the
  Fish
Fish Embryo
Fish: Master of Movement
Forest: Trees and Logs
Genetics
Grassland Ecology
Hidden World: Study of Insects
High Arctic Biome
Honeybee: A Social Insect
Human Body: Circulatory Sys-
  tem
Human Body: Digestive System
Human Body: Reproductive Sys-
  tem
Instincts of an Insect
Lakes - Aging & Pollution
Life Cycle of a Parasitic Flat-
  worm
Life Cycle of the Wasp
Liverwort: Alternation of
  Generations
Mayfly: Ecology of an Aquatic
  Insect
Mitosis
Pond
Populations

Private Life of the Kingfisher
Secret in the Hive
Snails
Species Specific Sorting
Story of the Blood Stream
Strange Partners
To Catch a Meal
Top of the World: Taiga,
  Tundra & Ice Cap

BIRDS

Bird of Prey
Bird Who is a Clown
Birds of Our Storybooks
Blind Bird
Canada Goose
Canada Goose Adventure
Five Colorful Birds (3rd Edit.)
Flurina
Great White Pelican
Kingfisher
Land of the Loon
Lost Pigeon
Pelican Island
Robin
Sounds of Nature
Where the Pelican Builds Her
  Nest
White Throat
Wild Wings
Winged World
Woodpecker Gets Ready for Winter

BLACK STUDIES

Africa Is My Home
Angry Prophet: Frederick
  Douglass
Attica
Black Roots
Blue Dashiki
Children in the City
Come Back, Africa
The Creation
Frame-Up!
Frederick Douglass: House on
  Cedar Hill
Holidays ... Hollow Days
The Hurdler
Immigrant from America

Inside the World of Jesse Allen
James Weldon Johnson
Legacy of a Dream
Negro Kingdoms of Africa's
    Golden Age
Oh, Freedom!
Peary and Henson: North to the
    Pole
Right On, Be Free
Rivers of Sand
The Slave Experience
Slavery and Slave Resistance
Under the Black Mask
Why the Sun and the Moon Live
    in the Sky

CANADA

Age of the Beaver
Best Damn Fiddler From Cala-
    bogie to Kaladar
Canada: Take It From the Top
Enduring Wilderness
Gold
Hutterites
In Search of the Bowhead Whale
Island Eden
The Kid From Canada
Land of the Loon
Manouane River Lumberjacks
Morning on the Lièvre
Paddle to the Sea
Quebec in Silence
Railroaders
Tour en l'Air

CAREERS

After High School - What?
All My Babies
Anything You Want to Be
Bob & Caren & Ted & Janice
Career & Costume Circus
Careers: Communications
Careers: Health Services
Careers: Leisure Industries
Country Vet
Cry for Help
Fire
Hamburger Sandwich
Information Explosion

Intern: A Long Year
Machine in Between
Making It in the World of Work
Manouane River Lumberjacks
Merchant to the Millions
Night People's Day
People Shop
The Road
Silent Drum
To Be Somebody
To Seek...To Teach...To Heal
Yankee Craftsman

CHEMISTRY

CBW: Secrets of Secrecy
Cell: A Functioning Structure,
    Pt. I
Handling Dangerous Chemicals:
    Acids
International Atom
Isotopes in Action
Magic Molecule

CHILDREN'S STORIES

Alexander & the Car with the
    Missing Headlight
Ali and His Baby Camel
Andy and the Lion
Apryl and Her Baby Lamb
As Long as the Grass Is Green
Balloon Tree
Big Red Barn
Bird Who Is a Clown
Blind Bird
Blow, Wind, Blow!
Canada Goose Adventure
Caterpillar
Caterpillar and the Wild Ani-
    mals
Chairmaker and the Boys
Changing of the Guard
The Chicken
Circus Town
Clue of the Missing Ape
Cockaboody
Conrad, Josie and the Zoom-
    erang
Crosstown Adventure
Dog and the Diamonds

Dorothy and the Pop Singer
Driscoll's Donkey
Drummer Hoff
Fable
False Note
Firefly Named Torchy
Flutterbye
Flurina
Follow Mr. Willoughby
Foolish Frog
For the Love of Fred
Fox Went Out on a Chilly Night
Francine, George and the Ferry-
    boat
Frederick
Frog Prince
The Gift
Go Kart Go
Goldilocks and the Three Bears
Greenhouse
Half-Masted Schooner
Happy Owls
Haunted House
Hoarder
Horses
How Beaver Stole Fire
How Death Came to Earth
"J. T."
Jacky Visits the Zoo
Joanjo: A Portuguese Tale
Johnny Appleseed: Legend of
    Frontier Life
The Kid From Canada
Legend of the Magic Knives
Lentil
Leopold, The See-Through
    Crumbpicker
Little Girl & a Gunny Wolf
Little Joys, Little Sorrows
Little Mariner
Little Red Hen
Little Red Lighthouse
Lost Pigeon
Martin & Gaston
Me and You, Kangaroo
Miguelin
Mystery on Bird Island
Naica and the Squirrels
Navajo Girl
Niko - Boy of Greece
Owl and the Lemming
Paddle To the Sea
Patrick

Paul Bunyan
Perils of Priscilla
Piccolo
Popcorn Lady
Pulcinella
Rainy Day Story
Red Balloon
Red Kite
Rescue Squad
River Boy
Rocket to Nowhere
Rosie's Walk
Sandman
Shepherd
Skinny and Fatty
Snowman
Sorcerer's Apprentice
Spotty: Story of a Fawn
Steadfast Tin Soldier
Stolen Necklace
Stolen Plans
Stone Soup
The Stonecutter
Story About Ping
Strange Story of a Frog Who
    Became a Prince
String Bean
Sunday Lark
The Thinking Book
Tommy, Suzie and the Card-
    board Box
Town Musicians
Uppity Albert McGuire
Why the Sun and the Moon Live
    in the Sky
Winkie, the Merry-Go-Round
    Horse
Winter of the Witch
Zebras

CITIES OF THE WORLD

A Valparaiso
City Out of Time
Jerusalem & Its Contributions
Jerusalem...Center of Many
    Worlds
London of Wm. Hogarth
Paris 1900
Pompeii: Once There Was a
    City
Rhythms of Paris

Tokyo: 51st Volcano
Venice Be Damned
Vivaldi's Venice

COMMUNICATIONS

Berfunkle
Bob Knowlton Story
Breakthrough to Language
Case History of a Rumor
Cockaboody
Communicating Successfully
Deaf Child Speaks
Debt to the Past: Language &
   Communication
Faces and Fortunes
The Great Gamble: Cyrus W.
   Field
Introduction to Holography
Language of the Bee
Laser Beam
Little Island
Love is for the Birds
Machine in Between
Microphone Speaking
Reaching Your Reader
Reporting & Explaining
Spires/Ballots Report
To Speak or Not to Speak
Trouble with Words
Words and Music

CONFORMITY

Adventures of *
Assembly Line
Blake
Boring Afternoon
Bullocky
Cages
Claude
Conformity
Don Quixote (vs. the System)
Flatland
Girls at 12
Greater Community Animal
Man Who Had to Sing
Master Kiteman
Mr. Grey
MROFNOC
Old Order Amish

Passing Days
Refiner's Fire
Sixteen in Webster Groves
Stop in the Marshlands
Summerplay
The Swing
To Speak or Not to Speak
Up Is Down

CONSUMERISM

Bunco Boys - And How to Beat
   Them!
Eat, Drink, and Be Wary
Just Sign Here
Matter of Fat
Why Do You Buy?

CRAFTS

Ancient Peruvian
At Your Fingertips - Boxes
At Your Fingertips - Grasses
Aurum
Basket Builder
Batik
Birch Canoe Builder
Chairmaker & the Boys
Clay (Origin of the Species)
Crayon
Creative Hands
Faces & Fortunes
Glass
Hand and Clay: A Celebration
India: Crafts & Craftsmen
Japanese Calligraphy
Kaleidoscope Orissa
Macramé
Magic Molecule
Masuo Ikeda: Printmaker
Music Rack
Navajo Silversmith
Paper Construction
Papier-Mache
People Might Laugh At Us
Posters
Prints
Reflections
Scraps
Stitchery
Story of a Craftsman

Vera Paints Ibiza in the Sun
Weaving
Windows
Woodblock Printer
Yankee Craftsman

CREATIVITY

An Actor Works
Creative Hands
Hello, Up There
Kinetic Sculpture of H. Barlow
Koestler on Creativity
La Linea
Rainy Day Story
Reach Out
Up Is Down
Why Man Creates

CRIME & PUNISHMENT

Attica
Dark Corner of Justice
Fall River Legend
Frame-up!
Holidays ... Hollow Days
Insiders
Law & Order
No Lies
Punishment Fits the Crime
Some Are More Equal than
    Others
Storm Over the Supreme Court
    Part I: 1790-1932
Storm Over the Supreme Court
    Part II: 1933-Present
This Child Is Rated X
Voices Inside

DANCE

Adolescence
Art Is ...
Ballerina
Ballet Girl
Bayanihan
Dance Squared
Dancing Prophet
Danze Cromatiche
Degas Dancers

Fall River Legend
Hopi Kachinas
Looking for Me
Matrioska
Opus Op
Pas de Deux
Plisetskaya Dances
Reflections in Space
Right On, Be Free
Shango
Tondo: A Round About A Round
Tour en l'Air
Two Ballet Birds
Witch Doctor

DISCOVERY & EXPLORATION

Abyss
Age of Exploration
Age of Exploration & Expansion
Age of the Beaver
Americans on Everest
Down to the Sea in Ships
Island Observed
Journey to the Outer Limits
Octopus Hunt
Peary & Henson: North to the
    Pole
Quest
Robert Scott & the Race for the
    South Pole
The Search for the Nile (series)
Solo

DISCUSSION

And Who Shall Feed This World?
The Audition
Beauty Knows No Pain
Betty Tells Her Story
The Box
But What if the Dream Comes
    True?
Can We Immunize Against
    Prejudice?
Chronology
Cosmic Zoom
The Daisy
Day that Sang and Cried
The Doodle Film
Essay On War

Exchanges
Faces
Fashion: The Second Skin
Follow Mr. Willoughby
Forces Make Forms
Free Fall
Genesis (Macmillan)
Genetics: Man the Creator
The Hand
How Do You Feel?
Is It Always Right to be Right?
Lady or the Tiger?
Lemonade Stand: What's Fair?
Like Other People
Lost Pigeon
Mammals
Master Kiteman
Meaning of Patriotism
Mexican or American?
Multiple Man
Mystery of Time
One Man's Opinion
Power and Wheels
President of the U. S. : Too
    Much Power?
Primitive Man in a Modern
    World
The Question
Refiner's Fire
Shooting Gallery
Tobacco Problem
Toys
Trumpet for the Combo
Tup Tup
Unanswered Question
Voter Decides
What is Life?
What Will Christy Do?

DRUGS

Acid (LSD)
Alcoholism: Model of Drug De-
    pendency
Allure of Drugs
Almost Everyone Does
Busted
Drugs Are Like That
11:59 Last Minute to Choose
Gale Is Dead
Grooving
Jump!

No Expectations
Not Me
Not the Giant ... Nor the Dwarf
Scag (Heroin)
Trip to Nowhere
Ultimate Trip
Ups /Downs
Us

EARTH SCIENCE

Aging of Lakes
Barrier Beach
City that Waits to Die
Continental Drift
Continents Adrift
Fire in the Sea
Fire Mountain
Geology of Yellowstone Park
Geyser Valley
Gold
Heartbeat of a Volcano
Krakatoa
Nahanni
Not-So-Solid Earth
Origins of Weather
Reflections on Time
Season of Fire
Understanding our Earth: Soil
Ways of Water
Who Killed Lake Erie?

ECONOMICS

Asian Earth
Bank Called Freedom
Close-up on Fire
Gold
Great Depression: A Human
    Diary
Harold & Cynthia
Hunger (La Faim)
Merchant to the Millions
Mr. Europe & the Common
    Market
Mountain People
Parkinson's Law
Scarecrow
Tobacco Problem
Who Killed the Sale?
Why Do You Buy?

EDUCATION

American Super 8 Revolution
Animation Goes to School
Bing, Bang, Boom
Breakthrough to Language
Cheating
Child Behavior - You
Childhood: Enchanted Years
Children Who Draw
Danny and Nicky
Deaf Child Speaks
Eternal Children
Eyes of a Child
Fireman is Sad and Cries
Focus on Ability
Give Us the Children
Helen Keller
Hello, Up There
How's School, Enrique?
I'm Going to School Today
Life Times Nine
Mathematics at Your Fingertips
Meet Comrade Student
Mimi
No Reason To Stay
One of Them is Brett
Passion for Life
Pillar of Wisdom
Place of Hearing
Pleasure is Mutual
Purple Turtle
Quiet One
Rock-A-Bye-Baby
School Without Failure
Silent Drum
Soviet Union: A Student's Life
Summerhill
The Test
That's Me
Three Looms Waiting
Thursday's Children
We're Gonna Have Recess

ENERGY

Energy
Footnotes on the Atomic Age
Ghosts of a River
International Atom
Juggernaut: A Film of India
Manhattan Odyssey

Problems of the Middle East
   (revised)
Rivers of Time
Room to Breathe
Water
World of Enrico Fermi

ESKIMO LIFE

Alaska!
Angotee
At the Time of Whaling
Eskimo Artist Kenojuak
Land of the Long Day Part II
Owl and the Lemming

EUROPE

City Out of Time
Farm Boy of Hungary
Industrial Region in Sweden
Joanjo: A Portuguese Tale
Land of the Swiss
Miguelin
Mila 23: Simion's World
Mr. Europe & the Common
   Market
New Life for a Spanish Farm-
   er
Niko - Boy of Greece
Norwegian Fjord
Orange and the Green
Paris 1900
Rhythms of Paris
Sky Over Holland
Spain - Proud Past & Promising
   Future
Venice Be Damned
Vera Paints Ibiza in the Sun
Western Germany: Land and
   the People

EVOLUTION

Changes, Changes
Chronology
Clay (Origin of the Species)
Darwin & the Theory of Natural
   Selection
Darwin's Galapagos Today

Ecology of a Hot Spring
Evolution
Evolution & the Origin of Life
Galapagos: Darwin's World
What is Life?

EXPRESSION

Alone and the Sea
Blue Dashiki
Brake Free
The Cabinet
Carrousel
Cow
The Doodle Film
Faces
Fantasy of Feet
Forces Make Forms
Jazzoo
A Journey
Life Times Nine
Multiple Man
Orange and Blue
Pandora's Box
Popsicle
Psychedelic Wet
Reflections
Right On, Be Free
The Swing
Tub Film
Tumbleweed
Walking
Wind

FAMILY LIFE

Adventures of *
Angotee
Best Damn Fiddler from Cala-
    bogie to Kaladar
Birth Day
The Cabinet
Cipher in the Snow
Escape
Family of the Island
Family of the River
I'll Never Get Her Back
Ivan and His Father
Life in Ancient Rome: The
    Family
Life of a Philippine Family

Mexican-American Family
Mimi
My Son Kevin
Navajo Girl
Old Order Amish
The Raft
What Color is the Wind?
Where Mrs. Whalley Lives
You See, I've Had a Life

FILM TECHNIQUES

American Super 8 Revolution
American Time Capsule
Animal Movie
Animated Cartoons: The Toy
    That Grew Up
Animation Goes to School
Animation Pie
Arthur Penn
Beginning of Life
Begone Dull Care
Blinkity Blank
Carrousel
Chronology
Closed Mondays
Color of Ritual, Color of
    Thought
Corral
The Critic
Cry of the Marsh
Day With Timmy Page
Desert Victory
Dom
Doodle Film
Dots
Double Portrait
Dream of the Wild Horses
Empty Hand
Experiments in Motion Graphics
The Face
Figures From a Fable
Fire Mountain
The First Flickers
Frank Film
Free Fall
Generation Gap
Glass
Golden Age of Comedy
Greenhouse
The Hand
Harmony of Nature & Man

Democracy: Your Voice Can Be
Heard
Federal Taxation (2nd edition)
Flowers on a One Way Street
Great Rights
The Hand
Have a Heart
Health
I. F. Stone's Weekly
Majority Vote
Our Living Declaration of In-
dependence
President of the U.S.: Too
Much Power?
Role of the Congressman
To Speak or Not to Speak
U.S. Congress (2nd edition)
Vote Power
The Voter Decides
Who Killed Lake Erie?
Who's Running Things?

HANDICAPS

Beethoven: Ordeal & Triumph
Being
Breakthrough to Language
Danny and Nicky
Deaf Child Speaks
Eternal Children
Eyes of a Child
Focus on Ability
Graduation
Helen Keller
Leo Beuerman
Like Other People
Looking For Me
Mimi
My Son, Kevin
One of Them Is Brett
Place of Hearing
Question of Attitude
Ricky's Great Adventure
Sheltered Workshop
Silent Drum
Thursday's Children
What Color is the Wind?

HEALTH

Acupuncture: An Exploration

Alexander Learns Good Health
All My Babies
Breast Self-Examination
Changing View of the Change of
Life
Cry For Help
Eat, Drink, and Be Wary
The Heart: Attack
Hospital
Hunger (La Faim)
If Kangaroos Jump, Why Can't
You?
Industrial Hygiene: Science of
Survival
Invader
Matter of Fat
Pain of Silence
People Shop
Proud Years
Report on Acupuncture
The Road
Robin, Peter and Darryl
Somebody Waiting
Sports Medicine
Tobacco Problem
Valley of Darkness
VD: A Plague on Our House
Venereal Disease
Wacky World of Wilfred Wicken-
bush
Who Stole the Quiet Day?

HISTORY - U.S.

America - Gone West
American Indian
American Revolution: Back-
ground Period
American Revolution: Postwar
Period
American Revolution: War
Years
American Super 8 Revolution
American Time Capsule
America's Foundations of Liber-
ty
Bellota
Benjamin Franklin
Capitol: Chronicle of Freedom
Chinese-American (2)
Christmas on Grandfather's
Farm (1890's)

Civil War: Background Issues
(1820-1860)
Colonial Life in New England
Colonial Life in the Middle
Colonies
Colonial Life in the South
Dawn of the American Revolu-
tion: Lexington Family
Fabulous Country
Folksongs of the Western
Movement
Folksongs of Western Settlement
Founding of the American
Colonies
Freedom's Finest Hour
George Washington
Geo. Washington's Inauguration
Ghost Towns of the Westward
March
Giants and the Common Men
Good Morning, Freedom
Great Depression: A Human
Diary
The Great Gamble: Cyrus W.
Field
Guadalcanal - Island of Death
History of Southern California
Part I
History of Southern California
Part II
Home Country, U.S.A.
James Monroe
Jamestown Colony (1607-1620)
Japanese-American
Jefferson's Monticello
John Paul Jones
Journey of Robert F. Kennedy
Kennedy: What Is Remembered
Is Never Lost
Making of the President, 1960
Making of the President, 1964
Making of the President, 1968
Maple Sugar Farmer
Mark Twain's America
Meet George Washington
Mirror of America
1964
Nobody Goes There
Our Country's Emblem
Over There, 1914-1918
Peary and Henson: North to the
Pole
Pioneer Journey Across the

Appalachians
Pioneer Living: Preparing
Foods
Progressive Era
Puritan Family of Early New
England
The Real West
Road to Gettysburg
The Sixties
The Slave Experience
Slavery and Slave Resistance
Statue of Liberty
Storm of Strangers
Tahtonka
They've Killed President Lincoln
Thomas Jefferson
Three From Illinois
U.S. Expansion: California
U.S. Expansion: Texas & Far
Southwest
Valley Forge
Washington, D.C., Story of Our
Capital
What Does Our Flag Mean?
White House: Past & Present
Who Are the People of America?
Witches of Salem: Horror &
Hope
Yanks Are Coming

HISTORY - WORLD

Age of Exploration
Age of Exploration & Expansion
Ancient Egyptian
Ancient Peruvian
Ancient Phoenicia & Her Con-
tributions
Changing World of Charles
Dickens
Colonial Expansion of European
Nations
Crusades (1095-1291)
Galileo
Hiroshima-Nagasaki
Holy Land
Images Medievales
The Incas
Israel
Jerusalem & Its Contributions
Let My People Go
Life in Ancient Rome: The Family

Memorial
Negro Kingdoms of Africa's
  Golden Age
Of Picks, Shovels & Words
Reformation
Spirit of the Renaissance
Stalin vs. Trotsky
Time Line
Where Are My People?

HOLIDAYS

Christ Is Born
Christmas Cracker
Christmas in Appalachia
Christmas on Grandfather's
  Farm (1890's)
Christmas Tree
Easter Season
Friends and Aliens
Great Toy Robbery
Littlest Angel
On the Twelfth Day
The Season

HUMAN RELATIONS

Being
Changes, Changes
Courtesy: Inside Story
Feather
Golden Rule
I Am Freedom's Child
I Just Work Here
Is It Always Right to Be Right?
Keith
King of the Hill
Mimi
Neighbors
Piccolo
Reflections in Space
Uppity Albert McGuire
The Wall
Woof Woof

HUMOR

Animation Pie
Assignment: Children
Bird Who is a Clown

The Box
Chairy Tale
The Critic
Day of the Painter
Dogs, Cats, and Rabbits
Dorothy and the Pop Singer
Dot and the Line
The Egg
Ersatz
Evolution
The First Flickers
Flower Lovers
The Gift
Golden Age of Comedy
Great Jewel Robbery
Great Toy Robbery
Happy Anniversary
Harold and Cynthia
Humor in Music
The Interview
Joachim's Dictionary
Junkdump
Keep Cool
La Joconde
Lecture on Man
Leopold, the See-Through
  Crumbpicker
My Financial Career
One-Eyed Men Are Kings
Piccolo
Pickles
Pigs vs. the Freaks
Pillar of Wisdom
Pow Wow
Rythmetic
7 Surprises
Soir de Fete
Sort of a Commercial for an
  Ice Bag
Sunday Lark
That's Me
Trikfilm
Walking
Why Do You Smile, Mona Lisa?

INDIA

Asian Earth
Farm Village of India
Ganges: Sacred River
Hindu Village Boy
In India the Sun Rises in the East

India and Her Food Problem
India: Crafts & Craftsmen
Juggernaut: A Film of India
Undala

ISLANDS

Bali Today
Children of Fogo Island
Darwin's Galapagos Today
Family of the Island: Her Name
   is Wasamantha
Fire on the Sea
Forest Without Spears
Galapagos: Darwin's World
High Arctic Biome
Island Eden
Land Divers of Melanesia
Season of Fire
Winds of Fogo

ISRAEL

Children of the Kibbutz
Golda Meir
Israel... Nation of Destiny
Jerusalem and Its Contributions
Jerusalem... Center of Many
   Worlds

LABOR RELATIONS

Decision at Delano
Games
Huelga!
Labor Relations: Do Not Fold,
   Staple, Spindle, or Mutilate

LATIN AMERICA

A Valparaiso
Boy of Mexico: Juan and His
   Donkey
Brazil, I Love You
Cajititlan
Child of Darkness - Child of
   Light
Cortez and the Legend
Highland Indians of Peru

Journey to Chinale
Miners of Bolivia
Over the Andes into Ecuador
Peru: Inca Heritage
Que Puerto Rico!
The Raft
Siqueiros: El Maestro
Viva Mexico!

LIFE AND DEATH

Abyss
Alone and the Sea
The Cabinet
Cipher in the Snow
The Day Grandpa Died
The Day Manolete Was Killed
Dead Bird
Garden Party
How Could I Not Be Among You?
How Death Came to Earth
Hunter
No Man Is An Island
Threshold
Unquiet Death of Ethel and
   Julius Rosenberg
What Man Shall Live & Not See
   Death?
You See, I've Had a Life

LITERATURE

An Actor Works
All Gold Canyon
America & the Americans
America, I Know You
Animal Farm
Archangel Gabriel & Mother
   Goose
Balzac
Bespoke Overcoat
Brown Wolf
Capt. Arbanos Marko
Changing World of Charles
   Dickens
Chickamauga
Cipher in the Snow
D. H. Lawrence in Taos
Don Quixote (vs. the System)
Down to the Sea in Ships
The Dull Griet

Edgar Allan Poe: Background
for His Works
The Father
Flatland
Garden Party
Genesis (CMC-Columbia)
Grey Metropolis
Hero
I Am Freedom's Child
L. F. Stone's Weekly
The Jewish Wife
Johnny Appleseed
Lady or the Tiger?
Man Without a Country
Mark Twain's America
Masque of the Red Death
Mr. Shephard & Mr. Milne
Mockingbird
Mutiny on the Bounty
Occurrence at Owl Creek Bridge
The Park
Paul Bunyan
The Pleasure Is Mutual
Quest
Richard II - How to Kill the
King
Search for Ulysses
Spanish Earth
Stolen Necklace
Story of My Life: Hans Chris-
tian Andersen
Strangest Voyage
The Stronger
Swan Song
Syrinx/Cityscape
This is New York
Virginia Woolf: The Moment
Whole

MAN AND WOMAN

Cats and Dogs
D. H. Lawrence in Taos
Dom
Exchanges
Fable of He and She
Harold and Cynthia
Hello Mustache
Hobby
I'll Never Get Her Back
In the Kitchen
I've Got This Problem

The Jogger
Love Is for the Birds
Opera Cordis
Pas de Deux
The Question
Sirene
Skater Dater
The Stronger
Tender Game
To Love
Zebras

MANAGEMENT

Berfunkle
Communicating Successfully
Discipline: Matter of Judgment
Engineering of Agreement
Eye of the Supervisor
It Starts at the Top
Management of Conflict
Manager Wanted
Overcoming Resistance to Change
Sam's Secret
Something to Work For
Training Memorandum
Trouble with Words
Welcome Aboard

MATHEMATICS

Anti-Matter
Central Similarities
Dance Squared
Dot and the Line
Flatland
Four Line Conics
Geometry Lesson
How Long Is a Minute?
I Got Six
Isometrics
Mathematics at Your Fingertips
Mathematics of the Honeycomb
Metric System
Notes on a Triangle
Prime Time
Rythmetic
Symmetries of the Cube
Symmetry
Weird Number

MENTAL HEALTH

Art of Age
Baggage
Cheating
Child Behavior - You
Cry Help!
The Jogger
Koestler on Creativity
Like Other People
Long Way Back
No Lies
Rock-A-Bye-Baby
Suffer the Little Children
This Man Is Not Dying of
  Thirst
Vertigo
Voices Inside

MEXICO

Boy of Mexico: Juan & His
  Donkey
Cajititlan
Child of Darkness - Child of
  Light
Siqueiros: El Maestro
Viva Mexico!

MIDDLE EAST

Bedouins of Arabia
Empty Quarter
Iran
Israel
Let My People Go
Middle East
Myth of the Pharoahs
Of Picks, Shovels & Words
Problems of the Middle East
Rivers of Time
Where Are My People?

MINORITIES

American Girl
American Indian
Archaeology
Ballad of Crowfoot
Between Two Rivers

Children in the City
Chinese-American (2)
Cities Have No Limits
Denmark 43
Games
Geronimo Jones
Good Night, Socrates
Henry...Boy of the Barrio
History of Southern California I
History of Southern California II
Hopi Kachinas
How's School, Enrique?
Hunger in America
Ivanhoe Donaldson
Japanese-American
Law and Order
L'Chaim - To Life!
Longhouse People
Manhattan Street Band
Memorandum
Mexican-American
Mexican-American Family
Mexican or American?
Migrant
Miguel - Up From Puerto Rico
Navajo Girl
Navajo Silversmith
Nobody Goes There
People Might Laugh at Us
Peru: Inca Heritage
Que Puerto Rico!
Reflections
Scraps
Some Are More Equal Than
  Others
Storm of Strangers
Summerthing
Tahtonka
This Is the Home of Mrs.
  Levant Graham
Unanswered Question
Washoe
The West of Charles Russell
Who Are the People of America?
Winter on an Indian Reservation
Yesterday's Tomorrow

MUSIC

Anatomy of an Orchestra
Antonia
As Long as the Grass Is Green

Beethoven and His Music
Beethoven: Ordeal & Triumph
Begone Dull Care
Black Roots
Blades and Brass
Bolero
Brake Free
Canon
Casals Conducts: 1964
Changes, Changes
Country Jazz
Crash, Bang, Boom
The Dreamer That Remains
False Note
Fiddle de Dee
Fidelio: Celebration of Life
Folksongs of the Western Move-
   ment
Folksongs of the Western Settle-
   ment
Forever Beethoven
Forms of Music: Instrumental
Glass
Guitar: From Stone Age through
   Solid Rock
Half-Masted Schooner
Harmony in Music
Hen Hop
High Lonesome Sound
Holy War
Humor in Music
I Know an Old Lady Who Swal-
   lowed a Fly
Indian Summer
Instruments of Band & Orchestra:
   Brasses
Instruments of Band & Orchestra:
   Introduction
It Ain't City Music
Jail Keys Made Here
Jazz in the Concert Hall
Jazzoo
Jealousy
Keep Cool
Le Merle
Legend of Jimmy Blue Eyes
Little Spoon
Lonely Boy
Manhattan Street Band
Music for the Movies
Notes on a Triangle
Oh! Woodstock!
On the Twelfth Day

Orozco Murals: Quetzalcoatl
Patrick
Piccolo
Pow Wow
Right On, Be Free
Sandman
Serenal
Shostakovich's Ninth Symphony
Short and Suite
Sorcerer's Apprentice
Story of a Craftsman
Street Music
Summerthing
Surprise Boogie
The Swing
Sydney Opera House
Synchromy
Taxi
Tender Game
Under The Black Mask
Venus and the Cat
Vivaldi's Venice
War... Man's Destiny?
Water's Edge
What Does Music Mean?
What Is a Melody?
Words and Music

NATURE

Alone and the Sea
Drop of Water
Fire in the Sea
Geyser Valley
Great White Pelican
In Search of the Bowhead Whale
Land of the Loon
Miner's Ridge
Pelican Island
Redwoods
Soliloquy of a River
Sounds of Nature
Take Time to See

NONVERBAL

Adventures of *
American Time Capsule
As Long As the Grass Is Green
Baggage
Begone Dull Care

Bighorn
Blades and Brass
Blinkity Blank
Blue Dashiki
The Box
Brake Free
Canada Goose
Canon
Carrousel
Catch the Joy
Chairy Tale
Cheetah
Chickamauga
The Chicken
Christmas Cracker
Chronology
Clay (Origin of the Species)
Corral
Cosmic Zoom
Cow
Cry of the Marsh
Dance Squared
Danze Cromatiche
Day of the Painter
Deep Sea Trawler
Degas Dancers
Dimensions
Dom
Dots
Dream of the Wild Horses
Drop of Water
Ecce Homo
Energy
Ersatz
Exchanges
Fable
Fantasy of Feet
Fiddle de Dee
Fire
Fire in the Sea
Fire Mountain
Free Fall
Freighter
Gate 73
Genesis (CMC-Columbia)
Geyser Valley
The Giants
Glass
Goal
Greater Community Animal
Great Toy Robbery
The Hand
Hang Ten

Happy Anniversary
Harmony of Nature & Man
Hen Hop
Highland Indians of Peru
Highway
Hoarder
Horses
How's School, Enrique?
In India the Sun Rises in the
    East
In the Kitchen
Industrial Region in Sweden
Iran
Jail Keys Made Here
Japanese Farmers
Jazzoo
Joachim's Dictionary
Junkdump
Les Escargots
Line Across Australia
Lines - Vertical & Horizontal
Little Mariner
Lonnie's Day
Loops
Machine
Mammals
Manhattan Street Band
Memento
Miners of Bolivia
Miner's Ridge
Mr. Gray
Mockingbird
Moods of Surfing
Mosaic
Mountain Day
MROFNOC
Multiple Man
Multiply and Subdue
Naica and the Squirrels
Neighbors
New Life for a Spanish Farmer
New York, New York
Newborn Calf
Norwegian Fjord
Notes on a Triangle
November
Nzuri: East Africa
Occurrence at Owl Creek Bridge
One-Eyed Men Are Kings
Op Hop - Hop Op
Opera Cordis
Orange and Blue
Over the Andes in Ecuador

Pandora's Box
Patterns
People Might Laugh at Us
Perils of Priscilla
Phantasy
Piccolo
Place in the Sun
Popsicle
Pow Wow
Psychedelic Wet
Rail
Red Balloon
Refiner's Fire
Rhythmetic
Rice Farmers in Thailand
Ricky's Great Adventure
River People of Chad
The Robin
Sandman
Scraps
Serenal
Shape of Things
Shooting Gallery
Short and Suite
The Sixties
60 Cycles
Skater Dater
Ski the Outer Limits
Sky
Sky Capers
Snow Solo
Street Musique
String Bean
Study in Wet
Sunday Lark
Surprise Boogie
Symmetry
Take Time to See
Third Avenue El
Thoroughbred
Threshold
Time Piece
To Love
Town Musicians
Treehouse
Tumbleweed
Undala
Variations on a Theme
Vivaldi's Venice
Volley Ball
The Wall
Watch Out for My Plant
Water's Edge

Waters of Yosemite
Ways of Water
We're Gonna Have Recess
White Throat
Wind
Winter Geyser
Winter on an Indian Reservation

NUTRITION

Eat, Drink, and Be Wary
Food, The Color of Life
Hamburger Sandwich
Kids and Cookies
Pioneer Living: Preparing
  Food
Why Not Be Beautiful?
Yeast Dough Shaping Made Easy

OCEANOGRAPHY

Barrier Beach
Deep Sea Drilling Project
Endless Sea
Fish: Master of Movement
Octopus Hunt
Sea Horse
Strange Partners
To Catch a Meal

OLD AGE

Alone and the Sea
Antonia
The Art of Age
Birch Canoe Builder
Casals Conducts: 1964
Changing View of the Change of
  Life
David
Greenhouse
Henry
Old-Fashioned Woman
Proud Years
Story of a Craftsman
String Bean
Where Mrs. Whalley Lives
Woo Who? Mary Wilson
Yudie

PANTOMIME

Baggage
Fable
Keith
Mime Over Matter

PHOTOGRAPHY

Biography of the Motion Picture
  Camera
Circle of Light
Daguerre: The Birth of Pho-
  tography
Imogen Cunningham, Photogra-
  pher
Naked Eye
New Beam, Laser
This Is Edward Steichen

PHYSICS

Anti-Matter
Carbon
International Atom
Introduction to Holography
Isotopes in Action
Laser Beam
Matter and Energy (2nd Edition)
Mystery of Time
New Beam, Laser
People and Particles
Physicists
Standing Waves and the Principle
  of Superimposition
World of Enrico Fermi

POETRY

Annabel Lee
Autumn: Frost Country
Concrete Poetry
The Creation
David
Days of Dylan Thomas
e. e. cummings: The Making of
  a Poet
Fog
Haiku (Oxford Films)
Haiku (Stanton Films)

Hangman
How Could I Not Be Among
  You?
How To Kill
James Dickey: Poet
James Weldon Johnson
Ladies & Gentlemen, Mr.
  Leonard Cohen
Legend of Jimmy Blue Eyes
Lover's Quarrel With the World
Making Haiku
Mr. Shephard & Mr. Milne
Morning on the Lièvre
No Man Is An Island
Poem
Poetry for Fun: Poems about
  Animals
Right On, Be Free
The Rose & the Mignonette
Sonnets: Shakespeare's Moods
  of Love
Sound of Poetry
Walt Whitman: Poet for a New
  Age
World of Carl Sandburg

POLITICS

Blue Collar Trap
Fayette Story
Flowers on a One Way Street
Majority Vote
Making of the President, 1960
Making of the President, 1964
Making of the President, 1968
My Childhood
Politics Film
Progressive Era
Role of the Congressman
To Speak or Not to Speak
U. S. Congress (2nd Edition)
Vote Power
Voter Decides
Who's Running Things?

POLLUTION

Ark
Bulldozed America
The Choice...Is Yours
From the Face of the Earth

Little Man, Big City
Livin' on the Mud
Mayfly: Ecology of an Aquatic
  Insect
Men at Bay
Time to Begin
Treehouse
Water
Who Killed Lake Erie?
Who Stole the Quiet Day?

PSYCHOLOGY

Betty Tells Her Story
Cheating
Emotional Development: Aggres-
  sion
Freud: Hidden Nature of Man
Games
Hidden Side of Selling
Imagination at Work
Like Other People
Management of Conflict
Perception of Orientation
Sense Perception
Shadow of an Apple
To See or Not To See
Vertigo
Victims
War Comes Home
Why Do You Buy?
Why Not Be Beautiful?

QUALITY OF LIFE

Assembly Line
Automation
Basket Builder
Because, That's Why
The Daisy
Flowers on a One Way Street
Frank Film
Genesis (Macmillan)
Hunger (La Faim)
Jail Keys Made Here
Livin' on the Mud
Master Kiteman
Matter of Survival
Men's Lives
Power and Wheels
Right On, Be Free

The Season
Story of a Craftsman
This Man Is Not Dying of Thirst
Time Piece
21-87
Valley of Darkness
What on Earth?

RACE RELATIONS

Ain't Gonna Eat My Mind
Bank Called Freedom
Battle of East St. Louis
Can We Immunize Against
  Prejudice?
Come Back, Africa
Exchanges
Fayette Story
Friendly Game
I'm A Man
Katutura
Ku Klux Klan
Law and Order
Let the Rain Settle It
The Matter with Me
My Childhood
No Hiding Place
Nothing But a Man
Now Is the Time
Punishment Fits the Crime
Southern Accents, Northern
  Ghettos
Spud's Summer
Time for Burning
Trumpet for the Combo
Unanswered Question

READING & LANGUAGE DE-
VELOPMENT

Alphabet
Ancient Phoenicia & Her Con-
  tributions
Birds of Our Storybooks
Cockaboody
Debt to the Past: Language &
  Communication
Ducks
Joachim's Dictionary
Korean Alphabet
Patrick

Playground
The Pleasure Is Mutual
Rainy Day Story
Reaching Your Reader
Reporting & Explaining
Safety As We Play
The Thinking Book
What Is Nothing?
Wind

RELIGION

Africa Is My Home
Blood and Fire
Christ Is Born
Christians at War
Cloistered Nun
The Creation
Ephesus
Evolution of a Yogi
Galileo: Challenge of Reason
Ganges: Sacred River
Genesis (CMC-Columbia)
Gospel According to St.
  Matthew
Holy Land: Background for
  History And Religion
Hopi Kachinas
Hutterites
Israel
Jerusalem and Its Contributions
Jerusalem... Center of Many
  Worlds
The Jesus Trip
Kaleidoscope Orissa
Land Divers of Melanesia
L'Chaim - To Life!
Life of Christ in Art
Longhouse People
Monastery
Myth of the Pharoahs
Old Order Amish
Orange and the Green
Rembrandt's Christ
Road Signs on a Merry-Go-
  Round
Satan in the Church
Secret of Michelangelo
The Smile
Story of the Blood Stream
Three From Illinois
Time for Burning

Ultimate Trip
Vesak
What Man Shall Live and Not
  See Death?

RIVERS

Colorado River (2nd Edition)
Family of the River: The
  River, My Home
Ganges: Sacred River
Ghosts of a River
Manouane River Lumberjacks
Morning on the Lièvre
Paddle to the Sea
The Raft
River People of Chad
River: Where Do You Come
  From?
Search for the Nile (series)
Soliloquy of a River
Street to the World

RUSSIA

Meet Comrade Student
Russia
Soviet Union: A Student's Life
Stalin vs. Trotsky

SAFETY

Another Man's Family
Bomb Threat! Plan, Don't
  Panic
Close-up on Fire
Dangerous Playground
Drownproofing
Fire
Fire in My Kitchen
First Aid Now
First Five Minutes
Focus on Ability
Have A Wonderful Evening
In a Fire... Seconds Count
Inner Mind of Milton Whitty
Just Once
Police Pursuit
Return of Milton Whitty
Roadbuilders

Roofer's Pitch
Safe Home
Safety in the Balance
Safety on the Way to School
Science of Fire
Something Concrete

SCIENCE, GENERAL

Bird Room
Cosmic Zoom
Drop of Water
Farmyard Babies
Forces Make Forms
Freedom in Flight
In One Day
Matter and Energy (2nd Edition)
Origins of Weather
Reptiles and Their Characteristics
Ricky's Great Adventure
River: Where Do You Come From?
The Robin
Science of Fire
Story of Electricity
Symmetry
Where Should a Squirrel Live?
Wind

SCIENTIFIC METHOD

Acupuncture: An Exploration
Anti-Matter
Aristotle & the Scientific Method
Continents Adrift
Darwin and the Theory of Natural Selection
Galileo
Galileo: Challenge of Reason
Grizzly Bear
How Do We Know?
Island Observed
Language of the Bee
Spirit of the Renaissance

SCULPTURE

Alberto Giacometti
A Boy Creates

Bronze
Closed Mondays
Ecce Homo
The Egg
Five British Sculptors Work and Talk
Genesis of a Sculpture
Henry Moore
Homage to Rodin
Kienholz on Exhibit
Kinesic Sculpture of Howard Barlow
Magic Machines
Nubia 64
Opus
Sculpture 58
Shape of Things
Sort of a Commercial for an Ice Bag
Textures
The Titan, Story of Michelangelo

SEASONS

America Goes Camping
Bighorn
Celebration of Winter
Color of Life
In One Day
Journey Into Spring
Journey Into Summer
Joy of Winter
Land of the Long Day, Part II
North With the Spring
November
Vivaldi's Venice
Winter on an Indian Reservation
Woodpecker Gets Ready for Winter

SEX EDUCATION

Adventures of *
Beginning of Life
Birth Day
Goodbye Lynn
Methods of Family Planning
Newborn Calf
Pain of Silence
Phoebe: Story of Premarital Pregnancy

Teen Scene
VD: A Plague on Our House
What Is Life?

SOCIAL PROTEST

America's Foundations of Liberty
Angry Prophet
Attica
Dark Corner of Justice
Decision at Delano
Denmark 43
Frame-up!
Frederick Douglass: House on
    Cedar Hill
The Hand
Holidays... Hollow Days
I. F. Stone's Weekly
I'm a Man
Legacy of a Dream
Mountain People
Now Is the Time
Orange and the Green
Pull the House Down
Saul Alinsky Went to War
Slavery & Slave Resistance
Vote Power
A Woman's Place
Women on the March

SOLAR SYSTEM

Cosmic Zoom
How Vast Is Space?
We Came in Peace

SPIRITUALISM

Evolution of a Yogi
Spirit Possession of Alejandro
    Mamani

SPORTS AND RECREATION

Abyss
America Goes Camping
Americans on Everest
Arena
Bicyclist

Blades and Brass
Catch the Joy
Celebration of Winter
Circus Town
Cross-Country Skiing
The Day Manolete Was Killed
Devil's Toy
Eighteen Footer
Empty Hand
Figure Skating
Flight
Flight in White
Focus on Ability
Glory of Their Times
The Goal
Hang Ten
Here's Hockey
If Kangaroos Jump, Why Can't
    You?
Lacrosse
Moebius Flip
Moods of Surfing
Pigs vs. the Freaks
Popsicle
Psychedelic Wet
Rodeo
Sabre and Foil
Sentinel: The West Face
60 Cycles
Skater Dater
Ski Racer
Ski the Outer Limits
Sky Capers
Solo
Sports Medicine
Sticky My Fingers, Fleet My
    Feet
Study in Wet
Style of Champions
Swimmer
Take Time to See
Tokyo Olympiad
Volley Ball
Watersmith
Wild Water
Will to Win
Wrestling

TEACHING

Animation Goes to School
Bing, Bang, Boom

Breakthrough to Language
Cheating
Child Behavior = You
Childhood: Enchanted Years
Children Who Draw
Danny and Nicky
Eternal Children
Eyes of a Child
Fireman Is Sad and Cries
Focus on Ability
Give Us the Children
Helen Keller
Hello, Up There
How's School, Enrique?
I'm Going to School Today
Mathematics at Your Fingertips
Meet Comrade Student
Mimi
No Reason to Stay
One of Them Is Brett
Passion for Life
Pillar of Wisdom
Place of Hearing
Pleasure Is Mutual
Purple Turtle
Quiet One
Rock-A-Bye-Baby
School Without Failure
Silent Drum
Soviet Union: A Student's Life
Summerhill
The Test
That's Me
Three Looms Waiting
Thursday's Children
We're Gonna Have Recess

THEATRE

An Actor Works
Art Is...
The Audition
Holidays...Hollow Days
The Jewish Wife
Summerthing
Swan Song
Three Looms Waiting

TRANSPORTATION

Brake Free

Cars In Your Life
Eurailpass Story
Francine, George and the Ferry-
  boat
Freedom in Flight
Freighter
From Here to There
Gate 73
Line Across Australia
Manhattan Odyssey
The Raft
Rail
Railroaders
Romance of Transportation
Shades of Puffing Billy
Snow
Street to the World
Taxi
Third Avenue El
Transportation: A Ship Comes
  Home

TV PROGRAMMING

Ain't Gonna Eat My Mind
Alaska!
Alone in the Midst of the Land
America and the Americans
America--Gone West
Anatomy of an Orchestra
Angry Prophet: Frederick
  Douglass
Arthur Penn
Atonement
Bank Called Freedom
Battle of East St. Louis
Beautiful River
Between Two Rivers
Blue Collar Trap
Bulldozed America
But What If the Dream Comes
  True?
Capitol: Chronicle of Freedom
Case History of a Rumor
Childhood: Enchanted Years
Christ Is Born
Christians at War
Christmas in Appalachia
Christmas Tree
City That Waits to Die
Close-up on Fire
Clue of the Missing Ape

TV PROGRAMMING (cont.)

Part I
Storm over the Supreme Court,
  Part II
Suffer the Little Children
Survival on the Prairie
They've Killed President Lincoln
This Child Is Rated X
This Is Edward Steichen
Three From Illinois
Three Looms Waiting
Tokyo--The 51st Volcano
Trip to Nowhere
Two Ballet Birds
The Unexplained
Venice Be Damned
What Does Music Mean?
What Is a Melody?
Who Killed Lake Erie?
Wild Fire!
Winged World
Wolves and the Wolf Men
A Woman's Place
Words and Music
World of Carl Sandburg

THE UNREAL

Ares Contre Atlas
Bad Day
Because, That's Why
Cassandra Cat
Concert of M. Kabal
Dom
Dream of the Wild Horses
Icarus Montgolfier Wright
Les Escargots
Masque of the Red Death
Maurice Escher: Painter of
   Fantasies
Moebius Flip
Omega
Phantasy
Renaissance
Sirene
Threshold
The Unexplained
Venus and the Cat
Witches of Salem: Horror &
   Hope

URBAN LIVING

A Valparaiso
Artist In Manhattan: Jerome
   Myers
Besieged Majority
Blue Dashiki
Boomsville
Caroline
Children In the City
Cities Have No Limits
Citizen Harold
City and the Future
City of Necessity
City Tree
Claw
Cosmopolis/Big City 2000 A. D.
Crosstown Adventure
Devil's Toy
Flowers on a One Way Street
Friends and Aliens
Future for the Past
Grey Metropolis
Henry
Hospital
Les Fleurs de Macadam
Little Man, Big City
Lonnie's Day
Manhattan Street Band
The Matter With Me
Men at Bay
Mirror of America
Mr. Grey
Mrs. Case
Monument to the Dream
Multiply and Subdue
New York, New York
On the Bowery
111th Street
Open Space
The Park
Population Explosion
Southern Accents, Northern
   Ghettos
Summerthing
Syrinx/Cityscape
Taxi
Third Avenue El
This Is New York
This Is the Home of Mrs.
   Levant Graham
Washington, D. C.

Watch Out for My Plant
Who Stole the Quiet Day?

VALUES

And Who Shall Feed This World?
The Audition
Beauty Knows No Pain
Beginning Responsibility: Books
  and Their Care
Debt to the Past
Fabienne
Frederick
Greenhouse
The Hoarder
Hunger (La Faim)
Livin' on the Mud
Oops, I Made a Mistake!
Ricky's Great Adventure
Toys
Uppity Al McGuire
Watch Out for My Plant
Zebras

VENEREAL DISEASE

Invader
Pain of Silence
VD: A Plague on Our House
Venereal Disease

VISUAL LITERACY

American Time Capsule
Around Perception
Blinkity Blank
Day With Timmy Page
Experiments In Motion Graphics
Forces Make Forms
Lines, Spines & Porcupines
Museum... Gateway to Percep-
  tion
Naked Eye
Searching Eye
Sense Perception
Take Time to See
To See or Not to See

WAR & PEACE

Archeology
Ares Contre Atlas (Mars vs.
  Atlas)
CBW: Secrets of Secrecy
Changing of the Guard
Chickamauga
Christians at War
Chronology
Death of a Peasant
Denmark 43
Desert Victory
Essay on War
Fields of Sacrifice
Goya: Disasters of War
Hiroshima-Nagasaki
Holy War
How to Kill
Memorial
Selling of the Pentagon
War Comes Home
War... Man's Destiny?
Where Are My People?

WOMEN'S STUDIES

African Girl... Malobi
Antonia
Anything You Want to Be
Asian Earth
Beauty Knows No Pain
Betty Tells Her Story
Birth Day
Caroline
Eleanor Roosevelt Story
Emerging Woman
Fabienne
Fable of He and She
Genevieve
Girls at 12
Golda Meir
Helen Keller
Imogen Cunningham, Photogra-
  pher
Intern: A Long Year
Men's Lives
Mrs. Case
Navajo Girl
No Lies
Old-Fashioned Woman
Popcorn Lady

WOMEN'S STUDIES (cont.)

Rivers of Sand
This Is No Time for Romance
To Be Somebody
Underground Film
Vera Paints Ibiza In the Sun
Virginia Woolf: The Moment
   Whole
Why Not Be Beautiful?
A Woman's Place
Women On the March
Woo Who? Mary Wilson
Yudie

PART III

FILM DESCRIPTIONS

A VALPARAISO
    30 min   BW   McGraw-Hill   '63
    *Critics' Award, Oberhausen
This documentary pointedly marks the observable contrast between
the poverty of the average resident of this Chilean port city and the
extravagant wealth of the elite upper-class families.   Directed by
Joris Ivens for Argos Films.   French narration with sub-titles.   A
Contemporary Films release.   (HS-Adult)

ABRAHAM LINCOLN: A Background Study
    16 min   color   Coronet
    *Participation, Venice
This biography is treated in relation to the period and places in-
volved in Lincoln's upbringing, working, writing, and governing.
Geographical realism is augmented by scenes of the Kentucky hills,
Indiana backwoods, and the Illinois prairie country ... achieved with-
out an enacted characterization of the subject himself.   (HS-Adult)

ABYSS
    17 min   color   Phoenix   '73
    *Blue Ribbon, American/EFLA
This mountain-climbing documentary follows R. Sorgato's ascent of
the west peak of Lavaredo in the Dolomite chain, one of the most
difficult in the Alps.   Re-enacts the drama of his self-rescue, after
being given up for lost and dead.   Directed by Gilbert Dassonville.
(Senior HS-Adult)

ACCELERATION
    3 min   color   Mass Media   '69
    *Merit Certificate, Phila.

Primitive man grows restless to accomplish something after lying
under a tree, drinking nectar. He sees a mountain and tries various schemes for climbing it. He does not succeed until he invents
a space ship that takes him to a high plateau. All he finds there,
though, is another tree, more nectar, and that same feeling of restlessness. Produced by John Taylor. (HS-Adult)

ACID (LSD)
      27 min   color   Encyc Brit   '70
      *Golden Eagle, CINE
The overdose death of a young man is the starting point for this
examination of the unpredictable power of this chemical tiger. Youthful acid-takers discuss their "trips," good and bad, and rationalize
about their fatalistic life style. Scientists report on the results of
their research on the relationship of LSD to creativity, physiology,
and self-image. Produced by Concept Films, Inc. (HS-College)

AN ACTOR WORKS
      20 1/2 min   color   Doubleday   '70
      *Bronze Award, Int. Film & TV
How does a 20th century actress absorb and project the personality
of a queen long dead and only partially transmitted by history?
Viveca Lindfors shows how she taps her own resources of memory
and imagination to identify personally with Queen Hecuba in Euripides'
masterpiece, The Trojan Women. (HS-Adult)

ACUPUNCTURE: An Exploration
      16 1/2 min   color   FilmFair   '73
      *Golden Eagle, CINE
Describes the current American experiments with this theory, and
confirms the accuracy of old Chinese body charts. Also describes
the history of acupuncture and its relationships (physical and philosophical) to the ancient concept of "Ch'i," the energy-flow pattern
in the body. A Franklin Konigsberg Film. (HS-Adult)

ADAPTATIONS OF INSECTS
      13 min   color   Stanton Films
      *Blue Ribbon, American/EFLA
Through cine-macrography, this production reveals four forms of
insect adaptation: structural, mimicry, numerical, and seasonal.
It also develops the broader concept of environmental adaptation of
all living things. (Junior-Senior HS)

ADAPTATIONS OF PLANTS AND ANIMALS
      13 1/2 min   color   Coronet   '60
      *Chris Award, Columbus
This film selects several examples to illustrate the adaptations of
living things to their environment, for food-getting and for protection. Observation of a variety of plants and animals can lead viewers to an awareness of the principles of survival. (Intermediate-
Junior HS)

ADOLESCENCE
     22 min BW Macmillan '65
     *Nomination, Academy Award
     *Golden Ducat, Mannheim
     *San Giorgio Prize, Venice
An insight into the world of dance and into the devotion to art shown by different generations of ballerinas. The schoolgirl of 14, Sonia Petrovna, takes ballet lessons from the great teacher, Madame Egorova, who is exactly 70 years older. When young Sonia tries out for a ballet company and is turned down, she returns to Madame Egrova for more study and practice, as did an earlier Egrova protégée, Maria Tallchief herself. Directed by Vladimir Forgency. (HS-Adult)

THE ADVENTURES OF *
     10 min color McGraw-Hill '69
     *Award Winner, Venice (Italy)
Man, represented by the asterisk symbol, is introduced in this animated film as a baby enjoying the sights and sounds of the new world around him. As he grows, his ability to enjoy life is gradually reduced until, ultimately, as an adult, he is unable to react spontaneously to anything ... except to the birth of his own child, through whom he is again able to discover the world around him. Produced by John Hubley. A Contemporary Films release. (HS-Adult)

AFRICA IS MY HOME
     22 min color Atlantis '61
     *Prize Winner, Melbourne
     *Chris Award, Columbus
A depiction of the life of a Nigerian woman from birth through marriage, including her perceptions of the issues of African nationalism, tradition versus progress, Islam vs. Christianity, and independence vs. colonialism. Produced by J. Michael Hagopian. (HS-College)

AFRICAN ELEPHANT
     7 min color AIMS '69
     *Golden Eagle, CINE
     *Chris Award, Columbus
An introduction to the basic concepts of habit and behavior of this largest of all land animals. (Intermediate-HS)

AFRICAN GIRL... MALOBI
     11 min color Atlantis '61
     *Honors, Edinburgh (Scotland)
     *Chris Statuette, Columbus
A portrayal of village community life in West Africa, featuring the activities of Malobi, a ten-year-old girl who dreams of becoming a teacher in her native Nigeria. Produced by J. Michael Hagopian. (Intermediate-Adult)

AFTER HIGH SCHOOL---WHAT?
     13 1/2 min color Vocational Films '73
     *Award, Nat. Voc. Guidance

A look at the options available to a young person graduating from 12th grade. Includes consideration of trade and technical programs, two- and four-year colleges, on-the-job training, and even military service. Film guide is available for utilization purposes. (HS-Adult)

AFTER THE FIRST
    14 min color TeleKETICS
    *Golden Eagle, CINE
    *Silver Medal, Atlanta
    *Blue Ribbon, American/EFLA
A sportsman presents his twelve-year-old son with a birthday present: the boy's first hunting trip. The camera suggests, in the scenes where the boy sees his father shoot a rabbit, the emotional and philosophical distance created between them. The parent's concluding words, "After the first time, it gets easier," can spark discussion on a variety of issues. (Intermediate-Adult)

THE AGE OF EXPLORATION
    8 1/4 min color Doubleday '70
    *Chris Award, Columbus
This film is an overview of the period between the fall of Rome and the Crusades. It offers viewers the opportunity of examining why men, from the beginning of recorded time, have searched for the unknown. (Intermediate-HS)

THE AGE OF EXPLORATION AND EXPANSION
    16 1/2 min color Centron '71
    *Chris Award, Columbus
Using the inquiry approach, this film questions specific related events of the 15th and 16th centuries. It delves into the issue of why European nations took the initiative in exploration, while other highly developed civilizations of that time chose not to. Emphasizes the cultural clashes between explorers and the native societies they encountered. (HS-College)

AGE OF THE BEAVER
    16 3/4 min BW Nat. Film Bd.
    *Canadian Film Award
A brief history of the fur trade, showing its effects on exploration and settlement of frontiers. Engravings and paintings from the periods treated convey impressions of the adventures and hardships of traders, Indians, and hunters. Animated maps indicate known routes. (Intermediate-Adult)

AGGREGATION OF DISSOCIATED SPONGE CELLS AND SPECIES-SPECIFIC SORTING
    8 min color BFA Educ Media
    *Golden Eagle, CINE
The cells from two different species of sponges are dissociated separately and are then shown to re-aggregate. Pseudopodal activity is also shown. The principles that emerge are: 1) cell movements appear to be random; and 2) re-aggregation is species-specific. Filmed by Tom Humphreys. (College)

THE AGING OF LAKES
    14 min   color   Encyc Brit   '71
    *Chris Certificate, Columbus
After introducing geological factors in the normal aging of lakes,
this film zeroes in on man's efforts at speeding up this process.
Examples shown are: indiscriminate disposal of fertilizers, sewage,
and industrial waste.   (HS-College)

AIN'T GONNA EAT MY MIND
    34 min   color   Carousel   '71
    *Award DuPont-Columbia U.
    *Emmy Award, Nat. Academy
When 25-year-old Cornell Benjamin (or "Black Benjy," as he was
known) was killed in a Bronx gang fight, the air there became
charged with revenge.   The gangs gathered but, unlike rivals of the
1950s and '60s, they are older and wiser organizations.   They called
a meeting of their leaders, to exchange views and to reduce tensions.
The result of that caucus is the story of this film and of the 200
young men involved.   Produced by Tony Batten, WNET-TV.   (HS-
Adult)

ALASKA!
    51 min   color   Films Inc   '66
    *Golden Eagle, CINE
Today most of its gold is gone but man continues to exploit this
area's vast potential wealth.   He persists in challenging nature, and
actually appears to be winning.   Or is he now, as in the past, simply plundering and profiting, only to leave when there's nothing left?
Or will he, for a change, make a reality of the prophecies of great-
ness made for Alaska long ago?   Produced by the National Geographic Society.   Also available in a 22-minute version.   (College-
Adult)

ALBERTO GIACOMETTI
    12 min   color   CMC-Columbia   '67
    *Golden Eagle, CINE
A presentation of the works exhibited in the major retrospective just
before the artist's death.   The narration consists of Giacometti's
own writings, edited to match the imagery presented.   This film
presents the essence of fifty years' productivity.   Produced by Sumner Glimcher.   (College-Adult)

ALCOHOLISM: A Model of Drug Dependency
    20 min   color   CRM Films   '72
    *Chris Award, Columbus
    *Best of Category, San Francisco
    *Bronze Medal, Atlanta
What are the answers to alcoholism?   This film shows how some
people have managed to conquer it by substituting other addictions.
It also shows how other methods have helped the alcoholic to realign
his dependency in order to effect a permanent cure.   Produced by
Tom Lazarus.   (Senior HS-Adult)

ALEXANDER AND THE CAR WITH THE MISSING HEADLIGHT
13 min   color   Weston Woods   '67
*Honor Diploma, Teheran (Iran)
An animated version of the picture book of the same name.   Also
available in Super 8 Sound.   Produced by Mort Schindel.   (Primary)

ALEXANDER LEARNS GOOD HEALTH
11 min   color   Coronet   '56
*Merit Certificate, Columbus
Alexander eats too much and sleeps too little, and is unable to play
ball with his team as a result.   He then improves his habits and,
with proper diet, rest, cleanliness, and exercise, goes out and
pitches and wins (naturally!) the ball game.   (Primary)

ALI AND HIS BABY CAMEL
11 min   color   Atlantis   '53
*Merit Award, Stamford (Conn.)
*Merit Certificate, Columbus
A light-hearted story of a Moslem boy and his playful desert pet
whose adventures take place in, and help to describe, a community
in Pakistan.   Produced by J. Michael Hagopian.   (Primary-Intermediate)

ALL GOLD CANYON
21 min   color   Weston Woods   '73
*Recognition Award, Columbus
This live-action adventure film is freely adapted from the story by
Jack London.   It deals with the effect of greed on man's character.
As a lone prospector discovers gold in a canyon and begins extract-
ing it, his former partner ambushes him.   Produced by Short Film,
Prague (Czechoslovakia).   (Junior HS-Adult)

ALL MY BABIES
55 min   BW   CMC-Columbia
*Special Flaherty Award
Shows the steps a midwife should follow between accepting a client
and taking the infant to its first Well Baby Clinic.   This was filmed
in Georgia, and features a certified midwife, her patients, and the
doctors and nurses who supervise the local midwife training program.
Restricted to use by professional audiences and cinema classes.
(College-Adult)

THE ALLURE OF DRUGS
24 min   color   Ext. Media Ctr.   '70
*Chris Award, Columbus
Examines the conflicting attitudes, social images, and realities of
the drug culture.   Compares the effects of coffee, tea, alcohol,
marijuana, hallucinogenic mushrooms, peyote, and intoxicating snuff.
Correlates the introduction of drugs with periods of change and tension, the outcome of which creates insecurity.   Produced by the
University of California (Berkeley).   (HS-Adult)

ALMOST EVERYONE DOES
    14 min   color   Wombat
    *Chris Award, Columbus
This film is about the different ways many people try to change
their feelings artificially.   And yet, what are the alternatives to
drug usage?   Instead of trying to change feelings, why not accept
them?   Or why not find out how to use them ... even the sad feelings?   Produced by Gene Feldman.   (Junior HS)

ALONE AND THE SEA
    13 min   color   Northwest Media   '70
    *Award Winner, Seattle
A gray-bearded and ruggedly noble fisherman is alone in his small
boat.   To himself he says, "There must be a rainbow out there.   I
haven't caught up to it yet, but I may some day."   A study of man
against the elements.   Influenced by Winslow Homer and Ernest
Hemingway.   Produced by Peter d'Amelio.   (HS-Adult)

ALONE IN THE MIDST OF THE LAND
    27 min   color   Films Inc   '70
    *Award, San Francisco State
    *Prize, Internat. Film & TV
    *Emmy, Nat. Academy
A dramatized account of man's destruction of his own environment.
In this story, the last person on earth is reduced to living within a
protectively imprisoning suit, after the rest of the population has
been annihilated by pollution.   Produced by WMAQ-TV.   (HS-Adult)

ALPHABET
    6 1/4 min   BW   Nat. Film Bd.   '69
    *Honors, Bilbao (Spain)
    *Award, Annecy (France)
    *Prize, LaPlata (Argentina)
A visual romp through the alphabet, in which each letter has its
own object, animal, or action to suggest words identified with it.
For example: A for Apple, and Z for Zebra.   None, however, retains its original form for long, as it fades or reforms at the artist's will.   (Primary)

AMERICA AND THE AMERICANS
    51 min   color   McGraw-Hill   '68
    *Golden Eagle, CINE
    *Emmy, Nat. Academy
Based on John Steinbeck's book and narrated by Henry Fonda, this
critique covers such contemporary subjects as conservation, air
pollution, and the self-defeating waste of natural assets.   Produced
by NBC-TV.   (College-Adult)

AMERICA GOES CAMPING
    28 min   color   Assn.-Sterl.   '67
    *Chris Award, Columbus
    *Honors, NY Internat'l
This is a description, as offered by a sporting goods supplier, of

the mass exodus of millions of Americans who annually heed the
call of the great outdoors. Suggests that the U.S. is a fun place to
discover and that camping is the best way to do it. Endorsing this
view, on film, is Ted Williams, among others lesser known. Available on free loan. Sponsor: Sears Roebuck and Co. (HS-Adult)

AMERICA--GONE WEST
        52 min   color   Time-Life   '72
        *Blue Ribbon, American/EFLA
One of 13 episodes in Alistair Cooke's personal interpretation of the
USA's history. This segment covers the period from the Louisiana
Purchase in 1803 to the California Gold Rush later that same cen-
tury. A co-production of BBC-TV and Time-Life Films. (College-
Adult)

AMERICA, I KNOW YOU
        5 min   color   FilmFair   '71
        *Award of Merit, Landers
        *Freedoms Foundation Award
America is a collection of beliefs, myths, and circumstances that
are often contradictory and need to be better understood. Through
historical photos, live-action film footage, and readings of the narration, the symbolism in our national life provides a rallying point.
Based on the book by Bill Martin, Jr. Produced by Sargon Tamimi.
(Elem.)

AMERICA ON THE ROCKS
        15 min   color   Nat. AV Center   '72
        *Golden Eagle, CINE
A study of alcohol and the American middle class. Narrated by
Robert Mitchum, the approach neither scolds nor scares but the dimensions of the problem are not ignored. Delves into ethnic influences on moderation, and recognizes industry's enormous interests
in eliminating the problem. Released by Airlie Productions. Also
available in a 28-min. version which is cleared for TV. (HS-Adult)

AN AMERICAN GIRL (The Problems of Prejudice)
        28 min   BW   Macmillan   '57
        *Chris Award, Columbus
How an adolescent young woman in a small town tests the democratic tradition in which she's been reared. Norma Davis, who is
not Jewish, wears a bracelet with Jewish symbols on it. She is
warned "Stick to your own kind," and is accused of trying to "pass."
She exposes these signs of bigotry and seeks a solution to it by
reading from her diary at a PTA meeting. Directed by Lee R.
Bobker for Dynamic Films. (HS-Adult)

THE AMERICAN INDIAN--Before the White Man
        19 min   color   Handel   '71
        *Chris Award, Columbus
Traces the early Asiatic descendants who migrated from Siberia to
Alaska and then fanned out into the Americas. The history of
tribes such as the Apaches and the Navajos is outlined. They were

deeply spiritual people who lived in harmony with neighbor and nature ... until the advent of the White Man. Produced by Leo Handel. (Intermediate-Adult)

THE AMERICAN REVOLUTION: The Background Period
 11 min color Coronet
 *Freedoms Foundation Award
What caused such political unrest among colonial farmers, laborers, craftsmen, merchants, and woodsmen? Each had his own reasons but all were united in the cause of self-determination, which persuaded the Colonists to rebel against their mother country. (HS)

THE AMERICAN REVOLUTION: The Postwar Period
 11 min color Coronet
 *Freedoms Foundation Award
Out of the battles that began at Concord, the work of forming an army followed. After the sufferings of seven years of war came victory over "benign neglect," and with victory came an enduring constitutional form of government. This film traces the steps that brought unity to the independent interests of America. Can we find a parallel solution today? (HS)

AMERICAN REVOLUTION: The War Years
 11 min color Coronet
 *Freedoms Foundation Award
Presents the major phases of the decision to rebel: the proclamation at Independence Hall, the crisis at Valley Forge, the military turning point at Yorktown, the diplomatic victory made possible at Paris, and the alliance of colonies that followed. Stresses the individual efforts of George Washington in his role as general, citizen, and statesman. (HS)

THE AMERICAN SUPER 8 REVOLUTION
 31 min color Int Film Found '72
 *Blue Ribbon, American/EFLA
A documentary about student film-making by fifth-graders, plus their finished production entitled "The American Revolution: Paul Revere's Ride, and the Battles of Lexington and Concord." Student-made scenes are live-action dramatizations enacted by students of the Hollow Tree School in Darien, Connecticut. Production supervision by Stan Woodward. (Elem.-College)

AN AMERICAN TIME CAPSULE
 3 min color Pyramid '68
 *Chairman's Award, US Industrial
Condenses 200 years of US history into the irreducible minimum. Using a kinestasis (i.e., still-based) technique, film-maker Charles Braverman "flash-frames" 1300 images from paintings, photographs, newspapers, film clips, posters, cartoons, and other visuals. This innovation was introduced over network TV by the Smothers Brothers. (HS-Adult)

AMERICANS ON EVEREST
        50 min   color   Pyramid   '67
        *First Prize, Trento (Italy)
        *Cindy Award, Info. Film
        *Golden Eagle, CINE
        *Blue Ribbon, American/EFLA
        *Chris Award, Columbus
Orson Welles recites the commentary for this pictorial record of
the first Americans to scale the world's highest mountain.   This
1963 expedition into the Himalayas was led by Norman Dyrenfurth,
who also produced the first motion pictures taken from that summit.
(College-Adult)

AMERICA'S FOUNDATIONS OF LIBERTY
        11 min   color   Handel   '63
        *Chris Award, Columbus
This first segment in the Americana Series is designed to introduce
the concept of liberty as interpreted by the original Revolutionists,
and to help viewers to see that same concept in the light of current
attitudes toward the relationship between citizen and government.
(Intermediate-HS)

ANATOMY OF AN ORCHESTRA
        52 min   BW   McGraw-Hill   '71
        *Series Award, Sat. Review
From the Young People's Concert series, with Leonard Bernstein as
master of ceremonies, narrator, and conductor of the N. Y. Philharmonic.   Produced by CBS-TV.   (Elem.-Adult)

THE ANCIENT PERUVIAN
        29 min   color   Int. Film Found.   '69
        *Golden Eagle, CINE
        *Blue Ribbon, American/EFLA
The magnificent civilizations of pre-Columbian America are deduced
from the artifacts and legends of the native cultures.   Includes references to the Inca Empire.   Along with animation by Gerald Mc-
Dermott are photographic views of present day archaeology and of
ancient textiles, pottery, and gold.   Original score.   Produced by
Sam Bryan.   (HS-Adult)

ANCIENT PHOENICIA AND HER CONTRIBUTIONS
        14 min   color   Atlantis   '68
        *Chris Statuette, Columbus
The main contributions of the people we now call the Lebanese are
the alphabet, the colonization of the Mediterranean, the discovery of
the Atlantic, and the opening of sea routes for commerce.   All of
these concepts are related to more current implications.   Produced
by J. Michael Hagopian.   (Intermediate-HS)

AND WHO SHALL FEED THIS WORLD?
        54 min   color   Films Inc.   '74
        *Blue Ribbon, American/EFLA
In its examination of the nature and causes of the world food problem,

this film presents two contrasting farm families, one in India and the other in North Dakota. They both personalize the many aspects of the issue in an open-ended format that encourages post-screening discussion and action. Director: Darold Murray. (College-Adult)

ANDY AND THE LION
    10 min   color   Weston Woods   '55
    *Merit Award, Columbus
An iconographic (art-based) version of the children's book of the same name. Also available with Spanish narration. Produced by Mort Schindel. (Primary)

ANGOTEE
    32 min   color   Int. Film Bur.
    *Awards: Durban, Trento, and Canada
Opens with the birth of Angotee, an Eskimo boy, in the eastern Arctic. Continues with his infancy and childhood when he learns the skills of hunting that he'll need as a man, along with the craft of igloo-building. His future wife learns the tasks associated with housekeeping and motherhood. Produced by the National Film Board of Canada. (Intermediate-Adult)

THE ANGRY PROPHET: Frederick Douglass
    24 min   color   Films Inc.   '70
    *Emmy, Nat. Academy
Frederick Douglass was perhaps the leading Black spokesman of his time, which ranged from the slavery years before the Civil War up to his death in 1894. The sountrack is composed entirely of his words, speeches, and writings, and the biographical footage was filmed in the historic locations identified with Douglass, who (as the only personality in this film) is portrayed by an actor. Produced by WRC-TV. (HS-Adult)

ANIMAL FARM
    75 min   color   Phoenix   '56
    *Award Winner, Cannes
    *Honors, American/EFLA
A feature-length animated version of George Orwell's modern classic, actually a metaphor (in the true literary sense of the word) that utilizes animal characters to enact and analyze the political aspects of human behavior. Produced in England by John Halas and Joy Batchelor. A Contemporary Films release. (HS-Adult)

THE ANIMAL MOVIE
    10 min   color   McGraw-Hill
    *First Prize, La Plata
    *Honors, Venice (Child.)
An animated cartoon to help children explore why and how animals move. A boy discovers that he can't compete with monkeys, snakes, and horses in the special ways they move, and that he can out-race them only with the help of a motor vehicle. Which all goes to prove that, while other animals are trapped by their environment, man, the inventor, isn't. Produced by the National Film Board of Canada. (Pre-school-Primary)

ANIMATED CARTOONS: The Toy that Grew Up
    17 min   BW   Film Images
    *Best Documentary, Brussels
A history of motion-picture equipment and the development of animated drawings. Explains the principle of persistence of vision as
creating the illusion of motion. Original music by Guy Bernard.
Produced by Roger Leenhardt. (HS-College)

ANIMATION GOES TO SCHOOL
    15 min   color   McGraw-Hill   '65
    *Golden Eagle, CINE
As students at the Horace Mann School plan their art production and
the animation of a class film, we see how and why animation is used.
We learn, too, about planning a single-concept film, preparation of
the subject, and animation with an Oxberry stand. Techniques include sixteen excerpts from student-made animations. Produced by
George H. Bouwman. (Junior HS-College)

ANIMATION PIE
    25 min   color   Bloomberg   '74
    *Blue Ribbon, American/EFLA
Presents five "slices" of animation, each one demonstrating a different style of art. The production itself grew out of a hands-on
workshop in Concord, California, and incorporates many examples
of student capabilities. (Junior HS-College)

ANNABEL LEE
    10 min   color   Oxford Films   '72
    *Golden Eagle, CINE
The poem this film is based on is dedicated to Edgar Allan Poe's
young cousin who died after only a few years of marriage to him--
about the only extended happiness ever enjoyed by that unfortunate
writer. Narrated by Lorne Greene. Music by Les Baxter. Film-
maker: Art Evans. (HS-Adult)

ANOTHER MAN'S FAMILY
    25 min   color   Film Communicators   '72
    *Bronze Plaque, Nat. Committee
    *Chris Award, Columbus
A dramatization of how an average family might react to common
fire hazards in the home, and how ignoring such dangers can lead
to peril to life and property. (HS-Adult)

ANTI-MATTER
    13 min   color   American Educ.   '74
    *Academy Award (Animation)
    *Golden Eagle, CINE
An animated film that presents the facts and fantasies associated
with theoretical science on matter and its antithesis. Offers to students of mathematics and physics an insight into the thought processes of modern scientific method. (Senior HS-College)

ANTONIA: A Portrait of the Woman
58 min color Phoenix '74
*Blue Ribbon, American/EFLA
An action profile of Antonia Brico, the former musical prodigy who, as a 73-year-old, still seeks the opportunity of leading a major symphony orchestra, in spite of the competition from younger persons in a field long dominated by men. Produced and directed by Judy Collins and Jill Godmilow. (College-Adult)

ANTONIO GAUDI
27 min color CMC-Columbia '65
*Prize, City of Barcelona
*Blue Ribbon, American/EFLA
Explores the work of one of architecture's greatest innovators. Shows how Gaudi's personal sense of space developed from the Mediterranean forms he knew so well. Starting with the Casa Vicens (1878), this film follows the major steps in his career, with individual buildings examined as representative of his use of color, materials, surfaces, and structural devices. Filmed in Barcelona by Ira LaTour. (College-Adult)

ANYTHING YOU WANT TO BE
8 min BW New Day '71
*Special Recognition, Ann Arbor
*Award, Sinking Creek (Tenn.)
*Blue Ribbon, American/EFLA
The conflicts, real and imagined, of a high school student. In her bid for class president, she settles for secretary. In her desire to become a doctor, she is persuaded to be a nurse. And so goes the familiar old story. Influenced by TV, the movies, and the magazines, she becomes a stereotype female: from sweet young thing, to harried housewife, to imperious matron. Film-maker: Liane Brandon. (HS-Adult)

APRYL AND HER BABY LAMB
13 min color Atlantis '56
*Award, U. of Illinois
*High Honors, Venice
About a girl's experiences and feelings in finding her lost pet. Produced in live-action photography by J. Michael Hagopian. (Primary)

ARCHAEOLOGY
14 min BW McGraw-Hill '69
*Silver Hobby Horse, Cracow
*Lion of St. Mark, Venice
This is a film of an excavation on the site of the Nazi death-camp at Auschwitz. There is no music or commentary; only the natural sounds of digging. Objects uncovered hint at the shocking climax to the film. Produced by Andrzej Brzozowski for the Education Film Studio of Lodz, Poland. (HS-Adult)

ARCHANGEL GABRIEL AND MOTHER GOOSE
28 min BW McGraw-Hill '70

*Silver Gondola, Venice
*First Prize, Oberhausen
A loose adaptation from Boccaccio's Decameron, this film by puppet-
animator Jiri Trnka tells of a diabolical monk who takes advantage
of a beautiful woman's love for the angel Gabriel. Produced by the
Short Film Studio of Prague, Czechoslovakia. A Contemporary
Films release. (College-Adult)

ARE YOU SAFE AT HOME?
15 1/2 min BW Nat. Film Bd.
*Award, Nat. Committee
Suggests home fire rules, and also demonstrates a variety of fire
extinguishers. Shows how a family that is well organized can escape
from a burning house, save the building and most of its contents.
(Intermediate-Adult)

ARENA
10 min color Pyramid '70
*Main Prize, Oberhausen
An empty stadium fills with people. The expectant stir, the bands,
and finally the game itself! The "Circus Maximus" of our time--
football--galvanizes the crowd as no other social rite can. Live-
action scenes and special optical effects reverse the original sequence,
as the stadium reverts to its empty state. Film-maker: Istvan
Ventilla. (HS-Adult)

ARES CONTRE ATLAS (Mars vs. Atlas)
7 1/2 min color Macmillan '66
*Grand Prix, Annecy (France)
Five animated episodes by Manuel Otero express the absurdity of
war. The first episode shows how a world filled with bird song becomes profaned by two humans' murder of each other. Other segments illustrate macabre examples of man's inhumanity, such as a
choir singing the Hallelujah Chorus just as the church bell falls on
them during an air raid. (HS-Adult)

ARISTOTLE AND THE SCIENTIFIC METHOD
13 1/2 min color Coronet '60
*Award, Scholastic Teacher
Against a background of the achievements of science in ancient
Greece, this film stresses Aristotle's contributions to the development of scientific method, i.e., observation, classification of data,
experimentation, and generalization. (Junior HS)

ARK
20 min color Barr Films '70
*Award of Merit, Landers
*Honors, San Francisco
The story of one man's attempt to maintain a pond community in a
glass house that protects it from the polluted world outside. But
rats and, finally, men destroy his "Walden under glass." Produced
by Rolf Forsberg. (HS-Adult)

AROUND PERCEPTION
    16 1/2 min   color   Nat. Film Bd.
    *Award, Buenos Aires
An experiment in using computers to animate film.   The result is a
vibration of geometric forms, achieved by varying the speed at which
alternate colors change.   Between these pyrotechnics, there appears
a single line gyrating in rhythm.   Sound effects are created by
registering shapes directly on the track of the film.   (College)

ART IS ...
    28 min   color   Assn. -Sterl.   '72
    *Gold Camera, US Industrial
    *Nomination, Academy Award
    *Bronze Award, Int. Film & TV
    *Award, San Francisco
    *Golden Eagle, CINE
Some new answers to the question, "What is art?" are suggested in
this exploration of our many opportunities to react to the world
around us.   Featured are composer Leonard Bernstein, dancer Edward Villella, painter Robert Murray, and mime Tony Montanaro.
Available on free loan to schools and adult groups.   Sponsored by
the Associated Councils of the Arts and the Sears Roebuck Foundation.   (HS-Adult)

THE ART OF AGE
    27 min   color   ACI Films   '72
    *Blue Ribbon, American/EFLA
The philosophy of four elders reminds us that personal growth and
learning need never stop.   Expressing their feelings on the subject
are a retired mailman; a woman whose age now allows her time to
sculpt; a former businessman who does volunteer tutoring; and an
elderly lady who dismisses her bone disease as "inconvenient."
Produced by Leonard S. Berman.   (College-Adult)

ARTHUR PENN: THEMES AND VARIANTS
    86 min   color   Macmillan   '70
    *Emmy Award, Nat. Academy
A portrait of the controversial American director on location with
Dustin Hoffman for the feature film Little Big Man.   Interview-im-
pressions are given by colleagues Arlo Guthrie and Warren Beatty.
Scenes from his other works are excerpted from The Chase, Mickey
One, The Left Handed Gun, and Alice's Restaurant.   (College-Adult)

ARTIST IN MANHATTAN: JEROME MYERS
    10 min   color   Film Images   '68
    *Golden Eagle, CINE
A tribute to the late American artist (1867-1940) whose drawings
and paintings reflected the city and the people of New York during
the first part of the 20th century.   The words spoken are those of
his autobiography, and help to explain his role in the so-called "ash-
can" school of American art.   Narrated by David Wayne.   Produced
by Barry Downes and Linda Marmelstein.   (College-Adult)

AS LONG AS THE GRASS IS GREEN
    11 min   color   Atlantis   '73
    *Golden Eagle, CINE
    *Recognition, Columbus
A non-narrated film about a summer experience with children of the
woodland Indians of North America. Depicts the development of relationships between a fawn and four Indian children. Original ethnic
music is used as background. Produced by J. Michael Hagopian.
(Elem.)

ASIAN EARTH
    22 min   color   Atlantis   '54
    *Merit Certificate, Columbus
    *Golden Reel Award (USA)
    *Award of Merit, Boston
    *First Prize, Cleveland
    *Honors, Stamford (Conn.)
This is the story of a Hindu mother in a village of the Lower Ganges
valley, as she and her family share the joys and sorrows that result
from their struggle against the hardships of their environment. Produced by J. Michael Hagopian. (HS-Adult)

ASSEMBLY LINE
    30 min   BW   Macmillan   '61
    *Citation, St. Lawrence U.
    *San Giorgio Award, Venice
    *First Prize, Oberhausen
A story of the loneliness that plagues our industrial society, especially the young people who labor in factories. A young man, who
spends his days on an assembly line and his evenings seeking pleasure downtown, personifies the frustrations suffered by many of his
contemporaries, and implies the need for new values and goals within our social format. Produced by the Annenberg School and the
Institute of Cooperative Research, Univ. of Pennsylvania. (HS-
Adult)

ASSIGNMENT CHILDREN
    20 min   color   AIM-Assn.   '57
    *Photo Achievement Award
This labor of love, undertaken by comedian Danny Kaye, brings
howls of laughter to hundreds of children throughout the world who
suffer from disease and malnutrition. Danny sees miraculous
changes in their spirits and their health through the medicine of
UNESCO--and from the therapy of his humor. Cleared for TV.
Suitable for all ages.

AT THE FOOT OF THE TREE--A HOMAGE TO STEINLEN
    24 min   BW   Roland Films
    *Quality Award, French Nat'l
    *Special Diploma, Bergamo
A well developed sense of social consciousness made Alexander Steinlen the most outspoken lithographer and painter of his day. He depicted the streets of Paris, their squalor and their drama, in the

early part of the Industrial Revolution. Steinlen, a Swiss, was born in 1859 and died in 1923. Directed by Alain Saury for SIPRO Productions. (College-Adult)

AT THE TIME OF WHALING
    37 min color U. of Alaska '74
    *Blue Ribbon, American/EFLA
Shows the activities in a contemporary Eskimo village during the whaling season. Includes scenes of dancing, fireside tales, the actual hunt, and the custom of dividing up the meat among the community. Produced by Leonard Kamerling. (HS-Adult)

AT YOUR FINGERTIPS--BOXES
    10 min color ACI Films '69
    *Silver Medal, Venice
    *Award, Bilbao (Spain)
    *Golden Eagle, CINE
Visiting a supermarket, we see a variety of boxes, cartons, and containers. At home, these same receptacles are transformed into playthings. Cereal boxes and milk cartons become cars, animals, and villages ... with just a little imagination and practice. (Preschool-Primary)

AT YOUR FINGERTIPS--GRASSES
    10 min color ACI Films '69
    *Honors, American/EFLA
An introduction to a familiar plant, but seen in several forms: lawn grass, tall grass, marsh grass, corn, and bamboo. Children make use of this plant in many ways: a pattern is made by shadows cast on paper; stalks are woven into a belt; marsh grass is designed to become a primitive head-dress. (Primary)

ATONEMENT
    51 min color Films Inc '71
    *Blue Ribbon, American/EFLA
The USA and Canada are shown working in unison to preserve threatened species on their border. Bison and bighorn sheep are inoculated; hatcheries are checked for water pollution; birds and polar bears are tagged for follow-up research; and whooping cranes' eggs are hatched artificially. Some of the work of "atonement" is shown being undertaken to save wildlife from man's misuse of chemicals. A National Film Board of Canada production. (College-Adult)

ATTICA
    80 min color Attica Films '74
    *Grierson Award, American/EFLA
    *Blue Ribbon, American/EFLA
An in-depth examination of the biggest prison rebellion in US history, and a report on the social shock-waves still being felt in the re-evaluation of American institutions of justice. Produced and directed by Cinda Firestone. (College-Adult)

THE AUDITION
    9 min   color   Counterpoint   '71
    *Chris Award, Columbus
An actor enters a darkened theater and is challenged by an unseen
voice there to display various emotions.   The surrealistic climax
makes this film suitable fare for discussion.   Film-maker: C. B.
Wismar.   (HS-Adult)

AURUM
    29 min   color   Assn. -Sterling
    *Bronze Medal, Atlanta
    *Award, US Industrial
About the element "aurum" (gold) of which we hear so much but
know so little.   In addition to artistic examples of goldsmithing, this
film shows the drilling of three tons of solid rock required to ex-
tract one ounce of gold.   Available on free loan.   Made by Gazelle
Film Productions.   Sponsor: the Union of South Africa.   (HS-Adult)

AUTUMN: FROST COUNTRY
    9 min   color   Pyramid   '70
    *Award, NY International
Explores the less-traveled roads of the New England poet, Robert
Frost.   The woods and mountains of Vermont suggest the natural-
ness of Frost's works.   The film is framed by his reading of "The
Road Not Taken" and "Reluctance. "   Produced by Fred Hudson.
(HS-Adult)

BABEL
    18 min   color   McGraw-Hill   '70
    *Exceptional Distinction, Anvers
Pieter Bruegel the Elder painted the activities of each season, the
delights and miseries of the world and, above all, the ambiguity of
human relations.   Drawing his inspiration from proverbs and popular
turns of speech, he showed (not without humor) the foolishness of
men who disrupt the natural harmony of life for the sake of vanity
and selfishness.   A Contemporary Films release.   (College-Adult)

BAD DAY
    12 min   color   Mass Media   '71
    *Winner, London Film Festival
An animationist's expression, through fantasy, of total disillusion-
ment.   Sixteen incidents occur during this film, all of them emphasizing the helplessness of human beings trapped by their own de-
sires, impulses, fears, and betrayal by other humans.   Produced
by Atelja Za.   (HS-Adult)

BAGGAGE
    22 min   BW   ACI Films   '69
    *Award Winner, Chicago
    *Honors, American/EFLA
A parable played by mime Mamako Yoneyama.   Through San Francisco, Mamako carries her "baggage," humanity's struggle to be
free from psychological restrictions.   The woman wrestles with her

burden but feels lost when she manages to rid herself of it. Re-
united with her "baggage," she greets it with grateful resignation.
Mamako finally surrenders the "baggage" in death. Musical score.
Without words. An Alexander Neel Film. (HS-Adult)

BALI TODAY
    17 min color ACI Films '69
    *Chris Award, Columbus
Records aspects of life of that Indonesian island. Dr. Margaret
Mead narrates from her extensive studies of South Seas people.
Sculpture, painting, music, and dance are seen in simple rituals
and elaborate ceremonies. A Hartley Productions Film. (HS-Adult)

THE BALLAD OF CROWFOOT
    10 min BW McGraw-Hill
    *Award San Francisco
    *Blue Ribbon, American/EFLA
    *Award, Filmcentron
    *Gold Hugo, Chicago
This history of the Canadian West was created by a film crew of
Indians who wanted to reflect the traditions, attitudes, and problems
of their people. Throughout the film runs a ballad in Dylan style
that surveys the broken treaties and speculates whether there will
be a better tomorrow. Produced by Willie Dunn, National Film
Board of Canada. A Contemporary Films release. (Intermediate-
Adult)

BALLERINA
    28 min BW Nat. Film Bd.
    *Chris Award, Columbus
About ballet dancer Margaret Mercier, prima ballerina of Les
Grands Ballets Canadiens, graduate of Sadler's Wells, and student
of the Bolshoi. The film follows her through rehearsal and a scene
from Cinderella. (College-Adult)

BALLET GIRL
    23 min BW Macmillan '53
    *Honors, Edinburgh
    *Honors, Venice
Narrated by Claire Bloom. Shows us the traditional world of ballet
through the eyes of a little girl--a member of the Royal Danish
Ballet--and enables us to see stars of the Royal Danish Ballet in
performance of "The Conservatory," the ballet by Bournonville. Directed by Astrid Henning-Jensen. (Intermediate-Adult)

THE BALLOON TREE
    10 min color Pyramid
    *Bronze Medal, Atlanta
A boy visits his aunt in New York. While playing with her antiques,
his finger becomes stuck in a jade carving. Unable to slip it off,
he runs away and has a series of adventures in the streets and parks
of the strange city. Tired and hungry, he returns, with the precious
jade still stuck on his finger, but that problem is solved when it's

accidentally smashed in the door. Produced by Ross Lowell. (Intermediate-Adult)

BALZAC
    23 min BW Film Images
    *Merit Award, <u>Scholastic Teacher</u>
    *Prize, Woodstock
    *Award, Boston
    *Best Biography, Rio de Janeiro
The great French novelist (1799-1850) is brought to life through
portraits and manuscripts, with attention to the influences of the
women in his life, Napoleon, the reign of Louis-Philippe, and the
revolution of 1848. Music by Guy Bernard. Production by Jean
Vidal. (College-Adult)

A BANK CALLED FREEDOM
    26 min color Films Inc. '68
    *Award, Freedoms Foundation
A report on the founding and operation of the black-owned Freedom
National Bank in Harlem and Brooklyn's Bedford-Stuyvesant area.
With loans to businessmen, mortgage help, and advances to purchase
cooperatives, this bank plays a role in helping to build the confidence
of the Black community. Produced by WNBC-TV. (HS-Adult)

BARRIER BEACH
    20 min color ACI Films '71
    *Honors, American/EFLA
A study of the changes in a barrier beach over a year. The result
is a time-lapse picture of the seasonal changes and shifting pattern
of cove, beach, and lagoon. Gives students of earth science, geology, oceanography, and ecology an experience difficult to duplicate,
even by means of personal observation. A Mary Hill Film. (HS-College)

BASKET BUILDER
    12 min color Blue Ridge '74
    *Golden Eagle, CINE
A Virginia craftsperson shows, step-by-step, how he makes white
oak baskets, while reminiscing about the people and way of life in
the mountains. Mood is enhanced by the inclusion of country fiddle
and harmonica music. (Junior HS-Adult)

BATIK
    10 min color ACI Films '70
    *Golden Eagle, CINE
This survey of Indian and Indonesian batik-making is a prelude for
a demonstration by artist Nancy Belfer. Viewers are shown techniques in creating traditional and current pieces. Unlike painting,
the image is dyed into canvas. Produced by the State University
College at Buffalo. (HS-Adult)

THE BATTLE
    5 min color Mass Media '71

*Award, Oberhausen

Life's conflicts are figuratively internalized and satirized in this animation. A soldier stands at attention, while the camera zooms in and takes an X-ray of his innards, where a massive war is about to begin. The war is carried to every part of his body. Teeth are chipped, hairs uprooted, and organs torn to shreds. Amidst the smoking carnage, a bugler blows "Taps." The camera zooms back to reveal, not a young soldier, but a bent old man leaning on his cane. Directed by Derek Phillips. (HS-Adult)

THE BATTLE OF EAST ST. LOUIS
46 min BW Carousel '69
*TV Award, Saturday Review

Fires were burning in Watts, Detroit, & Newark. And in East St. Louis a bomb was waiting to explode. Then a bi-racial group agreed to spend three days together in sensitivity training. Result: plans for encounters with larger numbers of people and a defusing of the riot atmosphere. A CBS News production. (HS-Adult)

BAYANIHAN
58 min color Bee Cross-Media '62
*Golden Eagle, CINE

The Bayanihan Philippine Dance Company traces, in the four sections of this film, the cultural heritage of its nation. Primitive tribes of the northern Luzon mountains, the Muslim (Moro) peoples of the south, and a series of dances showing Spanish influence reflect these historic origins today. Concludes with a suite of rural dances. Produced by Robert Snyder; directed and written by Allegra Fuller Snyder. (College-Adult)

THE BEAUTIFUL RIVER
26 min color Films Inc. '69
*Award, Int. Environment

This is the story of the once beautiful Connecticut River, now a raw sewage ditch by many standards. Industrial pollution and municipal abuse have made this river difficult to use for recreation or for clean water. Connecticut is now trying to save the river but it might be too late. Produced by WNBC-TV. (HS-Adult)

BEAUTY KNOWS NO PAIN
25 min color Benchmark '73
*Gold Medal, Atlanta

Each year for two weeks, coeds who aspire to join the Kilgore College Rangerettes and to share in the glamor of marching on football fields, submit to an ordeal of training and testing. The value the Rangerette ideal holds for them is demonstrated in scenes of hysteria when the results are posted. Whether the film appears cynical or sentimental is in the eye of the beholder. An Elliott Erwitt Film. (HS-Adult)

BECAUSE, THAT'S WHY
17 min BW Film Images
*Award of Merit, Cracow

    *Golden Gate, San Francisco
    *First Prize, Mannheim
What happens when two executives make the decision to get away
from it all? In a climax reminiscent of the early days of film
comedy, the executives-turned-sportsmen shoot down a runaway car
in the woods and then pose in front of their trophy--symbol of the
life from which they think they have escaped. Produced by Josef
Sedelmaier. (HS-Adult)

THE BEDOUINS OF ARABIA
    20 min color Films Inc. '69
    *Chris Certificate, Columbus
The desolate desert in the south of Arabia--the "Empty Quarter"--
is the setting for a look at the Bedouin's relationship with land,
family, and tribe. The Bedouin emerges as a figure of strength and
affection, of courtesy and loyalty--a person who has learned to live
with hardship and with nature. Today, as oil derricks begin to dot
the desert, the Bedouin can look forward only to an existence as an
unskilled laborer, grist for the mill of civilization. I. I. T. Production. (HS-Adult)

BEETHOVEN AND HIS MUSIC
    13 1/2 min color Coronet
    *Music Award, Cleveland
The music of Beethoven reflects the social upheavals of the late
eighteenth century, the composer's unusual strength and genius, and
a transition from the classical formality of Haydn and Mozart to
more romantic expression. The film develops the relationship between Beethoven's environment and his personal responses to it in
his music. (HS-Adult)

BEETHOVEN: Ordeal and Triumph
    52 min color McGraw-Hill
    *Award of Merit, Landers
Documents Beethoven's terrible struggle with deafness that began
when he was at the pinnacle of musical fame and ability. The story
is told against the background of his music played by the Boston
Symphony Orchestra under the direction of Eric Leinsdorf. Produced by ABC Television. (College-Adult)

THE BEGINNING OF LIFE
    30 min color Benchmark
    *Blue Ribbon, American/EFLA
This film records a human embryo's development from fertilized
ovum to birth. With innovative camera techniques, photographer
Lennart Nilsson catches the ever-growing, self-transforming evolution of a single cell into a human baby--the story of life repeating
itself without end. (HS-Adult)

BEGINNING RESPONSIBILITY: Books and Their Care
    11 min color Coronet '60
    *Award, <u>Scholastic Teacher</u>
Sue learns from her brother Tommy some important steps in the

care of books. When Tommy gets his new book, he is shown how it should be opened and handled, how to keep from soiling it, the proper bookmark to use, where the book should be kept when not in use, and how it should be mended. Children will also see that books are something to appreciate and enjoy. (Primary)

BEGONE DULL CARE
        9 min color Int. Film Bureau
        *Awards: Venice, Berlin, and others
By painting directly on film, Norman McLaren and Evelyn Lambart have created this cinematic expression. Opening with title page in eight languages, and with a hand-drawn sound track, the film moves into images that interpret the jazz of the Oscar Peterson Trio. In each of three movements of "ragtime," "blues" and "boogie-woogie," colors, forms, figures, and lines move against a continuously changing background in time with the music. (HS-Adult)

BEING
        21 min color ACI Films '73
        *First Prize, Rehab. Congress
A study of a handicapped young man who rejects an overture of friendship because he is afraid of pity, but who responds when he realizes it is genuine. A film on feelings and human relationships, that can provide insights into what it means to be handicapped. Produced by Musica Viva Limited. (HS-Adult)

BELLOTA
        34 min color Int. Film Bureau '69
        *Blue Ribbon, American/EFLA
Tells the story of a Southwestern cattle roundup, and chronicles a way of life that is rapidly disappearing. The traditions of the old cattle ranches are depicted with narration in part by five Mexican vaqueros (cowboys). Working the month-long roundup, they use long-acquired skills to solve problems that require immediate answers. Produced by the Radio-TV Bureau of the University of Arizona; photographed and edited by Harry Atwood and Philip L. Spalding. (HS-Adult)

BENJAMIN FRANKLIN--Scientist, Statesman, Scholar and Sage
        30 min color Handel '69
        *Freedoms Foundation Award
The subtitle reflects the versatility of this self-educated American who, at 17, ran away to become a master printer and then become one of the founders of our country and one of its most beloved figures. (HS-Adult)

BERFUNKLE
        10 min color Perennial Education
        *Award, Society/Management
What's in a word? This animated film presents the mysterious concept of "berfunkle" and what it means to different people. It follows the misadventures of a poor soul trying to find the exact meaning of the word. Produced by Portafilms. (HS-Adult)

BERLIOZ TAKES A TRIP
    53 min BW McGraw-Hill '70
    *Series Award, Saturday Review
From the Young People's Concert series, with Leonard Bernstein
as master of ceremonies, narrator, and conductor of the New York
Philharmonic. A CBS television production. (Elem.-Adult)

THE BESIEGED MAJORITY
    53 min color Films Inc. '70
    *Award, Freedoms Foundation
This film deals with urban crime from the victim's point of view.
It brings up points of law enforcement, criminal courts, and the
need for solutions to the social causes of crime. Produced by NBC
Television. (College-Adult)

THE BESPOKE OVERCOAT
    39 min BW Sterling Educ. Films
    *"Oscar," Academy Awards
This is a story of friendship. Of love. Of Morry, an east-end
tailor, and of Fender, a frail old clerk. For forty years, Fender
has stacked warm sheepskin coats in a warehouse. He is too poor
to buy one for himself, and his boss won't give him one. Fender
and Morry conspire to obtain a coat, even after death. (HS-Adult)

THE BEST DAMN FIDDLER FROM CALABOGIE TO KALADAR
    49 min BW Nat. Film Bd.
    *Award, Australia
    *Film of the Year, Canada
A story from an Ottawa logging community, about a man who chooses
the life and income of an itinerant bush worker, even though it
means his family lives poorly. A study of the effects on family life
of isolation and deprivation. Appearing as husband and wife are
Chris Wiggins and Kate Reid. (College-Adult)

BETHUNE
    60 min BW McGraw-Hill
    *Merit Diploma, Melbourne
    *1st Prize, Liepzig
    *Certificate, Edinburgh
    *Direction Award, Montreal.... and other honors
A biography of Norman Bethune, the Canadian doctor who served
with the Loyalists during the Spanish Civil War, and with the North
Chinese Army during the Sino-Japanese War. In Spain, he pioneered
mobile blood transfusion service; in China his work behind battle
lines to save the wounded made him a legend. Bethune has been described as a "Canadian Ghandi." This documentary pieces together
his career and provides a personal view of social progress in China.
Available in two parts of 28 & 32 minutes. Produced by the National Film Board of Canada. (College-Adult)

BETTY TELLS HER STORY
   20 min   BW   New Day
   *Honorable Mention, Bellevue
   *Blue Ribbon, American/EFLA
Betty recalls an incident. She needed "the perfect dress" for a special occasion, and describes how she found just the right one, mod-
eled it for friends, and then never got to wear it. Then Betty tells
her story again--this time revealing how she really felt: her anxiety, her discomfort at being praised for beauty she doesn't feel she
has, and her sadness at the way things turned out. The contrast
between the two stories can raise questions about self-concept, true
beauty, and social values. Producer: Liane Brandon. (HS-Adult)

BETWEEN TWO RIVERS
   26 min   color   Films Inc.   '69
   *Award, Robert F. Kennedy
Thomas James White Hawk, an American Indian who tried to make
it in the white man's world and failed, was a promising pre-med
student at the University of South Dakota. Now, the 21-year-old
Sioux Indian is serving a life sentence for murder and rape. No attempt is made to excuse his crimes, but the case is presented as
an example of the alienation of Indians caught in a cultural conflict.
NBC-TV News. (HS-Adult)

THE BICYCLIST
   15 min   color   Macmillan   '57
   *Blue Ribbon, American/EFLA
   *First Prize, Cork (Ireland)
A live-action film about a red bicycle owned by two kinds of riders:
one who obeys the rules and one who doesn't. Makes a pointed but
light-hearted contribution to safety education. Music by Bent Fabri-
cus-Bierre. Written and directed by Henning Carlsen. A Nordik
Films Junior production. (Elem.)

THE BIG RED BARN
   8 min   color   Oxford Films   '72
   *Gold Camera, US Industrial
Based on the book by Margaret Wise Brown, this film recreates a
day in the life of such creatures as mice, pigeons, and bats--plus
even a scarecrow. Moreland-Latchford, Ltd. (Elem.)

BIGHORN
   10 min   color   McGraw-Hill   '70
   *Merit Award, Philadelphia
   *Special Prize, Tourfilm
   *First Prize, Novisad
This production is about the Rocky Mountain Bighorn sheep that live

among rocks and snow, in the highest cliffs and most rugged terrain of Banff and Jasper National Parks, a landscape still untouched by man. The camera records the bighorn's adventures on the steep and dangerous slopes, highlighted by the gamboling of new-born lambs and slow-motion footage of two rams locked in combat. Nat. Film Bd. of Canada. (Intermediate-Adult)

BIGHORN!
        26 min color Stouffer Prod. '73
        *Special Award, CINDY
        *Award, Columbus
        *Award Winner, Chicago
        *Golden Eagle, CINE
This film shows the life history and ecology of the Rocky Mountain Bighorn Sheep. It concurrently depicts the birth and growth of a lamb and the death of the old ram of the band. Beginning in spring, it follows the band of wild sheep through the summer, autumn, and winter to the following spring. By M. and M. Stouffer. (HS-Adult)

BING BANG BOOM
        24 1/2 min BW Nat. Film Bd.
        *Award Winner, Australia
        *Award, American/EFLA
Composer-conductor R. Murray Schafer has seventh-grade students listen to sounds around them, even their own breathing, feet shuffling, bangles jingling, and noises outdoors. From such basics can children develop rhythm and phrasing, and then try their own composition. (Intermediate-Adult)

BIOGRAPHY OF A BEE
        14 min color Moody Institute
        *Award of Merit, Landers
Reveals the social structure of the hive and the part played by queen, drone, and worker. Follows a typical worker bee through a series of activities that includes cleaning, care of the young, wax building, ventilating, guarding, nectar processing, and foraging. Explains how bees communicate by means of a dance. Compares the bee community with human society. (Grades 4-7)

THE BIOGRAPHY OF THE MOTION PICTURE CAMERA
        21 min BW Film Images
        *Best Documentary, Brussels
About the first man to undertake a scientific study of recorded movement, Prof. Etienne-Jules Marey, a French physiologist. (Muybridge later confirmed his findings photographically.) Covers the related inventions of Edison, and shows scenes from Lumière's early films. Produced by Roger Leenhardt. (HS-Adult)

THE BIRCH CANOE BUILDER
        23 min color ACI Films '71
        *Gold Medal, Atlanta
        *Red Ribbon, American/EFLA
The craft of the Indian canoe builder has been revived by Bill

Hafeman of Big Fork, Minnesota, who has lived in the northern
woods for fifty of his seventy-two years. He is filmed as he works,
with his own comments on what he is doing and on the relationship
of man and nature. Flashbacks to old photos point up the changes
in the last fifty years. A Southern Illinois University film. (Intermediate-Adult)

A BIRD OF PREY: The Red-Tailed Hawk
        14 min color Encyc. Brit. '72
        *Special Mention, Rome
        *Golden Eagle, CINE
Shows how it is equipped for its environment and why birds of prey
must be preserved. Also shows how a raccoon climbs 60 feet above
ground, to snatch one of the bird's eggs. Close-up shots examine
the hawk's physical characteristics and its use of talons, beak, and
eyes. (Intermediate-Junior HS)

THE BIRD ROOM
        11 min color Doubleday '70
        *Honorable Mention, American/EFLA
A different slant on wild bird life: the care and feeding of young
helpless birds. Designed to stimulate the viewer's interest in environment and to give an understanding of a bird's life cycle and behavior patterns. (Intermediate-Junior HS)

THE BIRD WHO IS A CLOWN
        9 min color Encyc. Brit. '71
        *Golden Eagle, CINE
        *Chris Certificate, Columbus
The story of a rare bird, the blue-footed booby, is described with
humor and music on a small Galapagos Island, Daphne Major, an
inactive volcano. The bird's courtship and mating is seen on film,
as is its nest-building. (Primary-Intermediate)

BIRDS OF OUR STORYBOOKS
        11 min color Coronet '55
        *Award of Merit, Columbus
The robin, cardinal, crow, owl, blue jay, sparrow, redheaded
woodpecker, wren, and seal gull are the birds that children encounter most frequently in their stories and texts. Characteristics
of the birds--their coloring, calls, and easily observed habits--are
integrated with poems and stories. (Primary)

BIRTH OF THE RED KANGAROO
        21 min color Int. Film Bureau '68
        *Blue Ribbon, American/EFLA
Development from conception through the first year of life. This
film can be used to illustrate marsupial development, as well as
the reproductive organs and embryonic development of mammals.
Included are the differences between adult male and female reproductive cycles, mating behavior, and female behavioral patterns during
pregnancy and birth. Provides the opportunity to witness the birth
of a mammal. Produced by Australian Information Service. (College-Adult)

BLACK ROOTS
    60 min   color   Impact Films   '70
    *Experimental Award, Hollywood
A distillation of the history and culture of black Americans, with
five autobiographical sketches of Harlem blacks, their music, and
their anecdotes about their American "heritage." Film-maker:
Lionel Rogosin.   (College-Adult)

BLADES AND BRASS
    10 min   color   Int. Film Bureau   '72
    *Awards: Italy and Yugoslavia
Without commentary, this film combines Canadian hockey teams and
Mexican trumpets to portray the pace and hazards of one of the
world's fastest games.   By using slow-motion and zoom shots, the
camera relays the skill and grace necessary for this demanding
sport, as well as the violence that can erupt.   Filmed during National Hockey League games.   By the National Film Board of Canada.
(Intermediate-Adult)

BLAKE
    19 min   color   McGraw-Hill   '71
    *Nomination, Academy Award
Filmed by Bill Mason, the subject is his friend Blake James, an-
other film-maker, who pilots his own one-man plane.   The film is
Mason's view of this "hobo of the skies" but it is also an overview
of Canada, where flying is still an adventure.   Nat. Film Bd. of
Canada.   (HS-Adult)

BLIND BIRD
    45 min   color   McGraw-Hill   '69
    *Grand Prize, Venice
This story centers around a Russian boy, Vassia, and Pelka, a
blind pelican.   When Vassia learns that a famous eye surgeon is in
Moscow, he can think of nothing but trying to heal Pelka.   After
many difficulties, the two reach the doctor.   But the operation is
unsuccessful.   Vassia and his friend return home.   Then, one day,
Vassia notices Pelka is able to catch a ball he has thrown--his sight
is restored!   Vassia sets the pelican free, thankful that the bird
can fly to a warmer climate.   (Intermediat -Junior HS)

BLINKITY BLANK
    6 min   color   Int. Film Bureau   '55
    *Best Animation, Br. Film Inst. ... and other honors
An experiment by Norman McLaren in intermittent animation and
spasmodic imagery.   McLaren plays with the laws of persistence of
vision and after-images by engraving directly on black emulsion-
coated film, achieving a "now you see it, now you don't" effect.
The music is in the form of impro isation by instruments, with percussive effects added by synthet sounds scratched directly on film.
National Film Board of Canada.   (Intermediate-Adult)

BLOOD AND FIRE
    30 min   BW   McGraw-Hill   '67

*Canadian Film Award
*Certificate, Columbus
The Salvation Army in action. Band rehearsals, reminiscences of
an officer, unrehearsed "coming to Christ" in the Army Citadel--
these reveal the men and women dedicated to a life of service to
humanity. Produced by the National Film Board of Canada. (College-Adult)

BLOW, WIND, BLOW!
        11 min   color   Coronet
        *Participation, Venice (child.)
Johnny learns that the wind can turn windmills, shake the trees,
and make his toy sailboat go. From this knowledge, he gains a
background for understanding stories, poems, and songs about the
wind. (Primary)

THE BLUE COLLAR TRAP
        51 min   color   Films Inc.   '72
        *Award, duPont-Columbia
America's young blue-collar workers are a new breed. They want
a meaningful life. They do not want mass-production, standardized
jobs that do not provide opportunity for thinking and fulfillment.
This film examines their life styles, politics, views, and frustrations. NBC News. (College-Adult)

THE BLUE DASHIKI: Jeffrey and His City Neighbors
        14 min   color   Encyc. Brit.   '70
        *Chris Certificate, Columbus
The adventures of a black boy who wants to earn money to buy a
colorful African robe, a "dashiki. " This is a film without narration
or dialogue. It relies on visuals, sound effects, and musical background to spark ideas for interaction, group discussion, reading,
and writing. (Intermediate-Junior HS)

BOB & CAREN & TED & JANICE
        25 min   color   Datafilms   '72
        *Cindy Award, Info. Film
        *Golden Eagle, CINE
Young adults in real-life situations are asking, "What is vocational
education?" Bob, the son of a prosperous lawyer, wants commercial art. Caren, who's Spanish-American, chooses guidance counseling. Ted, a black dropout, returns to school to become a para-
medic. Janice, pregnant at 16, leaves her addict-husband, and
supports herself and her baby. Made by Parthenon Pictures.
(Grades 9-12)

THE BOB KNOWLTON STORY
        28 min   color   Roundtable
        *Award, US Industrial
Shows how psychological barriers can interrupt communication and
job performance. A production-oriented boss puts a brilliant in-
dividualist under an effective but team-oriented supervisor. The
team-oriented manager feels his new subordinate is taking over his

From THE BLUE DASHIKI (courtesy, Encyclopaedia Britannica Educational Corporation)

job--and the respect of his boss.   Raises questions about managing
a subordinate when he is the authority in his field.   (College-Adult)

THE BOLERO
        27 min   color   Pyramid   '72
        *Gold Medal, NY Film & TV
        *Gold Medal, Atlanta
        *Academy Award (Documentary)
        *Red Ribbon, American/EFLA
A montage of cinema-verité sequences shows the life of professional
musicians, on and off the concert stage of the Los Angeles Philharmonic Orchestra.   Climaxed by Zubin Mehta's conducting of the
Ravel masterpiece.   Produced by Allan Miller.   (Junior HS-Adult)

BOMB THREAT!   PLAN, DON'T PANIC
        15 min   color   Wm. Brose Prod.   '71
        *Award, U.S. Industrial
        *Winner, Int. Film & TV
        *Prize, Columbus
        *Award, American/EFLA
        *Golden Eagle, CINE
        *Award, Int. Security
Shows suggested procedures for institutional telephone calls, planning
detail, and bomb search follow-through.   Accompanied by Bomb
Threat Procedures Manual, available from the producer.   (College-
Adult)

BOOMSVILLE
        11 min   color   Learn. Corp.   '69
        *Blue Ribbon, American/EFLA
        *Chris Statuette, Columbus
This animated overview of the growth of cities shows what man has
done to his environment.   Without narration, the film recreates the
process by which man took virgin land and made it a frantic, con-
gested "boomsville."   The advent of railroads, cars and airplanes,
the industrial revolution, wars, the growth of a pleasure-loving so-
ciety--these are some of the factors sketched in.   The film concludes with man on another planet, preparing to start the whole process again.   Produced by the National Film Board of Canada.   (HS-
Adult)

A BORING AFTERNOON
        14 min   BW   Macmillan   '65
        *Nomination, Academy Awards
        *Young Critics' Prize, Locarno
        *Golden Ducat, Mannheim
This live-action short is about a man who tries to read a book in a
tavern on a busy afternoon.   It satirizes the "generation gap" and
the average man's contempt for the non-conforming outsider.   Its
surprise ending points out how little any of us sees of others.
Czech dialog with English subtitles.   Director: Ivan Passer.   (HS-
Adult)

THE BOX
    7 min   color   Macmillan   '67
    *Best Cartoon, Academy Awards
    *Critics' Award, Annecy (France)
A fable on communication: What does it "mean"? Perhaps each to
his own thing? No. It means that when a stranger enters a bar
with a mysterious box, and arouses curiosity about the inhabitant
(or contents) of the box, and when a young lady enters the same bar
with her box, and the two decide to ... but why spoil it for you?
Produced by Murakami-Wolf Films.   (HS-Adult)

A BOY CREATES
    10 min   color   Encyc. Brit.   '70
    *Golden Eagle, CINE
Demonstrates a boy's imagination in transforming "junk" into art
forms. He uses lifeless material found in a deserted amusement
park. From discarded bottles, plastic, cast-off wood, and metal,
he fashions a figure and places it on a log. His "found art" sculpture becomes a person in a roadster that soars airborne on a magical journey.   (Primary-Intermediate)

A BOY OF MEXICO: Juan and His Donkey
    11 min   color   Coronet
    *Award of Merit, Boston
Through the story of Juan and his donkey Pepito, children can learn
some of the characteristics of rural Mexico. The film conveys a
sympathetic feeling for Mexico, and provides a background for reading and language arts activities.   (Primary-Intermediate)

THE BOYHOOD OF ABRAHAM LINCOLN
    11 min   color   Coronet
    *Award, Freedoms Foundation
Filmed in the authentically reconstructed village and boyhood home
at Rockport, Indiana, this film recreates Lincoln's boyhood of near-
poverty and hard work. Encouraged by his stepmother in his desire
for learning, the boy Lincoln developed qualities of honesty, responsibility, humor, and a capacity for work.   (Intermediate)

THE BOYHOOD OF GEORGE WASHINGTON
    11 min   color   Coronet   '55
    *Award, Freedoms Foundation
The film shows Washington growing up around Ferry Farm and
Mount Vernon, and developing into young manhood on the Shenandoah
frontier. Begins when Washington was eight and shows his forma-
tive years--the experiences, standards of conduct, and capabilities
that fitted him for leadership.   (Intermediate)

THE BOYHOOD OF THOMAS EDISON
    13 1/2 min   color   Coronet   '61
    *Chris Award, Columbus
Photographed in the original buildings in Greenfield Village and at
Edison's boyhood home in Ohio, this film dramatizes incidents from
the boyhood of one of America's great practical scientists. Tom's

sitting on eggs to hatch them; his early experiments with chemicals and electricity; the newspaper he published on a train--all point up his curiosity, persistence, ingenuity, and ability to learn through observation. (Intermediate)

BRAKE FREE
    7 min color ACI Films '72
    *Silver Medal, Venice
    *Golden Eagle, CINE
A boy's fantasy excursion on a steam-driven cog railway, in tempo with Beethoven's 3rd and 7th symphonies. We climb White Mountain in New Hampshire, and speed through the countryside. The landscape flashes past our window, the pace accelerating until we reach our destination with an abrupt halt. This wordless film is almost equivalent to a ride on the last train of its kind in America. A Carson Davidson Film. (Intermediate-Adult)

BRAZIL, I LOVE YOU
    13 min color BFA Educ. Media
    *Chris Statuette, Columbus
To Brazil's samba beat, this film reveals the life and land of the world's fifth largest nation: her plains and mountains, beaches and jungles, her annual carnival, poor fishing villages, and cities with slums that house a large percentage of her multiracial population. Focuses on present problems and hopes as symbolized by the new capital, Brasilia. Filmed by Arthur Mokin Productions. (Intermediate-Adult)

BREAKTHROUGH TO LANGUAGE
    17 min color La. St. School '72
    *Golden Eagle, CINE
Describes the change-over to the Rochester Method of communication (language simultaneously spoken and finger-spelled) and its impact on the faculty, students, and families associated with the Louisiana State School for the Deaf, sponsor of this production. Available without charge to interested groups. An Avalon Daggett production. (College-Adult)

BREAST SELF-EXAMINATION: A Plan for Survival--A Lifetime Habit
    10 min color MIC/FP '74
    *Blue Ribbon, American/EFLA
Demonstrates techniques recommended for women, and explains differences in body types. Stresses the importance of personal surveillance. Director: Dolores E. Fiedler, M.D. Production company: William Clairborne, Inc. (Senior HS-Adult)

BRONZE
    14 min color Learn. Corp. '69
    *Silver Medal, Venice
Follows the work of sculptor Charles Daudelin. Without a word of dialogue or narration, director Pierre Moretti traces the process of sculpture by means of his photography. We see a gigantic sculpture

as it begins to take shape, and finally when it is placed in the National Arts Centre in Ottawa. Produced by Pierre Moretti of the National Film Board of Canada. (Intermediate-Adult)

BROWN WOLF
    26 min   color   Learn. Corp.   '72
    *Award Winner, Chicago
Photographed in the natural surroundings of the Klondike, this adaptation of Jack London's story of a dog and the people in his life brings out the conflict between the call of the wild and the demands of civilization. Filmed by George Kaczender. (Elem.-Adult)

BUFFALO: An Ecological Success Story
    14 min   color   Encyc. Brit.   '71
    *Merit, Human Environment
    *Golden Eagle, CINE
The life story of the bison ... and the effort made to preserve this species. Recaptures a vision of the vast herds that once roamed North America and of Indian tribes that depended upon the animal for food, clothing, shelter, weapons, and fuel. Settlers, railroads, and professional hunters decimated this important natural resource that is only now being gradually restored. (Junior HS-Senior HS)

BULLDOZED AMERICA
    25 min   BW   Carousel   '65
    *Blue Ribbon, American/EFLA
This film shows the triumph of the bulldozer and commercial interests as they devastate the countryside and turn it into un-needed supermarkets, un-wanted highways, and unproductive automobile dumps. Interviews with William O. Douglas and Stewart Udall present a defense of a point of view that puts human values above commercial interests. Produced by CBS News. (HS-Adult)

BULLOCKY
    14 min   color   Australia   '70
    *Gold Camera, US Industrial
A study of a disappearing character, the "bullocky," a man who prefers to use oxen (bullocks) rather than machines for hauling timber in the rugged Australian forests. Filmed by the Commonwealth Film Unit. (Intermediate-Adult)

THE BUNCO BOYS--And How to Beat Them!
    21 min   color   Wm. Brose Prod.   '72
    *Winner, NY TV & Film
    *Chris Statuette, Columbus
    *Golden Eagle, CINE
    *Merit Award, Chicago
The North Hollywood Federal Savings & Loan Assn. assisted with material for this exposition of common fraud schemes such as "The Bank Examiner," "The Pigeon Drop," and "The Charity Switch."
(College-Adult)

BUSTED
     17 min   color   Oxford Films
     *Award Winner, U.S. Industrial
     *Prize Winner, Columbus
What's it like to be tried in juvenile court? Filmed on actual locations, this production simulates the experience of the consequences
of an illegal use of drugs. An Art Evans Production. (Upper
Elem. -HS)

BUT WHAT IF THE DREAM COMES TRUE?
     52 min   color   Carousel   '71
     *Blue Ribbon, American /EFLA
Shows that there can be trouble in paradise--that once material
goals have been achieved, there still would seem to be a sense of
nonfulfillment, that perhaps the American Dream needs more than
money, status, and comfort. Produced by CBS News. (College-
Adult)

BY THE SEA
     14 min   color   Barr Films   '71
     *Golden Eagle, CINE
A variety of non-verbal impressions of the seashore: people by the
sea, changing moods of the sea, plant and animal forms beneath the
surface and along the shoreline. A film by Joern Gerdts. (Elem. -
Adult)

THE CABINET
     14 min   color   Carousel   '71
     *Golden Eagle, CINE
Inside a white frame house stands a wooden cabinet that is a personal museum of dolls, yellowing photos, family mementos, and
toys. They lie there, inanimate, until film-maker Suzanne Bauman
breathes life into them with her camera, allegorically re-enacting
the games, love, and tragedies of a little girl. Along with animated
sequences are some live-action episodes of maturing, aging, and dying. (Intermediate-Adult)

CAGES
     9 min   BW   McGraw-Hill   '69
     *Grand Prize, Annecy (France)
     *Bronze Hobby Horse, Cracow
An animated film made in the style of line drawings. Begins with
a man in prison whom the warden tries to cheer up by bringing him
some toy blocks. The prisoner's constructions, though, are more
elaborate than his captor's, and the latter, in jealousy, takes them
away. Neither can his jailers tolerate the thought-balloons that
form above his head, and these are captured in a butterfly net. But
who will guard the guards? For, as a door in the background opens,
viewers can see that the jailer is being watched by another jailer,
who's being watched by still another, and another, and another, and
so on, ad infinitum. Produced by the Short Film Studio, Warsaw.
(HS-Adult)

CAJITITLAN
    41 min color McGraw-Hill '66
    *Golden Eagle, CINE
This is a documentation of a Mexican village whose culture has re-
mained practically unchanged for more than a thousand years. A
Contemporary Films release, photographed and directed by Harry
Atwood. (College-Adult)

CAN WE IMMUNIZE AGAINST PREJUDICE?
    6 1/2 min BW Anti-Defamation
    *Prize Winner, Cleveland
    *Award Winner, Boston
Three pairs of parents use different methods to prevent prejudice in
their children. Nevertheless, racial and religious bias develops.
The film asks where the parents failed, and provides projector stop-
ping-points for viewer discussion. Narrated by Eddie Albert. Animation by Leo Lionni. (HS-Adult)

THE CANADA GOOSE
    6 1/2 min color AV Explor. '68
    *Honors, American/EFLA
Close-ups and naturally synchronized sound provide a study of the
courtship, nesting, flight, and behavior of this migratory bird.
Available with Study-Guide. Filmed by Dan Gibson. (Intermediate-
Adult)

A CANADA GOOSE ADVENTURE
    11 min color Encyc. Brit. '72
    *Golden Eagle, CINE
Authentic sounds take the place of narration as these geese are
shown nesting in a pond and romping with human friends. Slow-motion sequences emphasize the grace of birds in flight. Borden Productions, Inc. (Intermediate-HS)

CANADA: Take It From the Top
    23 min color Learn. Corp. '67
    *Certificate Winner, Columbus
From the Bay of Fundy to the Pacific Northwest, the topography of
this great nation unfolds in a helicopter view of diversified industries, recreation areas, historic points of interest, and changing
seasons in the provinces and major cities. By the National Film
Board of Canada. (Intermediate-Adult)

CANON
    10 min color Int. Film Bur.
    *Awards: New Delhi, Canada, Melbourne, Argentina
A visual definition of the musical form, the canon, with color and
shape representing vocal parts, and with designs showing patterns
and intervals of movement. An artistic interpretation of how sound
"looks." Producers: McLaren, Monroe, and Rathburn of the National Film Board of Canada. (College-Adult)

THE CAPITOL: Chronicle of Freedom
    22 min color Films Inc.   '65
    *Citation, US Capitol
    *3rd Place, TV Newsfilm
    *Merit Exhibition, CINE
    *Freedoms Foundation Award
Provides some points of interest about our nation's headquarters:
its architectural evolution, the important events that occurred within
this building, and the routine conduct of business.   Made by NBC-
TV.   (Intermediate-Adult)

CAPTAIN ARBANOS MARKO
    9 min color Pyramid '68
    *Silver Medal, Atlanta
A medieval Yugoslavian ballad is the basis for this story of the life
and death of a great swordsman.   In his reckless pride, he kidnaps
three maidens but, until morning dawns, he does not realize that
they were the Three Fates of Death.   Animated.   A Zagreb-Janus
Production.   (HS-Adult)

CARBON
    27 min color AIM-Assn.   '68
    *Blue Ribbon, American/EFLA
    *Chris Award, Columbus
    *Gold Medal, Atlanta ... and other honors
Attempts to survey the properties and uses of this versatile element.
Includes the reduction of a substantial diamond to a small heap of
graphite.   (HS-College)

CAREER AND COSTUME CIRCUS
    10 min color ACI Films   '70
    *Honors, American/EFLA
Two children play with a toy circus and, as they do, recall their
visits to real ones.   Meantime, the viewer sees a montage of the
garb of different occupations, each style obviously representing a
separate line of work.   Encourages youngsters to look for the real
person beneath surface indications, while providing a preliminary insight into job clusters.   A Communico Film.   (Elem.)

CAREERS: COMMUNICATIONS
    12 1/2 min color Doubleday   '70
    *Silver Medal, Atlanta
    *Hon. Mention, San Francisco
Three general areas are covered in this production: printing, advertising, and photography.   A printing salesman discusses his satis-
faction at seeing a color job well done; an advertising executive talks
about his willingness to work beyond the nine-to-five routine; and a
photographer is shown on the job, covering a road race.   (HS)

CAREERS: HEALTH SERVICES
    11 min color Doubleday   '70
    *Best Film, APGA
    *Bronze Medal, Atlanta

Dramatizes some real-life situations that can occur in work related to medicine. The lab technologist assists in diagnosing; the technician operates a heart-lung pump during surgery; and an occupational therapist helps patients to adjust and recover. (HS)

CAREERS: LEISURE INDUSTRIES
9 min   color   Doubleday   '70
*Chris Award, Columbus
This is a field that is growing and producing new job opportunities.
A few examples shown are represented: the owners of a motorcycle shop, a man who designs camper-trailers, and other people who build or sell these products. (HS)

CARNIVOROUS PLANTS
12 min   color   Nat. Geog.   '74
*Blue Ribbon, American/EFLA
Examines, in microscopic detail, the Venus's flytrap, sundew, bladderwort, and the Sarracenia pitcher plant--all bizarre plants that eat animals. Producer: Oxford Scientific Films. (Junior HS-Senior HS)

CAROLINE
28 min   BW   Nat. Film Bd.
*Prize Winner, Venice
*Canadian Film Award
To the public, she is the pleasant handler of complaints at the telephone office. But behind her calm exterior the camera reveals her doubts about her domestic world of husband and child. (College-Adult)

CARROUSEL
7 1/2 min   color   Univ. Educ.   '69
*Awards: Ceylon and Iran
A dream of merry-go-round horses that have come to life. The inside-out effect of the images was achieved by making a negative and a positive from the color negative, and then using all three as printing materials, together with color filters. By interposing one film on another during the printing, it was possible to change the color of part of a scene without changing all of it. National Film Board of Canada. (Intermediate-Adult)

THE CARS IN YOUR LIFE
29 1/2 min   BW   McGraw-Hill   '60
*Award, American/EFLA
A variety of camera work--slow motion and pop-on/pop-off technique--outlines this study of motormania and the urge for a place on the highway. A Contemporary Films release. Produced by Terence McCartney for the National Film Board of Canada. (HS-Adult)

CASALS CONDUCTS: 1964
17 min   BW   Encyc. Brit.   '65
*Golden Eagle, CINE
*Winner, Academy Award ... and other honors

A glimpse into Pablo Casals' workshop at the University of Puerto Rico. He conducts a rehearsal of the Bach Orchestral Suite in C-Major, then presents it at the actual performance. Produced by Edward Schreiber for Thalia Films. (College-Adult)

CASE HISTORY OF A RUMOR
    52 min BW Carousel '63
    *Blue Ribbon, American/EFLA
Describes the events following the rumor that the anti-communistic military maneuver (Operation Water Moccasin) was a foreign plot to occupy Georgia and eventually all of the U.S. This report, a product of ignorance and prejudice, shows how hate and extremism can threaten freedom. Produced by CBS News. (College-Adult)

CASSANDRA CAT
    87 min color Macmillan '63
    *International Award, FIPRESCI
    *Special Jury Prize, Cannes
A fantasy of how a town is turned upside down by the magical powers of a cat that, by donning special spectacles, reveals the true personalities of people. For example: lovers are red, liars are purple, and thieves are gray. Naturally, such disclosures are an embarrassment to too many of the townsfolk who, as a result, try to hunt the cat down. To the rescue come the children of the village, who return the animal to its traveling circus, leaving the town happier and (possibly) wiser. Live-action. Directed by Vojtech Jasny. (Elem.)

CATCH THE JOY
    14 min color Pyramid '70
    *Jack London Prize, Nat. Educ.
    *Special Award, Hemisfilm
    *Gold Medal, Atlanta
The makers of Moods of Surfing "catch the joy" of a new form of activity--speeding over the sand in dune buggies. Color filters and slow motion add their own mood, and motorized acrobatics provide a little humor. Producers: MacGillivray and Freeman. (HS-Adult)

CATERPILLAR
    16 min color Learn. Corp. '71
    *Merit Award, Landers
    *Certificate, Columbus
An animated tale of a boy and a green caterpillar that dances to the tune of a harmonica. This unique performance catches the eye of an impresario. Soon the boy and his pet are off on an international concert tour. At Christmas, of all times, the boy's friend disappears. His searching is to no avail but, one Spring day, as the boy plays his harmonica, he knowingly watches a beautiful butterfly, flying in rhythm to his music. From a story by Norman Corwin. Produced by Kresleny Film (Prague). (Elem.)

THE CATERPILLAR AND THE WILD ANIMALS
    7 min color American Educ.

*Golden Eagle, CINE
Based on an African Masai folk tale, this animated story is about a disenchanted insect that proceeds to bully the mighty animals of the jungle ... until he meets a curious frog. Film-maker: Gerard Baldwin. (Elem.)

CATS AND DOGS
    23 min BW ACI Films '71
    *Award, Rochester International
    *First Prize, Chicago
    *Award, Edinburgh (Scotland)
    *Golden Eagle, CINE
Explores the relationship between a man and a woman who share a walk-up apartment in New York, where most of the scenes take place. Their basic attitudes toward one another are revealed in their individuality and, after a quarrel, she leaves. They meet again but there seems little chance of their reconciliation. A Paul Gurian Production. (Senior HS-Adult)

CAVE ECOLOGY
    13 min color Centron '70
    *Chris Award, Columbus
    *Merit Award, Landers
    *Golden Eagle, ·CINE
An introduction to a unit of study on the human community. By observing relationships among organisms in a simple cave community, viewers may grasp the concept of interdependence more analytically and objectively. (Intermediate-Junior HS)

CBW: THE SECRETS OF SECRECY
    49 min color Films Inc. '69
    *Award, Polk Memorial
    *Geo. Foster Peabody Award
    *Award, duPont-Columbia
    *Emmy, Nat. Academy
The potential for mass annihilation is the subject of this examination of CBW (Chemical-Biological Warfare). Prepared without Defense Department approval, this report includes data long withheld from the public, and is composed of interviews with volunteers and scientists who worked on classified projects. Information from British and Canadian CBW centers round out the prospects for largescale destruction and "genocide by accident." Produced by NBC News. (College-Adult)

CELEBRATION OF WINTER
    28 min color Assn.-Sterl. '68
    *1st Prize, American/EFLA
A snow film that includes "turned on" ski instructors, snow-mobile races, dog-sled events, ice fishing, and après-ski parties. Sponsor: State of New Hampshire. Available on free loan to colleges and adult groups.

THE CELL: A Functioning Structure, Part I
    29 min color CRM Films '72
    *Gold Medal, Int. Film & TV
Dr. David Suzuki, University of British Columbia, narrates this
presentation. After a brief survey of the advances in microscopy
that have made cell study possible, the film illustrates the processes
by which cells nourish themselves and multiply. (College)

CENTRAL SIMILARITIES
    10 min color Int. Film Bur. '71
    *Golden Eagle, CINE
Dilatations (or central similarities) are introduced in order to solve
the problem of inscribing an ellipse to touch the sides of a triangle
at their midpoints. Coordinate geometry is applied toward solving
a related problem, stressing the importance of the geometric interpretation of algebraic equations. Mathematicians: Daniel Pedoe
and H. S. M. Coxeter. (HS-College)

CHAIM SOUTINE
    28 min color McGraw-Hill '70
    *Lion of St. Mark, Venice
This is a psychological profile of Chaim Soutine, the 20th century
expressionist painter. Filmed in documentary format, with actors
recreating his early life and his flight from Nazi persecution, this
production also includes interviews with some of Soutine's friends,
collectors, and other artists. All explore the relationship between
his character and his technique. Produced by Rita J. Morrison.
(College-Adult)

THE CHAIRMAKER AND THE BOYS
    21 min color Int. Film Bur.
    *Awards: Vienna (Austria), and Edinburgh
In this domestic drama, Ernest Hart of Cape Breton Island is black-
smith, carpenter, and all-round handyman to his farming neighbors.
While he makes chairs, his grandson makes mischief, and Grandpa
is forced into still another role. The result is a contrast between
the restraining wisdom of age and the carefree exuberance of youth.
By the National Film Board of Canada. (Elem.-Adult)

A CHAIRY TALE
    10 min BW Int. Film Bur. '57
    *Award, Br. Film Academy
    *Nomination, Academy Award
    *Experimental Prize, Venice ... and other honors
A live-action fantasy, told without words, of a man's confrontation
with a chair. He loses. Music is provided by Ravi Shankar and
others. Directed by Norman McLaren of the National Film Board
of Canada. (HS-Adult)

CHANGES, CHANGES
    6 min color Weston Woods '73
    *Golden Eagle, CINE
Wooden building blocks and two wooden dolls illustrate adaptability to

changing events and circumstances. This is itself an adaptation
(animated) of the picture book by Pat Hutchins, with music performed
only on wooden instruments. Produced by Mort Schindel. (Elem.)

CHANGING OF THE GUARD
       8 min   color   Macmillan   '59
       *Originality Prize, Cannes
       *Hon. Mention, Stratford (Canada)
An animated fairy tale in which all the characters are matchboxes.
They include a soldier of the Royal Guard, the King, the King's
daughter (naturally), and assorted inhabitants of the castle. By the
end, all go up in flame because they have not learned not to play
with fire. No narration or dialogue. A Film Miniatures Studio
production. (Elem.)

A CHANGING VIEW OF THE CHANGE OF LIFE
       28 min   color   Assn. -Sterl.
       *1st Place, Nat'l. Visual
This film attempts to answer some questions about menopause in
women. In non-technical language, and using animation, it explains
the biological factors causing menopause and its symptoms. It also
presents evidence of new attitudes and advances that are based on
information from medical journals. Available on free loan to wom-
en's groups, schools, and industry. Sponsor: the Wilson Research
Foundation. (College-Adult)

THE CHANGING WORLD OF CHARLES DICKENS
       27 min   color   Learn. Corp.   '69
       *Chris Statuette, Columbus
In the locale of the grimy and chaotic world of the Industrial Revolution, this film shows how the great novelist drew on reality and
transformed it into the ordered substance of his art. English actors
recreate passages from David Copperfield, Oliver Twist, Great Expectations, and Hard Times. (HS-College)

THE CHARM OF LIFE (The French Academy Painters, 1860-1914)
       17 min   BW   Pictura
       *1st Prize, Int. Film & TV
All the works in this film were winners of the Prix de Rome at a
time when paintings by such artists as Cézanne, Renoir, and Picasso
were being laughed off the walls. This film is a parody of a particularly vulnerable period of art criticism, a mockery of false
ideals. (College-Adult)

CHEATING
       9 min   color   Oxford Films
       *Gold Medal, Atlanta
       *Chris Statuette, Columbus
Mike, one of a group of students who have been falling behind in
math, is in conflict about a test to be given. His friend Jim obtains
an advance copy and offers Mike the chance to see it. That's where
the film pauses to permit discussion. It can be stopped again after
each of four alternative endings. Producer: Moreland-Latchford,
Ltd. (Junior HS)

CHEETAH
>11 min   color   Encyc. Brit.   '71
>*Golden Eagle, CINE
>*Bronze Medal, Atlanta

The fastest mammal of all is seen in action on the Serengeti Plains of Tanzania. Hunt scenes show how this cat uses its tail for balance, especially when achieving speeds up to 70 miles per hour! A mother cheetah and her two cubs stalk a gazelle and, when it comes time to feast on their prey, they are joined by the hyena and other scavengers. Non-narrated. Produced by P. and J. Chermayeff. (Elem. -Adult)

CHICKAMAUGA
>33 min   BW   McGraw-Hill   '63
>*Award, San Sebastian

This adaptation of Ambrose Bierce's Civil War story creates an awareness of the horrors of war. A boy wanders away from home, reaches a battlefield, plays soldier among the dead and dying, and ironically returns to find his home burned and his family slain while he was "playing war." Directed by Robert Enrico. (HS-Adult)

THE CHICKEN (Le Poulet)
>15 min   BW   McGraw-Hill   '65
>*Winner, Academy Award
>*First Prize, Venice
>*Award, NY International
>*Winner, Oberhausen
>*Award, Bordighera

This is the story of a boy so fond of a chicken that he can't let his pet become lunch for his family some day. So, he hits upon the idea of persuading his parents that their rooster is really a hen, thinking they'll be more interested in its ability to produce eggs than meat. His plan looks like a success--but the boy failed to reckon with the rooster itself. In French with sub-titles. Directed by Claude Berri. A Renn Production (France). (Elem.)

CHILD BEHAVIOR = YOU
>15 min   color   Benchmark   '72
>*Canadian Film Award

To modify behavior from infancy to adolescence, the basic principle is to reward desirable actions. In practice, it is often the undesirable actions that receive attention. By using humor and animation, this film tries to show what parent-child relationships can be like during those crucial years. (Intermediate-Adult)

CHILD OF DARKNESS, CHILD OF LIGHT
>28 min   color   Assn. -Sterl.
>*Blue Ribbon, American/EFLA

This is the story of two different children in the slums of South America. One four-year old, Marisol, is plagued by disease and hunger, her life dependent on scavenging from garbage and on her mother's begging. A luckier child, Luz, gets plenty of food, clothing, and medical care, and goes to school every day. She and her family are being helped by Foster Parents Plan, the sponsor of this production. Available on free loan to groups of Junior HS age and above.

CHILDHOOD: The Enchanted Years
    52 min color Films Inc. '71
    *Award, Ohio State Univ.
This film charts a child's progress from complete dependence to a self-determined will. While physical growth is relatively easy to understand, mental development is still a subject of much research and discussion. Through experiments and long-term studies, psychologists are beginning to ask the right questions, if not find the right answers. What are we humans? What is the nature of our minds? What forces influence our future? An MGM Documentary. (College-Adult)

CHILDREN IN THE CITY
    8 min color Oxford '74
    *Golden Eagle, CINE
    *Gold Camera, Ind. Films
This film depicts children of New York in their ingenuity at adapting to their complex environment. Stresses the need for safe and enlarged recreation facilities in recognizing the universal needs of growing up. Produced by Monroe-Williams. (College-Adult)

THE CHILDREN OF FOGO ISLAND
    17 1/2 min BW Perennial
    *Award, Conf. on Children
Gives some understanding as to what causes the people of a Newfoundland outpost to remain so deeply rooted to their isolated community. A case-study in comparative qualities of life. Produced by the National Film Board of Canada. (HS-Adult)

CHILDREN OF THE KIBBUTZ
    17 min color ACI Films '73
    *Golden Eagle, CINE
This film looks at life in Israel through the eyes of children in a cooperative agricultural community (a kibbutz). The narrator is the mother of several of the children who are observed studying, eating, playing, and visiting their families. Produced by Yehuda Yaniv. (Intermediate-Adult)

CHILDREN WHO DRAW
    44 min BW with color Macmillan '56
    *Robert Flaherty Award
    *First Prize, Japan
    *Educational Award, Venice
How children think, feel, and develop is the subject of this film of Japanese school children in their customary activities, individually and in groups. The film shows, for example, how children can express themselves through the art media of crayon, finger paint, oil, and clay. We can also observe some of the behavioral changes that

take place over a period of time.   An Iwanami Film, produced by
Teizo Oguchi.   (College-Adult)

CHINA!
     65 min   color   Impact Films   '65
     *First Prize, Melbourne
     *Merit Award, Edinburgh
Set in the natural beauty of the Far East, this is a report on the
people and quality of life there.   Citizens are found to be exception-
ally united to common interests and unusually devoted to the state,
in which each member shares equally.   This is essentially one man's
assessment of a huge civilization that, until recent years, was becoming practically unknown to Western man.   Film-maker: Felix
Greene.   (College-Adult)

CHINA: The East Is Red
     21 min   color   Doubleday   '71
     *Gold Camera, US Industrial
Presents modern China's economic and cultural problems in historic
perspective.   Her internal turmoil is traced from social and political traditions, and interpreted in the light of current international
politics.   (HS-College)

THE CHINESE-AMERICAN: Early Immigrants
     20 min   color   Handel   '72
     *Chris Award, Columbus
This is a review of the first Chinese to come to the United States
to seek their fortune in the California gold rush.   Explains the resentment of white miners, and reveals the torment they inflicted on
their "yellow" competitors.   Also covered in this history is the
Chinese Exclusion Act, passed during the panic of financial and political pressures.   Narrated by Sam Chu Lin.   (Junior HS-Adult)

THE CHINESE-AMERICAN: The Twentieth Century
     20 min   color   Handel   '72
     *Chris Award, Columbus
Narrator Sam Chu Lin examines the Chinese civil war that resulted
in the unifying of mainland China under Mao Tse-Tung, culminating
in President Nixon's 1972 visit there.   In another segment of this
review, a judge explains that, although the Chinese-American dis-
tricts used to be free of crime, new conditions are causing some
problems.   (Junior HS-Adult)

THE CHOICE ... IS YOURS
     13 1/2 min   color   AV Explorations   '68
     *Honors, American/EFLA
Appreciation for water resources is stimulated by visuals of water-
based recreation in its many forms.   In stark contrast are shown
the disastrous results of industrial pollution.   The film ends with an
abstract sequence in which the choice between purity and pollution is
again posed.   Produced by Dan Gibson.   (Intermediate-Adult)

CHRIST IS BORN
    54 min   color   Learn. Corp.
    *Gabriel Award, Cath. Broadcasters
    *Golden Eagle, CINE
Filmed in the Holy Land, this is a chronicle of the birth of Jesus,
depicting, too, the history of the Hebrew people from Abraham to
the Roman era.   Presenting the Nativity as history makes this material acceptable for members of all faiths.   Bible readings are by
John Huston.   Produced by John Secondari for the ABC Television
series, "The Saga of Western Man. "   (College-Adult)

CHRISTIANS AT WAR
    50 min   color   Time-Life   '72
    *Red Ribbon, American/EFLA
Shows the tragic effects of Ireland's civil war between Catholics and
Protestants.   We see what happens to ordinary people whose daily
lives are subject to violence and despair.   Produced by BBC-TV.
(College-Adult)

CHRISTMAS CRACKER
    9 min   color   McGraw-Hill   '64
    *Nomination, Academy Award
Created by four of Canada's artists and animators, this is a presentation of three short Christmas vignettes.   A National Film Board
of Canada production by Norman McLaren, Grant Munro, Jeff Hale,
and Gerald Potterton.   (Intermediate)

CHRISTMAS IN APPALACHIA
    29 min   BW   Carousel   '64
    *Blue Ribbon, American/EFLA
Of th e million Americans living in Appalachian poverty, the Kentucky
community of Whitesburg is a representative example.   This coal-
mining village is the home of discouraged out-of-work adults and undernourished out-of-school children.   Most of them live in hovels
and shacks where Christmas is a cold and barren experience within
a nation of supposed affluence.   Produced by CBS News.   (HS-Adult)

CHRISTMAS ON GRANDFATHER'S FARM (1890's)
    13 1/2 min   color   Coronet   '59
    *Award, Scholastic Teacher
This old-fashioned holiday begins, after a happy sleigh ride, with
dinner with Grandpa and Grandma at their big farmhouse.   It includes a reading of the Biblical account of the first Christmas.   Adding to the excitement are the candles (real ones!) on the tree (a real
one, too!), handmade gifts for cousins, aunts, and uncles, and a
very special surprise for grandson Josh.   (Elem. -Adult)

THE CHRISTMAS TREE
    57 min   BW   Sterling Educ.   '70
    *Hon. Mention, La Plata
This film is about the adventures of two young brothers and a sister
who try to get a Christmas tree for a hospital party.   Producer:
Children's Film Foundation (Britain).   (Ages 7-12)

CHRONOLOGY
　　1 1/4 min　color　daSilva　'71
　　*Award, Int. Film & TV
　　*Blue Ribbon, American/EFLA
A concise impression of Western civilization from pre-historic
times to the modern era. This film is structured in such a way as
to allow viewers to draw their own conclusions about the eventual
destiny of mankind. Based on 600 hand-drawn illustrations, shot on
a fully automatic Oxberry animation stand. Non-verbal, with electronic sound. Artwork by Ray daSilva; production by Raul daSilva.
(Intermediate-Adult)

CIPHER IN THE SNOW
　　24 min　color　Brigham Young U.　'74
　　*Golden Delfan Award, Teheran
　　*Year's Best, Learning Magazine
　　*Chris Statuette, Columbus
　　*Golden Eagle, CINE
The sad but true account of a boy whom nobody thought important
... until it was too late. Based on the story that won the 1964
NEA Teachers' Writing Contest. (Elem.-Adult)

CIRCLE OF LIGHT (The Photography of Pamela Bone)
　　32 min　color　Roland Films　'72
　　*First Prize, Cork (Ireland)
This film without words is composed of Pamela Bone's glass trans-
parency photographs. Inspired by nature, Ms. Bone has searched
for expression via photographic means alone. It took her 20 years
to find the techniques that would overcome the limitations of her
medium. Producer: Anthony Roland. (College-Adult)

CIRCUS TOWN
　　48 min　color　Films Inc.　'71
　　*Merit Award, Landers
　　*Golden Eagle, CINE
　　*Chris Award, Columbus
　　*Prize Winner, Chicago
　　*Honors, American/EFLA
Peru, Indiana, used to be the winter home for six American circus
companies. It is still the home of many retired performers, and
through them this film recalls the heights of this form of folk art.
Once a year, calling on the resources of its retired stars, Peru
puts on its own circus in which former greats lend a hand as train-
ers to young performers between the ages of 6 and 20. Produced
by NBC News. (Intermediate-Adult)

CITIES HAVE NO LIMITS
　　53 min　color　Films Inc.　'69
　　*Golden Eagle, CINE
An examination of modern urban crisis as exemplified in the decay
of the central city. Poverty amid prosperity is one source of social
division, along with unemployment, inflation, riots, addiction, and
other forms of "crime." All these elements are evidence of more

unrest to come, according to film-guests Daniel P. Moynihan and
Charles V. Hamilton. NBC News. (HS-Adult)

CITIZEN HAROLD
        9 min color Learn. Corp. '73
        *Award Winner, Columbus
The all too familiar frustrations of trying to get some action
through governmental channels is the subject of this animation by
Hugh Foulds, whose hero becomes aroused enough over bulldozer
violence to leave his TV set and to challenge City Hall. National
Film Board of Canada. (Elem. -Adult)

THE CITY AND THE FUTURE
        28 min BW Sterling Educ.
        *Chris Award, Columbus
        *Award, NY Int. Film & TV
In more and more parts of the world the inevitable choice must be
made between urban sprawl or a new form of regionalized city.
This last film of the Lewis Mumford series examines prospects for
the city and ways of restoring its role as the focus of man's highest
achievement. Produced by the National Film Board of Canada. (HS-
College)

CITY OF NECESSITY
        25 min color Carousel '62
        *Golden Gate Award, San Francisco
This film consists of impressions of Chicago, its beautiful facade,
its congestion, segregation, and unemployment. Chicago serves as
an example of a city in the throes of revolution. Implicit is the
struggle toward maturity, social and individual. Produced by Robert
Newman. (HS-Adult)

CITY OUT OF TIME
        15 3/4 min color Nat. Film Bd.
        *Award, Vancouver (Canada)
An appreciation of Venice that explores the legacy of Italian art be-
queathed to all peoples. Two hundred years ago Canaletto caught
and painted the elegance of spired churches and turreted palaces
that still seem to be soaring up to the blue Mediterranean sky. (HS-
Adult)

THE CITY THAT WAITS TO DIE
        57 min color Time-Life '72
        *Red Ribbon, American/EFLA
An examination of the geological prediction that the shifting San An-
dreas Fault may soon reduce the city of San Francisco to rubble,
while scientists race against time and apathy to head off disaster.
Produced by BBC-TV. (College-Adult)

CITY TREE
        9 min color ACI Films '73
        *1st Prize, Mich. St. Univ.
A story, told in verse, of a tree that is planted between sidewalk

and curb, and suffers from the carelessness of passersby. Nobody looks after it and, as a result, it is dying of neglect. Produced by Barbara Kerans. (Elem.)

THE CIVIL WAR: Background Issues (1820-1860)
        16 min   color   Coronet
        *Freedoms Foundation Award
Analyzes forty years of compromise that bridged differences between the way of life in the South and the North. The breakdown of legislation to resolve the differences is seen in the crucial decisions that led to the War Between the States. (HS)

CLAUDE
        3 min   color   Pyramid   '65
        *Silver Hugo, Chicago
        *Animation Prize, Nat. Student
        *Best Animation, Cinestud
Claude is a boy with a head like a football. He lives in an opulent house and is owned by conformist parents who tell him, "You'll never amount to anything." But Claude has ideas of his own and gets his revenge by the use of a little black box. Animation by Dan McLaughlin. (Elem.-Adult)

CLAW
        30 min   BW   Pyramid   '67
        *First Prize, Yale Univ.
        *Golden Eagle, CINE
Manhattan's grand old buildings and intricate statuary are being demolished, one after another, by a claw-like machine designed to make room for more look-alike skyscrapers. The real enemy, though, is not "the claw" but the motivation of the money men behind the machinery. Filmed by Manfred Kirchheimer. (HS-Adult)

CLAY (Origin of the Species)
        8 min   BW   McGraw-Hill   '64
        *Best Beginner, Int. Animated
By animating three-dimensional objects, Eliot Noyes, Jr. has created a visual variation on Darwin. Beginning with simple graphics on a clay "sea," forms of life emerge, then play, now devour one another, and metamorphose into worms, gorillas, mermaids, clams, lions, whales, and eventually into man himself. (But what about the female of our species?) (Intermediate-Adult)

THE CLOISTERED NUN
        18 min   color   Films Inc.   '69
        *Award, White House News
        *Honors, National Press
This film essay, narrated by one of the sisters, goes behind the walls of a convent to show the simple yet multi-dimensional motivations of the religious order. Parts of her outward life are the chores, recreation, and organized prayer. But the contemplative experience is the search for serenity and for truth. Produced by NBC News. (HS-Adult)

CLOSED MONDAYS
    8 min   color   Pyramid   '75
    *Nomination, Academy Award
    *Gold Hugo, Chicago
    *Golden Eagle, CINE
In a combination of animation graphics and three-dimensional clay
figures, a museum comes to life in this subconscious awareness of
what is involved beneath the surface of a work of art and its housing. A Lighthouse Production. (Junior HS-Adult)

CLOSE-UP ON FIRE
    54 min   color   Phoenix   '73
    *Blue Ribbon, American/EFLA
A television documentary on the economic impact of fire damage in
the U.S., along with the more disturbing proof that America leads
the industrialized world in annual deaths by fire. As a result of
government failure to protect its citizens from the malfeasance of
property owners, 12,000 died in one year, and another 300,000 suffered the agony of burns. An ABC-TV production by Jules Bergman
and Pamela Hill. (College-Adult)

THE CLUE OF THE MISSING APE
    58 min   BW   Sterling Educ.   '70
    *Co-winner, Venice (Children)
The adventures of a sea cadet and a little girl who round up crooks
who are trying to destroy the British Fleet in Gibraltar. Produced
by the Children's Film Foundation, England. (Ages 7-12)

COCKABOODY
    9 min   color   Pyramid   '74
    *Golden Reel, San Francisco
    *Golden Eagle, CINE
An animated study of children learning to use words in order to
communicate. Produced by John and Faith Hubley. (Elem.)

COLONIAL EXPANSION OF EUROPEAN NATIONS
    13 1/2 min   color   Coronet
    *Golden Reel Award
Shows the importance of trading and other factors that led to exploration and settlements by Spain, Portugal, the Netherlands, England, and France. Shows also the shift in global power, the social
and political reasons for imperialism, and their economic motivations for colonization. (HS)

COLONIAL LIFE IN NEW ENGLAND
    11 min   color   Coronet
    *Freedoms Foundation Award
Costumed re-enactments portray how colonists lived in rural New
England communities. A young lawyer describes life in cosmopoli-
tan Boston and the restlessness caused by the remote British gov-
ernance. (Intermediate)

COLONIAL LIFE IN THE MIDDLE COLONIES
    11 min   color   Coronet
    *Freedoms Foundation Award
Suggests the character of life in pre-Revolutionary times.   Re-enacts
a trip of a post rider carrying mail between Philadelphia and New
York.   Explains how the population and geography contributed to our
national traditions.   (Intermediate)

COLONIAL LIFE IN THE SOUTH
    13 1/2 min   color   Coronet
    *Freedoms Foundation Award
The journey of a surveyor points out the social and economic characteristics of that period and that region.   Filmed at authentic restorations, where many objects of that time are seen by viewers:
utensils, household articles, and clothing.   (Intermediate)

THE COLOR OF LIFE
    23 1/2 min   color   Univ. Educ.   '70
    *Award Winner, Edinburgh
Probes the transformation of a spring seedling into the green foliage
of a mature tree.   Time-lapse photography and animation show the
processes of plant growth and the chemical changes that create autumnal color.   National Film Board of Canada.   (Intermediate-HS)

THE COLORADO RIVER (2nd Ed.)
    13 1/2 min   color   Coronet
    *Chris Award, Columbus
High in the Rocky Mountains begin the headwaters of this river and
its tributaries that drain an area almost a quarter million square
miles in the southwestern U. S.   In addition, its dams provide power
and recreation, as well as helping to control the floods and droughts
that used to occur so often.   (Intermediate)

COME BACK, AFRICA
    83 min   BW   Impact Films   '60
    *Year's Best, Chevalier
    *Year's 10 Best, Time
    *Special Achievement, Vancouver
    *Critics' Award, Venice (Italy)
This story of a Zulu family reflects the reality of 20th century segregation in the Union of South Africa.   Shot on location in Johannesburg and restricted areas, where 50,000 African homes were being
annihilated to make room for whites.   Film-maker: Lionel Rogosin.
(College-Adult)

COMMUNICATING SUCCESSFULLY
    25 min   color   Time-Life   '73
    *Blue Ribbon, American/EFLA
Actor Robert Morse hosts this dramatized lesson on how to face an
audience, with emphasis on productive meetings, effective speeches,
and persuasive presentations.   (College-Adult)

THE CONCERT OF M. KABAL
   6 min color Pyramid '64
   *Jury Prize, Int. Animation
   *Quality Prize, Nat. Center
   *Outstanding Film, NY Film & TV
   *Film of the Year, London
An animated performance of Grand Guignol vaudeville. Madame
Kabal, with the profile of a vulture, secures her henpecked husband's
attention to her playing of Chopin by application of a meat-cleaver.
A Janus Film by Valerian Borowczyk. (HS-Adult)

CONCRETE POETRY
   12 min color Pyramid '70
   *Golden Eagle, CINE
A filmic interpretation of a new art form: poems that are meant to
be seen as well as heard. Nine poems, selected from Emmett Williams' Anthology of Concrete Poetry, appear as typographical designs and as recited words. Each poem imprints itself as a type-
picture, interplaying meaning and structure. Film-maker: Michael
Warshaw. (HS-College)

CONFORMITY
   49 min BW Carousel '63
   *Award, Christians & Jews
This indictment of "me-tooism" in a nation's populace focuses on
advocates of book-burning, bigots, supporters of the late Senator
Joseph McCarthy, buck-passing parents, "yes men," and group-think
education. The firing of a freedom-of-choice librarian is one illustration, along with the panic selling of a house because of a new
Black family in the neighborhood. Produced by WCAU-TV, Philadelphia. (College-Adult)

CONRAD, JOSIE AND THE ZOOMERANG
   15 min color Oxford '72
   *Award Winner, Canada
As one of the main characters, the "Zoomerang" becomes three different things in the three different stories within this film. Designed to show how several stories can be based on the same general
eral elements. Produced by Moreland-Latchford, Ltd. (Elem.)

CONTINENTAL DRIFT
   10 min color Univ. Educ.
   *Award, London (England)
This animated film presents the idea that continents were formed
from one super-sized land mass that broke up, whose pieces sank
and then rose again but far apart from the original unit. Produced
by the National Film Board of Canada. (HS-College)

CONTINENTS ADRIFT
   15 min color American Educ.
   *Red Ribbon, American/EFLA
   *Merit Award, Landers
In explaining Alfred Wegener's hypothesis that all continents were

once one large land mass, this production applies the principles of scientific method to make its point. Through animation and live-action photography, it examines paleomagnetism, sea-floor spreading, magnetism in rock, and the drifting magnetic poles. Also available in Spanish. (HS-College)

CORRAL
   11 1/2 min BW Int. Film Bur. '54
   *First Prize, Venice
   *Merit Diploma, Edinburgh ... and other honors
An impressionistic study of the taming of a high-spirited horse. Hand-held shots show the unharnessed dignity of an unbroken animal and its reluctant subservience to man. No narration; guitar accompaniment. National Film Board of Canada. (Intermediate-Adult)

CORTEZ AND THE LEGEND
   52 min color McGraw-Hill '68
   *Merit Award, Landers
Shows the forces that enabled Spain to build a colonial empire, and the effect of European culture on early American civilization. Recreates the Spanish conquest of the Aztec empire and the epic clash between Cortez and the emperor Montezuma. Produced by ABC-TV. (College-Adult)

COSMIC ZOOM
   8 min color McGraw-Hill '69
   *Award, Philadelphia
Probes the infinite vastness of space and its reverse parallel, the ultimate minuteness of inner matter. Animation and camera span the journey to the farthest conceivable point in the universe, and then into the tiniest particle of existence--an atom of a living human cell. Produced by Eva Szaz of the National Film Board of Canada. (Junior HS-Adult)

COSMOPOLIS/BIG CITY 2000 A. D.
   52 min color McGraw-Hill '69
   *Critics' Citation, AIA
   *Award, Christopher Society
What will big cities be like in the next century? This film visits with architects Philip Johnson and I. M. Pei, along with Senator Paul Douglas. A few of the forecasts discussed are floating cities, pre-fabricated buildings, megastructures, and green "belts" around new British towns. Produced by ABC News. (College-Adult)

COUNTRY JAZZ
   10 1/2 min color Australia '71
   *Gold Camera, US Industrial
A quiet Australian country town is depicted as it cuts loose for its annual invasion by jazz musicians and fans. This production features Australia's leading jazz figures. Produced by the Commonwealth Film Unit. (College-Adult)

COUNTRY VET
    12 min   color   Encyc. Brit.   '71
    *Chris Certificate, Columbus
This follows a South Dakota veterinarian in his rounds to treat farm
animals and pets.   It shows the doctor preparing to operate on a
dog, giving shots to animals, setting the broken leg of a raccoon,
and dehorning cows.   (Intermediate-HS)

COURTESY: The Inside Story
    10 min   color   Nat. Educ. Media   '71
    *Chris Certificate, Columbus
From the Professional Food Preparation and Service series, this
film demonstrates restaurant service under realistic conditions, with
professional personnel in authentic locations.   Related printed materials, including tests, are available upon request.   (HS-Adult)

THE COW
    10 min   color   Churchill   '68
    *Blue Ribbon, American/EFLA
A visual exploration of this tranquil and versatile animal: the texture of its nose, the surprising grace of its awkwardly shaped body,
the grinding action of its jaws, the mystery of its cud, the magic of
its udders, and the functional but fascinating swish of its tail.   No
narration.   A Dimension Film by Michael Murphy.   (Elem. -Adult)

CRASH, BANG, BOOM
    9 1/2 min   color   Xerox Films   '70
    *Golden Eagle, CINE
This film introduces musical percussion via a chorus of voices that
identifies eleven instruments, each of which is played solo in order
to allow viewers to see what it looks like, how it sounds, and how
it is played.   Made by Eric Productions, Inc.   (Primary-Intermediate)

CRAYON
    15 min   color   ACI Films '64
    *Merit Award, Landers
    *First Prize, Venice
    *Chris Award, Columbus
    *Golden Eagle, CINE
    *Honors, American/EFLA

Demonstrates the qualities of crayon which, when used by itself or
in combination with other media, offers a variety of ways for students to express their ideas.   Specific scenes include: crayon carving, graffito, lamination, encaustic, and batik.   Produced by Stelios
Roccos.   (Elem. -Adult)

THE CREATION
    12 min   color   Oxford Films   '71
    *Golden Eagle, CINE
    *Award Winner, Atlanta
This story of Genesis is told in the language of the Black tradition.

From THE CRITIC (courtesy Learning Corporation of America)

It is one of seven sermons in verse by James Weldon Johnson. The poem is recited by the Black actor Raymond St. Jacques, and is then re-read by Margaret O'Brien with the words simultaneously superimposed on the screen. An Art Evans Production. (HS-Adult)

CREATIVE HANDS
    12 min color FilmFair '72
    *Award, Nat. Educational
Three artisans demonstrate and discuss their skills: building life-size dolls, making banjos, and sculpting with plastics and resins. This treatment presents a balance of craftspersons who preserve the old while searching for new means of expression. Film-maker: Sargon Tamimi. (HS-Adult)

THE CRITIC
    4 min color Learn. Corp. '62
    *Winner, Academy Award
A spoof on audiences and offerings in today's theaters and art galleries. This animation ridicules art that is really a subtle hoax against the dilettantes who confuse clichés with wisdom. Created by Ernest Pintoff. (HS-Adult)

CROSS-COUNTRY SKIING
 6 1/2 min color Nat. Film Bd.
 *Award, Cortina d'Ampezzo
Here is a vicarious experience of the sport of skimming over white
fields and forest trails. The film shows how four experts do it,
observing their coordination and the color they add to the open landscape. No narration. (Elem. -Adult)

CROSSTOWN ADVENTURE
 14 min color Encyc. Brit. '70
 *Jury Award, Int. Film & TV
 *Gold Medal, Atlanta
This is the what-happens-next story of an eight-year-old boy who is
accidentally closeted in a city delivery truck. He can only guess
where he is by listening to the sounds outside. At natural points,
the teacher can stop the projector to let students make their own
decisions before seeing three filmed alternatives. Produced by
Moreland-Latchford, Ltd. of Canada. (Elem.)

THE CRUSADES (1095-1291)
 16 min color Centron '69
 *Chris Award, Columbus
This film simulates the rumble of battle, the storming of citadels,
and the socio-religious climate that motivated the Crusades. Its
content may be particularly relevant in comparing more current conflicts in Northern Ireland and in the Middle East. (HS-Adult)

CRY FOR HELP
 15 min color Oxford Films
 *Award, National Committee
This enactment of a drowning points up the need for first-rate emergency medical service to protect every member of a community.
Shows how specialists are vital in preventing the loss of life, not
just applying remedies after accidents. Produced by Paramount
Communications in conjunction with the American College of Emergency Physicians. (HS-Adult)

CRY HELP!
 83 min color Films Inc. '70
 *Award, Ohio State Univ.
 *Honors, Mental Health
 *Winner, American/EFLA
Mentally disturbed adolescents total six million forgotten souls.
Only ten per cent of them receive care that is anywhere near ade-
quate. This study focuses on three teenagers who are part of the
lucky ten per cent. It observes their participation in a program
that uses videotape self-analysis, psychodrama, and body awareness
to help them regain emotional stability. Produced by NBC News.
(College-Adult)

CRY OF THE MARSH
 12 min color ACI Films '69
 *Merit Award, Landers

*Chris Statuette, Columbus
*Golden Eagle, CINE
*Blue Ribbon, American/EFLA
A wordless indictment of man's wanton destruction of his environment. The ruination of marshes has already wiped out, with them,
an infinite variety of inter-related forms of life. Now the consequences threaten our very life, not to mention our appreciation of
its natural wonders. (Before presentation, <u>preview</u> for emotional
impact that may be excessive for certain audiences.) A Robert
Hartkopf production. (Intermediate-Adult)

CYCLES
    13 1/2 min   color   Assn.-Sterl.
    *Blue Ribbon, American/EFLA
    *Gold Camera, US Industrial
Reveals how man's future is building banks or stockpiles of miner-
als for recycled usage. Documents the involvement of youth in the
collection of glass and its conversion for road paving, jewelry, in-
sulation, and reflective paint. Sponsor: The Glass Container Manufacturers Institute. Available on free loan to adult groups and
schools. (HS-Adult)

DAGUERRE: The Birth of Photography
    29 min   BW   Film Images   '70
    *Lion of St. Mark, Venice
The birth of photography is documented by the complementary pioneer work of Daguerre, Niepce, and Talbot. All three span the
period 1765-1871. Original music by Guy Bernard. Produced by
Roger Leenhardt. (HS-Adult)

THE DAISY
    6 min   color   Macmillan   '64
    *Cartoon Award, Chicago
For lovers of animation in the tradition of Jiri Trnka. The daisy
is the symbol of beauty, yielding only to those who love and enjoy
it. The "rectangular character" is a boor, with a whole arsenal of
weapons to destroy beauty; but his rudeness and narrowmindedness
only make him ridiculous, and the daisy is untouched. Animated by
Todor Dinov. (Intermediate-Adult)

DANCE SQUARED
    3 1/2 min   color   Int. Film Bureau   '61
    *Awards: Chicago, Portugal, Iran, Argentina
This film is an encounter with geometrical shapes. Employs move-
ment, color, and music to explore the symmetries of the square.
Every movement of the square and its components presents a new
opportunity to observe its properties. Animated by Norman Mc-
Laren. Produced by the National Film Board of Canada. (HS-Adult)

THE DANCING PROPHET
    25 min   color   Pyramid   '70
    *Golden Eagle, CINE

*Gold Medal, NY Film and TV
A documentary about Ruth St. Denis. A major figure through several decades of the American dance, Ms. St. Denis recounts her beginnings and major triumphs, with specially staged dance sequences and reminiscences by Alicia Markova, Jack Cole, and Anton Dolin. Produced by Edmund Penney. (HS-College)

DANGEROUS PLAYGROUND
19 min   color   Association Films
*Merit Award, Nat. Committee
Suggests methods of guiding children in forming conclusions about the hazards of playing on construction sites. Encourages them to recognize the dangers to their safety there. (Primary-Intermediate)

DANNY AND NICKY
56 min   color   Films Inc.   '70
*3rd Prize, Int. Scientific
Danny lives at home with his brothers and sisters, and is able to attend a special neighborhood school. Nicky was placed in a public institution as a baby. Both are mentally retarded. The differences in their temperaments and personality are indicated in actual scenes recorded at home and school. Produced by the National Film Board of Canada. (College-Adult)

DANZE CROMATICHE
8 1/2 min   color   Xerox Films   '69
*Golden Eagle, CINE
The dancers in this non-verbal abstraction are colors, shapes, and light--all moving in tempo with a musical score that ranges from classical to contemporary. With no recognizable objects in it, this film is actually a continuing arrangement of matter and space in relation to time. Produced by Ugo Toricelli. (HS-Adult)

DARK CORNER OF JUSTICE
38 min   color   Films Inc.   '70
*Award, Religious PR
*Award, Int. Film & TV
*Honors, Columbus
*Prize, American Bar
*Emmy, Nat. Academy
Most prisoners in a county jail are innocent, yet they suffer the worst of conditions while awaiting trial. They are held in buildings that are overcrowded and badly designed. They have few facilities for the necessities of life, much less for the niceties or for recreation and rehabilitation. For those proven guilty, life becomes an occasion of frustration and hostility that builds to volcanic intensity. Produced by WKYC-TV. (HS-Adult)

DARWIN AND THE THEORY OF NATURAL SELECTION
13 1/2 min   color   Coronet
*Chris Award, Columbus
Through Darwin's observations of the coasts and islands of South America, and his experiments in England, we see how this scientist

developed his theory of natural selection. Rare views of animal and plant life were photographed on the Galapagos Islands. (HS)

DARWIN'S GALAPAGOS TODAY
14 min color ACI Films '70
*Chris Award, Columbus
Through the eyes of a boy at the Darwin Research Station, we observe the species discovered there over 100 years ago. The creatures that influenced Darwin are pointed out and examined in the light of modern biology. An insight into the delicate balance between organisms and their environment. A Hartley Production. (HS)

DAUMIER (1808-1879)
14 min BW Roland Films
*Special Mention, Locarno
Keenly aware of the social disorders and injustices that pervaded his society, Honoré Daumier portrayed a broad spectrum of humanity in a prolific output of satirical lithographs. Producer: Les Films Roger Leenhardt. (College-Adult)

DAVID
35 min BW Films Inc.
*Golden Reel, American Film Assembly
*Award, Edinburgh (Scotland)
An aged Welsh janitor relives the time when he started working in the coal mines at 12 years old. Now in his later years, friends know him as a good and kind person but not as a major contemporary poet. Produced by the British Film Institute. (College-Adult)

DAWN OF THE AMERICAN REVOLUTION: A Lexington Family
16 min color Coronet
*Award, Freedoms Foundation
Produced in Lexington and other historical sites, this is a review of events that led to the American Revolution. As seen from the perspective of a boy of that period, a critical situation involving his family and an uncle from England helps to describe the mood of the colonists and the important issues of that era. (Intermediate)

THE DAY GRANDPA DIED
11 1/2 min color BFA Educ. Media '70
*Gold Medal, Int. Film & TV
In this vignette of a boy's first experience with death, we watch David's struggle with reality. In sepia flashbacks, he relives memories of a kindly grandfather and happy times. In the end, he begins to understand the words of the rabbi at the burial: "People die only when we forget them." A King Screen Production. (Intermediate-Adult)

THE DAY MANOLETE WAS KILLED
20 min BW Films Inc. '58
*Prize Winner, Oberhausen
*First Prize, Tours

An account of the day when Manolete, idolized as the greatest matador in the world, came out of retirement to match skills in the bull
ring with young Luis Dominguin--and met death. Produced in animated stills by film-maker Barnaby Conrad. (HS-Adult)

DAY OF THE PAINTER
        14 min   color   Macmillan   '59
        *Academy Award (Live Action)
        *Co-Winner, San Francisco
The "biography" of a work of modern art. A painter who knows
how to make money in the contemporary market spends the day hurl-
ing and splashing paint onto a masonite board. An art dealer
chooses one segment that the painter has sawed off. The other
parts of the "masterpiece" float downstream with some puzzled gulls
and swans. No narration. Directed by Robert P. Davis. (HS-
Adult)

THE DAY THAT SANG AND CRIED
        28 min   color   Centron   '70
        *Chris Award, Columbus
        *Finalist, American/EFLA
About the loneliness, joy, and reflection of youth, presented from a
teenage point of view. Particularly oriented toward urban adolescents as a stimulus for discussion of their feelings and common
problems. A Dale Smallin Production. (Junior-Senior HS)

A DAY WITH TIMMY PAGE
        18 min   BW   Macmillan   '68
        *Award, American/EFLA
        *Honors, San Francisco
        *Prize, Chicago
When this film was made, 11-year old Timmy had been a film-
maker for ten months. Using his father's old camera, he completed
twenty films, each ten minutes long. Composed of interviews with
the young director, and with excerpts from his work, this film is a
microcosm of his world. Produced by David Hoffman. (Intermediate-Adult)

THE DAYS OF DYLAN THOMAS
        21 min   BW   McGraw-Hill   '65
        *Golden Eagle, CINE
Music, photographs, and narration, including selections spoken by
Thomas himself, present the life and works of this Welsh poet who
became a legend in his own lifetime. Directed by Graeme Ferguson.
(HS-Adult)

DDT--Knowing It Survives Us
        30 min   color   Xerox Films   '69
        *Silver Medal, Atlanta
Assesses the status of the insecticide and, with the help of scientists, explains how DDT has become a paradoxical symbol of man's
genius and his stupidity; how it has become a danger to us and to
innocent wildlife, too. Exposes the fact that DDT will continue to

kill organisms for decades after its original application. Produced by Steve Rosen and Darrell Salk. (HS-Adult)

THE DEAD BIRD
13 min color Oxford Films
*Award Winner, Atlanta
This film is based on the short story by Margaret Wise Brown, the theme of which lends itself to discussion about the nature of death and the appraisal of the fundamental values of life. Moreland-Latchford Productions, Ltd. (Elem.-Junior HS)

A DEAF CHILD SPEAKS
16 min color Ext. Media Center '73
*Golden Eagle, CINE
Illustrates aspects of the Oral Education Center of Southern California, where children with severe hearing loss learn to function in the world of speech and sound. Stresses individualized instruction that leads to the acquisition of language and the development of academic skills. Produced by the University of California. (College-Adult)

DEATH OF A LEGEND
50 1/2 min color Nat. Film Board
*Canadian Film Award
The wolf is threatened with extinction, principally because of negative myths about it. Film-maker Bill Mason seeks to set the record straight by photographically disproving many fallacies. Footage contains scenes of Canada's North and not only of the wolf but of deer, caribou, and moose. Produced for the Canadian Wildlife Service. (College-Adult)

DEATH OF A PEASANT
10 min color Mass Media '72
*Honor Diploma, Cracow
*Special Award, Bogota
*Gold Medal, Atlanta
This is based on a true story of the last minutes in the life of a Yugoslav farmer who had to face a German firing squad in 1941 and yet defiantly decided to choose his own way of death. This film should be followed up by discussion, whatever the age level of the viewers. A Fastava Film Production. (HS-Adult)

DEBT TO THE PAST
21 min color Moody Institute
*Chris Award, Columbus
*Honors, American/EFLA
A statement about our dependence on past gifts of language, agriculture, science, mathematics, architecture, commerce, government, and law. Also demonstrates what modern life would be without these traditional gifts. (Junior-Senior HS)

DEBT TO THE PAST: Language and Communication
16 min color Moody Institute

*Award, American/EFLA
Presents three stages in the development of written language: pictographic, ideographic, and phonetic. Traces the history of the alphabet and the power of language for good and evil, stressing the need for man to use language for worthy purposes. (Junior-Senior HS)

DECISION AT DELANO
26 min color Nat. Educ. Media '68
*Blue Ribbon, American/EFLA
Records one chapter in the struggle between migrant workers and American industry. Traces the background of the California grape strike that, in 1965, resulted in the first collective bargaining election in the history of American agriculture. Key figures in this conflict are Cesar Chavez, the Mexican-American organizer, and former U. S. Senator Robert F. Kennedy. A QED Production. (College-Adult)

DEEP SEA DRILLING PROJECT
27 1/2 min color Assn.-Sterling
*Gold Camera, US Industrial
*Golden Eagle, CINE
*Blue Ribbon, American/EFLA
The voyage of the Glomar Challenger, a drilling ship capable of probing beneath the ocean floor. Her purpose is to retrieve samples of sediment that have accumulated for millions of years. Scientists, from this laboratory, make direct measurements of how fast the sea floor is actually spreading. Sponsored by the National Science Foundation, this film is available on free loan to classes and groups interested in science. (HS-Adults)

DEEP SEA TRAWLER
18 min color Films Inc. '68
*Chris Certificate, Columbus
A modern trawler steams from its port to the Grand Banks off Newfoundland. It is an ocean-going factory, complete with electronic fishing aids and packing facilities. An animated sequence shows how nets drag the ocean bed and how fish are processed and frozen immediately after being caught. Once the ship's hold is filled, the trawler heads for home after months at sea. Produced by the Institut für Film und Bild. (Intermediate-Adult)

DEGAS DANCERS (1834-1917)
13 min BW Roland Films
*Silver Cup, Salerno
*Chris Award, Columbus
Edgar Degas discovered ways of composing figures on canvas, and used new angles of vision that only today are being utilized by the film medium. His techniques are all the more apparent in these black-and-white studies. Produced by Les Films de Saturne. (HS-Adult)

DELACROIX (1798-1863)
13 min BW Roland Films

*Commendation, Wiesbaden
*Chris Award, Columbus
*First Prize, Yorkton
*Honor Diploma, Cannes
*Silver Cup, Salerno ... and other awards
Through tightly edited sequences, this treatment simulates movement
in the human and animal form. Delacroix's work helps us under-
stand his thoughts and his inventiveness. This film is the only one
of its kind made in the Louvre Drawing Collection. Director:
Anthony M. Roland. (HS-Adult)

DEMOCRACY: Your Voice Can Be Heard
     18 1/2 min color Coronet
     *Wm. F. Knowland Award
     *Award, Freedoms Foundation
     *Chris Award, Columbus
Recreates the campaign by Detroit high school students for improvements at a public hospital. Their involvement provides an example
of the advancement of a cause and of how individuals can be effective within a democracy. (HS-Adult)

DENMARK 43
     22 min color Learn. Corp.   '70
     *Certificate, Columbus
     *Gold Medal, Atlanta
     *Golden Eagle, CINE
Inspired by the story of how Denmark saved its Jewish population
from the Nazis, this film follows Danish students through a reenact-
ment of events in 1943 in the fishing village of Gilleleje. A class
project conducted by a Danish teacher as an experiment in history.
(HS-Adult)

THE DESERT
     28 min color Films Inc.   '70
     *Chris Statuette, Columbus
A complex variety of plants and animals has adapted to the desert's
difficult conditions: the giant cactus, woodpeckers, horned lizards,
kangaroo rats, skunks, rabbits, and coyotes. This unfolding of
varied forms of life lends itself to an appreciation of the beauty and
value to mankind. Produced by the Canadian Broadcasting Corporation. (HS-Adult)

DESERT PEOPLE
     51 min BW McGraw-Hill '68
     *Special Award, Venice
     *High Honors, Prades
     *Merit Diploma, Edinburgh
     *Golden Bucranium, Padua
The aborigines of Western Australia are united by a common culture,
as depicted here in the lives of two families of the Western Desert.
Reveals what a great portion of their time is spent in the search
for food. Produced by Ian Dunlop for the Commonwealth Film Unit.
(College-Adult)

DESERT VICTORY
      60 min   BW   McGraw-Hill   '43
      *Academy Award (Documentary)
The filmed report of Britain's victory at El Alamein and the drive
toward Tripoli.   It begins in the grim days when Rommel's Afrika
Korps had driven to within 60 miles of Alexandria, and then follows
Montgomery's 8th Army to its final triumph.   Produced by Maj.
David MacDonald and the Royal Air Force Film Unit.   (College-
Adult)

DEVELOPMENT OF THE CHICK EMBRYO
      5 1/2 min   color   Coronet
      *Award of Merit, Boston
This introductory study of embryology shows a living chick during
key stages of early growth.   Includes embryonic movement, circula-
tion of blood, heartbeat, and the action of shell breaking by means
of the egg tooth.   (HS-College)

THE DEVIL'S TOY
      15 min   BW   Nat. Film Bd.
      *Award Winner, Teheran
Though frowned on by grown-ups, the skateboard gives youngsters a
sensation of speed unexcelled by any other street sport.   This film
captures the exuberance of boys and girls in free and fast locomotion.   (Intermediate-Junior HS)

D. H. LAWRENCE IN TAOS
      41 min   color   McGraw-Hill   '70
      *Chris Certificate, Columbus
      *Blue Ribbon, American/EFLA
Based on recollections of friends of the author when he lived in New
Mexico, this treatment is an informal biography of the noted literary
figure who enjoyed fame in his own time.   Produced by Peter and
Joy Davis.   (College-Adult)

DIGGING FOR THE HISTORY OF MAN
      55 min   color   Roland Films
      *Recognition, German Govt.
      *Gold Ribbon, Berlin
      *Commendation, Wiesbaden
Excavations in Asia Minor, the Near and Middle East reveal man's
development from a primitive state to advanced ones in which civilization flourished.   This film shows the art and architecture of the
Babylonians, Sumerians, Hittites, Greeks, Romans, and Sassanians
(who brought about the end of ancient Persia).   Can be shown in two
or four parts.   Producer: H. J. Hossfeld.   (College-Adult)

DIMENSIONS
      12 1/4 min   color   Nat. Film Bd.   '68
      *Awards: Venice, Edinburgh, Canada, and Guadalajara
A man wants a door in a wall, so he draws a rectangle there and--
voilà!--there's an opening.   He likewise conjures up furniture which,
if too low or high, he can correct by a flick of the finger.   This
nonverbal animation is a lesson in proportion for youngsters.   (Elem.)

DINING ROOM SAFETY
    10 min   color   Nat. Educ. Media   '71
    *Merit Award, Nat. Committee
Stresses awareness of commercial hazards and how to avoid them.
Includes procedures for carrying food, stacking dishes, and lists
rules of safe dress.   Demonstrates precautions against falls, cuts,
burns, spilled foods, and scalding.   For waiters, waitresses, and
busboys.   (Adult)

DISCIPLINE: A Matter of Judgment
    12 min   color   Nat. Educ. Media   '73
    *Bronze Plaque, Columbus
Uses a courtroom setting to dramatize the need for objectivity on
all levels of employee relations.   Emphasizes the importance of
putting rules in writing, chastising in private, maintaining files of
infractions, and of consistency in application of rewards and penal-
ties.   (College-Adult)

DR. LEAKEY AND THE DAWN OF MAN
    26 min   color   Films Inc.   '66
    *Award Winner, Florence
Certain that Africa was the cradle of civilization, Louis Leakey and
his wife spent over 40 years there in painstaking excavations.   Their
persistence was rewarded in 1959 when they unearthed the remains
of a specimen dating back 1. 76 million years.   Narrated by Alexander Scourby.   Adapted from the National Geographic TV program.
(HS-Adult)

THE DOG AND THE DIAMONDS
    55 min   BW   Sterling Educ.   '70
    *Children's Prize, Venice
A group of children, living in apartments where pets are forbidden,
use a deserted house as a private zoo and, by chance, capture three
jewel thieves.   Made by the Children's Film Foundation of Britain.
(Ages 7-12)

DOGS, CATS AND RABBITS
    7 min   color   Texture Films   '72
    *Golden Eagle, CINE
A three-part film including 41 Barks, animated (and barked) by Eliot
Noyes, Jr.; Catsup by Tana Hoban; and Rabbits by Bill Stitts.   Pro-
ducer: Cyclops Films.   (Elem.)

DOM
    12 min   color   McGraw-Hill '61
    *Grand Prix, Brussels
A woman waits at home ("dom") for her man whose footsteps she
hears on the street outside.   He comes in, places his hat on an old-
fashioned hatrack, and appears to her as a handsome mannequin's
head which she caresses ... only to have it disappear into thin air.
Produced by Waldemar Borowcyk and Jan Lenica.   (College)

DON QUIXOTE (VS. THE SYSTEM)
    11 min   color   Film Images   '62

*Animation Prize, Oberhausen
Through a strange urban land of busy little people ride Don Q. and
his servant Pancho. The people in power fear these intruding pres-
ences as threats to the establishment. So the police are called,
then the army. There is almost mass confusion, what with all those
men, trucks, planes, radar, etc. But Quixote rides blithely on.
A Zagreb Film. (HS-Adult)

THE DOODLE FILM
      11 min color Learn. Corp.   '71
      *Silver Medal, Atlanta
This animated film traces the history of a compulsive doodler whose
"problem" begins in penmanship class. We watch his writings grow
from scribbles on school notebooks, to correspondence, tax returns,
and other unconventional surfaces. Animator: Donald Winkler,
National Film Board of Canada. (Junior HS-Adult)

DOROTHY AND THE POP SINGER
      9 min color Phoenix '72
      *Golden Plaque, Teheran (Iran)
Dorothy's pet parrot, Koko, is her alter ego, and would do anything
for its mistress but is jealous of a pop star and one of his recordings. The story tells about what Koko does to reclaim Dorothy's
attention and affection. Produced by Short Film, Prague. (Elem.)

THE DOT AND THE LINE
      9 min color Films Inc.
      *Academy Awards (Cartoon)
This animation about two geometric figures explores their plane relationships in a fashion designed to heighten mathematical interest
in young and old alike. Produced by MGM Studios. (Elem.-Adult)

DOTS
      3 min color Int. Film Bur.
      *Awards: Rome and Canada
Visuals and sound were created by drawing directly onto the film
surface with ordinary pen and ink. An early experiment in film
animation by Norman McLaren of the National Film Board of Canada.
(HS-Adult)

DOUBLE PORTRAIT
      8 min color Macmillan '64
      *Gold Ducat, Mannhein
A single picture is painted on the screen. As it produces a double
portrait of a man and a woman, a continuous throbbing of the paint
can be seen, and the viewer perceives different interpretations. By
the Pannonia Studio of Budapest. (HS-Adult)

DOWN TO THE SEA IN SHIPS
      54 min color Films Inc.   '68
      *Golden Eagle, CINE
      *Award, Int. Review (Milan)
This story of man in deep waters is told from the standpoint of

history and the present. Documentary footage shows the clipper
ships rounding Cape Horn. Newer scenes are shown from aboard a
Coast Guard training ship. Through the words of Melville and Conrad, this film suggests the sense and feel of the sea. Produced by
NBC News. (College-Adult)

DREAM OF THE WILD HORSES
       9 min color McGraw-Hill '60
       *Nomination, Academy Award
       *Merit Award, Edinburgh ... and many other honors
Utilizes show motion against soft focus backgrounds to simulate
dreamlike effects of the wild horses of the Camargue in France.
Produced by Denys Colomb de Daunant. (Junior HS-Adult)

THE DREAMER THAT REMAINS: A Portrait of Harry Partch
       27 min color Macmillan
       *Golden Eagle, CINE
Harry Partch, the 73-year-old visionary, has built his own world
by creating musical instruments, his own notation system, his own
theory--all without much aid or comfort from the Establishment.
Here is a film study of an extraordinary combination of prophet,
eccentric, iconoclast, and philosopher. (HS-Adult)

A DROP OF WATER
       12 min color ACI Films '70
       *Honors, American/EFLA
In a drop of water are found organisms that are the basis for all
life. Cine micro photography reveals a hidden world which, if
studied, can lead to a better understanding of the one we inhabit.
Of special interest to students of biology and microscopy. (HS-
College)

A DROP OF WATER
       14 min color Barr Films '71
       *Golden Eagle, CINE
The camera follows a drop of water as it falls into a forest glade,
then becomes a part of a creek, joins a river, and eventually
reaches the sea to rise as a vapor and return to the forest once
more. Non-narrated. Photographed and edited by Joern Gerdts.
(Intermediate-Adult)

DROWNPROOFING
       24 min color Films Inc. '68
       *Winner, San Francisco State
       *Award, Columbus
       *Award, National Safety
Demonstrates a technique of floating and breathing so that even non-
swimmers can remain comfortably afloat, without fatigue, for hours
at a time. Drownproofing, as a method of survival, is taught in a
number of U. S. schools. Produced by WKYC-TV. (HS-Adult)

DROWNPROOFING
       14 min color Amer. Film Prod. '72

*Golden Eagle, CINE
*Chris Award, Columbus
This lifesaving film teaches the techniques for water survival which
are taught to trainees assigned to the Naval Underwater Swimmers
School. Produced under Lt. Irve C. LeMoyne, U. S. Navy. (HS-
Adult)

DRUGS ARE LIKE THAT
17 min color Benchmark '72
*Citation, White House
In six episodes, children can perceive the nature of addiction, the
reason for drug laws, the effects of drugs on coordination, and the
risks to health that are involved in consumption. (Grades 3-4)

DRUMMER HOFF
6 min color Weston Woods '69
*Certificate, American/EFLA
An animated version of the children's picture book of the same name.
Also available in Super 8 Sound. Produced by Mort Schindel. (Pri-
mary)

DUCKS
7 min color ACI Films '69
*Chris Award, Columbus
*Honors, American/EFLA
From the Starting to Read series, featuring subjects of natural interest to children, accompanied by a lively song. Key words are
superimposed on the screen in unison with the pronunciation on the
soundtrack. Also available without captions. (Primary)

THE DULLE GRIET
13 min color McGraw-Hill '70
*Diploma, Cracow (Poland)
*Honors, Bergamo (Italy)
*Winner, Prix du Conseil
*Jury Prize, Belgium
Elements of Bruegel's work--his expression of man's conflict with
society and nature and the confrontation between death and the will
to life: these are interpreted by the combination of photography and
narration produced by the Belgian Ministry of Education and Culture.
(HS-Adult)

DUNES
7 min color Pyramid '68
*Merit Award, Landers
*Golden Eagle, CINE
A poet's view of desert wilderness, including among the imagery:
a sunrise, barren dunes, a sidewinder snake, grass and tumbleweed
in the wind. In all, a wide range of desert moods that begin at
sunrise and continue until sunset. Produced by Fred Hudson.
(Elem.-Adult)

EARLY HANDLING OF SPINAL INJURIES
    17 1/4 min BW Nat. Film Bd.
    *Award Winner, Cleveland
What to do and what to avoid when back injuries occur. Animation illustrates the structure of the spinal column, and how paralysis can happen. Demonstrations, in a factory and a logging camp, show how an accident victim should be handled to prevent further complications. (HS-Adult)

THE EASTER SEASON
    11 min color Coronet '56
    *Participant, Venice (Child.)
Explores some of the cultural origins of Eastertime, comparing customs of different lands and other times. Explains the tradition of eggs, rabbits, and the display of bright colors during this season. (Elem.)

EAT, DRINK AND BE WARY
    19 min color Churchill '74
    *Blue Ribbon, American/EFLA
A consumer-oriented study of the level of quality ... and the lack of it ... in many of today's foods available in and promoted by the marketplace. Written, filmed, and edited by George McQuilkin. (HS-Adult)

ECCE HOMO
    9 min color Roland Films
    *Merit of Honor, Bergamo
The Gothic influence, elegant and instructive, was manifested in the richly painted and gilded wood sculpture of the birth, death, and resurrection of Christ as interpreted by artists of the 15th and 16th centuries. Producer: Kratky Film. (HS-Adult)

ECOLOGY OF A HOT SPRING: Life at High Temperatures
    14 min color Encyc. Brit. '71
    *Golden Eagle, CINE
Yellowstone Park's hot springs provide answers to what form of life survived when the earth was so much hotter billions of years ago. Micro-tropical environments, created by the constancy of temperature, show the relationships of organisms that are limited due to the heat. (HS-College)

EDGAR ALLAN POE: Background for His Works
    13 1/2 min color Coronet '59
    *Chris Award, Columbus
Paintings created in the style of Poe's writings are presented against a background of his life. Revealing elements of his contributions to literature are excerpts from To Helen, Fall of the House of Usher, Murders in the Rue Morgue, and The Raven.   (HS)

e. e. cummings: The Making of a Poet
    24 min color Films/Humanities '72
    *Honors, Brussels (Belgium)

*Golden Eagle, CINE

A personal and literary insight into this revolutionary poet, interpreted in the language of e. e. cummings himself. Produced by Harold Mantell. (HS-College)

THE EGG
10 min   color   McGraw-Hill   '70
*Honor Award, Atlanta
*Bronze Medal, Venice

About a sculptor and his masterpiece--an egg. As his friends come to see his work of art, each adds an "improvement" until the egg is covered by a pyramid of foreign objects. Everyone is happy, even the sculptor. But what about the egg? It cracks under the burden, and finally collapses altogether. Animated by Zagreb Films. (HS-Adult)

EGG INTO ANIMAL (Roundel Skate)
12 min   color   Macmillan   '67
*Golden Hugo, Chicago

The life cycle and environment of the skate. A blend of outdoor surroundings and laboratory photography, this film makes use of animation to accentuate life functions not otherwise visible. It also details the anatomy and organs of reproduction and digestion, embryonic development, fertilized egg, and fully grown baby. A Reela Film. (HS-College)

EIGHTEEN FOOTERS
19 1/2 min   color   Australia   '68
*Gold Camera, US Industrial

They say that Sydney's 18-foot sailboats carry sail like the Vikings. With three barefoot trapeze artists perched on the rail, and a daredevil at the helm, the audience experiences the excitement of the race. Produced by the Commonwealth Film Unit. (College-Adult)

EL GRECO
27 1/2 min   color   Graph. Curric.   '70
*Chris Statuette, Columbus

Interwoven with El Greco paintings are the threads of his life, including scenes of Crete (his birthplace), Venice, the Escorial, and Toledo. He lived in an era not unlike our own, a time of crisis and anxiety, and his search for answers is the theme of this study. (College-Adult)

THE ELEANOR ROOSEVELT STORY
90 min   BW   Macmillan
*Academy Award (Documentary)

A tribute to a woman who became an institution, a rarity in modern times. This film is a record of the life and deeds of a great lady, and a documentary study of one human's commitment to world betterment. Producer: Sidney Glazier. Written by Archibald MacLeish. (College-Adult)

ELECTRIC SAFETY ... FROM A TO ZAP
    9 1/2 min color Perennial '70
    *1st Place, Nat. Committee
This animated film focuses on three aspects of electricity: what is
meant by power; how it travels through homes; and hazards and precautions. Strongly oriented towards safety. Produced by Portafilms. (HS-Adult)

11:59, LAST MINUTE TO CHOOSE
    27 min color BFA Educ. Media
    *Award, American Personnel
    *Golden Eagle, CINE
Utilizing split-screen technique, this unstaged film alternately presents interviews with young heroin addicts in San Francisco, and
scenes of their treatment in emergency and psychiatric wards. Addicts themselves tell of the pleasure of drugs as well as the panic
of withdrawal. (HS-College)

EMBRYONIC DEVELOPMENT OF THE CHICK
    25 3/4 min color Univ. Educ. '67
    *Award Winner, Salerno
    *Golden Reel Award (USA)
Animation and time-lapse show the process from germinal disc to
hatching, along with natural speed photography to portray a sequen-
tial view of the inside of a fertilized egg. Microscopic views of the
embryo help to clarify the entire process. By the National Film
Board of Canada. (HS-College)

THE EMBRYONIC DEVELOPMENT OF THE FISH
    27 1/2 min color Univ. Educ. '67
    *Award Winner, Berlin
    *Honors, Buenos Aires
Covers the four-day period from fertilization to hatching. Cameras
at normal and time-lapse speeds were trained on the egg of the
transparent-shelled Zebra fish. Diagrams explain the more complex
stages. By the National Film Board of Canada. (HS-College)

THE EMERGING WOMAN
    40 min BW Film Images '74
    *Blue Ribbon, American/EFLA
This documentary utilizes photographs and newsreels to trace the
history and role of women in American society. Historical engravings provide background for treatment of the colonial period of our
history, and these contrast with more modern footage to suggest the
changes that have taken place in the interim. Director: Helena
Solberg Ladd. (HS-Adult)

EMIL NOLDE (1867-1956)
    15 min color Roland Films
    *Quality Award, German Govt.   .
    *Commendation, Wiesbaden
This leading German expressionist produced a depth of feeling in
stormy coasts, radiant hills, and people's moods. Forbidden to

paint by the Nazi regime, Nolde surreptitiously made postcard-size
sketches that were triumphs of miniature vitality. Producer: Th. N.
Blomberg. (College-Adult)

EMOTIONAL DEVELOPMENT: Aggression
    20 min   color   CRM Films   '73
    *Golden Eagle, CINE
Are we born "killer apes"? Or do we develop our aggressions?
Cinema verité catches an act of aggression in a nursery school.
The scene is replayed, and a psychologist comments on the incident
and on the reaction of the teacher which inadvertently rewards the
aggressor with attention. Film-maker: Barbara Jampel. (College-
Adult)

THE EMPTY HAND
    10 min   BW   ACI Films   '68
    *Golden Eagle, CINE
    *Award, San Francisco
    *Honors, Festival dei Popoli ... and winner of four other events
Karate, Japanese for "empty hand," is the subject of this film, a
realistic account of training by black belt practitioners. Quick cuts,
zooms, tight shots, and a grunt-filled soundtrack create a sense of
body contact and physical presence. A Stephen Verona Production.
(HS-Adult)

THE EMPTY QUARTER
    48 min   color   Films Inc.   '66
    *Award of Merit, Landers
Wilfred Patrick Thesiger, an Englishman, was the first white man
to explore the "Empty Quarter," the desert south of Arabia. This
film describes one of his expeditions with Bedouin colleagues. The
chanting and music form the background to photography of the maze
of dunes and open sky that constitute the area under study. An ITT
Production. (College-Adult)

THE END OF ONE
    7 min   color   Learn. Corp.   '69
    *Film Essay Award, Chicago
The camera watches seagulls soar and scavenge for food from a
huge garbage dump. A lone frail bird is seen at a distance, limp-
ing along a polluted stretch of beach. Through a blend of sound and
image, the film interprets its eventual death as symbolic of earth's.
Preview for possibly offensive emotional impact. (HS-Adult)

THE ENDLESS SEA
    76 min   color   Macmillan   '72
    *Golden Eagle, CINE
Shows how life may have evolved in the sea; the role of plankton;
the water cycle; ocean farming and its implications for feeding the
world. Narrated by James Mason. Producer: Owen Lee. (College-
Adult)

THE ENDURING WILDERNESS
27 3/4 min color Sterling Educ. '65
*Award, Marseille (France)
*Honors, NY International
Scenes of nature, photographed by Christopher Chapman, provide the
material for this film on the need for wilderness sanctuaries. Offers a springboard for discussion on the importance of such preserves in an increasingly mechanized society. (HS-Adult)

ENERGY
12 min color Pyramid '70
*Golden Eagle, CINE
*Chris Award, Columbus
Through non-verbal animation, this film examines the ways that different forces affect each other. The manifestations of this concept
are treated in a loose historical fashion that suggests how man
gradually classified such phenomena as gravity, heat, electricity,
magnetism, and radioactivity. Produced by Timothy Wade Huntley.
(Intermediate-Adult)

THE ENGINEERING OF AGREEMENT
21 min color Roundtable
*Prize, Internat. Industrial
*Honors, American /EFLA
*Award, Seattle Film Festival
Designed for use in management and sales training, this film is an
aid in demonstrating examples of how to foster cooperation, and to
instill acceptance of ideas, products, and services. (College-Adult)

EPHESUS
25 min BW Macmillan
*Documentary Award, Foothill
*Zellerbach Award, San Francisco
A study of religious ceremonies in a "Black Holiness" church, involving pentecostal participation by worshippers. The sermon
reaches its climax in unison with gospel music by organ and choir,
as all join in with handclapping and dancing. Filmed by Fred Padula.
(College-Adult)

ERSATZ
10 min color McGraw-Hill '69
*Winner, Academy Award
Depicts a make-believe world of inflatable substitutes for everything,
including man. The main character creates, then destroys at will,
but in the end is himself done in by a puny thumbtack. Animation
by Zagreb Studio of Yugoslavia. (HS-Adult)

ESCAPE
14 min BW Mass Media '67
*Gold Medal, Belgium
*Award Winner, Malta
*Ten Best, Photo Society
An unloved boy has a fierce argument with his parents that sends

him running away from home. With nothing else for solace, he
wanders into an empty church and gazes at its attestations to a lov-
ing heavenly father. But the sound of someone approaching drives
him out of the building into the path of fatal tragedy. Ironically,
his final escape is permanently effectual. Produced by Alan Laven-
der. (Intermediate-Adult)

ESKIMO ARTIST KENOJUAK
    20 min   color   McGraw-Hill
    *Special Mention, Venice
    *Best Short, British Academy
    *Art Prize, Cork (Ireland)
    *Nomination, Academy Award
Besides being an artist, Kenojuak is also a wife and a mother who
makes her drawings when free of the duties of camp or trail. Hers
is a world where, in the Arctic twilight, the whole environment
seems heavy with shadows. The thoughts of this woman are recorded as commentary and, as such, add to an appreciation of the
images she creates. National Film Board of Canada. (College-
Adult)

ESPOLIO
    7 min   color   Films Inc.   '70
    *Chris Statuette, Columbus
    *Red Ribbon, American /EFLA
A carpenter builds a cross for the execution of the son of another
carpenter. As he works, he speaks of his pride in his craft and of
his reluctance to become involved in the morality of the crucifixion.
Are his "situation ethics" much different from those of the designer
of bombs and napalm? From the National Film Board of Canada.
(HS-Adult)

AN ESSAY ON WAR
    23 min   color   Encyc. Brit.   '72
    *Bronze Plaque, Columbus
    *Bronze Medal, Atlanta
    *Golden Eagle, CINE
Explores the contradictions of war. Flashbacks provide perspective
as statesmen and generals expound their opinions. Their reasoning
is confronted with that of combatants whose own emotional responses
are stated. Released by Essay Productions. (HS-Adult)

ETERNAL CHILDREN
    30 min   BW   Int. Film Bur.
    *Chris Certificate, Columbus
    *Award, NY International
The special problems of the retarded who, through heredity or other
causes, are unable to keep up with other children. Gives an appraisal of their care and training, focusing attention on the need to
improve and expand facilities. National Film Board of Canada.
(College-Adult)

ETHIOPIA
      51 min   color   Films Inc.   '70
      *Golden Eagle, CINE
The diversity of this land in northeastern Africa is reflected in the
occupations of her people: hunters on the Omo River, fishermen on
Lake Chama, herdsmen in the deserts, business and factory workers
in modern Addis Ababa.   Narrated by Joseph Campanella.   Produced
by the National Geographic Society.   (College-Adult)

THE EURAILPASS STORY--Too Much for Your Money
      30 min   color   Assn. -Sterling
      *Chris Award, Columbus
Promotes the advantages of train travel in Austria, Belgium, Denmark, France, Germany, Italy, Luxembourg, the Netherlands, Nor-
way, Portugal, Spain, Sweden, and Switzerland.   Shows the facilities
and related privileges available with purchase of a Eurailpass.
Free loan to adult groups.

THE EVERGLADES
      51 min   color   Films Inc.   '71
      *"Emmy," Nat. Academy
Observes the unusual animal and plant life of the Florida preserve
that is under the National Park Service now.   Still, even today when
the importance of ecology is recognized, the area is still threatened
by poachers, engineers, and developers.   Produced by NBC Television News.   (HS-Adult)   (Not to be confused with the following CBC
production.)

THE EVERGLADES
      28 min   color   Films Inc.   '70
      *Gold Medal, Atlanta
      *Chris Statuette, Columbus
This wilderness in southernmost Florida depends for its survival on
decisions far outside its boundaries; that is, business decisions, political decisions, and vested interests.   At stake are fresh water
sources, unique plants and animals including the cypress tree, the
white heron, the giant pelican, the alligator, and the bald eagle.
Apparently, the priorities for the development of natural resources
don't include the preservation of the Everglades.   Produced by the
Canadian Broadcasting Corporation.   (HS-Adult)   (Not to be confused
with the above NBC-TV production.)

EVERYDAY CHRONICLE
      11 min   color   Mass Media   '71
      *First Prize, Bergamo
A story, told in animation, that is deliberately topsy-turvy.   It concerns a blind man whose dog becomes lost in pedestrian traffic, and
goes on to show how--even in a giant turnstile of a modern city--
love between beings can persist.   Made by Zagreb Films.   (Intermediate-Adult)

EVERYTHING UNDER THE SUN
      27 min   color   Australia   '70

*Gold Camera, US Industrial
A promotional view of typical Australians at work, at home, and at play.   Contrasts the sophistication of Australia's cities with the simplicity of her "outback" regions.   Produced by the Commonwealth Film Unit.   (HS-Adult)

EVOLUTION
11 min color Learn. Corp.   '71
*Award, San Francisco
*Gold Medal, Atlanta
*Nomination, Academy Award
How life began on earth, according to the imagination of animator Michael Mills. His zany characters mix, match, and eventually multiply in a full range of beings from one-celled amoebae to homo sapiens. Produced by the National Film Board of Canada. (HS-Adult)

EVOLUTION AND THE ORIGIN OF LIFE
33 min color CRM Educ. Films '72
*Category Prize, San Francisco
*Gold Medal, Int. Film & TV
This treatment is designed as an introduction to biology. Beginning with the creation of the universe (as conceived by the "big bang" theorists), the film takes as its premise the Miller-Urey theory that the right chemical and climatic conditions led to the building-blocks of human life. (HS-College)

EVOLUTION OF A YOGI
28 min color Hartley Prod.
*Blue Ribbon, American/EFLA
Ram Dass was formerly named Richard Alpert, Harvard professor and associate of Dr. Timothy Leary. He is now America's foremost teacher of Raja Yoga. This film observes him and his followers at a spiritual teach-in on the philosophy and practice of Yoga. (College-Adult)

EXCHANGES
10 min BW ACI Films '69
*Merit Award, Philadelphia
*Golden Eagle, CINE
An encounter between two train passengers, a black man and a white woman. By showing how an ordinary experience can be complicated by prejudice, this film provides an examination of a fundamental social issue. A John Camie Film. (HS-Adult)

EXPERIMENTS IN MOTION GRAPHICS
13 min color Pyramid '68
*Golden Eagle, CINE
*Best Art, American/EFLA
Film-maker John Whitney explains the processes involved in programming and animating his designs. He compares motion graphics with music and language but concludes that it really is a different form that impinges directly upon emotions and perceptions. An

From EXCHANGES (ACI Films Inc.)

introduction to abstract or kinetic film study.   Produced by John
Whitney.   (HS-College)

EYE OF THE SUPERVISOR
        12 min   color   Nat. Educ. Media   '72
        *Chris Certificate, Columbus
Discusses two sides of the seeing process, stressing that supervision involves both the collection and the analysis of information.
Emphasizes the need for an open mind behind the open eye.   Includes the importance of listening, human needs on the job, and consistency of standards.   (College-Adult)

EYES
        4 min   color   Int. Film Bur.
        *Bronze Plaque, Nat. Committee
An attractive young woman puts on glasses just as she is hit by a
popped champagne cork, a fishing fly, welder's sparks, an exploding
fire cracker, and other flying objects.   The message, expressed
non-verbally: Wear safety glasses on the job.   Produced by Craw-
ley Films.   (Adult)

EYES OF A CHILD
        30 min   BW   Time-Life
        *Award Winner, Venice
Follows children in the primary grades through a typical day at a
school for the blind in England.   We watch them in classes where
they learn standard subjects and are taught to make maximum use
of their sense of touch and of hearing.   Demonstrates that it is possible for the handicapped to lead productive lives with other human
beings.   Produced by BBC-TV.   (College-Adult)

FABIENNE
        27 1/4 min   BW   Nat. Film Bd.
        *Award, Evian (France)
She is a night club entertainer, a successful exponent of her art,
but there are moments when the admiration of her Montreal following is not enough.   A portrait of a woman who has achieved fame
but is still far from content.   (College-Adult)

A FABLE
        18 1/2 min   color   Xerox Films   '72
        *Golden Dove, Atlanta
        *Chris Statuette, Columbus
        *Golden Eagle, CINE
Stars Marcel Marceau who mimes his way through the story of a
man who builds a wall around his bit of paradise, only to discover
that his "paradise" has become his prison.   The sound-track consists of musical score by the London Royal Orchestra.   There are
no words or spoken narration.   Film-maker: Fred A. Niles.   (Intermediate)

THE FABLE OF HE AND SHE
        12 min   color   Learn. Corp.   '74

*Blue Ribbon, American/EFLA
Designed to encourage early-age discussion of male and female roles,
this animation dramatizes life on the mythical island of Baramel.
There the Hardibars (men) and the Mushamels (women) have clearly
separate roles ... until an unusual event occurs. Producer: Eliot
Noyes, Jr. (Elem.)

THE FABULOUS COUNTRY
52 min color Films Inc. '72
*Award, Freedoms Foundation
As it portrays the development of our country, this film follows Ben
Franklin from Boston to Philadelphia. Other pioneer spirits--hunt-
ers, trappers, miners and finally farmers--felt the same drive for
opportunity, so they pushed the frontier farther west. By depicting
both the true and the Hollywood versions of the West, this essay encompasses the legendary and the real heroes of American history.
NBC News. (College-Adult)

THE FACE
3 min color Macmillan '66
*Awards: San Francisco Museum, St. Lawrence U., Newton
College, N.Y., and Ann Arbor
A film by Herbert Kosower. An animated whimsy based on the
premise that ideas lead to ideas. In "film absurdity," Herbert
Kosower manipulates original engravings by Piero Fornasetti into
the bizarre and beautiful. (HS-Adult)

FACES
5 min color Schloat Prod. '72
*Chris Statuette, Columbus
*Bronze Medal, Atlanta
"What you see depends on how you look at it," says Max, the freck-
le-faced young star of this film. His questions, comments, and con-
tortions are intended to demonstrate the value of communication and
sensitivity. Based on the book by George Ancona and Barbara Bren-
ner. Produced by George Ancona. (Primary)

FACES AND FORTUNES
18 min color Kimberly-Clark '60
*First Place, Turin
A sponsored product-information film that stresses the importance
of printed matter in corporate identity or public relations programs.
Available on free loan. (HS-Adult)

FALL RIVER LEGEND
10 min color ACI Media '70
*Golden Eagle, CINE
Choreographer Agnes de Mille has fashioned a capsule version of
her ballet based on Lizzie Borden. Against the period background
of New England's Sturbridge Village, dancers enact the passions and
repressions that led to Lizzie's alleged murder of her father and
stepmother. Griffin Productions in association with Group W-West-
inghouse Broadcasting. (HS-Adult)

THE FALSE NOTE
     10 min color Int. Film Bur.
     *Grand Prix, Belgian Nat'l. Animation
     *Award, Benelux
Follows a crippled little beggar-musician through a modern city with
his hand organ. Bank-note collages suggest the main interest of the
inhabitants whose reaction to the musician is impatience or indifference. When he comes to an old section of the city, the sad tune he
plays evokes a sympathetic response: a tear from a carrousel
horse. The tear is caught and becomes the means through which
the man's dreams come true. Written and animated by Raoul
Servais. (Elem. -Adult)

FAMILY OF THE ISLAND: Her Name is Wasamantha
     11 min color McGraw-Hill '69
     *Chris Certificate, Columbus
Wasamantha, a ten-year-old girl in the Fiji Islands, learns a lesson
in responsibility. The film focuses on the role of each member of
the family: the mother's work in the fields and food preparation;
the father's fishing; and Wasamantha's care of the baby. We learn
that each member must carry his or her share of responsibility if
the family is to survive. (Intermediate)

FAMILY OF THE RIVER: The River, My Home
     12 min color McGraw-Hill '69
     *Chris Statuette, Columbus
Razi, a nine-year-old girl, narrates this film about her life, her
family, and the river. Razi's family makes its living by selling
salt and other goods to people along the Chao Phrara River in Thailand. On the trip from Bangkok, we see Razi and her family sharing the housework and earning their living on their boat, in contrast
to our urban society where father goes away to work, children go to
school, and mother is often left home with the housework. Produced
by McGraw-Hill Films in collaboration with Vision Associates. (Intermediate)

FANTASY OF FEET
     8 min color Encyc. Brit. '70
     *Golden Eagle, CINE
     *Chris Certificate, Columbus
In this film, feet walk, dance, run, jump, hop, and wear sandals,
flippers, slippers, boots, wooden shoes, and no shoes at all. A
pair of cowboy boots does a lively square dance--all by themselves!
This approach can help children talk about the different shoes there
are, why there are so many, and how feet serve many functions.
(Primary)

FARM BOY OF HUNGARY
     19 min color Barr Films '74
     *Bronze Plaque, Columbus
Lajos explores the village market and tells us about his family's
farm and the way of life in the rural regions of Central Europe today. (Intermediate)

FARM VILLAGE OF INDIA: The Struggle with Tradition
    22 min color Perspective
    *Golden Eagle, CINE
Working their farm on the Ganges Plain, Gopal and his wife plan a
better future for their son. Complications in obtaining a loan, and
delay in the delivery of seed and fertilizer, point up problems in
attempting to change the patterns of the past. Produced by Phillips
Foster, Professor, Dept. of Agricultural Economics, University of
Maryland. (Senior HS-College)

FARMYARD BABIES
    11 min color Coronet
    *Participation, Venice (Child.)
As we follow Daisy, the farm dog, on her morning rounds, we see
a variety of babies of the farmyard--lambs, calves, colts, chicks,
and others. We learn the answers to questions such as: What do
farmyard babies look like? What do they sound like? What do they
eat? (Kindergarted-Primary)

FASHION: The Second Skin
    22 min color Document Assoc. '71
    *Gold Medal, Atlanta
One of a series of 25 films that explore areas of major significance
in the future of man. Enlists authorities, educators, and scientists
to discuss concepts of an open-ended nature. (HS-Adult)

THE FATHER
    28 min BW New Line Cinema
    *Blue Ribbon, American/EFLA
Directed by Mark Fine. Burgess Meredith plays a lonely hansom
cab driver in this retelling of Chekhov's short story, "Grief." (HS-
Adult)

THE FAYETTE STORY
    54 min color Schloat Prod.
    *Golden Eagle, CINE
    *Chris Statuette, Columbus
    *Blue Ribbon, American/EFLA
About the impact of Charles Evers' election as the first black mayor
since Reconstruction in a bi-racial southern town. Fayette citizens
--young and old, black, white, office holders, those with high status
and those with lower status--describe their feelings, fears, and
hopes in their own words. There is no narrator's commentary or
interpretation. As the camera and microphone move back and forth
from Mayor Evers to a state senator, local newspaper publisher,
businessman, landowner, worker, students and other town residents,
viewers can judge for themselves the political and personal issues
at stake in Fayette, Mississippi. (College-Adult)

FEATHER
    8 min color ACI Films '72
    *Golden Eagle, CINE

*Best of Show, Seattle
A story about a child's emotions and relations with others. A girl
finds a pheasant feather, offers it to many people, suggesting new
uses for it each time. Everyone refuses it, but then she finds that
her little brother has found his own use for it. Happily, she joins
him in play. No narration; only the natural conversation of the girl.
Produced by Teaching Research of Oregon. (Elem.)

FEDERAL TAXATION (2nd Edition)
   11 min   color   Coronet
   *Award, Freedoms Foundation
Analyzes the sources and uses of revenue, with emphasis on defense
and the general welfare as authorized by the Constitution. The student, as a future voter and taxpayer, is encouraged to evaluate federal taxation in light of such questions as equality and privileged
status. (HS)

FIDDLE DE DEE
   4 min   color   Int. Film Bur.   '47
   *Awards: Brussels, Rome, and others
Celluloid dyes, inks, and paints were applied directly onto film.
The surface was then stippled, etched, and pressed with cloths to
create unusual patterns. The music is "Listen to the Mockingbird,"
played on a folk fiddle. Animated by Norman McLaren, National
Film Board of Canada. (Intermediate-Adult)

FIDELIO: A Celebration of Life
   54 min   BW   McGraw-Hill   '70
   *Series Award, Saturday Review
From the Young People's Concert series, with Leonard Bernstein
as master of ceremonies, narrator, and conductor of the New York
Philharmonic. CBS Television. (Elem.-Adult)

FIELDS OF SACRIFICE
   38 1/4 min   color   Nat. Film Bd.
   *Canadian Film Award
   *Award, Victoria (B.C.) Canada
   *Chris Award, Columbus
A tribute to the 100,000 Canadians who gave their lives in the serv-
ice of their country on foreign battlegrounds. Photographed from
Hong Kong to Sicily, the film visits battlefields of the World Wars
and cemeteries where servicemen are buried. (College-Adult)

FIFTH STREET
   32 min   color   CRM Films   '73
   *Best Documentary, Vancouver
   *Gold Medal, Atlanta
The crushing humiliation, the oppressive boredom, and the degrada-
tion of addiction to alcohol is portrayed in this visual and verbal

tour of skid row. Because this documentary is a frank look at one of our society's most harsh and degenerate environments, preview the film before screening it for audiences. Produced by Bob Mc-Andrew. (HS-Adult)

FIGURE SKATING
14 1/2 min color Nat. Film Bd.
*Award, Cortina d'Ampezzo
An opportunity to experience the sensation of spinning, jumping, skimming, and dancing on skates. Champions appear briefly in the film in exhibition, but the main object of the film is to show that figure skating is for everyone--children, young people, adults. (Elem.-Adult)

FIGURES FROM A FABLE
10 min color ACI Films '69
*Award, American/EFLA
*Golden Eagle, CINE
An animated film that charts the rise and fall of a civilization. Relies not on narration, but on music, sound effects, and experimental technique: three-dimensional dwarfs and two-dimensional graphics. (Intermediate-Adult)

FIRE
11 min color FilmFair '70
*Hon. Mention, San Francisco
The routine of firehouse life and work is given dimension by these non-narrated glimpses into fire-fighters' recreation, meals, and surroundings. This leisurely pace is accelerated as they then answer the alarm and battle a fire. Produced by Istvan Ventilla. (Elem.-Adult)

FIRE IN MY KITCHEN
12 min color Film Communicators '72
*Bronze Plaque, Nat. Committee
Provides guidance on wastebasket fires, overloaded circuits, grease ignitions, hazards of clothing ignitions, child safety in the kitchen, with special emphasis on correct way to call the fire department. (Intermediate-Adult)

FIRE IN THE SEA
10 min color Encyc. Brit. '73
*Golden Eagle, CINE
Close-up views of the lava flow during the eruption of Mount Kilauea in Hawaii are combined with music and natural sounds to try to capture the feeling of presence. No narration. (Intermediate-Adult)

FIRE IN TOWN
26 min color Int. Film Bur.
*Awards: Canada and Chicago

Reviews basic requirements for adequate community fire protection,
with emphasis on thorough and frequent building inspections by
trained firemen. Designed to improve community fire department
service. Produced by the National Film Board of Canada. (HS-
Adult)

FIRE MOUNTAIN
        9 min color Encyc. Brit. '70
        *Trophy, Nat'l Educational
        *Silver Medal, Venice
        *Award, City of Trent (Italy)
        *Golden Eagle, CINE
        *Bronze Medal, Atlanta ... and several other awards
Orange flames of lava, burned-out tree trunks shrouded in steam,
and molten lava cascading over a precipice--these are seen in close-
up views of the second greatest eruption of Mt. Kilauea in Hawaii.
Music and the natural sounds of the volcano's roar permit viewers
to create individual interpretations without the need for narration.
(Intermediate-Adult)

A FIREFLY NAMED TORCHY
        7 1/2 min color Xerox Films '73
        *Golden Eagle, CINE
Is it fun to be different? Torchy doesn't think so. Instead of twin-
kling, Torchy flashes. "TURN OFF THAT LIGHT!" the forest creatures demand. But try as he might, Torchy can't tone down to a
twinkle. Torchy gets a new lease on life when he meets his match
in the big city--and flashes all the way home. From the "Desire to
Read" series. A Stephen Bosustow Production. (Primary-Intermediate)

THE FIREMAN IS SAD AND CRIES
        10 min color McGraw-Hill '65
        *Best Short, Nat. Film Inst.
        *1st Prize, La Plata, Argentina
Portrays children's expressions and emotional reactions through
scenes of the children at work with crayon, paint and brush, and
clay. Directed by Pablo Szir and Elida Stantic. Photography by
Rocardo Aronovich. Electronic music by Tom Dissevelt and Kid
Baltan. A Contemporary Films Release. (College-Adult)

FIRST AID FOR AIRCREW
        27 1/2 min color Nat. Film Bd.
        *Award Winner, Chicago
A training film, produced originally for military personnel. Demonstrates the application of four principles of first aid to show that,
by keeping cool, a victim of a plane crash can often render first aid
to the more seriously injured. (College-Adult)

FIRST AID NOW
        28 1/2 min color Assn. -Sterling
        *Golden Eagle, CINE
A man drowning, a woman unconscious, an automobile accident, a

fire--situations that illustrate how a life can be saved if first aid
is administered in time. Shows what to do in case of burns or
broken bones; how to control bleeding; and how to administer mouth-
to-mouth resuscitation. Free loan. Johnson & Johnson, sponsor.
(HS-Adult)

THE FIRST FIVE MINUTES
27 min BW Assn. -Sterling
*Winner, Golden Reel Award
The importance of industrial fire brigades in plant fire prevention
and protection is emphasized in this film. Sponsor: American Insurance Association. (Adult)

THE FIRST FLICKERS
27 min BW Films Inc. '69
*Award, San Francisco St.
*Award Winner, Atlanta
For more than 50 years, still prints of motion pictures produced
between 1894 and 1912 were stored in the Library of Congress.
These paper print positives were filed in order to copyright films
in an era when motion pictures could only be registered as still pictures. Most of the original films, made on nitrate base, have literally disappeared. But a process developed in the 1950s converted
the paper prints into motion picture film and a lost period of movies
was recovered. Appearing are such early stars as Mary Pickford
and Mack Sennett, and two versions of The Great Train Robbery.
Produced by WRC-TV. (HS-Adult)

THE FISH EMBRYO: From Fertilization to Hatching
12 min color Encyc. Brit. '63
*Award, Congress of Int. Assns.
Illustrates how fish eggs are fertilized in a stream, then traces the
development of the zygote from the first cell cleavage to the formation of a young fish. Producer: National Film Board of Canada.
(HS-College)

FISH: MASTER OF MOVEMENT (Locomotion in the Sea)
12 min color Macmillan '69
*Golden Eagle, CINE
*Honor Certificate, American/EFLA
Although sea creatures seem to move effortlessly, the mechanics of
locomotion can be complex and beautiful. This film is an explora-
tion of fish moving in their own environment. Produced by Reela
Films. (HS-College)

FIVE BRITISH SCULPTORS WORK AND TALK
28 min color McGraw-Hill '64
*Lion of San Marco, Venice
Each of the five sculptors--Barbara Hepworth, Reg Butler, Kenneth
Armitage, Lynn Chadwick and Henry Moore--has a different aura.
Armitage working in his artists' colony surrounded by the sea, Chad-
wick in Dick Whittington's castle--each is an individual. Their
homes meld with their studios, their egos with their work. Art is

their life, and their way of life, art. Filmed and directed by Warren Forma. A Contemporary Films release. (College-Adult)

FIVE COLORFUL BIRDS (3rd Edition)
      11 min   color   Coronet
      *Award, Golden Reel
Using new footage, new sound, and authentic bird calls, this revised
version presents the American goldfinch, cedar waxwing, scarlet
tanager, redheaded woodpecker, and eastern bluebird in their natural surroundings. Shows the characteristic colorful plumage and
nesting and feeding habits of each bird. (Intermediate-Adult)

FLATLAND
      12 min   color   McGraw-Hill   '65
      *Silver Award, Chicago
This animated film, based on the short novel by Edwin A. Abbott,
offers a social commentary. It depicts the tale of a square who
lives in Flatland, and the difficulties he encounters in trying to convince his two-dimensional society of the existence of a third dimension. Produced by John Gardner for Harvard University. (HS-College)

FLIGHT
      8 min   color   Int. Film Bur.   '72
      *Awards: Montreal, Italy, and others
Filmed over the Laurentians and the Canadian Rockies, this film
follows gliders as they soar over the countryside. Many shots were
taken in actual flight. Without commentary, the film expresses the
feel of piloting an engineless craft. National Film Board of Canada.
(Intermediate-Adult)

FLIGHT IN WHITE
      14 3/4 min   color   Nat. Film Bd.
      *Award Winner, Brussels
Nothing a person does brings him closer to flight than skiing.
Filmed in the Canadian Rockies, this picture reveals the blend of
exhilaration, risk, prowess and speed that is part of this sport.
(HS-Adult)

FLOWER LOVERS
      11 min   color   Film Inc.   '70
      *Short Film Award, Krakow
Business is bad for an old flower peddler, so he experiments with
chemicals to increase his flowers' size. He stumbles onto a formula
that makes the flower explode. Exploding flowers become the latest
rage. Everyone buys them. It is a matter of status to have the
biggest and best explosion. Animation by Zagreb Films. (Intermediate-Adult)

FLOWERS ON A ONE WAY STREET
      58 min   BW   Films Inc.   '67
      *TV Award, Chicago
      *Merit Award, Philadelphia

*Blue Ribbon, American/EFLA
Centers on the hippie community on Yorkville Avenue in Toronto.
The youngsters want their street closed to traffic. They petition
the Board of Control. What emerges is a look at two generations
coming to grips, trying vainly to explain and understand each other's
thinking. By the time the sit-downs, arrests, and demonstrations
are over, only a few of the city councillors have begun to examine
their own position concerning the young people's demands. National
Film Board of Canada. (College-Adult)

FLURINA
    14 min color ACI Films '69
    *Awards: Edinburgh, Teheran, and Venice
An animated story of a little Swiss girl, Flurina, who, on a visit
in the Alps, rescues a small bird from an eagle. She tries to make
the bird into a pet, but realizes she must let him go. Her bird
friend swoops down in a farewell salute of gratitude, suggesting that
the two may somehow meet again. (Primary-Intermediate)

THE FLUTTERBYE
    9 min color ACI Films '70
    *Award Winner, Zagreb
    *Golden Eagle, CINE
    *Honors, American/EFLA
Animation based on children's drawings, and a narration spoken by
children about the distant time past when the creature, the Flutterbye, appeared on earth to end conflict, and everyone lived in peace.
When people began to ignore the Flutterbye, he disappeared, but
just might reappear some day. A Ron Phillips Rilm. (Primary-
Intermediate)

FOCUS ON ABILITY
    22 min color Red Cross '74
    *Blue Ribbon, American/EFLA
Deals with the teaching of swimming to the handicapped. As such,
it goes beyond the mechanics of instruction, and explains the importance of establishing relationships between teacher and student, if
technique is going to succeed. Producer: John S. Allen. (HS-Adult)

FOG
    9 min color Encyc. Brit. '71
    *Red Ribbon, American/EFLA
Carl Sandburg's poem was the inspiration for this non-narrated film.
Views of fog in valleys, clouding sea and ships, and landmarks such
as the Golden Gate Bridge encourage observation and comment by
viewers. (HS-Adult)

FOLK MUSIC IN THE CONCERT HALL
    53 min BW McGraw-Hill '67
    *Series Award, Saturday Review
From the Young People's Concert series, with Leonard Bernstein
as master of ceremonies, narrator, and conductor of the New York
Philharmonic. A CBS Television production. (Elem.-Adult)

FOLKSONGS OF THE WESTERN MOVEMENT
    13 1/2 min   color   Coronet
    *Award, Freedoms Foundation
The American westward movement has been told in many histories,
but none is presented with such immediacy as in the songs of the
people.   Songs in this film: Bounding the U.S. , Cumberland Gap,
Driver's Song, The Sioux, The Handcart Song, Clementine, and the
Wayfaring Stranger.   (Intermediate-HS)

FOLKSONGS OF WESTERN SETTLEMENT (1865-1900)
    16 min   color   Coronet
    *Chris Award, Columbus
    *Award, Freedoms Foundation
Miners and merchants, farmers and ranchers, lawmen and railroaders settled the American West, and their hardships are mirrored in
folksongs of the people: Down in the Mine, The Rambler, The
Farmer is a Man, The Greer County Bachelor, I Ride an Old Paint,
The Chisholm Trail, The Cowboy's Lament, and Billy the Kid. (Intermediate-HS)

FOLLOW MR. WILLOUGHBY
    14 min   color   Encyc. Brit.   '70
    *Chris Certificate, Columbus
A race against time involves eight-year-old Jamie in numerous adventures.   His friend, Mr. Willoughby, an absentminded ship's
cook, leaves a present for his grandson at a bus stop.   Jamie tries
to catch Mr. Willoughby before his ship leaves port.   Youngsters
can plot their own endings before viewing three possible climaxes.
A Moreland-Latchford Production.   (Elem.)

FOOD, THE COLOR OF LIFE
    26 min   color   Assn. -Sterling
    *Golden Eagle, CINE
The story of nutrition, a science that grew out of the quest for information about the components of food.   Demonstrates how the
knowledge man has acquired enables him to combat starvation and
malnutrition.   Emphasis is placed on the importance of a balanced
diet.   Free loan.   National Dairy Council-Sponsor.   (HS-Adult)

THE FOOLISH FROG
    8 min   color   Weston Woods   '71
    *Chris Certificate, Columbus
An animated version of the children's picture-book of the same name.
Produced by Morton Schindel.   (Elem.)

FOOTNOTES ON THE ATOMIC AGE
    46 min   color   Films Inc.   '70
    *"Emmy," Nat. Academy
Since the dawn of the atomic age, 2 1/2 billion dollars have been
spent testing nuclear devices at the rate of two explosions per month.
This report documents the programs of the nuclear establishment and
the dangers and the promise of peacetime use of the atom.   An NBC
News production.   (College-Adult)

FOR THE LOVE OF FRED
    49 min   color   Films Inc.   '70
    *Winner, Gabriel Awards
    *Award, Christopher Movement
    *Award, Catholic Broadcasters
Fred, the caterpillar in this story performed by puppets, has
yearned all his life to become a butterfly.   But he doesn't know how
to make a cocoon.   Fred's friend, Albert the chipmunk, has tried
wrapping Fred in gauze, but it fails.   Finally Sir Geoffrey the
giraffe and Magnolia the ostrich advise them to see a doctor.   The
doctor says that the only thing that will help Fred is love.   With
that, the puppets begin their search for love.   Produced by NBC
Television.   (Elem. -Adult)

FORCES MAKE FORMS
    12 1/2 min   color   FilmFair   '73
    *Gold Medal, Atlanta
Encourages multiplicity of interpretation of images by displaying
common and unusual objects and events.   Can also motivate critical
observation and logical association between forces in operation and
their resultant forms.   A Kinek Production.   (Upper Elem. -Junior
HS)

FOREST FISHERMAN: Story of an Otter
    16 min   color   ACI Films   '72
    *Science Prize, Birmingham
A forest ranger receives an orphaned otter.   As summer passes,
the otter becomes more curious about his world.   He swims in the
highlands all winter but, come spring, the mature otter returns to
his natural world ... illustrating the need of a wild animal, raised
in captivity, to return to his native environment.   (Elem. -Adult)

FOREST: Trees and Logs
    15 min   color   American Educ. Films
    *Silver Medal, Venice
Portrays the life cycle of a rain forest, stressing that the forest
ecosystem (as a mirror of all other environments) is in delicate
balance.   At the same time we see the miracle of rebirth that can
occur when nature is allowed to heal her wounds.   (HS-Adult)

FOREST WITHOUT SPEARS
    26 min   color   Australia   '68
    *Gold Camera, US Industrial
The remote and mysterious Bulolo Valley, once a tribal battleground,
now echoes to the sound of economic development: a new timber industry in Australia.   Filmed by the Commonwealth Film Unit.   (HS-
Adult)

FOREVER BEETHOVEN
    53 min   color   McGraw-Hill   '69
    *Series Award, Saturday Review
From the Young People's Concert series, with Leonard Bernstein as
master of ceremonies, narrator, and conductor of the New York
Philharmonic.   Produced by CBS Television.   (Elem. -Adult)

FORMS OF MUSIC: INSTRUMENTAL
    16 min BW Coronet '61
    *Chris Award, Columbus
Visualizes most of the major forms of instrumental music, using
animated drawings. Specially selected music by Bach, Haydn, Mozart, Beethoven, and other important composers, illustrates the historical development of the sonata form, the classical sonata, the
concerto, the symphony, and the tone poem, as well as earlier
forms of music. (HS)

FOUNDING OF THE AMERICAN COLONIES
    10 1/4 min color Doubleday '70
    *Chris Award, Columbus
Surveys the period from the discovery of America by Columbus to
the end of the 17th century. It is an overview of the Spanish,
French, and English colonization efforts. Explores the general reasons for colonization and the specific reasons of each European
country. (HS)

FOUR LINE CONICS
    10 3/4 min color Nat. Film Bd.
    *Awards: London and Budapest
An experimental mathematics film by T. J. Fletcher. This is a
film of potential value in advanced mathematics but also of aesthetic
interest. It may be shown at sound speed or at slower silent speed
so that one's own commentary can be added. (HS-College)

1492
    54 min color McGraw-Hill '65
    *Golden Eagle, CINE
From the Italian Renaissance to the high adventure of Christopher
Columbus' "impossible" journey, this film focuses on the freeing of
man's spirit in a new age. The great art and architectural treasures of the era illustrate the sweep and grandeur of the age of enlightenment. An ABC-TV production. (College-Adult)

THE FOX WENT OUT ON A CHILLY NIGHT
    8 min color Weston Woods '68
    *Honors Certificate, American/EFLA
An iconographic (still picture) version of the children's picture-book
of the same name. Also available in Super 8 Sound. Produced by
Mort Schindel. (Elem.)

FRAME-UP! THE IMPRISONMENT OF MARTIN SOSTRE
    30 min color Pacific St. '73
    *Blue Ribbon, American/EFLA
    *Grierson Award, American/EFLA
The subject is an outspoken Black bookstore owner who persisted in
expressing his political beliefs, in spite of harassment from the FBI
and local police. As a result, he was indicted on a trumped up
drug charge, and condemned to serving a sentence of 41 years for a
crime he didn't commit. (Junior HS-Adult)

FRANCINE, GEORGE AND THE FERRYBOAT
    15 min   color   Oxford '72
    *Bronze Plaque, Columbus
This three-character story is one that can entertain children and
also serve as motivation for listening, communicating, and evaluat-
ing. As such, it is actually three stories in one. Produced by
Moreland-Latchford, Ltd. (Elem.)

FRANK FILM
    9 min   color   Pyramid '72
    *Jury Prize, Montreal
    *Gold Medal, Atlanta
    *Grand Prix, Annecy
    *First Prize, Aspen Design
    *Award, Ann Arbor ... and many others
A flood of images explains and expands each phase of growing up in
America. This "cinematic family album" is a collage of 11,592
shots of filmed stream-of-consciousness-of-life experiences of this
generation. Narrated by film-maker Frank Mouris in intentional
monotone, with contrasting sound effects by Tony Schwartz. (HS-
Adult)

FREDERICK
    6 min   color   Connecticut Films '71
    *National Cup, Teheran
    *Gold Medal, Atlanta
While the other mice collect nuts and grain for the winter, Frederick savors the colors and feelings of summer and fall, so that
he'll be able to share them with his brothers during the bleak days
of winter. This animated fable was produced by Leo Lionni and
Giulio Gianini. (Elem.)

FREDERICK DOUGLASS: The House on Cedar Hill
    17 min   BW   McGraw-Hill '53
    *Award, Freedoms Foundation
A biography of Frederick Douglass (1817-1895), Negro leader in the
struggle against slavery. The narration was taken from Douglass'
writings. The musical score is based on Negro folk songs. A Contemporary Films release. (HS-Adult)

FREE FALL
    9 min   BW   McGraw-Hill '64
    *Awards: Montreal, San Francisco
Composed of film trimmings, especially assembled to make comment on modern man and his world. Suggests a surrealist dream
of mankind's fall from grace into banality. Produced by the National Film Board of Canada. A Contemporary Films release. (HS-
Adult)

FREEDOM IN FLIGHT
    29 min   color   Moody Institute '71
    *Chris Award, Columbus
Places the student in the cockpit during an instrument landing.

Demonstrates the limitations of man's balance mechanism. Observes the many facets of air traffic control at a major airport. Emphasizes the importance of total commitment by the pilot to his instruments. (HS)

FREEDOM RIVER
    8 min   color   Roundtable   '71
    *1st Prize, Nat. Educational
An animated parable on two levels. One level talks about "freedom river," an ecologically pure river that gradually becomes polluted. On another level, it shows how a society can become too busy to look at the pollution of its own freedoms, its own responsibilities, and its own moral environment. The film raises questions of individual and corporate responsibility. Narrated by Orson Welles. A Stephen Bosustow Production. (HS-Adult)

FREEDOM'S FINEST HOUR
    54 min   color   McGraw-Hill   '67
    *Gold Medal, Freedoms Foundation
    *Golden Eagle, CINE
A film of the Revolutionary War, using some of the art works of that period to illustrate its story. Narrated by Governor Ronald Reagan of California; introduced by Robert Taylor; ballads and themes sung by Jimmy Rodgers. (College-Adult)

FREIGHTER
    13 min   color   AIMS   '69
    *Golden Eagle, CINE
Without words, the camera dwells on harbor sights and sounds: the work of dock crews and of seamen; lunch breaks; the ships themselves. The beauty, toil, and trade of maritime service are all evident here. (Intermediate-Adult)

FREUD: The Hidden Nature of Man
    29 min   color   Learn. Corp.   '70
    *Best Educ. Script, Montreal
This film uses live-action, art, and photographs. Freud, as an old man, talks to us and becomes our guide to his own dreams. We see him as a young man in Vienna. We watch his early work with patients. We learn how he developed his theories on psychoanalysis, the Oedipus complex, the role of the unconscious, and infantile sexuality. A dramatization reveals Freud's radical concept of the human personality. (HS-Adult)

FRIENDLY GAME
    10 min   BW   Mass Media   '68
    *Award, Martin Luther King
    *Golden Eagle, CINE
This interpretation of racist and capitalistic mentality takes the form of a chess game: Whitey, a manicured Ivy League gentleman, vs. Blackie, a Black who is worldly-wise, thanks to his experiences at the hands of white trickery. Film-maker: Robert Glatzer. (HS-Adult)

FRIENDS AND ALIENS
    21 min   color   Oxford Films
    *Golden Eagle, CINE
The scene is a city bus shortly before Christmas.   Each individual
rides along in his own cocoon of apathy and mistrust.   Then two
girls get aboard and start to sing carols.   Gradually a feeling of
openness, and consideration for others invades the formerly depersonalized atmosphere.   Produced by Johnson-Nyquist.   (Elem.-Adult)

THE FROG PRINCE
    7 min   color   Encyc. Brit.   '69
    *Silver Medal, Venice (Child.)
The story of a stubborn princess who doesn't want to keep her
promise.   After her father, the king, makes her honor her word,
she discovers that doing the right thing can have its own reward.
Produced by Halas & Batchelor Films, Ltd.   (Primary)

FROM HERE TO THERE
    9 min   color   Pyramid '64
    *Jury Award, Chicago
    *Critics Award, Cracow
    *Special Prize, Melbourne
A "commercial," in kaleidoscopic form, of the experiences of travel
--the excitement and the poignancy of partings and greetings--and
the visual simulation of aerial flight.   Producer: Saul Bass.   (HS-
Adult)

FROM THE FACE OF THE EARTH
    16 min   color   BFA Educ. Media   '70
    *Silver Medal, Atlanta
Set in the year 2020, this is science-fiction used to dramatize the
delicate ecological balance of our planet.   A girl and her grandfather make a perilous pilgrimage from their underground prison to
the now-uninhabitable surface of the earth--a world she has never
seen, a world he has known and lost.   A King Screen Film.   (Intermediate-Adult)

FROM YELLOWSTONE TO TOMORROW
    51 min   color   Films Inc.   '72
    *Award, Freedoms Foundation
The slopes of Mt. McKinley in Alaska, lava fields in Hawaii, and
coral reefs in the Virgin Islands are representative of the diversity
of the National Parks system.   This salute to the National Park
Service is narrated by George C. Scott and was filmed at fifty different locations within the Park Service system.   NBC News.   (College-Adult)

A FUTURE FOR THE PAST
    30 min   color   Films Inc.   '73
    *Blue Ribbon, American/EFLA
Presents the benefits for city growth and vitality that emanate from
restoring and maintaining historic sections of town.   Cites some
specific examples of how preservation can successfully integrate the
the new with the old.   Produced by World Wide Pictures, Ltd. (HS-Adult)

THE GALAPAGOS: Darwin's World Within Itself
20 min   color   Encyc. Brit.   '71
*Chris Statuette, Columbus
This is an on-site study of the diverse biology of the volcanically
formed Galapagos Islands, discovered by Charles Darwin as the
basis for the theory of evolution.   This film recounts his observations on the rare plants and animals there.   It also suggests man's
harmful influences on the balance of nature.   (HS-College)

GALE IS DEAD
51 min   color   Time-Life   '72
*Award, National Council
In documentary style, this is the story of a young woman's losing
battle with drugs.   Beginning and ending with scenes from Gale's
funeral, the film visits the people who tried to help her.   One sequence is a hospital interview with Gale a few months before her
death.   Her situation is a study of the motives behind drug addiction
and of the responsibilities of society for its young victims of neglect.
From the BBC-TV Network.   (College-Adult)

GALILEO
13 1/2 min   color   Coronet   '60
*Chris Award, Columbus
Made in Italy, this film recreates elements of this scientist's struggles against prevailing tradition and opinion.   In locations associated
with Galileo, viewers see how he disproved earlier theories of Aristotle, how he verified the astronomical theories of Copernicus, and
how he continued making discoveries in physical science, despite
strong opposition.   (HS)

GALILEO: The Challenge of Reason
26 min   color   Learn. Corp.   '70
*Chris Statuette, Columbus
This is a study of Galileo as a man and as the founder of experimental science.   Because of his unorthodox beliefs, he was brought
before the Inquisition.   In dramatizing this confrontation between Individual and Establishment, a more contemporary and universal
theme is exposed for discussion and comparison.   Produced by Dennis Azzarella.   (HS-Adult)

THE GALLERY DOWN UNDER
9 min   color   Australia   '69
*Merit Award, Philadelphia
*Creative Prize, Yorkton
*Honors, San Francisco
*Gold Camera, US Industrial
A filmed tour of the National Gallery of Victoria in Melbourne.   In
a building that is itself a work of art, the film-makers capture
numerous impressions of texture, shape, sound, and image.   Pro-
duced by the Commonwealth Film Unit.   (HS-Adult)

GAMES
25 min   color   Nat. AV Center   '72

*Best of Show, Ind. Photo.
A simulation of situations of disguised job prejudice and favoritism
against minority applicants such as Blacks, Jews, Chicanos, Puerto
Ricans, and immigrant Europeans. Sponsored by the Aberdeen
Proving Grounds. A Larry Ross Production. Available on free
loan. (HS-Adult)

GANGES: Sacred River
      27 min   color   Encyc. Brit.   '66
      *Golden Eagle, CINE
Follows the Ganges from its Himalayan origins, through the heart
of India, to Calcutta and the Bay of Bengal. This panorama of
modern India shows the contradictions between its culture and social
needs, and stresses India's dependence on the water cycle. Produced by the National Broadcasting Company and re-edited from its
original 54-minute TV length. (HS-Adult)

GARDEN PARTY
      24 min   color   ACI Films   '74
      *Maxi Award, Media & Methods
      *Red Ribbon, American/EFLA
      *Jury Award, San Francisco
      *Silver Plaque, Chicago
An adaptation of the short story by Katherine Mansfield that experi-
entially probes a young woman's first encounter with death. Directed
by Jack Sholder. Co-producer: Paul Gurian. (HS-Adult)

GATE 73
      12 min   color   Pyramid   '70
      *Golden Eagle, CINE
This non-verbal examination of airplanes and airports is highlighted
by split-screen and tinted images, speeded-up motion, and superimposed action shots. Traffic streaming into the terminal, baggage on
conveyor belts, engineers checking instrument panels--all suggest
the complex demands for safe operation of modern air travel. Produced by Michael Bloebaum. (Intermediate-Adult)

GENESIS
      6 min   color   Macmillan   '66
      *Grand Prize, Oberhausen
Czech animators demonstrate the theory that the origin of mankind
is not a mystery at all but rather a mechanical phenomenon. A
man is stamped out in all his parts: an egg-shaped head, scarlet
boutonnière, implanted heart--all on an assembly line consisting of
box-machines of polished wood. Just when the wooden head seems
able to act, a guillotine chops it off. Produced by the Studio for
Puppet Film, Prague. (HS-Adult)

GENESIS
      13 min   color   CMC-Columbia
      *Gran Premio Winner, Bergamo
An animated visualization of the seven days of Creation, as written
in the Old Testament. The imagery is symbolic rather than literal,

and it concentrates on the element of mood. The abstract approach
makes this film suitable for non-denominational use. Animator:
Abe Liss. (Intermediate-Adult)

THE GENESIS OF A SCULPTURE
 13 min BW Roland Films
 *Prize, Paris Biennale
 *Hon. Mention, Cannes
A demonstration of the various stages of a sculpture, ranging from
the representational form to abstraction. The work performed is
by Maxim Adam-Tessier, as the camera follows his choices, his
decisions, his hesitations, and his regrets. Directed by Oliver
Clouzot and Julien Pappe. (HS-Adult)

GENETICS: Man the Creator
 22 min color Document Assoc. '71
 *Educ. Winner, Canadian
 *Bronze Medal, Atlanta
Investigates the possibility and the morality of genetic engineering;
that is, the manipulation of genes and sperm production. Comments
are provided by leading geneticists of the U.S. and Canada. One of
a series of 25 films on the study of the future. (HS-College)

GENEVIÈVE
 29 min BW McGraw-Hill '72
 *Series Award, Venice (Italy)
The dilemma of two friends in love with the same man. Geneviève
and Louise go to a Quebec winter carnival, and are joined there by
Louise's boyfriend Bernard. Louise oversleeps and Geneviève, not
wanting to miss any of the carnival, goes there with Bernard. As
they both return to Louise's room, Louise catches sight of them
kissing quickly. On the train-ride home, Geneviève invents a story
of how she spent that morning alone; Louise keeps silent about what
she saw. Who was more dishonest? Dialogue in French-Canadian
with subtitles. Director: Michel Brualt. (HS-College)

GEOLOGY OF YELLOWSTONE PARK
 15 min color McGraw-Hill '68
 *Golden Eagle, CINE
A view of the varied natural wonders of these 3,472 square miles.
Many of the park's characteristic marvels are shown, especially
those associated with its volcanic origins. Also included are such
terminology as fumarole, geyser, hot spring, canyon, and mud volcano. (Intermediate-Adult)

A GEOMETRY LESSON
 13 min BW Macmillan '47
 *Prize Winner, Venice
By showing the geometric bases of natural forms, and by indicating
how geometry functions in art and science, this film reveals principles of that subject in everyday existence. It suggests a correlation
between abstract art and the spatial forms of higher mathematics,
and demonstrates how abstract forms can be derived from mathematics. Produced by Carlo Ponti. (HS-College)

GEORGE WASHINGTON
30 min color Handel '67
*Freedoms Foundation Award
A study of Washington's boyhood and education, his work as a surveyor, and his military career. This led to his involvement in the French and Indian War, Braddock's expedition, and finally to his civil activities prior to the Revolution. (HS-Adult)

GEORGE WASHINGTON'S INAUGURATION
22 min color Handel '72
*Freedoms Foundation Award
A "You Are There" format, with modern newscasters giving background and coverage of this event as it happens. After the ceremony, reporters then interview prominent political leaders such as Hamilton, Madison, and King George. There are also authentic songs and even appropriate commercials. (Intermediate-HS)

GERONIMO JONES
21 min color Learn. Corp. '70
*Best Document., San Francisco
Geronimo is an Indian boy caught between two cultures: that of his Apache grandfather and that of his forward-looking cousin, an astronomer. We follow Geronimo from his reservation home to an after-school trip to town. There, he is persuaded by a storekeeper to trade a treasured Apache medallion for a second-hand TV set for his grandfather. But instead of joy, his gift brings pain. Producer: Burt Salzman. (Intermediate-Junior HS)

GEYSER VALLEY
9 min color Encyc. Brit. '72
*Bronze Medal, Atlanta
*Silver Hugo, Chicago
*Golden Eagle, CINE
Yellowstone's geysers and other thermal curiosities are seen and heard in this non-narrated film. Viewers travel through valleys, over precipices, and into caverns. Unusual forms, colors, and movements offer possibilities for writing, drawing, and storytelling. (Intermediate-Adult)

GHOST TOWNS OF THE WESTWARD MARCH
18 min color Higgins Prod. '73
*Bronze Plaque, Columbus
*Golden Eagle, CINE
This is the history of the Westward movement told against a background of ghost towns and abandoned mines. Mood is reinforced by related sound effects and by music of the era. (Intermediate-Adult)

GHOSTS OF A RIVER
20 1/4 min color Nat. Film Bd.
*Awards: Brussels, NYC, Teheran, and Canada
The subject is the powerful Columbia River, preserved in this film as it is as of now. Soon, however, many of the ghost towns, abandoned mines, and other reminders of livelier times will vanish,

From THE GIANTS (SIM Productions, Inc.)

---

while hydro-electric construction changes the face of the valley. (HS-Adult)

THE GIANTS
    10 min   color   SIM Prod.   '69
    *Chris Statuette, Columbus
A satirical non-verbal cartoon that explores, with some documentary footage, man's aggressive impulses. This film is a protest against all forms of intolerance and tyranny. Directed by Gene Deitch for Kratky Film, Prague. (HS-Adult)

THE GIANTS AND THE COMMON MEN
    54 min   color   Films Inc.   '68
    *Award, San Francisco State
    *Freedoms Foundation Award
    *Prize Winner, Atlanta
    *Emmy Award, Nat. Academy
Chicago's history is recounted through profiles of its pioneers. Using photographs and tombstones as focal points, individual stories are woven into an historic whole. Famous people are identified, such as: William Hulbert, founder of baseball's National League; George Pullman, railroad-car tycoon; Louis Sullivan, innovative architect; and Governor John Peter Altgeld. The not-so-famous contributed more. Produced by WMAQ-TV, Chicago. (College-Adult)

THE GIFT (Le Cadeau)
      6 min   color   McGraw-Hill   '61
      *Cabildo d'Oro, Buenos Aires
      *Best Cartoon, Cork (Ireland)
      *Animation Prize, Oberhausen
A little man gives a present to his fiancée--a golden horn.   But
when she blows it, it makes a noise like a cow mooing.   Trying to
find the proper sound for it, our hero finds himself at large in a
world where sounds have gone haywire.   Produced by Dick Roberts
and Jacques Vausseur.   (Intermediate-Adult)

GIRLS AT 12
      30 min   color   Educ. Dev. Ctr.   '74
      *Blue Ribbon, American/EFLA
This film traces the daily lives of three girls who are growing up
in a small industrial city.   The pressures on them toward socializa-
tion originate from family, school, and peers.   Designed for use
within curricula on decision points in living, this dramatization can
also increase adult awareness of the same social forces that con-
front adolescents.   Produced by Adeline Naiman.   (Junior HS-Adult)

GIVE US THE CHILDREN
      82 min   color   Films Inc.   '70
      *Award, Ohio State Univ.
      *Prize, San Francisco State
      *Emmy Award, Nat. Academy
This film looks at the crisis that exists under the surface of all
schools; especially those in the inner city.   Then it considers some
alternatives.   It also studies some innovative plans tested across the
nation, from the Parkway experiment in Philadelphia to the 49th
Street School in Los Angeles.   Produced by WKYC-TV.   (College-
Adult)

GLASS
      11 min   color   McGraw-Hill   '58
      *Academy Award (Documentary)
A subjective treatment of the ancient art of glass-blowing and of the
men who create this useful elegance.   A jazz score accompanies the
rhythmic images of the men, the glass, and the machines.   Produced by Bert Haanstra.   Released by Contemporary Films.   (Intermediate-Adult)

THE GLORY OF THEIR TIMES
      50 min   BW   AIM-Assn.
      *Chris Award, Columbus
Rare footage and tape-recordings recall the era of John McGraw,
Christy Mathewson, Babe Ruth, and other baseball immortals.   This
film is based on the best-selling book by Lawrence Ritter.   Narrated by Alexander Scourby.   (HS-Adult)

GO KART GO
      55 min   BW   Sterl. Educ.   '70
      *Arquero de Bronce, Gijon

*Special Mention, La Plata
*Bronze Medal, Venice (Child.)

The story-line of this adventure is built upon rival groups who build go-carts and overcome obstacles in their efforts to win the local races. Produced by the Children's Film Foundation, Britain. (Ages 7-12)

GO TO BLAZES
29 1/2 min BW Nat. Film Bd.
*Award Winner, Chicago
*Golden Reel Award (USA)
*Award, Nat. Safety Council

Investigates fires that have happened or could happen but that, more importantly, could have been prevented. Concludes that, frequently, fires are crimes of carelessness that needlessly cost too much in human life and property. (HS-Adult)

THE GOAL
10 min color McGraw-Hill '69
*Award, Cortina d'Ampezzo

This impression of a French basketball team in action is an interpretation of the sport itself. Almost a basketball ballet, it employs slow motion, jump cutting, and unusual angles to convey the poetry and tension of the game. Produced by Dominique Delouche. (Intermediate-Adult)

GOLD
10 1/2 min BW Nat. Film Bd.
*Award Winner, Edinburgh

A description of placer gold mining in the Yukon. Giant dredges cut deep into creek beds, leaving behind monstrous coils of waste in the wake of the gold-bearing gravel. Shows how gold is trapped, washed, and hand-sorted. (Intermediate-Adult)

GOLDA MEIR
52 min color Time-Life '72
*Red Ribbon, American/EFLA

An interview with Mrs. Meir as prime minister of Israel. Covers the milestones of her political career, and also the highlights of her people's struggle to create a new nation. Produced by BBC-TV. (College-Adult)

THE GOLDEN AGE OF COMEDY
86 min BW Carousel '60
*Winner, Academy Award

A backward glance at Hollywood comedy from the early 1900s to 1960. Features such cinema stars as Jean Harlow, Will Rogers, Carole Lombard, Harold Lloyd, and Laurel and Hardy. Adapted for sound with original music and new narration. Producer-writer: Robert Youngson. (HS-Adult)

THE GOLDEN RULE: A Lesson for Beginners
11 min color Coronet

*Award of Merit, Boston
*Merit Certificate, Columbus
The Golden Rule is visually examined and interpreted as a standard
for behavior. Everyday situations are dramatized to encourage children to apply this norm to their own actions. (Intermediate)

GOLDEN TRANSVAAL
14 min color Assn. -Sterl.
*Chris Award, Columbus
Within the borders of the Transvaal is found a diversity of attrac-
tions, natural and manmade. They include Johannesburg, Pretoria,
and the game reserve of Kruger National Park. Sponsored by the
South African Tourist Corporation. Available on free loan. (HS-
Adult)

GOLDILOCKS AND THE THREE BEARS
11 min color Coronet
*Award of Merit, Boston
*Merit Award, Stamford (Conn.)
Starring three real-life bears, this children's classic is retold in a
presentation that remains faithful to the original fairy tale and bed-
time story. (Primary)

GOOD MORNING, FREEDOM
22 min color ACI Films '70
*Golden Eagle, CINE
Juxtaposing music and live-action scenes against recitation of historical facts, this film shows the landmark locations of important
Revolutionary events that took place at Lexington, Concord, Philadelphia, Valley Forge, and Washington's Crossing. This exploration
of Revolutionary towns and battlefields can serve as an introduction
to that entire period. Produced by Richard S. Burdick. (Intermediate-Adult)

GOOD NIGHT, SOCRATES
34 min BW McGraw-Hill '63
*Golden Lion Award, Venice
As a poetic documentary, this film shows the death of a tradition.
It is related by a man reflecting on a certain Spring of his boyhood.
Through his eyes as a 10-year-old, we see native traditions fade
away as the Greek community and culture are assimilated into an
American city. Produced by Maria Moraites. (College-Adult)

GOOD TIMES, WONDERFUL TIMES
73 min BW Impact Films '65
*Golden Dove, Leipzig
*Cine Forum Award, Venice
War newsreels of human anguish, destruction, and waste are inter-
cut with the empty chatter of a London cocktail party and interviews
with veterans about "the old times." Documentary footage was col-
lected from archives in London, Paris, Berlin, Warsaw, New York,
Tokyo, Belgrade, Budapest, and Moscow. Produced by Lionel Rogosin. (College-Adult)

GOODBYE LYNN
21 min color Centron '72
*Gold Camera, US Industrial
*Mention, Nat. Council/Family
*Silver Hugo, Chicago
A teenage unwed pregnant girl tells of her ordeal in facing reality
with her family, friends, teachers, doctors, and even her boyfriend.
Focuses on the social reactions to Lynn's plight and the related emotional stresses. To be used for counseling with audiences composed
of any of the above individuals likely to experience Lynn's anguish
and need for understanding. (HS-Adult)

THE GOSPEL ACCORDING TO ST. MATTHEW
136 min BW Macmillan '63
*Cine Forum Award, Venice
*Prize, Catholic Film
*Jury Prize, Venice
*Unicrit Award
This treatment does not pretend to parallel the complete letter or
spirit of its New Testament origins. It does, however, purport to
show the urgency with which Jesus preached, realizing that his time
on earth was limited. The use of amateur actors and of images
analogous to great paintings expands the mysteries inherent in Biblical interpretation. By paradoxical reasoning, the rugged Sicilian
landscape, costumes, and people reflect a realistic vision of the
Holy Land during the First Century A.D. Available in Italian with
subtitles. Directed by Pier Paolo Pasolini. (HS-Adult)

GOYA: The Disasters of War
20 min BW Film Images
*Winner, Le Prix Lumière
*Grand Prize, Venice
In 1807 the Napoleonic Wars came to Spain, and the great Spanish
painter, Francisco de Goya, became a self-appointed war correspond-
ent. His series of lithographs of 1810, entitled "The Disasters of
War," reveals the futility and the destruction he witnessed. Imagine
his reactions to the nature and extent of hostilities one hundred years
later during World War I, to say nothing of World War II and its
sequels! Produced by Pierre Kast. (College-Adult)

GRADUATION
17 min color Stanfield House '73
*Winner, USC (Special Educ.)
Narrated by Burt Lancaster, this film examines the question of what
happens to retarded children when they grow up. Presented are the
sheltered workshop and activity center programs available to some
of the graduates. Also portrayed is the life style of "Johnny," a
young adult who has not left his home to work or to visit friends
since his graduation from his special school. Unfortunately, Johnny
represents 44 per cent of his classmates, according to studies of a
large Southern California school district, 1968-70. Produced by
James Stanfield. (College-Adult)

GRASSLAND ECOLOGY--Habitats and Change
     13 min color Centron '70
     *Merit Award, Landers
     *1st Prize, Nat. Visual
     *Golden Eagle, CINE
     *Trophy, Nat. Educational
An historical approach to the ecology of the American prairies.
Wildlife scenes show how bison, prairie dogs, and other organisms
affected the nation's grasslands. Explores various habitats and the
reasons why certain forms of life are found in one biome but not in
others. Challenges the wisdom of man's changing his prairies
through agriculture, chemicals, and construction. (HS-College)

THE GREAT BARRIER REEF
     54 min color Films Inc. '70
     *Golden Eagle, CINE
     *Award, American/EFLA
An ecosystem off the coast of Australia is in danger. The Crown
of Thorns, a species of starfish that eats live coral, is multiplying
and thereby threatening to destroy the Great Barrier Reef. The
Reef is a shelter for many unusual creatures. Its function, beauty,
and variety of life make it a habitat like no other in the world.
Mankind must decide whether to risk introducing new elements there
or to leave the Reef alone and wait for nature to repair it. Produced by NBC News. (College-Adult)

THE GREAT DEPRESSION: A Human Diary
     52 min BW Mass Media '72
     *Jury Award, Chicago
The stock market crash of 1929 made the thirties a dire period in
our history. Here we have material that pertains to the aftermath
of that crash. The visuals consist of photos from the Library of
Congress, the Farm Security Administration, the Office of War Information, and the private collections of journalists. All this documentation helps recall--lest history repeat--the squalor of the Dust
Bowl, mass migration to California, the jobless millions standing in
breadlines, and other evidence of the economic punishment suffered
by so many American citizens. Produced by Jean and Cliff Hoel-
scher. (College-Adult)

THE GREAT GAMBLE: Cyrus W. Field
     20 min BW Indiana U.
     *First Award, Thomas A. Edison
An authenticated enactment of the laying of the trans-Atlantic tele-
graphic cable. Stresses not the technical problems but the vision
and intellectual courage of Cyrus Field (1819-1892). Edited from a
full-length theatrical film production that was re-edited by Teaching
Film Custodians. (Intermediate-HS)

THE GREAT JEWEL ROBBERY
     9 min color Film Images '61
     *Jury Prize, Oberhausen
This tale of an attempted heist, betrayal, and capture involves a

rich lady who owns the largest gem in the world. She keeps it hidden in her mansion, guarded by a detective whose eventual greediness makes him oblivious of the other hired detective sneaking up to catch him in the act. Moral: Who will guard the guards? Animation by Zagreb Film Studio of Yugoslavia. (HS-Adult)

THE GREAT MOJAVE DESERT
    52 min color Films Inc. '70
    *Golden Eagle, CINE
A study of the 20,000 California-Nevada square miles that naturalists fear can no longer withstand the encroachment of "civilization." Airplanes, trains, and automobiles have cut deep scars into this region's surface, and air pollution threatens the sparse vegetation. If this trend continues, man will soon destroy this showcase of natural adaptation. Produced by the National Geographic Society. (College-Adult)

THE GREAT RIGHTS
    14 min color Macmillan '64
    *Award of Merit, Landers
    *Recognition, Nat. Conference
    *Gavel Award, American Bar
Twelve-year-old Millie and her father Marve are touring the landmarks of the capital. Millie is curious about the "Memorials" and particularly about the Bill of Rights. In a fantasy, by way of explanation, their family is confronted with different forms of tyranny that would be their fate if they had no rights under our system of government. Animation by Wm. T. Hurtz. Produced by Thomas Brandon. (Elem.)

THE GREAT TOY ROBBERY
    7 min color McGraw-Hill '67
    *Blue Ribbon, American/EFLA
A cartoon, in the style of a Western movie, starring the world's most wanted good guy--Santa Claus, alias Father Christmas, alias Kris Kringle, alias Saint Nicholas. When he becomes ambushed, a hero comes to his rescue with a guitar more potent than his pistol, and Santa's bag of goodies is restored. Animation by Jeff Hale and Cameron Guess. Produced by Wolf Koenig and Bob Verrall for the National Film Board of Canada. (Elem.)

THE GREAT WAR--Fifty Years After
    25 min color Films Inc. '68
    *Award, San Francisco State
    *Freedoms Foundation Award
    *Honors, Christopher Society
    *Prize Winner, Atlanta
The Great War of 1914 remains unique. There was gallantry and a sense of mission ("The war to end all wars") but also a new disregard for civilian casualties. The camera visits several battle sites and interweaves film clips of past clashes. Through recollections of U.S. veterans, the film reviews American involvement in the campaigns between 1917 and 1918. Produced by WKYC-TV. (HS-Adult)

THE GREAT WHITE PELICAN
19 min color AV Explor. '69
*Award, San Francisco
Life in a pelican colony in the Great Salt Lake: the hatching of
eggs and their protection; the feeding of the young; learning to fly.
Offers reasons for the gradual decline of this unique bird, one of
the largest of all. Photographed by Bob Davidson. Film study-
guide is available upon request. (Intermediate-Adult)

THE GREATER COMMUNITY ANIMAL
7 min color ACI Films '68
*Blue Ribbon, American/EFLA
This animated film makes its point without the use of words. We
see an "I" that is being put through the normalizing process required
by "The Company" that supplies "I's" needs but which, in turn,
takes over complete control. The ornate "I" soon becomes extinct,
replaced by standard company-approved typeface. Produced by
Derek Phillips. (Intermediate-Adult)

GREENHOUSE
11 min color Barr Films '74
*Silver Medal, Atlanta
*Bronze Plaque, Columbus
About a boy who works to repair the damage he did to an old man's
property. He finds that the man's plants mean something to him,
too. When the greenhouse is vandalized again, the oldster and the
boy discover a new friendship and mutual respect. (Intermediate-
Adult)

THE GREY METROPOLIS
15 min BW Film Images
*Award, Scholastic Teacher
Impressions of Edinburgh in the words of Robert Louis Stevenson
who was born there. Views of ancient landmarks are combined with
scenes of newer developments. Music arranged by Norman Shires.
Filmed by the Norton Park Group. (HS-Adult)

GRIZZLY!
52 min color Films Inc. '67
*Golden Eagle, CINE
Scientists Frank and John Craighead roam the trails of Yellowstone
Park, armed with drug-filled darts. Their purpose is not to kill,
but to learn the habits of the grizzly bear. Using electronic track-
ing devices, the brothers risk their lives to find out how the animals live, their weight changes, pulse rate, blood type, and territory patterns. They even analyze the grizzly sow's milk. Also
available in a 21-minute version. Produced by the National Geographic and Metromedia. (College-Adult)

THE GRIZZLY BEAR--A Case Study in Field Research
21 min color Films Inc. '67
*Award of Merit, Landers
The condensed version of the full-length TV version, Grizzly!,

described immediately above. Emphasizes how the collection of
data can provide information of future importance to human life and
other forms of animal life. National Geographic Society and Metromedia Producers Corporation. (HS-Adult)

GROOVING
    31 min   color   Benchmark
    *Ten Best, Council on Drugs
This film employs professional actors, uses no prepared script, and
shows no adults. It brings together a group of teenagers--drug
users, non-users, and ex-users--in a series of discussions that lasts
several days. As superficial reasons for smoking pot are challenged,
deeper motivations gradually come to the surface. Sponsored by the
New York State Narcotics Addiction Control Commission. (HS-Adult)

GUADALCANAL--Island of Death
    53 min   color   Films Inc.   '70
    *Honors, Radio-TV/Cleveland
    *Award, Christopher Society
    *Prize Winner, Chicago
    *Gold Medal, Atlanta
    *Freedoms Foundation Award
The battle for Guadalcanal was a turning point in the Pacific "theatre" of World War II. For the 23,000 Marine fatalities, it was an
empty victory. This report, filmed on the 25th anniversary of the
end of that war, includes historical footage and captured Japanese
film. Rather than painting a picture of the glories of battle, this
treatment pays tribute to those who died there. Produced by WKYC-
TV. (College-Adult)

THE GUITAR: From Stone Age Through Solid Rock
    14 min   color   Xerox Films   '70
    *Golden Eagle, CINE
    *Chris Award, Columbus
As the favorite instrument of today's youth, the guitar transcends
regional, class, and racial differences. This history explores the
musical styles that the guitar and its predecessors created, including flamenco, bossa nova, the blues, hard rock, and the classics.
It concludes with a selection by Brazilian virtuoso Laurindo Almeida.
Produced by Stephen Bosustow. (HS-Adult)

HAIKU
    7 1/2 min   color   Oxford Films   '71
    *Award Winner, Columbus
    *Golden Eagle, CINE
The Japanese poetry of awareness is written in three lines totaling
seventeen syllables. Haiku is about nature, almost always referring
to one of the seasons of the year. Producer: Art Evans. (Upper
Elem.-Junior HS)

HAIKU
    14 min   color   Stanton Films   '72
    *Award Winner, Atlanta

Live-action photography and original music help capture the character of Haiku, a form of Japanese poetry devoted to or based upon
nature. This film helps create understanding between cultures, and
helps develop appreciation of the relationship of literature to art.
(Elem.-Adult)

THE HALF-MASTED SCHOONER
    7 min color McGraw-Hill '70
    *Medal, Balboa
Balladeer Bruce Mackay provides a kaleidoscope of images to ac-
company his own song, "The Half-Masted Schooner," with accompaniment on his guitar. This young entertainer chooses illustrations
that do not literally translate his words into images but rather suggest the same free-wheeling commentary as the words of his song.
Producer: National Film Board of Canada. (Intermediate-Adult)

THE HAMBURGER SANDWICH
    10 min color Nat. Educ. Media '71
    *Chris Certificate, Columbus
Demonstrates ways to prepare and present this popular sandwich.
Shows organization of work area and procedures for grilling and
broiling. Emphasis given to creative embellishment through use of
cheeses, garnishments, and other accompaniments. Twenty-one
variations are shown. (HS-Adult)

THE HAND
    19 min color McGraw-Hill '65
    *Main Jury Prize, Annecy (France)
The contented life of a potter is interrupted by an omnipotent hand
demanding that he abandon his work and make nothing but reproduc-
tions of itself. The potter resists but, in trying to escape, is
killed by one of his own potted plants. Discussion topic: What does
the hand symbolize? Puppet animation (non-verbal) by Jiri Trnka
for the Short Films Studio, Prague. (HS-Adult)

HAND AND CLAY: A Celebration
    18 1/2 min color Film Fair '69
    *Merit Award, Chicago
    *Creative Award, US Industrial
    *Bronze Award, Int. TV & Film
Two Japanese potters demonstrate different techniques for creating
pottery, while more subtly showing viewers the relationship of art
to artist, and contrasting ways that are typical of American potters.
A Dave Bell Associates Film. (HS-Adult)

HANDLING DANGEROUS CHEMICALS: Acids
    8 1/2 min color Centron '70
    *Chris Award, Columbus
Includes definition and characteristics of acids, viscosity of concentrated acids, proper handling and storage, hazard and safety precautions in handling. (Senior HS-College)

HANG TEN
    9 min   color   Pyramid   '70
    *Golden Eagle, CINE
An exploration of the beauty and thrills of surfing. The action of
the sport is interpreted and its techniques are shown--all to the accompaniment of an original rock score. Film-maker: David Adams.
(HS-College)

THE HANGMAN
    12 min   color   McGraw-Hill   '63
    *Luther Rose, Oberhausen
    *Merit Diploma, Vancouver
    *Silver Medal, San Francisco
    *Silver Sail, Locarno
    *Golden Eagle, CINE
    *Recognition Diploma, Tours
Maurice Ogden's allegorical poem, which won the President's Award
of the National Poetry Society in 1961, has overtones of recent history, appealing to specific associations and memories. The mood
is accentuated by the simple ballad form narrated by Herschel Bernardi. The coward who lets others die, to protect himself, becomes
the Hangman's final victim. Produced by Les Goldman. Music by
Serge Hovey. (Intermediate-HS)

HAPPY ANNIVERSARY
    13 min   BW   Int. Film Bur.
    *1st Prize, West Germany
    *Best Short, Academy Awards
France's Pierre Étaix directed and acted in this comic portrayal of
a man trying to reach home to celebrate his wedding anniversary.
Étaix presents without words the humorous but frustrating plight of
the husband who encounters delay after delay in Paris traffic.   (HS-
Adult)

THE HAPPY OWLS
    7 min   color   Weston Woods   '69
    *Certificate, American/EFLA
An animated version of the children's picturebook of the same name.
Also available in Super 8mm sound. Producer: Mort Schindel.
(Elem.)

HARMONY IN MUSIC
    13 1/2 min   color   Coronet
    *Award of Merit, Boston
How harmony enriches music. This film shows the relationship of
harmony to chords, how these chords are created, and how harmony
supports melody and rhythm, adding vitality and variety to music.
(Intermediate)

HARMONY OF NATURE AND MAN
    12 min   color   BFA Educ. Media   '70
    *Gold Medal, Atlanta
Originally produced in 70-millimeter wide-screen format on a

quarter-million-dollar budget, HARMONY played 44 times a day for
six months at the 1970 World's Fair in Osaka, Japan. HARMONY
was designed to present Americans believably and warmly to their
counterparts in the Orient. Its setting is the American Northwest:
the mountains, lakes, rivers, ocean, forests, grainfields, orchards;
the heritage of Indian tribes and pioneer settlers; the blending of
modern architecture with the outdoors; the cities functioning in harmony with the beauty of unspoiled frontiers. Filmed for the State
of Washington by King Screen Productions. (Intermediate-Adult)

HAROLD AND CYNTHIA
        10 min   color   Eccentric Circle   '71
        *Prize Winner, Sinking Creek
Two simple people struggle to get in touch with themselves and each
other. Their search is complicated by the endless barrage of advertising we are all subjected to. This warns them that unless they
wear the right clothes and makeup, eat the right foods, etc., they
cannot make it in this society. Animation by John Strawbridge.
(HS-Adult)

THE HAT: Is This War Necessary?
        18 min   color   McGraw-Hill   '67
        *Special Medal, Independent
        *Animation Award, Tours
        *Best Cartoon, Venice
Two soldiers, patrolling a border, keep a suspicious eye on each
other. The hat of one falls off and into enemy territory. Whose
hat is it now? What are the rights in this matter? Who is to decide, particularly when national honor is at stake? Arguments turn
into threats, and soon a full-scale crisis is on. When night falls,
the two soldiers discuss means of reaching a peaceful decision, coming to the conclusion that a higher authority is needed. As the film
ends, they disappear into the distance, patrolling the line but ear-
nestly discussing a better world system. (HS-Adult)

THE HAUNTED HOUSE
        14 min   color   Encyc. Brit.   '70
        *Gold Medal, Atlanta
Two brothers and their little sister timorously explore the big, empty house on the next street. Is it haunted, as rumored? A slam-
ming door and a large trunk in the middle of the bedroom set the
stage for the sound of footsteps coming up the stairs and a door that
begins to open slowly. Which of three endings will children enjoy
the most: a magical tea-party; a "ghost" who turns out to be a
housepainter; or one boy's bad dream? Produced by Moreland-
Latchford, Ltd. (Elem.)

HAVE A HEART
        15 min   color   Pyramid   '74
        *Gold Cindy, Info. Film
        *Gold Medal, Atlanta
        *Bronze Hugo, Chicago
        *Gold Camera, Ind. Films

In simple and concise terminology, children narrate this overview of
the workings of the heart, showing how a healthy pattern of living,
established while young, can help protect that organ throughout adult-
hood. Produced by Saul Rubin. (Intermediate-Adult)

HAVE A WONDERFUL EVENING
    16 min color Film Communicators '73
    *Merit Award, Nat'l. Committee
A babysitter's guide to fire safety, dramatized by a story of a near
disaster. Demonstrates the importance of anticipating and preparing
for emergency situations requiring escape, rescue, and Fire Department notification. (HS-Adult)

THE HEART: Attack
    25 min color CRM Films '72
    *Gold Medal, Int. Film & TV
    *Golden Eagle, CINE
Why do Americans have a higher chance of attack than people in any
other country? Heart attack is examined from both a biological and
social viewpoint. The film opens with presentation of what it is like
to have a heart attack. This leads to a presentation of the basic
structure and functions of the heart and a pictorial discussion of the
three most common forms of heart attack--myocardial infraction,
ventricular fibrillation, and angina. (College-Adult)

HEARTBEAT OF A VOLCANO
    20 min color Encyc. Brit. '70
    *Golden Eagle, CINE
    *Silver Medal, Atlanta
One of the earth's most powerful and land-building processes--a volcano eruption. Shows the two-week buildup and nine-hour eruption
of Kilauea in Hawaii. Views of "degassing" and cessation of the
eruption add to the mood of this film. Produced in collaboration
with the American Geological Institute, Howard Powers, the U. S.
Geological Survey, and the Hawaii Volcanoes Observatory. (Intermediate-Adult)

HECTOROLOGIE--Hector Guimard
    13 min color Roland
    *Gold Lion, Venice
    *Prize, Paris Biennale
    *Quality Award, French National
Hector Guimard, the leading French Art Nouveau designer and archi-
tect, was the rage of his time and a highly controversial figure.
Today he is considered the most individualistic artist of that era.
(Born 1867, died 1942.) Direction and commentary by Yves Plantin and
Alain Blondel. Music: Jeff Gilson. Producer: Films ABC. (Col-
lege-Adult)

HELEN KELLER
    15 min color McGraw-Hill '69
    *Silver Medal, Venice
    *Blue Ribbon, American/EFLA

The story of a child, left blind and deaf by disease, who grew from
an unruly infant into a sensitive human being whose writings and
work for the handicapped are known the world over.   In this film,
Helen Keller and Anne Sullivan explore the belief that no one is un-
worthy or incapable of being helped.   (Intermediate-Adult)

HELLO MUSTACHE
    32 min BW Films Inc.   '70
    *Blue Ribbon, American/EFLA
"She" is a product of the high-rise; her eyes are hidden beneath
layers of goo, and most of her hair isn't hers.   She has a date with
Alan and Alan wears a mustache.   He wears a cape and rides a bicycle.   They realize their values are different but, like many of
their generation, they try to "work it out. "   Produced by Larry Lu-
beck & Associates.   (HS-Adult)

HELLO, UP THERE
    8 min color Learn. Corp.   '69
    *Certificate, Columbus
Children's drawings, paintings, and comments express the way they
see--and feel about--the adult world.   Through their artwork, children give form to their emotions of jealousy, anger, and love.   Useful for special education, art and language arts.   (Intermediate-
Adults)

HEN HOP
    4 min color Int. Film Bur.
    *Award: Brussels
Drawn directly on film with a pen, lines are used to form the shape
of a hen, illustrating an example of design economy.   To the tune
of a familiar folk-dance fiddle, the lines move in combinations, re-
cessions, convolutions, and progressions.   Animator: Norman Mc-
Laren for the National Film Board of Canada.   (Elem. -Adult)

HENRY
    10 min BW Oxford Films
    *Golden Eagle, CINE
    The words of the film are those of an old man living on a
covered barge in New York Harbor.   But the harbor no longer has
a place for big, rundown, old barges.   Where will Henry go?   Is
there still room in the world for an old man to have a place of his
own?   Produced by Anne Belle.   (Intermediate-Adult)

HENRY ... BOY OF THE BARRIO
    30 min BW Atlantis '68
    *Chris Award, Columbus
    *Recognition, Hemisfilm
A two-year documentary study of a Mexican-American boy's search
for identity as he grows up in conflict with his Indian mother, his
Mexican heritage, and Anglo society.   (Intermediate-Adult)

HENRY MOORE (London 1940-1942)
    11 min BW Roland

*Silver Cup, Salerno
*Honor Award, Vancouver
*Chris Award, Columbus
*Honor Certificate, Leipzig
*Quality Prize, French National ... and other honors

Documentary material, filmed during the war, shows the beginnings
of an air attack on London. From the deserted streets, the film
moves underground into the world of Henry Moore's shelter drawings.
People sit along subway platforms, looking after their children, set-
tling down for the night, sleeping in bunks and on the floor. Above
ground, London burns. Henry Moore used the eye of a sculptor in
portraying the stolidity and patience of a beseiged people. This film
brings together a series of drawings believed to be some of the most
remarkable achievements by an artist during wartime. Director:
Anthony M. Roland, Music: Marius Constant, Producer: Les Films
de Saturne. (College-Adult)

HERE'S HOCKEY
        10 3/4 min BW Nat. Film Bd.
        *Award Winner, Venice
From the Pee Wee League to professional stars, this film climbs
the ladder of skill, showing what it takes to become a hockey player.
(Intermediate-Adult)

THE HERITAGE
        11 min color Centron '72
        *1st Place, Nat'l. Agric.
Filmed at Old Sturbridge Village in Massachusetts; Living History
Farms at Des Moines, Iowa; and Heritage Park, Calgary, Alberta,
Canada. Traces the history of farming in North America. Costumed actors in authentic settings work with oxen, horses, and an-
tique implements such as the scythe and flail, to show how agriculture progressed from the hand labor of 18th century mechanization.
Includes sequences on family activities, the westward movement, and
growth of cities. Though originally produced by the John Deere
Company as a tribute to farmers, it contains no commercial messages. (Intermediate-Adult)

HERO
        18 min color Films Inc. '72
        *Award Winner, Chicago
Why do styles in heroes change? What is a hero? Presents stories
of famous Greek heroes, Hercules and Theseus, to try answering
these questions. One hero is muscular--the soldier, the athlete.
The other is loyal, wise and chivalrous. Graphics and still photos
illustrate heroes of other lands, and then explore today's political,
pop music, and sports heroes; film, television and comic book heroes; the heroine and the anti-hero. Produced by the Ontario Educational Communications Association. (HS-Adult)

THE HIDDEN SIDE OF SELLING
        34 min color Roundtable
        *Chris Award, Columbus

Presents methods that salesmen can use to improve abilities. Shows how to find common areas of interest; how to get a customer to answer his own objections. Indecisive, silent, aggressive, complaining authoritative, and deceivingly agreeable customers are shown, along with techniques for handling them. (College-Adult)

THE HIDDEN WORLD--A Study of Insects
24 min color Films Inc. '66
*TV Award, Monte Carlo
*Award, Ohio St. Univ.
*Award, Venice (Child.)
Condensed from the TV original. A revealing study of the color and drama of insect life. Close-ups show how, by means of a dance, one bee tells others where to find nectar, and how winged termites are sent from the home colony to establish new colonies. Includes experiments on how insect populations can be controlled to insure protection of food, livestock, and human life. Made by National Geographic Society and Metromedia Producers Corporation. (HS-Adult)

HIGH ARCTIC BIOME
21 1/2 min color Encyc. Brit. '59

From THE HIGH ARCTIC BIOME (courtesy, Encyclopaedia Britannica Educational Corporation)

*Award, LaPlata (Argentina)
*Chris Award, Columbus

An ecological study of plant and animal life on the Queen Elizabeth Islands, and of the life cycles in that frozen wasteland. Musk-oxen, lem-
mings, and arctic hares are seen as part of the evolution that pre-dates
history and continues today. Made by the National Film Board of Canada. (HS-College)

HIGH IN THE HIMALAYAS
27 min color Assn. -Sterling '65
*Honors, Toronto
*Golden Eagle, CINE

A mountain-climbing expedition atop Mount Taweche, 21,000 feet above
sea level. The expedition, led by Sir Edmund Hillary, conqueror of
Mount Everest, inched its way into the Himalayan range on a mission
to bring running water to a native village. Free loan. Sears, Roebuck
and Co. , sponsor. (Intermediate-Adult)

THE HIGH LONESOME SOUND (Kentucky Mountain Music)
30 min BW Macmillan '53
*Honorable Mention, Midwest

An audio-visual document of folk music and gospel songs sung by the
mountain people of Eastern Kentucky as a way of holding on to tradition
and dignity amid the hard times in this depressed area, where farms
have worn out and machinery has replaced men in the coal mines. Music is seen as an integral part of their life, and is sung here by an un-
employed worker, by miners, by church congregations, and by members of a miner's family at home. A film by John Cohen. (HS-Adult)

HIGHLAND INDIANS OF PERU
18 min color Films Inc. '68
*Chris Certificate, Columbus

The film raises the question, "Is the Indian better off in the highlands,
or moving to Lima to live in a slum?" From modern Lima, the film
moves to the highlands, where the Indians labor as farmers and herdsmen on land owned by absentee landlords. We see them working with
primitive tools on arid land, for long hours. They receive no pay for
this labor; instead they are given small plots of land that barely provide
subsistence. They chew the coca leaf (from which cocaine is derived)
to relieve hunger and fatigue. There are no schools, except in the villages, and 50 per cent of the highland Indians are illiterate. Occasionally the Indians go to the village to trade or to participate in a religious
festival, the only color in their lives. Produced by the Institut für
Film. (Intermediate-Adult)

HIGHWAY
6 min color Film Images
*Experimental Prize, Brussels

Hilary Harris produced this film from behind the wheel of an auto. It
evokes the exhilaration of high-speed driving, using every tempo from
slow to fast. Rock music by David Hollister. (College-Adult)

HIMALAYA--Life on the Roof of the World (Revised)
     21 min color Atlantis '68
     *High Honors, Venice
     *Prize Winner, Edinburgh
     *Award, Rio de Janeiro
     *Golden Eagle, CINE
     *Chris Award, Columbus ... and other honors
About the world's loftiest mountains--meeting-ground of diverse peoples and cultures--as related to the strategic importance of Asia, its geography and economy. Filmed by J. Michael Hagopian. (HS-Adult)

HINDU VILLAGE BOY (Revised)
     11 min color Atlantis '70
     *Chris Award, Columbus
     *Award, Nat'l. Educ. Film
     *Silver Reel Award (USA)
     *Award Winner, Stamford (Conn.)
     *High Honors, Venice
     *Award Winner, Cleveland
The vision and hopes of a village boy in an ancient land, as he evaluates the changes in agricultural tools and human relationships in his native India. Producer: J. Michael Hagopian. (Elem.-Junior HS)

HIROSHIMA-NAGASAKI (August 1945)
     16 min BW CMC-Columbia '71
     *Silver Dragon, Cracow
The destruction brought to Hiroshima and Nagasaki in August 1945 by two bombs, ushering in the atomic age, was recorded by nine Japanese cameramen, but their film was withheld from the public by United States authorities for more than twenty years. Made from that original footage, this is a candid report on a crucial moment in the story of mankind. Produced by Erik Barnouw. (HS-Adult)

HISTORY OF SOUTHERN CALIFORNIA (Part I)
     16 min color Atlantis
     *Chris Award, Columbus
     *High Honors, Edinburgh
The first of a series of two motion pictures that review the Indian and Spanish periods of influence on the people of the region. (Elem.-Junior HS)

HISTORY OF SOUTHERN CALIFORNIA (Part II)
     18 min color Atlantis
     *High Honors, Edinburgh
     *Chris Award, Columbus
The second in a series of two films. This one covers the Mexican-American period in the development of the lower region of the state. (Elem.-Junior HS)

THE HOARDER
     7 1/2 min color Benchmark '70

*Special Award, Teheran
*Award Winner, Bogota
*Winner, Buenos Aires
*Blue Ribbon, American/EFLA
A story about greed and sharing. Evelyn Lambart's animated blue-jay carries away and hides all it can see--including the sun. National Film Board of Canada. (Elem.)

HOBBY
　　7 min color McGraw-Hill '69
　　*Animation Prize, Oberhausen
In a strangely distorted landscape, winged men are flying about aimlessly. From time to time, a lasso can be heard, as the bird-men are captured by a peculiar young woman. She sits knitting while the men are lured into iron cages where they rattle the bars in protest. The woman, for no apparent reason, releases the bird-men, only to return to her knitting and plan their re-capture. The story could be interpreted as a depiction of the war between the sexes. Produced by the Featurette Studio, Lodz, Poland. (College-Adult)

THE HOLE
　　15 min color McGraw-Hill '70
　　*Blue Ribbon, American/EFLA
　　*Special Jury Prize, Annecy
　　*Best Cartoon, Academy Awards
The team of John and Faith Hubley has turned its talents on one of the concerns of our time: the danger of accidents in the atomic age. Two workers enter into an argument on the cause of accidents. In the course of their discussion, the men reveal their disparate backgrounds. The Black is convinced carelessness is the villain; the more suspicious white man argues that accidents are subconsciously willful and can be controlled. The debate turns from job injuries to nuclear warfare, until the crash of falling machinery suddenly interrupts. The two workers climb out of the hole, expecting to be the sole survivors of an atomic blast--willful or accidental. (HS-Adult)

HOLIDAYS ... HOLLOW DAYS
　　59 min BW Indiana U. '73
　　*Blue Ribbon, American/EFLA
A documentary plus a drama of role-playing as directed by Rhozier T. "Roach" Brown, Jr., a convicted murderer, and performed by his Black inmates of the District of Columbia Loxton Reformatory. The play has a Christmas season theme that prompts reflections on law and our penal system. Produced by Whitney LeBlanc. (College-Adult)

THE HOLY LAND: Background for History and Religion
　　11 min color Coronet
　　*Award of Merit, Columbus
Adding to the study of the geography, history, and the literature of ancient Palestine, this film presents scenes of important historical events. Maps and natural scenes show Jerusalem, Nazareth, the Lake of Galilee, the River Jordan, Jericho, Mount Nego and other places of ancient history and Biblical literature. (HS-Adult)

HOLY WAR
>8 min   color   Billy Budd   '69
>*Merit Award, Philadelphia

Narrated by Cliff Robertson, this film tells the story of Dr. Gordon Livingston in Vietnam and how he came to write "The Blackhorse Prayer." With a folksong by Juniper, the film presents war as it is, neither holy nor romantic, but savage and brutal. This film is not too popular with people who think God's on our side in every war. Produced by Frank Moynihan. (HS-Adult)

HOMAGE TO RODIN
>19 min   color   Pyramid   '68
>*Gold Medal, Int. Film & TV
>*Chris Award, Columbus

A tribute to the French sculptor who transcended the styles of his period to bridge classic tradition and modern freedom of form. Covers the full range of his work, from the days before the Impressionists (1868) to the modern art-world of 1917. The counterpoint of visuals and narration carries three levels of content: the beauty of Rodin's work, his life, and the critics' account of his developing style. Most of his great works are filmed. Producer: Herb Golden. (Senior HS-Adult)

HOME COUNTRY, U. S. A.
>53 min   color   Films Inc.   '68
>*Award, Freedoms Foundation

Tension and strife are so often emphasized in reports on the quality of American life that it is easy to forget that there are people who have stayed close to their roots and found fulfillment. This film looks at that side of American life. People whose life styles are diverse--boatbuilders in Maine, cowboys in Montana, a schoolteacher in California--discuss their attitudes on the good life. NBC News. (College-Adult)

THE HONEYBEE: A Social Insect
>5 1/2 min   color   Coronet   '55
>*Award of Merit, Boston

Honeybees are seen as a typical example of social insects: 1) they cooperate with each other; 2) there is a division of labor among them; and 3) they live in a community. While observing these characteristics, the film studies the activities of the honeybees, their life-cycle of complete metamorphosis, and their value to man. (Intermediate-HS)

HOPI KACHINAS
>10 min   color   ACI Films   '61
>*Chris Award, Columbus

A study of an Indian tribe's religion, expressed mainly through spiritual dances. Kachina dolls, wooden images of the dancers, are made for Hopi children as representations of supernatural spirits, other Indians, or creatures from mythology. This film can help dispel stereotyped notions about the American Indian. (Intermediate-Adult)

HORSES
>6 1/2 min   color   FilmFair   '70
>*Merit Award, Landers Associates

As a deserted carousel lights up, its horses start to move in free and exuberant slowmotion. Non-narrated, with original music. A Jerry Brady Film. (Elem.-Adult)

HOSPITAL
>84 min   BW   Zipporah Films   '70
>*Two "Emmy" Awards, Nat. Academy

One of a series of studies of American institutions, based on meticulous editing of voluminous footage, and allowing situations to speak for themselves without adding commentary or narration. Produced by Frederick Wiseman. (College-Adult)

HOT STUFF
>9 1/4 min   color   Nat. Film Bd.
>*Canadian Film Award

A cartoon, tracing fire from its very origin (as this film would have it) as a flame sent from heaven to Adam and Eve on an icy mountain top--with the warning that it be handled with care. The examples shown are a warning to householders. Produced for the Dominion Fire Commissioners of Canada. (Intermediate-Adult)

THE HOUSE
>32 min   BW   McGraw-Hill '61
>*Honors, Cork (Ireland)
>*Award, Arnheim (Germany)
>*Prize, Edinburgh (Scotland)
>*Gold Medal, San Francisco
>*Award, Int. Federation
>*Ribbon, Berlin (Germany)

Flashes back and forth through the history of an old house that is being demolished. Out of the fragments grows the mosaic of many lives, the story of a house and its occupants. Half a century is compressed into these thirty-odd minutes of suggestions in image and sound of falling walls, collapsing rooms, and a hailstorm of rubble. A film by Louis van Gasteren. (HS-Adult)

HOW BEAVER STOLE FIRE
>12 min   color   ACI Films   '72
>*Award Winner, Brussels
>*Golden Eagle, CINE
>*Golden Camera, US Industrial

A recreation of an American Indian myth on the origin of fire, this film offers inquiring children a fanciful explanation of an important natural element. Expressed in Caroline Leaf's sand-animation and an original Indian score. A Communico Film. (Primary-Intermediate)

HOW COULD I NOT BE AMONG YOU?
>30 min   color   Eccentric Circle   '70
>*Prize Winner, Sinking Creek

*Blue Ribbon, American/EFLA
A visual accompaniment to the writings of the late Ted Rosenthal who, at the age of 30, learned he had leukemia. In free verse and spontaneous prose, Rosenthal expresses his feelings and shares his philosophy. Film-maker: Tom Reichman. (HS-Adult)

HOW DEATH CAME TO EARTH
        14 min color McGraw-Hill '72
        *Ten Best, Philadelphia
        *Award, Adelaide (Australia)
        *Children's Award, American/EFLA
A legend from India, animated by a film-maker from India. It is a story of gods and men, of planets and earth, interpreted via painted cels and cut-out figures. National Film Board of Canada. (Elem.)

HOW DO WE KNOW?
        10 min color Neubacher-Vetter '73
        *Red Ribbon, American/EFLA
        *Statuette Award, Columbus
Designed to create an awareness of the senses and their importance in discovering and experiencing the world. Also useful for language arts. (Pre-school through 2nd grade)

HOW DO YOU FEEL?
        10 min color FilmFair '71
        *Golden Eagle, CINE
Designed to encourage children to think and talk about their feelings of love, happiness, sadness, and fear. They voice their innermost feelings about the happiest times in their lives and about their fears. Children's art helps make the point. An original song amplifies their remarks. A Ben Norman Film. (Elem.)

HOW GOOD IS A GOOD GUY?
        21 min color Roundtable
        *Chris Award, Columbus
An on-screen narrator analyzes three typical cases of supervisory failure. In each case, undesirable relationships result from a supervisor's failure to fulfill his responsibilities. The situations are then repeated to show that if the supervisor didn't try to be a "good guy," he would be more effective, efficient, respected, and confident. (College-Adult)

HOW LONG IS A MINUTE?
        11 min color Malibu Films
        *First Prize, Atlanta
Shows, by optically dividing the screen into five images, an exact minute without reference to clocks or seconds. Different examples and exercises are given to demonstrate shorter and longer periods. Partly animated, with freeze frames. Also available in Spanish. Produced by Claire Menken. (Primary)

HOW TO KILL
    11 min color Benchmark '73
    *Golden Eagle, CINE
    *Honors, San Francisco
Six poems (in effect a diary of Keith Douglas) take us from his
cloistered Oxford student days in 1941 through the carnage in North
Africa during World War II, to a premonition of his own death in
1944. The visuals are watercolors done expressly for the film by
Robert Andrew Parker. Original music by Hal McKusick. Producer: Walter Goodman. (HS-Adult)

HOW TO KILL THE KING--RICHARD II
    23 min color Films Inc. '69
    *Award, Ohio State U.
Illustrates a recurring historical situation: rebellion and assassination are constant threats to the statesman. Excerpts from the
Shakespearean play emphasize the clash between the principal characters: the old world of Richard (based on the false security of
divine sanction) and the more realistic world of Bolingbroke (in
which personal merit and strength are the dominant factors). Contemporary parallels are provided by scenes of recent riots along
with popular music. (HS-College)

HOW TO MAKE A DIRTY RIVER
    27 min color Films Inc.
    *Honors, Int. Film & TV
    *Award, Int. Environment
    *Prize, Associated Press
At its source, the Passaic River is fresh and clean. By the time
eleven New Jersey communities have dumped their municipal and
industrial wastes, it becomes one of the dirtiest rivers in the country. This report takes a look at what the river once was and investigates projects to clean it up. Produced by WNBC-TV. (Junior
HS-Adult)

HOW VAST IS SPACE?
    19 min color Atlantis '60
    *Merit Award, San Francisco
    *Award Winner, Edinburgh
An imaginary journey through the universe. Produced by J. Michael
Hagopian. (Junior HS-Adult)

HOW'S SCHOOL, ENRIQUE?
    18 min color AIMS '70
    *Blue Ribbon, American/EFLA
Designed to stimulate discussion and cultural awareness. Contrasting a subject-oriented department chairman whose attitude toward
minorities is "Let them learn a trade," with a compassionate "English is a Second Language" teacher, the film helps us learn the
problems faced by Mexican-American youngsters in an often hostile
Anglo society. (College-Adult)

HUELGA!
    50 min color McGraw-Hill '69
    *Merit Award, Vancouver
    *Award, Int. Film & TV
    *Award, Int. Labor
    *Winner, Liepzig
In September, 1965, a loosely-knit group of Mexican and Filipino-American grape pickers began a walkout demanding union recognition, the right to collective bargaining, and a minimum wage. Thus began the now famous Delano Grape Strike. HUELGA (Spanish for "strike") is a documentary about the struggle to raise standards of living for all farmworkers. In cinema-verité, the film records the genesis of a union and its effects on the lives of its members. Written by Mark Harris for King Screen Productions. (College-Adult)

THE HUMAN BODY: Circulatory System
    13 1/2 min color Coronet '56
    *Award, Scholastic Teacher
    *Award, Golden Reel (USA)
This anatomical function is analyzed by means of animation, cine-fluorography, drawings, and close-ups of live organs. Included are the heart, lungs, and kidneys; the key processes of the circulatory system; and the network of arteries and veins that carry blood throughout the body. (Junior-Senior HS)

THE HUMAN BODY: Digestive System
    13 1/2 min color Coronet '58
    *Chris Award, Columbus
Animation, X-ray and live-action scenes of the major digestive organs give an account of the function of this system: to break down chemically the complex nutrients, carbohydrates, proteins, and fats into simple food materials. The roles played by the salivary glands, esophagus, stomach, pancreas, liver, gall bladder, and small and large intestines are described and related to each other. (Junior-Senior HS)

THE HUMAN BODY: Reproductive System
    13 1/2 min color Coronet '59
    *Chris Award, Columbus
Through animation and photomicrography, including fertilization of a human ovum, the film presents a description of the human reproduction system. It shows similarities and differences between male and female organs, locates them in the body, and describes the functions of each in the creation of new life. Note: the producer recommends that this film be shown to boys and girls in separate groups. (Junior-Senior HS)

HUMOR IN MUSIC
    59 min BW McGraw-Hill '67
    *Series Award, Saturday Review
From the Young People's Concert series, with Leonard Bernstein as master of ceremonies, narrator, and conductor of the New York Philharmonic. Produced by CBS Television. (College-Adult)

HUNGER (LA FAIM)
       12 min   color   Learn. Corp.   '73
       *Blue Ribbon, American/EFLA
Using the technology of computer-assisted animation, simple line
drawings are employed in creating a picture of affluent indulgence
and conspicuous consumption ... even while millions of people are
starving.   Written by Peter Foldes for the National Film Board of
Canada.   (Elem. -Adult)

HUNGER IN AMERICA
       54 min   color   Carousel   '68
       *Current Events Award, WGA
       *"Emmy," Nat. Academy
       *Geo. Foster Peabody Award
Ten million citizens go hungry every day in one of the world's most
affluent nations--America.   This film shows Black sharecroppers in
Alabama, Navajo Indians in Arizona, starving tenant farmers 25
miles outside the nation's capitol, and impoverished Mexican-Ameri-
cans in San Antonio.   It shows the dull-eyed, the undernourished,
dead and dying children--and a federal program that provides lard
and peanut butter to people who desperately need fruit, fresh milk,
meat and eggs.   Produced by CBS News.   (College-Adult)

From HUNGER IN AMERICA (Carousel Films, Inc.)

THE HUNTER
    10 min   color   ACI Films   '72
    *Award Winner, Brussels
    *Golden Eagle, CINE
    *Honors, American/EFLA
"Why kill?" is the theme, and the landscape of the Ozarks is the
setting. A boy gets a BB gun for his birthday. When he succeeds
in killing a bird, he is overwhelmed by grief. This film tells its
story wordlessly. Produced by Communico Films. (Intermediate-
Adult)

THE HURDLER
    16 min   color   Sterling Educ.   '70
    *Randolph Award, Int. Film & TV
This is the biography of the late Dr. Charles Drew, whose pioneer-
ing research in blood plasma led to the establishment of the first
blood bank system. (HS-Adult)

THE HUTTERITES
    28 min   BW   Nat. Film Bd.
    *Awards: Melbourne, Columbus, and Florence
The followers of Jacob Hutter live in farm communities, devoutly
holding to the rules their founder laid down. Through the cooperation of a Hutterite colony in Alberta, this film shows aspects of the
Hutterites' communal way of life. (College-Adult)

I AM FREEDOM'S CHILD
    5 min   color   FilmFair   '71
    *Award of Merit, Landers
This film is concerned with personal and social meanings, sum-
marized by and ending with the statement, "So, as I learn to like
the differences in me, I learn to like the differences in you. "
Based on the book by Bill Martin, Jr. Produced by Ben Norman.
(Elem.)

I. F. STONE'S WEEKLY
    62 min   BW   Open Circle   '73
    *Emily Award, American/EFLA
    *Grierson Award, American/EFLA
    *Blue Ribbon, American/EFLA
A cinema-verité profile of the recently retired publisher whose per-
sonal journalism was dedicated to exposing federal corruption and
peccadilloes. His newspaper was read regularly by Philip and Daniel
Berrigan and other social activists. Produced by Jerry Brick, Jr.
(College-Adult)

I GOT SIX
    3 1/2 min   color   Xerox Films   '73
    *Series Honors, ACT
    *Best Picture, ASIF-East
One of a series of eleven cartoons that translate elements of arithmetic into original varieties of music. This film features a boy
with six balloons who uses them to illustrate multiplication and

From I THINK (Wombat Productions, Inc.)

addition. Consulting institution: the Bank Street College of Education. Produced by Scholastic Rock. (Primary-Intermediate)

I JUST WORK HERE
        17 min   color   Roundtable
        *Merit Award, NAM Institute
        *Chris Award, Columbus
Purpose: to demonstrate the importance of maintaining good customer relations. The first part of this film dramatizes the damaging effects of negative, self-centered attitudes. The second segment resets the stage with the same people in the same situations but with a totally different outcome as the result of applying common-sense rules of business-like courtesy. (Adult)

I KNOW AN OLD LADY WHO SWALLOWED A FLY
        6 min   color   Int. Film Bur.
        *Awards: Santa Barbara, Chicago, Czechoslovakia
An old folk tale, sung by Burl Ives accompanying himself on his guitar. Using animation, the story is told of how an old lady swallowed a fly. Other predators followed: spider, bird, cat, dog, goat, pig, cow, and horse. Sorry, but all this could not account for the fact that the old lady died. Produced by the National Film Board of Canada. (Primary-Intermediate)

I, LEONARDO DA VINCI
        54 min   color   McGraw-Hill   '66
        *Emmy Award, Nat. Academy
The life story of the great Renaissance man and the influence of his ideas on the history of the western world--as a painter, sculptor, architect, musician, engineer, and scientist. Filmed in Italy and France, the motion picture shows two of Leonardo's great, but ill-starred works of art: the immense fresco, "The Battle of Anghiari," and the giant sculptured horse, the Sforza monument. Frederic March speaks the words of Leonardo da Vinci. Produced by ABC for the "Saga of Western Man" Series. (College-Adult)

I MISS YOU SO
        8 min   BW   Macmillan   '66
        *Award, Rhode Island
        *First Rank, Ann Arbor
A soldier's wife is writing him a letter: "Everything reminds me of you--I miss you so." As we see, hear, feel everything that reminds her of him, image and sound become a paean to life and an outcry against war. Going about her job as a model in London, taking her son to school, returning to places that they enjoyed together, coming home alone to bath and bed, the young woman is real. Photographed and edited by Gino Ardito. (College-Adult)

I THINK
        19 min   color   Wombat
        *Award of Merit, Landers
        *Chris Award, Columbus
A youngster today is under many influences from home and from

school. Mass media also have a great impact. However, the greatest influence of all is probably from peers. But where does a young person make a stand even though it is in opposition to the attitudes of friends? (Elem. -Junior HS)

ICARUS MONTGOLFIER WRIGHT
     23 min color Pyramid '63
     *Golden Eagle, CINE
     *Nomination, Academy Award
Ray Bradbury, the science-fiction writer, composed the script for this film. It is prophecy, fantasy, history, and philosophy--all rolled up in the story of a young astronaut. While asleep in his quarters on a rocket-launching base in New Mexico, our space-boy dreams of the pioneers of flight: Icarus who flew too close to the sun; the Montgolfiers' first balloon; and the Wright brothers at Kitty-hawk, North Carolina. Produced by Osmond Evans. (Intermediate-HS)

IF KANGAROOS JUMP, WHY CAN'T YOU?
     8 min color Atlantis '71
     *Award, Nat. Educ. Films
The value of jumping rope for exercise and enjoyment is outlined in the format of this film designed to stimulate ideas about recreation and health. Non-narrated. Produced by J. Michael Hagopian. (Elem.)

IF YOU HEAR THE EXPLOSION, THE DANGER HAS PASSED
     9 1/2 min color Xerox Films '69
     *Citation, US Industrial
     *Golden Eagle, CINE
Covers a wide range of industrial safety problems, including the most frequent single cause of work loss--the achin' back. It also points out three factors that show up in any accident: 1) the unsafe act itself; 2) an unsafe facility or piece of equipment; 3) an unsafe procedure. Produced by Holland-Wegman. (Adult)

I'LL NEVER GET HER BACK
     24 min BW Films Inc. '65
     *Award, Radio-TV/Cleveland
     *Award, National Press
     *Gabriel Award, Cath. Broadcast.
The story of the unwed mother. She relates her experience: her arrival at the maternity home, the birth of her daughter, the signing of the adoption papers in the realization that she will never again get her child back. Produced by WKYC-TV. (HS-Adult)

I'M A MAN
     20 min color (with BW) McGraw-Hill '70
     *Chris Certificate, Columbus
     *Award, Oberhausen
     *Golden Eagle, CINE
     *Blue Ribbon, American/EFLA
Documents the personal and ideological struggle for freedom and

manhood of black militant John Barber. Explains why years of racial strife and of non-violent pleas for understanding have converted John Barber and his fellow black intellectuals to radical black militancy. Photographed and edited by Peter Rosen at Yale University. (College-Adult)

I'M GOING TO SCHOOL TODAY
27 min   color   Australia   '71
*Gold Camera/US Industrial
Children learn by doing--and acquire self-discipline without inhibiting the natural learning process. The teacher is narrator of this day in an Australian primary school. Photographed by the Commonwealth Film Unit. (College-Adult)

IMAGERY IN SPACE
11 min   color   ACI Films   '71
*Golden Eagle, CINE
Encourages a visual awareness of space as it affects our perception of the world. Involves the viewer in a changing stream of images, as though actually moving through space. Photography, score, and terse commentary emphasize spatial relationships in art and design. Produced by Paul Burnford. (Junior HS-Adult)

IMAGES MEDIEVALES
18 min   color   Film Images
*Grand Prize for Color, Cannes
Life in the Middle Ages as recorded in the miniature paintings and illuminated manuscripts of the 14th century. Photographed in the Bibliothèque Nationale in Paris. Music based on medieval melodies. Narration also available in French. Produced by William Novick. (HS-Adult)

IMAGINATION AT WORK
21 min   color   Roundtable
*Merit Award, San Francisco
Illustrates how anyone can do more creative thinking, improve imagination, utilizing ingenuity and initiative. The film outlines four factors necessary for creative thinking: sensitivity, fluency, flexibility, and originality. (College-Adult)

IMMIGRANT FROM AMERICA
20 min   color   Sterling Educ.
*Bronze Award
*Int. Film & TV
A film that confronts us with the injustices of racism in a nation of immigrants. Designed to stimulate discussion and awareness of the contributions of American Blacks and other minorities. (HS-Adult)

IMOGEN CUNNINGHAM, PHOTOGRAPHER
20 min   color   Time-Life   '72
*Red Ribbon, American/EFLA
A study of the pioneer portrait photographer, now in her eighties. Captures her vitality and radiance through interviews, candid footage,

and a lengthy look at her work. A film by John Korty and the American Film Institute. (College-Adult)

IN A FIRE ... SECONDS COUNT
   18 min color Film Communicators '72
   *Silver Medal, Atlanta
   *Bronze Plaque, Nat. Committee
A dramatization of an average family that rehearses their nightime home escape plans. A tragedy is averted when a young friend is visiting and an actual fire strikes. (Intermediate-Adult)

IN INDIA THE SUN RISES IN THE EAST
   14 min color McGraw-Hill '70
   *Chris Certificate, Columbus
An uninterrupted view of India. There is no narration or dialogue, only the natural effects surrounding people and places, and the music native to the country. One sees and hears farmers with buffaloes, and city dwellers with bikes; chemists, printers, weavers, and potters; politicians, teachers, priests, sailors; transistor radios and the sounds of a local language; temples and houses; cities and villages; harvests and celebrations; bazaars and beggars; sunrise and sunset. Produced by Richard Kaplan. (Intermediate-Adult)

IN ONE DAY
   17 1/2 min color Nat. Film Board
   *Chris Award, Columbus
Scientific look at weather forecasting, from far-flung observation-post to the weather-plotting station of the Meteorological Service of Canada with its automated mapping machines. An examination of what weather is and how it is anticipated on a world scale. (HS-Adult)

IN SEARCH OF INNOCENCE
   27 3/4 min color Nat. Film Bd.
   *Award Winner, Chicago
A film-maker from Quebec finds out how Vancouver's poets and painters look at life and art. Among the people seen are sculptor Donald Jarvis; painters Jack Shadbolt, Joy Long, and Margaret Peterson; and print-maker Sing Lim. (College-Adult)

IN SEARCH OF THE BOWHEAD WHALE
   50 min color Nat. Film Bd. '74
   *Blue Ribbon, American/EFLA
Filmed in the treacherous ice and water off the coast of Alaska and northern Canada, a nine-man expedition seeks out the giant sea-going mammal and, in the process, obtains the first footage of this 70-ton endangered species. Produced by Bill Mason. (College-Adult)

IN THE KITCHEN
   12 min BW Mass Media '70
   *Merit Certificate, Philadelphia
Only one sequence of action takes place and that is contained in one sustained shot. Contrast is seen between two opposite styles of life. In the foreground, we see a family in their kitchen, eating lunch.

In the background, seen through a window only by the viewer, two lovers on a balcony have a quarrel that ends in suicide. Neither group is aware of the other, but together in the same picture-frame they form a contrast: life that is neat, ordered, sometimes monotonous, alongside another that is desperate and unpredictable. (HS-Adult)

THE INCAS
11 min   color   Coronet
*Chris Award, Columbus
Filmed at authentic sites, and using archeological remains and existing Peruvian Indian materials, this film presents a historical, geographical, and cultural view of their civilization. Discussed are the distinctive features of Incan government and an economy based on agriculture and small business. We witness a re-enactment of worship to the pagan sun-god. (Intermediate-HS)

INDIA AND HER FOOD PROBLEM
16 min   color   Atlantis   '66
*Award, Asian Pacific
How the future of India depends on her ability to increase her food supply faster than population. Produced by J. Michael Hagopian. (Elem.-Junior HS)

INDIA: Crafts and Craftsmen
15 min   color   ACI Films   '68
*Golden Eagle, CINE
*Honors, American/EFLA
Combining authentic settings, sound, and music, this film documents a variety of craft techniques. It interweaves the influence of tradition (religious, aesthetic, and sociological) with the changing nature of Indian life, and shows some consequences. (HS-Adult)

INDIAN SUMMER
28 min   BW   McGraw-Hill   '63
*Honored at Edinburgh, Venice, and San Francisco
*Excellence Citation, Boston
The Catskill valley, rich in the lore of Revolutionary times, is soon to be submerged by a new reservoir for New York, the huge city to the south. An old farmer, famed in the countryside as story-teller par excellence, must face the future with courage; a new life for a man with few years more to go, and a two-hundred year heritage behind him. Produced by Jules Victor Schwerin, assisted by Julius Tannenbaum. Music composed by and performed by Mike and Pete Seeger. (College-Adult)

INDUSTRIAL HYGIENE: Science of Survival
9 min   color   Xerox Films
*Citation, US Industrial
*Chris Award, Columbus
The smog-filled air, the oil-slicked river, and the noise-sated ozone are approaching the perimeter of man's environmental limits. In industry it is the job of the hygienist to know the dangers of dust,

toxic materials, intense light, excessive noise, and elimination of
waste materials in and around a plant. A Holland-Wegman Production. (College-Adult)

INDUSTRIAL REGION IN SWEDEN
   18 min   color   Films Inc.   '68
   *Chris Certificate, Columbus
Can a country become industrialized and still maintain beautiful
forests and clear rivers and lakes? This film shows how it is done
in Sweden. We meet Einar Jonasson, a crane operator who works
in a modern steel mill and lives in an attractive town of 16,000 people. Industrial centers like this are scattered throughout the region,
instead of being concentrated in major centers. Jonasson and his
family enjoy a summer cottage on a lake still unspoiled by industry.
Produced by Institut für Film und Bild. (Intermediate-HS)

INFORMATION EXPLOSION
   11 min   color   AIMS   '73
   *Gold Medal, Atlanta
Explores problem-solving possibilities of computers and careers in
the computer industry. Made by Miller Productions. (HS-College)

THE INNER MIND OF MILTON WHITTY
   18 1/2 min   color   AIM Assn.
   *Chris Award, Columbus
   *Bronze Plaque, Nat. Comm.
This picture says things about safety that apply to employers, fore-
men and workmen. (Adult)

INSIDE NORTH VIETNAM
   85 min   color   Impact Films
   *Nomination, British Film Academy
About the Vietnamese and how they live in harmony with themselves
while at war with the wealthiest and most powerful nation in the
world. Probes their tenacity while revealing the beauty and strength
of a united people. Includes footage of Ho Chi Minh, their political
leader and symbol. (College-Adult)

INSIDE RED CHINA
   51 min   color   Carousel   '66
   *Blue Ribbon, American/EFLA
The daily life of the Chinese under Communism, particularly within
Peking, Wuhan, and Shanghai. The film shows life on a farm com-
mune, the interior of a bourgeois home, a steel mill, and the methods by which school children are taught. Also shown are the Red
Guards--the militant young group. Three writers, Hans Konigs-
berger, Robert Guillan, and Dr. Han Suyin, visitors to China, offer
personal observations. (College-Adult)

INSIDE THE WORLD OF JESSE ALLEN
   30 min   color   Vorpal   '73
   *Blue Ribbon, American/EFLA
An introduction to the artist and his way of life as seen through his

paintings and original prints. Insight is amplified by a score that
includes flute, guitar, and various African instruments. Directed
by Muldoon Elder and Steve Grumette. (HS-Adult)

THE INSIDERS
    22 min color Films Inc. '70
    *Merit Certificate, American Bar
A convict film-maker at the Missouri State Penitentiary documents
the unique society of a prison. The members of this society make
their life a little more endurable by having "hustles" or jobs to help
camouflage the reality of their situation. Prisoners' conversations
center around drugs, sex, escape, or crime. Rarely do thoughts or
activities in prison lead toward rehabilitation. (HS-Adult)

INSTINCTS OF AN INSECT
    16 min color Macmillan
    *Golden Eagle, CINE
    *Blue Ribbon, American/EFLA
The female beetle's instinctive behavior. How she rolls a leaf cradle for the egg she lays, and the ways the cradle provides protection
and food for the young beetle. Reveals how the mother beetle follows the coded instruction in her genes to repeat this complex and
ancient ritual. (HS-College)

INSTRUMENTS OF THE BAND AND ORCHESTRA: Introduction
    11 min color Coronet
    *Merit Certificate, Cleveland
A general introduction to bands and orchestras, explaining the three
sections of the band--the brasses, the woodwinds, and the percus-
sions--and showing how the addition of strings gives the orchestra
its different sound. The most common instruments of each section
are demonstrated. (Intermediate-HS)

INSTRUMENTS OF THE BAND AND ORCHESTRA: The Brasses
    11 min color Coronet
    *Merit Certificate, Columbus
The distinctive sounds of the brass section. After the film explains
the basic principle on which brasses operate, we are introduced to
the cornet, the French horn, the trombone, the baritone, the tuba,
and the Sousaphone. (Intermediate-HS)

INTERN: A Long Year
    20 min color Encyc. Brit. '73
    *Bronze Plaque, Columbus
Philadelphia General Hospital is understaffed and underequipped.
That's why Dr. Karin Mack chose it for her intern year. Dr. Mack's
patients are society's dispossessed: the homeless, the jobless, people
suffering from malnutrition, cancer, heart disease, and alcoholism.
Viewers witness Dr. Mack's activities at the hospital and at home.
Made in cooperation with Philadelphia General Hospital. (HS-College)

THE INTERNATIONAL ATOM
    26 min color McGraw-Hill '61

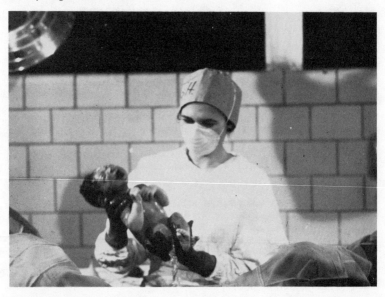

From INTERN: A Long Year (courtesy, Encyclopaedia Britannica
Educational Corporation

---

  *Blue Ribbon, American/EFLA
Reviews peaceful applications of atomic energy in various parts of
the world. Specialists in agriculture, industry, and medicine describe the uses of radioactive isotopes. A sequence on nuclear research and education, highlights international cooperation. Produced
by the United Nations Visual Information Board. (College-Adult)

INTERREGNUM (GEORGE GROSZ'S BETWEEN THE WARS)
  29 min BW McGraw-Hill '59
  *Nomination, Academy Award
  *Golden Lion, Venice
Life Magazine devoted an article to social satirist George Grosz
upon his death in July, 1959. The Whitney Museum published a
book of his art. But this marks the first time the work of Grosz
has appeared on the screen. Produced by Charles and Altina Carey.
Original score by Paul Glass. (College-Adult)

THE INTERVIEW
  5 min color Learn Corp. '64
  *Nomination, Academy Award
An imaginary interview between two so-called knowledgeables of the
music world. This film spares neither questioner nor guest as it
pokes fun at the pretensions that often surround a "cultural discussion." A comment on our society, where pretense is often more
respected than substance. Created by Ernest Pintoff. (HS-Adult)

INTERVIEWS WITH MY LAI VETERANS
    22 min color New Yorker '71
    *Best Documentary, Academy Award
Brings the reality of war to the office, the easy chair, and the
front porch, by allowing us to observe the reactions of five men who
describe the horrors of war as experienced at close range. (HS-
Adult)

INTRODUCTION TO HOLOGRAPHY
    17 min color Encyc. Brit. '72
    *Science Award, Nat. Education
    *Golden Eagle, CINE
Types of holograms and holographic interferometry. Illustrates the
hologram's three-dimensionality, data storage, and multi-channel
capacity. Explains wave interference and laser coherence. (HS-
College)

THE INVADER
    29 min BW CMC Columbia
    *Merit Diploma, Edinburgh
    *Golden Reel Award (USA)
An introduction to the subject of venereal disease, this film presents
man's efforts since the fifteenth century to cope with syphilis. Medical advances and changes in public attitude emphasize how syphilis
is a disease that can be cured. Woodcut engravings, paintings, and
drawings by artists including Dürer, Breughel, Hogarth, and Daumier

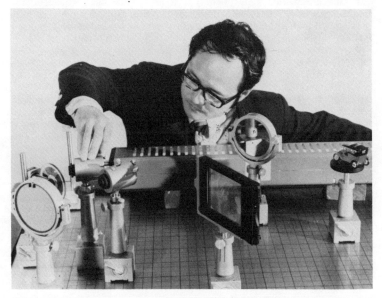

From **INTRODUCTION TO HOLOGRAPHY** (courtesy, Encyclopaedia
Britannica Educational Corporation)

portray earlier periods. The later years are reconstructed with photographs of Ehrlich, Hata, and others, and with motion-picture records of the work of Fleming and Mahoney. An illustrated teachers' guide is available. Directed by George C. Stoney. (HS-Adult)

IRAN
    18 min color Pyramid '72
    *Documentary Award, Venice
    *Blue Ribbon, American/EFLA
    *Grand Prize, Teheran (Iran)
    *Judges' Award, Sydney
A non-narrated tour of this ancient nation and culture that so visibly blends the old with the new. Spans the spectrum of life within that society by showing not only the caviar of palace parties, but the fishermen who provide that luxury product. Original music by Francis Lai. Directed by Claude Lelouch. (HS-Adult)

IS IT ALWAYS RIGHT TO BE RIGHT?
    8 min color N.W. Media '71
    *Special Award, N.Y. Int.
    *Peace Prize, Atlanta
    *Blue Ribbon, American/EFLA
    *Chris Award, Columbus
    *"Oscar" Winner, Academy Award
"There once was a land where men were always right"--so begins this parable that identifies the sources of divisiveness in our society: war, the generation gap, poverty, racism. Stressing the need for establishing a spirit of interdependence, this film can provoke discussion without alienating any single group. Narrated by Orson Welles. (HS-Adult)

ISLAND EDEN
    25 min color Canada Travel '71
    *Best of Show, Ind. Photo
Designed to stimulate interest in touring or living in the Canadian province of British Columbia. Features aerial and underwater footage, plus optical effects. Available on free loan. Produced by the Canadian Travel Service. (HS-Adult)

ISLAND OBSERVED
    28 min color Nat. Film Bd.
    *Award, Buenos Aires
A record of a medical expedition to Easter Island, headed by a Mc-Gill University research team. While mainly concerned about charting the physical condition of Easter Islanders, the film also glimpses island activities, a wedding, and the long-faced stone sculptures. (College-Adult)

ISOMETRIES
    26 min color Int. Film Bur. '71
    *Golden Eagle, CINE
Live-action and animation introduce isometry. The mathematician and film artist show basic theorems on plane isometries. The film

concludes with the theorem that produces a complete classification
of plane isometries. Mathematicians: Seymour Schuster and
W. O. J. Moser. (HS-College)

ISOTOPES IN ACTION
        28 1/4 min   color   Universal Educ.   '69
        *Awards: London and Rome
What isotopes are and do is developed in this exploration into one
great force of the atomic age: radiation. Illustrated are the ways
radioactive isotopes have been put to use in preserving food and
strengthening plastics, in industry, medicine, and agriculture. The
composition and function of Cobalt 60 is also delineated. (HS-College)

ISRAEL
        32 min   color   Int. Film Found.
        *Award of Merit, Landers
Sweeping back 4,000 years into Biblical times, Philip Stapp's animation portrays Jewish history, beginning with the patriarchs and concluding with the Nazi persecutions. Documentary footage depicts the
years from the zionist movement in 1900 through the birth of the
Jewish nation in 1948. Modern footage presents descriptions of Israel as seen through the lives of Israeli families and individuals.
Produced by Julien Bryan. (HS-Adult)

ISRAEL ... NATION OF DESTINY
        27 min   color   Atlantis   '72
        *Silver Medal, Atlanta
        *Chris Award, Columbus
An insight into the spirit and achievements of the Israeli people, as
a step towards understanding and solving problems of the Middle
East. Viewed in the perspective of the Arab-Israeli conflicts of
this century. Produced by J. Michael Hagopian. (HS-Adult)

IT AIN'T CITY MUSIC
        15 min   color   Davenport
        *2nd Prize, Baltimore
A light-hearted celebration of grass roots America and its music.
Filmed at the national Country Music Contest, Whipoorwhill Lake,
Warrenton, Virginia. Produced by Tom Davenport. (HS-Adult)

IT COULDN'T BE DONE
        53 min   color   Films Inc.   '70
        *Golden Eagle, CINE
        *Award, Atlanta
        *Chris Award, Columbus
        *Freedoms Foundation Award
        *Award, Int. Film & TV
        *Award, Ohio State U.
Four faces on Mt. Rushmore, a bridge over the Mississippi, and a
canal linking the Atlantic with the Pacific were all visions of determined men. The music of the Fifth Dimension helps tell the story
of artistry and engineering that seemed impossible. Produced by
NBC. (College-Adult)

IT STARTS AT THE TOP
18 min   color   Macmillan   '70
*Best of the Year, Canada
*Creative Excellence, US Industrial
Management must become involved in any safety program devoted to
the prevention of falls suffered by workers in the construction industry.   Close-ups illustrate potential dangers on the job and suggest
methods of prevention and action to be taken when falls occur.   (Adult)

IVAN AND HIS FATHER
13 1/2 min   color   Churchill
*Medalist, Atlanta
The difficulty of change is the issue here.   Ivan cannot communicate
with his father.   "What would you like to say to your father, if you
could?"   This question leads Ivan into a powerful role-play in which
he struggles to break out of his shell.   (Young Adult)

IVANHOE DONALDSON
57 min   BW   Macmillan   '63
*Gold Medal, Mannheim
The first full-length documentary on the civil rights workers in the
deep south, showing the experiences of a field secretary of the Stu-
dent Nonviolent Coordinating Committee.   Also featured are CORE
(Congress on Racial Equality), voter registration volunteers, and Dr.
Aaron Henry, NAACP Chairman in Mississippi.   (HS-Adult)

I'VE GOT THIS PROBLEM
8 min   BW   Macmillan   '65
*Three Best of the Year, Cork
A satire on non-communication in which a boy and a girl carry on
a conversation about life and sex without ever getting across to each
other.   The two are shown in close-up against plain backgrounds, in
the style of Godard, so as to emphasize every significant blink,
twitch, and fumble as they try to express and hide their feelings.
Produced by Don B. Klugman and Ron Clasky.   (HS-College)

"J. T. "
51 min   color   Carousel   '69
*Geo. Foster Peabody Award
The story of a Harlem boy who, while wandering through a vacant
lot, finds a friend--a lost cat, wounded in some recent skirmish.
"J. T. " makes a shelter for the cat, leaves his jacket for warmth
and his radio for company.   Later, bullies steal the radio and tease
the cat.   The cat gets away but, in escaping, is killed in traffic.
Though J. T. loses a good friend he finds a new ability to love and
to be responsible, too.   From the CBS Children's Hour.   (All Ages)

JACKY VISITS THE ZOO
11 1/4 min   color   Nat. Film Bd.
*Award Winner, Rome
A tour of the zoo is given extra interest as an irate animal keeper
chases Jacky for teasing the beasts.   The camera catches close-ups
of the polar bear, lion, giraffe, elephant, rhinoceros, camel, zebra
and, finally, Jacky himself, in a cage labelled "Wild Boy. " (Elem.)

From J. T. (Carousel Films, Inc.)

JAIL KEYS MADE HERE
    10 min BW McGraw-Hill '65
    *Award, San Francisco
Advertising signs in streets and alleys and highways were filmed all
across America, and were recorded here for their novelty or their
insights. For example: The Sweetsex Bridal Salon and The Co-
Existence Bagel Shop were selected as humorous, often fumbling,
efforts to catch the attention of passersby. Music by Dave Brubeck.
Produced by Lee Boltin and Frank DeFelitta. (HS-Adult)

JAMES DICKEY: Poet
    37 min color Encyc. Brit. '70
    *Chris Certificate, Columbus
The sub-title (rather lengthy) is: "Lord, Let Me Die But Not Die
Out." These words, and others of the poet, project an insight into
his personality and his work. He is a man trying "to break through
this kind of glass wall we all live behind." From the EBE Humanities Series. (HS-Adult)

JAMES MONROE--The Man and The Doctrine
    30 min color Handel
    *Award, Freedoms Foundation

The fifth president of the United States, Monroe maintained that expansion of European influence to the Western Hemisphere could be dangerous to American interests there. Has history proven him right? (Junior-Senior HS)

JAMES WELDON JOHNSON
        12 min   color   Oxford Films   '71
        *Cindy Award, Info. Film
        *Award Winner, Atlanta
        *Prize Winner, Columbus
        *Golden Eagle, CINE
This is an account of the life of the Black poet whose versatile career included music, teaching, Latin American diplomacy, and NAACP leadership. It concludes with a reading and visualization of his poem, The Creation. Produced by Art Evans. (HS-Adult)

THE JAMESTOWN COLONY (1607 through 1620)
        16 min   color   Coronet   '58
        *Chris Award, Columbus
This enactment of events originates from the historically accurate re-construction of the Jamestown village. The colony's early days are chronicled, suggesting the faith and dedication of the first settlers from England. (Intermediate-Junior HS)

JAPAN
        27 min   color   Int. Film Found.
        *Award, Scholastic Teacher
        *Blue Ribbon, American/EFLA
This introduction to modern Japan shows an ancient people's success in rebuilding after a disastrous defeat. It stresses how they were able to create the new without destroying the old traditions. Aspects shown are: farming, fishing, crafts, television, city life, and industry. Filmed by Kenneth Snelson and Julien Bryan. (HS-Adult)

JAPAN: The Land and the People
        11 min   color   Coronet
        *Award of Merit, Boston
Investigates how this small nation supports its large population. The relationship between climate and crops is indicated, along with the importance of industry in achieving a balanced economy. (Intermediate-Junior HS)

THE JAPANESE
        52 min   color   Carousel   '69
        *Award, Overseas Press Club
        *Prize, Christopher Movement
        *"Emmy," Nat. TV Academy
        *Geo. Foster Peabody Award
Harvard professor and former ambassador Edwin Reischauer shows us Japan's citizens at home, at work, and at play. He reports on Japan's rapid recovery from war, its Westernization, and problems related to the process. Shown, too, are examples of their culture: Haiku poetry, Kabuki theatre, and Zen sports. Produced by CBS-TV. (College-Adult)

THE JAPANESE-AMERICAN
    30 min   color   Handel   '72
    *Award, Nat'l. Education
Concepts include Perry's mission, emigration to Hawaii and California, the Exclusion Act, Pearl Harbor, the "relocation camps" of
World War II, Nisei bravery in European combat, and the Immigration and Nationality Act of 1952.   (HS-Adult)

JAPANESE CALLIGRAPHY
    17 min   BW   Macmillan   '58
    *Prize Winner, Mannheim
A painter's rediscovery of the beauty of this ancient and continuing
art form.   Western art--with its theories of abstraction--is then
compared with this Japanese craft that has existed for ten centuries.
Produced by Pierre Alechinsky.   (HS-Adult)

JAPANESE FARMERS
    17 min   color   Films Inc.   '68
    *Chris Statuette, Columbus
Despite the mountainous terrain of his country, the Japanese farmer
has achieved a level of productivity that is among the world's very
highest.   His secret: ingenuity and special cultivation techniques.
But, with many farmers moving to the cities, what will happen to
this historically high state of agriculture?   Produced by the Institut
für Film und Bild.   (Intermediate-Adult)

JAZZ IN THE CONCERT HALL
    53 min   BW   McGraw-Hill   '67
    *Series Award, Saturday Review
From the Young People's Concert series, with Leonard Bernstein as
master of ceremonies, narrator, and conductor of the New York
Philharmonic.   Produced by CBS-TV.   (Elem.-Adult)

JAZZOO
    18 min   color   ACI Films   '68
    *Silver Phoenix, Atlanta
    *Golden Eagle, CINE
    *Honors, American/EFLA
Here is the rare beauty of early morning at the zoo ... before we
humans intrude.   Filmed at the St. Louis Zoo, these images are
joined with an original jazz score in creating a mood without the use
of words.   Also available in 13-min. form.   Produced by John
Camie.   (Elem.-Adult)

JEALOUSY
    8 min   color   Macmillan   '63
    *Gold Rose Award, Varna
A cartoon parody that mimics the style of the Western hero by animating musical notes, using the staff as the ground, groups of notes
as horses and riders, and a treble clef as a lasso.   Produced by
Todor Dinov.   (Elem.-Adult)

JEFFERSON'S MONTICELLO
    25 min   color   Films Inc.   '70

*Award, NY Int. Film & TV
*Honors, Freedoms Foundation
*Prize Winner, Atlanta

Jefferson's diverse and exceptional life is viewed in relation to the construction of his mansion over a period of forty years that coincided with his other activities during the Revolution, and his duties as Secretary of State, Vice President, and President. Produced by WRC-TV. (HS-Adult)

JERUSALEM AND ITS CONTRIBUTIONS
    16 min   color   Atlantis   '70
    *Honors, Photo. Society
    *Chris Award, Columbus

The importance of Jerusalem, explained through the three major religions that control the city: Judaism, Christianity, and Islam. Produced by J. Michael Hagopian. (Elem. -HS)

JERUSALEM ... CENTER OF MANY WORLDS
    29 min   color   Atlantis   '69
    *Chris Statuette, Columbus
    *1st Prize, Photo. Society
    *Award Winner, Industrial

The historical origins of Jerusalem, the significance of her location, and her eminence in the religious and political role of several civilizations. Producer: J. Michael Hagopian. (HS-Adult)

THE JESUS TRIP
    50 min   color   Time-Life   '72
    *Blue Ribbon, American/EFLA

Thousands of teenagers release their energies in the Jesus movement. Cameras penetrate the communes of "Jesus Freaks" to record the impact of one of the more recent cults to engage the youth of America. From the BBC-TV network. (College-Adult)

THE JEWISH WIFE
    20 min   color   Doubleday   '71
    *Merit Award, Philadelphia
    *Honorable Mention, San Francisco
    *Gold Award, Int. Film & TV
    *Red Ribbon, American/EFLA

This story by German playwright Bertold Brecht takes place in Hitler's era as a Jewish woman says goodbye to her Aryan husband before she flees to safety. It is basically an examination of every person's responsibility for social sins. (HS-Adult)

JOACHIM'S DICTIONARY
    9 min   color   Macmillan   '65
    *Diploma of Honor, Locarno
    *Diploma of Merit, Bergamo
    *Critical Prize, Oberhausen

In the rhythm of one gag per idea, one idea per drawing, and one drawing per word, animator Walerian Borowczyk makes good on this film's subtitle, "un film distractif. " Whether translated as "disturb-

From JOANJO: A PORTUGUESE TALE (ACI Films, Inc.)

ing" or as "diverting," this is a sophisticated adult-level alphabet.
No narration. (College-Adult)

JOANJO: A PORTUGUESE TALE
    12 min color ACI Films '70
    *Golden Eagle, CINE
    *Honors, American/EFLA
    *Awards: Bilbao (Spain), Rome, and Venice
Based on the book by Jan Balet, this is a story of a boy whose
relatives are fishermen. He dreams of becoming a storekeeper,
then mayor, governor, and finally, king. But his dreams aren't all
pleasant ones, and when he awakes, he's glad to find he's back home
by the sea again. The dream sequence is in animation; the rest in
live-action. Shot on location in Nazare by Stelios Roccos. (Elem.)

THE JOGGER
    9 min color ACI Films '70
    *Golden Eagle, CINE
A man is seen jogging through New York's Central Park. As he
runs, we hear voices of a man and woman at various stages of their
relationship. As the runner's landscape changes, so does the relationship we overhear, ending--as it began--with a cold formality of
indifference. A Webber-Garthwaite Film. (Senior HS-Adult)

JOHN PAUL JONES
     14 min   color   Schloat Prod.
     *Honor Medal, Freedoms Foundation
Studies the qualities that made this man one of the most admired of
early Americans.   Also gives insights into the mode of life in the
18th century colonies.   (Intermediate-Junior HS)

JOHNNY APPLESEED
     13 1/2 min   color   Coronet
     *Award of Merit, Stamford
The story of this man of peace is enacted against the background of
pioneer America in a live-action portrayal.   The enactment is accompanied by a descriptive folk ballad.   (Intermediate)

JOSEF HERMAN
     13 min   BW   Roland Films
     *Chris Award, Columbus
     *Quality Award, French National
The drawings of this British realist continued the humanist traditions
of Millet, Daumier, and Van Gogh, with subjects of men close to nature.   Non-verbal.   Producer: Anthony Roland.   (College-Adult)

JOSEPH SCHULTZ
     13 min   color   Wombat   '72
     *Gold Medal, Belgrade

From JOSEPH SCHULTZ (Wombat Productions, Inc.)

Does war nullify moral responsibility? That is the issue implicit in this film, based on a World War II incident in which a German soldier dared to question an order to execute innocent hostages. His action (or inaction) can become a point of departure for discussion on matters related to current issues. (HS-Adult)

A JOURNEY
12 min   color   Wombat   '72
*Subject Award, Birmingham
It was an ordinary day. To all appearances, it was also an ordinary group of people riding a train. But then a series of events casts an entirely different light on what had once seemed common. No dialogue and no narration. A Zagreb Film. (HS-Adult)

JOURNEY INTO SPRING
30 min   color   McGraw-Hill   '58
*Nomination, Academy Award
This film observes the coming of Spring to the English countryside. Shown are scenes of animal life, pond life, and plant life--all adding up to a celebration of life itself. The chief locale is Selborne in Hampshire, the parish of the 18th century naturalist, Rev. Gilbert White. (HS-Adult)

JOURNEY INTO SUMMER
51 min   color   Xerox Films   '70
*Bronze Medal, Atlanta
This is a record of natural history of summer in America, and a commentary on the relationships of living things. But all is not ideal, for the camera reveals how Lake Erie, a once magnificent body of water, is now practically dead. Still, evidence of some correction is seen in the comeback of the bison and in measures taken to save our water, woods, fields, and hills. Produced by Hobel-Leiterman. (College-Adult)

THE JOURNEY OF ROBERT F. KENNEDY
73 min   color   Films Inc.   '70
*Red Ribbon, American/EFLA
*Chris Statuette, Columbus
Through newsreels, rare photos, and home movies, this film, written by Pulitzer Prize-winning author Arthur Schlesinger, recounts Bob Kennedy's life from childhood to that tragic night of June 6, 1968 in Los Angeles where he met his violent and unexpected death. A David Wolper Production. (College-Adult)

JOURNEY TO CHINALE
25 min   color   McGraw-Hill   '70
*Chris Certificate, Columbus
This ethnographic film tells of an Indian family who, as the only survivors of an epidemic, leave its village in Brazil and travel down an unknown river to join relatives in Surinam. Covers many aspects of life among Carib-speaking Oyanas, along with the ritual of the Marake in which huge ants are pressed against the bodies of initiates. Produced by Willard Baldwin. (College-Adult)

JOURNEY TO THE OUTER LIMITS
    52 min color Nat. Geog. '73
    *Blue Ribbon, American/EFLA
Attending the Colorado Outward Bound School, teenagers struggle
with rock climbing, rappeling, rope bridges, and zipwires. Their
training is climaxed by scaling the 18,715 foot peak of Santa Rosa
in the Peruvian Andes, a challenge that takes them beyond previously imagined capacities of physical and emotional endurance. Producer: Alex Grasshoff. (Senior HS-Adult)

THE JOY OF WINTER
    15 min BW Nat. Film Bd.
    *Award, Necochea (Argentina)
    *Honors, Gijon (Spain)
How to adjust to a long snowy season. Shows people making the
best of what they cannot change. From tots to polar bears, all beings prove that winter can be more fun than summer. (Elem.-Adult)

JUGGERNAUT
    28 min color Learn. Corp. '70
    *Red Ribbon, American/EFLA
India is revealed through the eyes of her people as they watch the
incongruous journey of a nuclear reactor on its 600-mile trip across
the landscape. Scenes touch on many aspects of their life, their
work, their customs, and religion. By the National Film Board of
Canada. (HS-Adult)

JUMP!
    25 min color BFA Educ. Media
    *Golden Eagle, CINE
Explores the forces of parental and group pressure and how both can
lead to decisions about drugs. A teenage boy finds himself under
pressure, at a party, to "jump" to hard drugs; this scene is contrasted with one of his younger brother at a birthday party where
the latter is being taunted to "jump" from a tree. (Intermediate-
Junior HS)

JUNKDUMP
    15 min color ACI Films '70
    *Gold Medal, Atlanta
The problem of disposal of wastes is presented in this film. It
shows one day in the life of a couple who pursue "normal" activities
in a garbage dump. The humor is brought up short, though, with
the realization that what is portrayed could eventually happen. A
Communico Film. (Intermediate-Adult)

JUST ONCE
    16 min color AIM-Assn.
    *Best Educ. Film, Canadian
    *Bronze Plaque, Nat. Committee
Many hazardous job functions are shown to demonstrate the necessity
for eye protection. Designed to emphasize the importance of sight-
saving devices for workmen, foremen, and supervisors. (Adult)

JUST SIGN HERE
        14 min   color   Macmillan
        *Blue Ribbon, American/EFLA
With credit and interest charges under scrutiny, this film is a re-
minder of how purchasers can protect themselves from usury. Four
different misrepresentations of credit are dramatized, and the viewer is instructed on how to recognize and avoid them.   (HS-Adult)

KALEIDOSCOPE ORISSA
        37 min   color   Int. Film Bur.   '67
        *Blue Ribbon, American/EFLA
Orissa, one of the poorest states in India, is renowned for its intricate art produced with almost primitive instruments. Included
here are examples of ceramic pottery, weaving, and fabrics. Religious beliefs are reflected in paintings, and ritual is expressed in
ceremonial garments and decorative tents. Film-maker: Mary
Kirby, Pilgrim Films, London. (College-Adult)

KANDINSKY
        15 min   color   Roland Films
        *Honor Diploma, Cannes
        *First Prize, Mannheim
        *Merit Award, Berlin
        *Bronze Medal, Brussels
        *Silver Lion, Venice ... and other awards
Working his way from familiar to abstract forms, Kandinsky changed
the course of contemporary art in his exuberant mastery of color.
His Russian origins are stressed, as is his later turn toward the
Fine Arts with a metaphysical outlook. Producer: H. G. Zeiss.
(College-Adult)

KANGAROOS--Part One, Biography
        12 1/2 min   color   Australia   '70
        *Award, San Francisco
        *Gold Camera, US Industrial
Feeding, mating, and growth are studied, including the birth and
development of the embryo in the pouch. Filmed under natural conditions. Produced by the Commonwealth Film Unit. (College)

KANGAROOS--Part Two, Varieties
        12 min   color   Australia   '70
        *Hon. Mention, San Francisco
The kangaroo family has 50 known types. Many of them, including
rare species, are seen in this film. Filmed in natural environments.
Made by the Commonwealth Film Unit of Australia. (College)

KATUTURA
        37 min   color   Phoenix   '73
        *Red Ribbon, American/EFLA
The title is an African word for total insecurity, a feeling that describes the lives of the Blacks in the dormitory towns run by whites
in the southeast of that continent. Outlines the history of the English and Dutch colonization of the area, and how their roles remain

dominant to this day.   Directed by Ulrich Schweizer.   (Senior HS-Adult)

KEEP COOL
   3 1/2 min   color   BFA Educ. Media   '71
   *Best Music, Zagreb
A humorous essay on how one black man tries to make it by a new
Golden Rule: "Keep cool." Oscar Brown's swinging blues ballad
and Barrie Nelson's animation suggest that this rule may be harder
to observe than the original. (HS-Adult)

KEITH
   9 min   color   Billy Budd   '73
   *Diploma of Excellence, Montreal
Keith Berger performs his pantomime, the "mechanical man," as a
warning that we, too, can become frozen in our prejudices and automatic in our responses. This lack of human spontaneity can be just
as inhibiting as barbed wires or iron bars. Produced by Frank
Moynihan. (Intermediate-Adult)

KENNEDY: What Is Remembered Is Never Lost
   23 min   BW   Films Inc.   '65
   *Golden Eagle, CINE
This tribute to JFK simulates the march of the funeral caisson to
Arlington National Cemetery. The verbal continuity is provided by
recordings of John Kennedy's own words, supplemented by commentary from correspondents who knew him. Re-edited from the NBC
special, "JFK Remembered." (HS-Adult)

THE KID FROM CANADA
   57 min   BW   Sterling Educ.   '70
   *Spec. Award, Venice (Child.)
Andy comes from Canada to stay with his cousins in Scotland. During a pony ride, he antagonizes the others but an exciting climax
takes care of all problems. Produced by the Children's Film Foundation, Britain. (Ages 7-12)

KIDS AND COOKIES
   14 min   color   Assn-Sterling
   *Silver Hugo, Chicago
   *Award, Calvin Workshop
   *Blue Ribbon, American/EFLA
   *Golden Eagle, CINE
This trip through a cookie factory--a dream come true for kids--is
described by children themselves as they wonder at the rows and
rows of treats before their eyes. They also marvel at the technol-
ogy involved in ovens 300 feet long, giant dough mixers, and other
"magic" machines. Available on free loan. Sponsor: the National
Biscuit Company (Nabisco). (College-Adult)

KIENHOLZ ON EXHIBIT
   21 min   BW   McGraw-Hill   '69
   *First Prize, Nat. Student

The unorthodox sculpture of Edward Kienholz had such impact that it was partially censored during its showing at the Los Angeles County Museum of Art, and barely escaped being banned as pornographic. Viewers were either attracted to his work or were repulsed by it; very few were indifferent. These reactions on film form a spontaneous study of the interaction between art and society. Produced by June Steel of UCLA. (College-Adult)

KIFARU: The Black Rhinoceros
    52 min color Films Inc. '71
    *Award, Ohio State U.
    *Golden Eagle, CINE
The rhino (or "Kifaru" in Swahili) is close to extinction, so Canadian biologist John Goddard was asked to conduct an investigation of this ecological crisis. This film is a report of his six-year study in which he counted, cataloged, and photographed 180 black kifarus, the first scientific compendium of this rare species. An MGM Documentary. (College-Adult)

THE KINETIC SCULPTURE OF GORDON BARLOW
    7 min color Perspective '74
    *Golden Eagle, CINE
    *Silver Medal, Atlanta
    *Chris Award, Columbus
This artist makes things move. He takes rows of dominoes and makes them rise and fall in wavy patterns. Barlow paints ping-pong balls and bounces them through plastic boxes. His is sculpture that speaks for itself. A Rainbow Production. (College-Adult)

KING OF THE HILL
    13 min color Barr Films '71
    *Award Winner, Chicago
    *Prize Winner, Atlanta
A human relations analogy, designed to motivate rather than explain, and expressed in a comparison between a forest and a cornfield. The rigid individual is portrayed in the form of a child's game, while the flexible personality is interpreted as being a folk dance. Produced by Rolf Forsberg. (Intermediate-Adult)

THE KINGFISHER
    15 min color ACI Films '69
    *Red Ribbon, American/EFLA
Introduces members of the Kingfisher family of birds, and shows the life cycle of the European or Common Kingfisher. The process of catching fish is shown at normal speed and in slow motion. A Gateway Educational Film. (Intermediate-Adult)

KITCHEN SAFETY: Preventing Fires
    10 min color Nat. Educ. Media '73
    *Merit Award, Nat. Committee
Commercial hazards are reviewed with emphasis on grease fires and cleaning of hood and duct systems. There is also information on extinguishers, alarms, and use of the telephone in emergencies.

Demonstrates fires in deep fat fryers, on grills, in trash cans, and from electrical gear. (HS-Adult)

KOESTLER ON CREATIVITY
40 min   color   Time-Life   '72
*Blue Ribbon, American/EFLA

An interview with the author and philosopher, analyzing the creativity and pathology of the human mind which are, Koestler believes, "two sides of the same medal." From the BBC-TV Network. (College-Adult)

KOREAN ALPHABET
7 1/4 min   color   Univ. Educ.   '68
*Award Winner, Teheran

The style of animation and background music (the latter produced without instruments) gives this work by a young Korean artist more utility than that implied by the title. Produced by the National Film Board of Canada. (Primary-Junior HS)

KRAKATOA
28 min   BW   Macmillan
*Awademy Award (Documentary)

About the rebirth of the volcanic island in the Sunda Straits. Contains comparative scenes of eruptions of Mt. Vesuvius and Mt. Aetna. Krakatoa, after spouting a mile into the sky, gradually settles down again, as the long process of rebuilding the island begins anew. Narration is by Joseph Cotten. Producer: Joe Rock. (HS-Adult)

KU KLUX KLAN: The Invisible Empire
47 min   BW   Carousel   '65
*Geo. Foster Peabody Award
*Festival Winner, Florence
*Blue Ribbon, American/EFLA

The objectives and mentality of this band of men are examined in an effort to understand their apparently destructive motivations. One instance of mob violence involves a Black who survived the whip and fire. Included are scenes from the early classic film, Birth of a Nation, which presented the Klan in a sympathetic light. Produced by CBS News. (College-Adult)

LA JOCONDE: The Smile of the Mona Lisa
16 min   color   McGraw-Hill   '70
*Grand Prize, Cannes
*Grand Prix, Tours

A live-action and animated diversion (if not distortion) of da Vinci's famous subject in a variety of new guises: as a deep-sea diver, X-ray photo, football player, and skeleton, to name a few. Animated by Henri Gruel; produced by Argos Films. (HS-Adult)

LA LINEA
11 min   color   BFA Educ. Media   '71
*Critics' Prize, Zagreb

A series of unconventional episodes involving an animator and his creation, Mr. Line. The artist bedevils his little character by surprising him with a variety of incongruities. Produced by Brunetto del Vita. (Intermediate-Adult)

LABOR RELATIONS: Do Not Fold, Staple, Spindle or Mutilate
    50 min   BW   McGraw-Hill   '68
    *First Prize, Intnat'l. Labor
Contrast is drawn between union-management relations in the early part of this century and as they exist today. Produced by the National Film Board of Canada. (College-Adult)

LACROSSE
    14 1/2 min   color   Nat. Film Bd.
    *Award, Cortina d'Ampezzo
    *Award Winner, Belgrade
Demonstrates how the game is played, how lacrosse sticks are made by Mohawk Indians, and how the Canadian Lacrosse Association helps to instruct teams. (HS-College)

LADIES AND GENTLEMEN, MR. LEONARD COHEN
    44 min   BW   CMC-Columbia   '65
    *Blue Ribbon, American/EFLA
Cohen is known as a poet and novelist. Cinema-verité reveals his self-mocking irreverence that is part of the mystique of his artistic personality. Examines his early life and his schooling, then his more recent days as a stand-up comic. The film traces Cohen's way through bars, hotels, streets, and recording studios. He recites some of his poetry in this film that is climaxed by his own amused reactions to the film itself. Produced by Donald Owen and Donald Brittain. (College-Adult)

THE LADY, OR THE TIGER?
    16 min   color   Encyc. Brit.   '70
    *Chris Statuette, Columbus
    *Gold Hugo, Chicago
    *Red Ribbon, American/EFLA
This 1882 short story by Frank Stockton has been re-staged in the space age. It preserves the suspense of the original classic but adds helicopters, sports cars, penthouses, and other modern touches. (HS-College)

LAKE WILDERNESS
    30 min   color   Assn.-Sterling
    *Best Film, Comité Internat'l.
    *1st Place, Nat'l. Visual
Along South Africa's Lake St. Lucia lies an animal preserve that this film tours. It shows an array of strange beasts and birds that inhabit this kingdom, recording the forces of nature that maintain the balance of jungle life. Available on free loan to adult groups. Sponsor: the South African Tourist Corporation. (HS-Adult)

LAKES--AGING AND POLLUTION
    15 min   color   Centron   '71
    *Golden Eagle, CINE
Features underwater scenes, microcinephotography, and other
graphics in explaining the aging process of bodies of water.   Examines, in addition, typical plants, animals, and fish, with special
stress on man's role in affecting the quality and succession of organisms.   (Elem. -Junior HS)

LAND DIVERS OF MELANESIA
    30 min   color   Phoenix   '73
    *Red Ribbon, American/EFLA
Shows how the men of Pentecost Island anchor their feet with vines,
and then dive head-first onto soft earth ... to ensure a good crop
of yams from their gods.   This is only one of several annual rites
that keep these inhabitants in touch with the forces that control their
world.   Produced by Karl Muller and Robert Gardner of the Harvard
University Film Study Center.   (Senior HS-Adult)

LAND OF THE LONG DAY, Part II: Summer and Autumn
    19 min   color   Int. Film Bur.
    *Robt. Flaherty Award
    *Golden Reel Award
    *Honors, Salerno (Italy)
While the women make clothes, the hunter's father helps prepare
seal skins, and the boys look after the fish nets.   White whales are
spotted feeding.   A chase follows with Eskimos in their kayaks.   As
autumn arrives and daylight fades, the Eskimos prepare for winter.
Produced by the National Film Board of Canada.   (Elem. -Adult)

LAND OF THE LOON
    26 min   color   AV Explor.   '67
    *Best TV Film, Canadian
Deep in the wilderness of a Canadian nature sanctuary, Algonquin
Park, the camera roams through lakes and trails.   The result is
this close-up of birds and mammals in synchronous authentic sound,
as recorded by film-maker Dan Gibson.   (Intermediate-Adult)

THE LAND OF THE SWISS
    21 min   color   Neubacher-Vetter
    *Statuette Award, Columbus
A look at modern, highly developed Switzerland.   In spite of geographical limitations and language differences, the enterprising citizens of this democracy have created a prosperous and unified nation,
with good relations and trade with the rest of the world.   (Intermediate-Adult)

LANGUAGE OF THE BEE
    15 min   color   Moody Inst.
    *Award, San Francisco
Explains and demonstrates communication among honeybees.   The
structure of the compound eye is also examined, including the instinct that enables a bee to fly at a given angle to the sun.   Scien-

tific method is employed, and the viewer is encouraged to perform experiments and to verify results. (HS)

THE LASER BEAM
        16 min   color   Handel   '68
        *Merit Award, Landers
The laser produces an intense, pencil-thin beam of light. The process is explained in detailed animation, along with some applications in medicine, industry, communications, space exploration, and the hologram which may lead to three-dimensional TV. (HS-Adult)

LAURETTE
        19 3/4 min   BW   Nat. Film Bd.
        *Award, Conf. on Children
A subjective view of a middle-class working woman, separated from her husband and bringing up a daughter. As she tries to make sense of the realities of her life, Laurette must somehow convince herself that life can go on for her and her child, that living as a solo parent is possible. (College-Adult)

LAW AND ORDER
        81 min   BW   Zipporah   '68
        *Best Documentary, Nat. Academy
One of a series of studies of American institutions, accomplished by meticulous editing of live-action footage, and by letting the situations speak for themselves without adding any commentary or narration. Filmed by Frederick Wiseman. (Senior HS-Adult)

L'CHAIM--TO LIFE!
        82 min   BW & color   Harold Mayer   '72
        *Golden Eagle, CINE
        *Award Winner, Florence
The story of the real fiddlers on the roof--the East European "shtetle" Jews. In a bitter world, they tasted sweetness. Stills, stock footage, and music depict their history over the past 100 years. Narrated by Eli Wallach. (College-Adult)

LE MERLE
        4 min   color   Int. Film Bur.   '58
        *Awards: Brussels, New York, Bilbao, Montevideo
Animator-producer Norman McLaren imparts graphic activity to an old French-Canadian nonsense song. White cut-outs on pastel provide the visuals, as the song relates how a blackbird loses parts of his body one by one, only to regain them twofold and threefold. Sung in French by the Trio Lyrique of Montreal. Produced by the National Film Board of Canada. (All Ages)

A LECTURE ON MAN
        4 min   BW   Macmillan   '61
        *Satire Prize, Annecy
        *Gold Prize, Mannheim
The dry and well-trained voice of a lecturer, removed by time and space from the follies of his subject, is the framework for this

satire on humanity's hypocrisies and manners. This collage consists of news clips, stills, diagrams, and drawings by cartoonist
Richard Williams. (HS-Adult)

LEGACY OF A DREAM
        29 min   color with BW   King Found.   '74
        *Blue Ribbon, American/EFLA
This production by Richard Kaplan outlines the career and campaigns
of Dr. Martin Luther King, Jr. , showing also how his life's work is
being carried on by Mrs. Coretta King and Rep. Andrew Young.
Narrated by actor James Earl Jones.   (HS-Adult)

THE LEGEND OF JIMMY BLUE EYES
        22 min   color   Macmillan
        *Winner, Edinburgh (Scotland)
        *Nomination, Academy Award
The story of a debonair New Orleans character of the 1920s who
wins a battered old trumpet in a card game but loses his girl to Joe,
a jazz trumpeter. After 20 years of practicing on the horn in prison, Jimmy finally meets the Devil who shows him how to hit the
perfect note. With it, Jimmy wins a trumpet "blow off" against his
rival Joe, recaptures his girl, but is claimed by the Devil and disappears in a cloud of smoke. Produced by Fleetwood Films. (HS-
Adult)

LEGEND OF THE MAGIC KNIVES
        11 min   color   Encyc. Brit.   '71
        *Chris Certificate, Columbus
        *Golden Eagle, CINE
This legend is expressed through figures on a totem and authentic
Indian masks. An old chief realizes that his apprentice's carvings
are better than his own and, in jealousy, lashes out with a knife, accidentally killing himself. In death, however, he is allowed to return in any form he wishes. He chooses to become a river, one
that flows close to his native tribe. Collaborator: Tony Hunt,
Kwakiutl Indian artist, British Columbia, Canada. (Intermediate-
Adult)

LENTIL
        9 min   color   Weston Woods   '56
        *Chris Award, Columbus
An iconographic version of the children's picture book of the same
name. Also available with Spanish narration. Produced by Mort
Schindel. (Primary)

LEO BEUERMAN
        13 min   color   Centron   '68
        *Best, National Visual
        *Cindy Award, Info. Film
        *Merit Award, Landers
        *Nomination, Academy Award ... and many other honors
The true story of a contemporary American, born with almost every
imaginable physical handicap. He learns not only to care for himself

From LEO BEUERMAN (Centron Educational Films)

but also manages to make his own contribution to society far into his old age. (Intermediate-Adult)

THE LEMONADE STAND: What's Fair?
    14 min   color   Encyc. Brit.   '70
    *Chris Certificate, Columbus
Focuses on the meaning of obligations and fairness to others, using the team-operation of a lemonade stand as the basis for discussion. This film also introduces concepts of economics such as investment of time and money. (Elem.)

LEONARDO DA VINCI: Man of Mystery
    68 min   color   Pictura   '52
    *Robert Flaherty Award
    *Documentary Prize, Venice
This full-length biography was two years in the making. It provides a record of da Vinci's contributions to world art and science, and offers an insight into what drove him toward solving the mysteries of mind and matter in that way so unique to the Renaissance mentality. Produced by Leonard Kipnis and Herman Starr. (College-Adult)

LEOPOLD, THE SEE-THROUGH CRUMBPICKER
    9 min   color   Weston Woods   '72
    *Golden Eagle, CINE
The havoc that invisible Leopold creates is described as he devours
every morsel in sight.   Based on the Harcourt-Brace picture book,
written and illustrated by William Flora.   Producer: Firebird
Films.   (Primary)

LES ESCARGOTS
    11 min   color   McGraw-Hill   '69
    *Pelican Award, Mamaia
    *Silver Seal, Trieste
    *Golden Dragon, Cracow
An unsuccessful farmer discovers that his tears have the power to
make his sickly crops grow.   The absurd but logical results of this
magic form the basis of this science-fiction tale with moral overtones.   A Rene Laloux production; animated by Jacques Laloux.
(Intermediate-Adult)

LES FLEURS DE MACADAM (The Asphalt Flowers)
    3 1/4 min   color   Nat. Film Bd.
    *Award, Yorkton (Saskatchewan)
After a brief introduction in English, a French song by Jean-Pierre
Ferland provides the narration for this study of the industrial work-
ers of Montreal, tied to the grind and grime of the city.   Animated.
(HS-Adult)

LET MY PEOPLE GO
    54 min   BW   Films Inc.   '65
    *Award, Nat. Academy
    *Nomination, Academy Award
    *Geo. Foster Peabody Award
    *Honors, Ohio State Univ.
    *Award, San Francisco
    *Golden Eagle, CINE
Traces the history of the Jews from their exile in the first century
A. D. until the creation of the modern Israeli state in 1948.   Includes
film never seen publicly before the original telecast from which this
film was made.   Also incorporates footage obtained from the Haganah
and the Irgun, depicting how they transported "illegals" on their way
to Palestine.   A David Wolper Metromedia Production.   (College-
Adult)

LET THE RAIN SETTLE IT
    13 min   color   TeleKETICS
    *Golden Eagle, CINE
A man's car breaks down on a Texas road in the middle of a humid
day.   He leaves his son with a Black couple and their grandson while
he goes on for help.   The two boys become friendly soon enough,
but their parting is jarred by the bigotry of an outsider.   (Intermediate-Adult)

THE LIFE CYCLE OF A PARASITIC FLATWORM (Cryptocotyle lingua)
14 min color BFA Educ. Media
*Award, American/EFLA
*Prize, Nat. Educational
Shows the life cycle of a flatworm in relation to its sequence of
hosts: the sea gull, snail, and cunnerfish. Among the processes
filmed are copulation, release of eggs, and amplification of numbers
through polyembryony. Photographed by Paul Krupa, City College
of New York. (College)

LIFE CYCLE OF THE WASP
18 min color Macmillan '71
*Golden Eagle, CINE
How wasps aid agriculture by pollinating plants and destroying harmful insects. Also shows how engineers, by copying the ways of the
wasp, learned to reinforce structures with lightweight materials.
(HS-College)

LIFE IN ANCIENT ROME: The Family
11 min color Coronet '59
*Award, Scholastic Teacher
Filmed in Rome and other authentic settings, this picture describes
the activities of a typical day in that era: its educational system,
the marketplace and shops, public baths, costumes, architecture,
and other facets of Roman civilization. (Intermediate)

LIFE OF A PHILIPPINE FAMILY
11 min color Coronet '57
*Award, Scholastic Teacher
A Philippine farm family exemplifies how village people meet their
needs. The father describes, through the narrator, his work in the
rice fields, the children's chores, their schooling, their games, and
finally a birthday party for his son. (Intermediate)

THE LIFE OF CHRIST IN ART
21 min color Coronet '56
*Merit Certificate, Columbus
Through paintings from seven centuries of religious art, this film
outlines the major events of Christ's life. The narrative consists
mostly of passages from the Revised Standard Version of the New
Testament. (HS-Adult)

LIFE TIMES NINE
15 min color Pyramid '73
*Academy Award Nomination
*Silver Hugo, Chicago
An anthology of nine short films, each written by students between
11 and 16 years old who directed their own productions with professional actors and film crew. Released by Insight Productions. (Intermediate-Junior HS)

LIKE OTHER PEOPLE
37 min color Perennial '72

*Silver Medal, Red Cross
*1st Grand Prix, Milan
*Silver Medal, British Society
*Silver Boomerang, Melbourne

The sexual, emotional, and social needs of the handicapped are dealt with here. The two central characters are cerebral palsy patients who make a plea for treatment as "real people." Note: the first eight minutes of narration are intentionally difficult to understand, in order to simulate speech patterns of some handicapped persons. Produced by Kastrel Films. (College-Adult)

THE LINE ACROSS AUSTRALIA
19 min   color   Australia   '69
*Gold Camera, US Industrial

(Originally entitled The Line.) Views from the first train to cross Australia on standard-guage tracks capture the contrast between the fertile coasts and the barren desert. A ballad replaces narration. Photographed by the Commonwealth Film Unit. (Intermediate-Adult)

LINES, SPINES, AND PORCUPINES
7 1/2 min   color   Doubleday   '70
*Chris Award, Columbus

Drawings, accompanied by light verse, are designed to help increase visual awareness in viewers. This film is a source of potential art appreciation material with added potential for story telling. (Primary-Intermediate)

LINES--VERTICAL AND HORIZONTAL
13 min   color   Int. Film Bur.
*Awards: Edinburgh, Venice, London, and others

This creation by Norman McLaren and Evelyn Lambart is non-objective art that joins design with music. The design consists of straight lines that are constantly in motion against colored backgrounds. For the segment Lines Vertical, Maurice Blackburn plays the electronic piano; for Lines Horizontal, Pete Seeger is on wind and string instruments. Both segments are available separately, and each is 6 1/2 minutes. Produced by the National Film Board of Canada. (Intermediate-Adult)

A LITTLE GIRL AND A GUNNY WOLF
6 min   color   ACI Films   '71
*Golden Eagle, CINE
*Red Ribbon, American/EFLA

The inner-city kindergarten children of the California Elementary School use cut-out designs to illustrate a story based on The Gunniwolf by Wilhelmina Harper. They also provide the narration and the song. These elements were animated by their teacher. A Steve and Marion Klein Film. (Primary)

THE LITTLE ISLAND
30 min   color   McGraw-Hill   '58
*Award, British Academy

A cartoon based on the inability of men to communicate. One man believes in truth, one in beauty, the third in goodness. The incompatibility of their narrow frames of moral reference results in catastrophe. Produced by Richard Williams. (HS-Adult)

LITTLE JOYS, LITTLE SORROWS
        10 min   BW   McGraw-Hill   '70
        *Silver Hobby Horse, Cracow
A girl happily nurses her doll until distracted by a cat. The doll is then cast aside in favor of the cat. The capricious animal, though, refuses to play, so the little girl, disappointed, returns to her abandoned toy, her faithful friend, the consolation of her childish sorrows. Produced by the Featurette Film Studio in Lodz, Poland. (Intermediate)

LITTLE MAN, BIG CITY
        10 min   color   CMC-Columbia   '68
        *Blue Ribbon, American/EFLA
In animation this film shows the city's relentless assault on the health of its inhabitants. The little man in the story lives in a typical urban setting where poor planning and inadequate health controls have depleted him emotionally and physically. Even in the confines of his small apartment, he cannot escape the noxious effects of his environment. (Intermediate-Adult)

THE LITTLE MARINER
        20 min   color   Encyc. Brit.   '66
        *Golden Eagle, CINE
Music and visuals, with no narration, reveal the dreams and actions of a boy who sails his boat in the Long Beach (California) harbor. Released by Tiger Productions. (Elem.)

THE LITTLE RED HEN
        11 min   color   Coronet   '54
        *1st Prize, Venice (Child.)
This is a retelling of the fable about sharing in work and in rewards. It is a combination of artwork and live-action photography. (Primary)

THE LITTLE RED LIGHTHOUSE
        9 min   color   Weston Woods   '55
        *Chris Award, Columbus
An iconographic version of the children's picture book of the same name. Also available in Spanish and in Super 8 Sound version. Produced by Mort Schindel. (Primary)

THE LITTLE SPOON (La Petite Cuillière)
        11 min   color   McGraw-Hill   '60
        *Golden Palm, Cannes
        *Jury Prize, Tours
This film is a fleeting and mysterious glance that turns--and returns--around a museum exhibit. Is it an object? Or a woman? It might be--and it is--an ancient Egyptian cosmetic spoon. It might also be--and it is, too--an exquisite little swimmer, a slave girl! (You figure it out for yourself.) The music is adapted from the

second movement of Beethoven's first quartet.   Produced by Carlos
Vilardebo.   (Junior-Senior HS)

THE LITTLEST ANGEL
      13 1/2 min   color   Coronet   '53
      *Participation, Venice (Child.)
To the gates of Heaven one day came a lonely cherub who, though
he tried, just couldn't stay out of trouble.   Then eventually the kind
old Understanding Angel granted the Littlest Angel his wish: when
Jesus was born, he was chosen by God to shine as an inspiration to
all men on earth.   (Elem.)

THE LIVELY ART OF PICTURE BOOKS
      57 min   color   Weston Woods   '64
      *Chris Certificate, Columbus
John Langstaff is the host of this presentation that is intended to
heighten appreciation of literature for children.   It includes inter-
views with professional illustrators, plus excerpts from Weston
Woods films based on popular stories.   Produced by Mort Schindel.
(College-Adult)

THE LIVERWORT: Alternation of Generations
      16 min   color   Coronet
      *Golden Eagle, CINE
Close-up and time-lapse photography enable viewers to examine this
specimen, Marchantia.   The role of water is seen in the transfer of
sperm from antheridia to archegonia.   A laboratory experiment dupli-
cates chemotaxis.   The complete cycle is accomplished in scenes of
vegetative reproduction.   (Senior HS-College)

LIVIN' ON THE MUD
      23 min   color   Northwest Media   '71
      *Grand Prize, Bellevue (Wash.)
The shanty bohemians of North Vancouver are shown in their happy
self-sustaining community whose somewhat seedy utopia is threatened
by urban "development" and finally destroyed by bulldozers.   Produced by Sean Malone.   (HS-Adult)

THE LONDON OF WILLIAM HOGARTH
      27 min   BW   McGraw-Hill   '56
      *Award, Golden Reel
Attempts to capture the spirit of mid-eighteenth century London: the
nobility, the street people, the bourgeois, the beggars, the theaters,
and the fairs--all as interpreted by the engravings of Hogarth.   (College-Adult)

LONELY BOY
      27 min   BW   McGraw-Hill   '69
      *1st Prize, Vancouver
      *Main Prize, Oberhausen
      *Grand Prix Eurovision, Cannes
The life of teenage idol Paul Anka, as described and sung by the pop
star himself.   Based on his autobiographical book, the film stresses

the creation of an image that sells.   Produced by the National Film
Board of Canada.   (HS-Adult)

THE LONG WAY BACK
        22 min BW Int. Film Bur.
        *Chris Certificate, Columbus
Designed to show lay persons how they can provide a link between
the community and mental hospital patients.   After comparing old
and new approaches to treatment, the film shows the role of the
volunteer in such areas as recreation, study, and shopping trips.
Produced by the National Film Board of Canada.   (College-Adult)

THE LONGHOUSE PEOPLE
        23 min color Nat. Film Bd. '49
        *Canadian Film Award
The life and religion of the Iroquois Indians of years past is linked
with these same people today.   Their proud past is recreated in the
performance of a rain dance, a healing ritual, and a celebration in
honor of a newly elected chief.   (Intermediate-Adult)

LONNIE'S DAY
        13 1/2 min color Perspective '65
        *Award, So. Calif. Social Sci. Assn.
        *Honors, American/EFLA
Through documentary techniques, the viewer looks in on a city boy's
life throughout a typical day.   Being with him at home, at school,
and in the streets helps convey a feeling of what life is like for an
eight-year-old Black in the city.   Made by New Document Productions.   (Elem.)

LOOKING FOR ME
        29 min BW Ext. Media Ctr. '70
        *Golden Eagle, CINE
This one is about experiencing one's body.   As such, this film supports Janet Adler's teaching theory that awareness of movement is
essential for all children and that, for disturbed or handicapped children, body language is an important means of communication.
Briefly narrated.   Produced by the University of California.   (College-Adult)

LOOPS
        3 min color Int. Film Bur.
        *Awards: Salerno and Canada
Another of McLaren's experiments in using the technique of drawing
the visuals and the sound directly on the film with ordinary pen and
ink.   Other creations of his in this category are Dots and Pen Point
Percussion.   Produced by the National Film Board of Canada.   (HS-
College)

LOST PIGEON
        15 min color Barr Films '74
        *Best Film, San Francisco
        *Golden Eagle, CINE

*Bronze Plaque, Columbus

This story begins as 3,000 homing pigeons race from their lofts--all except "Oscar," who lands near home and is injured. A boy nurses him back to health, only to realize he has found somebody else's pet. How does he resolve the problem? (Elem.)

LOVE IS FOR THE BYRDS
    28 min   color   Brigham Young U.
    *Chris Award, Columbus
The subjects of this film, Tom and Donna Byrd, dramatize the need for understanding and for communication ... especially in marriage. (College-Adult)

A LOVER'S QUARREL WITH THE WORLD
    40 min   BW   Pyramid   '67
    *"Oscar," Academy Award
Robert Frost is filmed here while reading poetry at Sarah Lawrence College, then while puttering around his Vermont home, and while speaking at a poetry seminar. In recording the public and the private person, this film gives an insight into his relationship with nature and his feelings about the gamble of life. Produced by Shirley Clarke. (HS-Adult)

MACHINE
    10 min   color   Pyramid   '66
    *Prix de Qualité, France
    *Catholic Award, Oberhausen
A combination of European animation, photos and line-drawings, along with an unusual soundtrack. As such, this is a wordless allegory on people and their inventions. An artist draws whatever worldly goods his characters need, then draws machines for them to make more of the same. But then his figures begin to compete and to make weapons with their new machines. Finally they produce a machine that enslaves their artist-creator. Producer: Wolfgang Urchs. (Intermediate-Adult)

THE MACHINE IN BETWEEN
    11 min   color   AIMS   '73
    *Silver Medal, Int. Film & TV
An animated film that portrays communication technologies that allow our society to share ideas. A Miller Production. (Junior-Senior HS)

MACRAME
    15 min   color   ACI Films   '71
    *Bronze Plaque, Columbus
    *Honors, American/EFLA
The ancient art of knotting has had a revival in recent years. Belts, necklaces, handbags, and totebags are among the objects that can be knotted. Artists use the same materials and techniques to create wall-hangings, and this film shows how to make basic knots, combine them to form objects, and create various effects. (HS-Adult)

From MACRAME (ACI Films, Inc.)

THE MAGIC MACHINES
        14 min   color   Learn Corp.   '69
        *Award Winner, Cannes
        *Winner, Academy Award
American sculptor Robert Gilbert, whose works and philosophy are
the subject of this film, describes himself as a grown-up flower
child.   Shunning conventional materials, he searches the scrap heaps
for junk that he converts into kinetic sculptures.   His creations
range from playful contraptions to angry forms of social protest.
Narrated by Gilbert himself in a stream-of-consciousness style.
Film-maker: Joan Keller.   (College-Adult)

MAGIC MOLECULE
        9 min   color   Nat. Film Bd.
        *Awards: London, Antwerp, and Budapest
The techniques and processes of the plastics industry.   Transmuted
from coal, oil, or wood, these synthetic substances can make thousands of new products, from silken threads to furniture.   (Junior
HS-Adult)

MAINE'S HARVESTERS OF THE SEA
        28 min   color   Assn.-Sterling
        *Golden Eagle, CINE

      *Silver Medal, NY Int.
      *Chris Award, Columbus
      *Award, US Industrial
      *First Place, Nat'l. Visual
That special breed of fishermen who work the waters of New England by hunch, experience, and a seaman's knowledge of the fishing grounds, as their fathers did before them. They are shown in all weather and at all times of the year, harvesting cod, haddock, whiting, ocean perch, shrimp, and lobster. Maine Department of Sea and Shore Fisheries, sponsor. Free Loan. (HS-Adult)

THE MAJORITY VOTE
      7 min BW Nat. Film Bd.
      *Award, Film Council of America
Should the representative of a group support a measure that is unpopular with voters? Students voice disapproval of support given by their student council to a move curtailing extra-curricular activities. Their representative gives his reasons for his actions. Do you agree with his logic? (HS)

MAKING HAIKU
      9 min color Encyc. Brit.
      *Red Ribbon, American/EFLA
Children's drawings, coupled with youngsters reading their own verse, explain poetic form. A projector-stop allows viewers time to compose their own Haiku, stimulated by scenes and sounds of streams, leaves, flowers, rainstorms, clouds, and animals. (Intermediate-Junior HS)

MAKING IT IN THE WORLD OF WORK
      26 min color FilmFair '72
      *Chris Certificate, Columbus
Nine recent graduates describe the work they're doing, why they chose it, its benefits, and personal goals. The workers are: a letter carrier, a copy writer, a meter reader, a woman who designs and makes jewelry, a Chicano telephone operator, a mechanic, a junior executive, a young man who operates a cleaning firm, and a woman who chose teaching. Ben Norman Films. (HS-Adult)

THE MAKING OF A PRESIDENT (1960)
      80 min BW Films Inc. '63
      *Award, Florence
      *Program of Year, Nat. Academy
      *Honors, Cannes
      *Award, Vancouver ... and several other awards
American politics in action, centering on John F. Kennedy's campaign for the Presidency. Includes footage made available by the candidates themselves: earlier campaigns for lower office, primary elections, conventions, the JFK-Nixon television debates, and finally, one of the closest votes in our nation's history. Produced by Metromedia. (College-Adult)

THE MAKING OF A PRESIDENT (1964)
    80 min BW Films Inc. '65
    *TV Award, Sat. Review
    *Emmy, Nat. Academy
    *Thomas Edison Award
A behind-the-scenes chronology of one of the most colorful presidential races in recent history. The Presidential campaign of 1964 begins with the efforts of supporters of Senator Barry Goldwater and
the efforts of fellow Republicans (such as Rockefeller, Scranton,
Romney, and Lodge) to derail the Goldwater express. Finally we
see President Lyndon B. Johnson's record-shattering victory at the
polls. Metromedia Producers Corp. (College-Adult)

THE MAKING OF A PRESIDENT (1968)
    82 min color or BW Film Inc. '69
    *Emmy Award, Nat. Academy
    *Chris Statuette, Columbus
A view of the role played in that election by the war in Vietnam, by
student unrest, and by uprisings in the inner-city. Follows candidates Richard Nixon, Eugene McCarthy, and George Romney. Cameras cover Robert Kennedy's entry into the race and Lyndon Johnson's withdrawal. The assassinations of Dr. Martin Luther King,
Jr. and Bob Kennedy are also covered, as well as the bloodshed in
Chicago during the Democratic convention. Finally, Hubert Humphrey's defeat by Richard Nixon. A Metromedia Production. (College-Adult)

MAMMALS
    10 min BW McGraw-Hill '62
    *Red Ribbon, American/EFLA
    *Merit Diploma, Oberhausen
    *Grand Prix, Tours
The fourth and last of Roman Polanski's early short films. This is
the story of two men traveling in the snow with only one sled. The
two strive to take advantage of each other in order to spend the
most possible time riding and the least walking. Slapstick, sight-
gags, and visual puns are in ample supply. This is a metaphor of
the unending conflict and precarious balance between man the exploit-
er and man the exploited, and how easily the roles can shift. Directed by Roman Polanski. (College-Adult)

THE MAN HUNTERS
    52 min color Films Inc. '71
    *Gold Medal, Atlanta
    *Golden Eagle, CINE
    *TV Award, Sat. Review
    *Red Ribbon, American/EFLA
Imagine a line three miles long representing the four million years
of humanity on earth. Walking back only 40 foot would cover all of
recorded history. The rest of the four million years is pre-history.
About 100 years ago scientists began to probe this void in search of
the earliest evidence of man's existence. From France to China,
from Israel to South Africa, scientists have discovered remains of

humanoid creatures, some dating back 3.5 million years. As each piece of the puzzle is assembled, we are brought one step closer to understanding not only our past but our future. An MGM Documentary. (College-Adult)

THE MAN WHO HAD TO SING
10 min   color   Mass Media   '71
*Jury Award, Hemisfilm
The story of a luckless Charlie Brown-type character. Throughout his life of being pushed, shoved, kicked, and bounced around, he meets one disaster after another, simply because he has only one thing to offer the world--a song represented by the animationist as "Ya, Ya, Ya, Ya-Ya." Even in his grave we hear, "Ya, Ya, Ya, Ya-Ya." This little singing man may be thought of as the student whom the teacher never understood, the genius suppressed, the handicapped person, the non-conformist, a Christ figure, or an Everyman. A Zagreb Studio Production. (Intermediate-Adult)

THE MAN WITHOUT A COUNTRY
25 min   BW   McGraw-Hill   '55
*Award, Scholastic Teacher
A dramatization of Edward Everett Hale's patriotic story of Phillip Nolan, the Navy officer who renounced his country. Bing Crosby Productions. (Junior-Senior HS)

MANAGEMENT OF CONFLICT
20 min   color   Int. Assn./Police   '74
*Blue Ribbon, American/EFLA
Dramatizes situations in which police officers may have to exercise certain human relations techniques in order to function effectively. Explains the psychological bases for such techniques. Produced by Bruce Seth Green for Universal Studios, a division of MCA. (College-Adult)

MANAGER WANTED
28 min   BW & color   Roundtable
*Golden Eagle, CINE
*1st Prize, Int. Management
*Certificate, San Francisco
Purpose: To show the requirements for managerial training and the importance of delegation of authority. The story develops around a situation that occurs when a junior executive feels he is not ready to take over a senior position. As the reasons for this reluctance are analyzed, it is shown that management must create the right atmosphere and accept responsibility for the development of subordinates. (College-Adult)

THE MANHATTAN ODYSSEY
7 3/4 min   color   Nat. Film Bd.
*Award: Milan (Italy)
The voyage of the giant American oil tanker, the U.S.S. Manhattan, and the Canadian icebreaker, the John A. Macdonald, through the Northwest Passage of the Canadian Arctic to test its navigability as

a year-round commercial sea lane. Filmed from the ice, from a helicopter, and from aboard the two ships. Produced for the Department of Transport by the National Film Board of Canada. (Intermediate-Adult)

MANHATTAN STREET BAND
        24 min color Carousel '70
        *First Prize, Salerno
        *Certificate, US Industrial
        *Chris Certificate, Columbus
        *Red Ribbon, American/EFLA
        *Silver Medal, NY Int. Film
        *Golden Eagle, CINE
Take a mixed bag of guys from the ghetto. Add sense of musical style, steel drums, bongos and vibraphone, and you have the Manhattan Street Band. And when the music slows and changes key, they dream a bit with flowers in their hands. And you can see how vulnerable these young men from the Lower East Side of New York are. Produced by Gene Searchinger. (Intermediate-Adult)

MANOUANE RIVER LUMBERJACKS
        27 3/4 min BW Nat. Film Bd.
        *Awards: Los Angeles and Locarno
The forests of Quebec supply much of the paper for North America's printed news. From fall until spring, the woods echo with the whine of saws and the shouts of men. The temperature may register fifty-below but the work continues. (Intermediate-Adult)

MAPLE SUGAR FARMER
        29 min color ACI Films '72
        *Bronze Medal, Atlanta
        *Sociology Prize, San Francisco
        *Chris Statuette, Columbus
        *Golden Eagle, CINE
A portrait of an old farmer who maintains a family tradition of making maple syrup. He works with his hand-hewn spikes, buckets, and an iron kettle. As he goes about his activities, he describes the one-room schoolhouse, the country dances, neighborliness, farming with horses, and the attitudes of an earlier, less complicated era. A W. Craig Hinde and Robert Davis Film. (Intermediate-Adult)

MARIA OF THE PUEBLOS
        15 min color Centron '71
        *Chris Statuette, Columbus
The life of Maria Martinez, probably the world's most famous Indian potter. Maria, as a young woman, accidentally discovered the long-forgotten process for creating iridescent black pottery. Through her artistry and her desire to help her people, she shared her techniques and helped lift her village out of poverty. The film gives an insight into the culture, philosophy, art and economic conditions of the Pueblo Indians of San Ildefonso, New Mexico. A Coleman Film Enterprises Production. (Intermediate-Adult)

MARK TWAIN'S AMERICA
    54 min BW McGraw-Hill '61
    *Award, American/EFLA
Using 1,000 pictures from a collection of 3,500 photographs and engravings, this film re-creates the life of Mark Twain and the age in which he lived. Prototypes of Tom Sawyer, Huck Finn, and Becky Thatcher are shown as well as characters who piloted and traveled the magnificent old side-wheelers. Highlights include the elegance of what Twain called "the Gilded Age" in the 1880s; the frontier towns; Manhattan in the gay 90s; Twain's stagecoach journey across the western plains. An NBC "Project 20" Production. (College-Adult)

MARTIN AND GASTON
    11 min color McGraw-Hill '53
    *Award Winner, Edinburgh
    *First Prize, Golden Reel
The tale of two small but fearless boys who set out to sea. This film is made from animated color cutouts of drawings by French children, ages 8 to 10, of the school in Avenue Thierry, Ville d'Avary, France. Produced by George K. Arthur. (Intermediate)

THE MASQUE OF THE RED DEATH
    10 min color McGraw-Hill '70
    *Blue Ribbon, American/EFLA
Edgar Allan Poe's classic tale has been converted into a spectrum of colors in this animated short. Count Prospero has locked himself and his court inside his castle as a protection against the plague. The castle ball is interrupted by a seductive woman who entices the count through the luxurious rooms of the castle. At the end, in a passionate embrace, Prospero discovers that the mysterious guest is, in fact, the plague. Pavao Stalter and Vladimir Jutrisa handpainted each frame of this film. (Junior-Senior HS)

MASTER KITEMAN
    11 1/2 min color Barr Films '74
    *Winner, San Francisco
Dinesh Bahadur's unique friends--his kites--provide him with a way of approaching the world and coping with life. Through his hobby (or more accurately, his outlet) he finds time to meditate and to know himself. Produced by Murray Mintz. (Elem.-Adult)

MASUO IKEDA: Printmaker
    14 min color ACI Films '73
    *Golden Eagle, CINE
Japanese artist, living in New York, explains how he finds ideas, and how he creates his prints. Ikeda draws inspiration from nature, from city streets, and from photographs. A montage of many of his prints demonstrates the work of a master of contemporary art. An Ellis Edmonds, KEI Production. (HS-Adult)

MATHEMATICS AT YOUR FINGERTIPS
    27 1/2 min color Nat. Film Bd.

*Chris Award, Columbus
*Award Winner, Canada
Shows the system developed by a Belgian schoolmaster, Georges
Cuisenaire, who made colored sticks designed to help children grasp
mathematical relationships. His method is demonstrated in a class-
room. (College-Adult)

MATHEMATICS OF THE HONEYCOMB
13 min color Moody Institute
*Award of Merit, Landers
The elegance of the honeycomb, admired by the Greek mathematician
Pappus, was not fully realized until modern mathematical methods
were applied. Through an historical and analytical approach to the
honeycomb problem (including closeup scenes of bees exuding and
manipulating wax), the student is led to appreciate mathematics in
science and engineering. A case history in scientific methods and
bionics. (HS-College)

MATRIOSKA
5 min color McGraw-Hill
*Blue Ribbon, American/EFLA
This is a dance of Russian dolls, as lively in its way as any performance of the Moiseyev Company. But these are painted wooden
dolls, hollow and congruent, so that the largest holds all the rest.
The animator makes them twirl, swing, and sway to gay Russian
tunes without losing their fixed reserve. When the dance ends, they
each return into the mother figure, and hurry off the screen. National Film Board of Canada. (Primary)

MATTER AND ENERGY (2nd edition)
13 1/2 min color Coronet
*Honors, American/EFLA
We see examples of properties and states of matter, the relationship
between kinetic and potential energy, and the role of energy in chemical changes. The law of conservation of matter and energy as related to nuclear fission and fusion leads to the modern concept of
the equivalence of matter and energy. (Junior HS)

A MATTER OF FAT
98 3/4 min color Nat. Film Bd.
*Canadian Film Award
*Award Winner, Atlanta
*Honors, American/EFLA
How one man shed half his body weight--140 lbs.--by starvation under hospital observation. What brought him to so desperate a
course, and how he managed to cope with it, is told by the fat man
himself. Lorne Greene narrates the rest. Examines what other
overweight people are doing to reduce. Visits body contouring parlors, "weight watchers" clubs, and summer camps. Authorities
comment on misconceptions and malpractice. (College-Adult)

A MATTER OF SURVIVAL
26 min color McGraw-Hill

*Blue Ribbon, American/EFLA
*Merit Award, San Francisco

Probes the effects of automation on a man who thought he was im-
mune from that threat. The installation of a computer in his ac-
counting firm forces him to re-assess his life, his career, and the
values associated with them. Produced by the National Film Board
of Canada. (HS-Adult)

THE MATTER WITH ME
15 min color Oxford Films
*Award Winner, Atlanta

Photographed in a modern American city. The film follows a boy
about 12 years old through two worlds, one white, one black. The
viewer sees both worlds through the boy's eyes. The contrasts
emerge naturally and a fragment at a time. On this particular day,
they are destructive to this particular boy. Produced by Monroe
Williams. Non-verbal. (Elem. -HS)

MATTHEW MERIAN
14 min BW Roland Films
*Recognition, German Govt.
*Commendation, German Center

Merian's engravings illustrate his life history, that of the greatest
commentator of Europe of his time (1593-1650). He etched in great
detail the geographic and historic facts, the nations, different occupations, landscapes, and the towns. Director/producer: Th. N.
Blomberg. Commentary: Dr. von Loehneysen. (College-Adult)

MAURITS ESCHER: Painter of Fantasies
28 min BW Coronet '71
*Honors, American/EFLA

The works of this graphic artist are a curious blend of fact and
fancy, with mirror images and interlocking figures flowing from
symmetrical shapes. He discusses his art and philosophy, and the
camera explores such works as "Day and Night" and "Ascending and
Descending." Produced by Document Associates. (HS-Adult)

MAX ERNST (Journey into the Subconscious)
11 1/2 min color Roland Films
*Commendation, Wiesbaden
*Grand Prix, Oberhausen

The inner world of the contemporary painter Max Ernst. One of the
founders of Surrealism, Max Ernst explores the nature of materials
and the emotional significance of shapes. The director and Ernst
together use the film as a medium to explain the artist's development. Directed by Peter Schamoni and Dr. Carl Lamb. (College-
Adult)

THE MAYFLY: Ecology of an Aquatic Insect
15 min color Encyc. Brit. '73
*Golden Eagle, CINE

Reveals the Hexagenia's curious life history, its importance in
fresh water food chains, and its dependence on pure water for

survival. Includes scenes of its emergence from nymph to winged insect. From the EBE Biology Program. (HS-College)

ME AND YOU, KANGAROO
       18 min color Learn. Corp. '74
       *Blue Ribbon, American/EFLA
In telling the story of a wild pet that outgrows its new domestic surroundings, this treatment portrays the relationship between a boy and an animal and the often conflicting responsibilities that are involved. A live-action production, directed by Bert Salzman. (Elem.-Adult)

THE MEANING OF PATRIOTISM
       13 1/2 min color Coronet
       *Chris Award, Columbus
In a series of vignettes depicting American patriots of the past, this film points out that lawmakers, school teachers, newspapermen, and housewives can each achieve the uncommon service to their country that we identify as patriotism. (Intermediate-Junior HS)

MEDIEVAL ENGLAND: The Peasants' Revolt
       31 min color Learn. Corp. '69
       *Best Educational Film, San Francisco
       *Certificate, Columbus
       *Merit Award, Chicago
An English cast portrays the men and women of the Middle Ages who worked the soil, paid their taxes, survived from the plague, yet continued to struggle until the day they could not and would not endure suffering any longer. The Peasants' Revolt of 1381 reveals the condition of virtual slavery that persisted throughout the Middle Ages and the weaknesses of the feudal system--its oppressive tax structure, its cruelty, its social inequity. By John Irvin. (HS-College)

MEET COMRADE STUDENT
       54 min BW McGraw-Hill '61
       *Thomas Alva Edison Award
An examination of the Soviet primary, secondary, and trade school education systems. Also examines the extracurricular programs, the cultural activities, physical fitness, and political indoctrination. An ABC News Production. (College-Adult)

MEET GEORGE WASHINGTON
       54 min color Films Inc. '69
       *Award, Ohio St. Univ.
       *Award, Freedoms Foundation
       *Golden Eagle, CINE
History has managed to convert a boy with a hatchet into an awe-inspiring idol, but somewhere in between these extremes is a person. The script draws on Washington's own words as well as those of his contemporaries. Produced by NBC News. (College-Adult)

MEETING IN PROGRESS
       43 min color Roundtable

  *Award, US Industrial
Purpose: to teach conference leadership through group participation.
Takes viewers through a typical conference in which they witness 12
critical problem-solving conflicts such as digression from the subject, personality clashes, and similar impediments to group productivity. (College-Adult)

MEMENTO
  9 min color CMC-Columbia '68
  *Golden Eagle, CINE
  *Gold Medal, Atlanta
  *Excellence Mention, Antwerp
  *Merit Award, Nat'l. Safety
  *Grand Prix, Vienna
Uses picture and sound contrapuntally. Photographed in an automobile graveyard, the film presents a study of cars irreparably
smashed in accidents, while the sound track reconstructs the voices
of the participants of three particular accidents. Kaleidoscopic
montages, single-frame images, and subjective sound-effects. Produced by Sumner Glimcher. (HS-Adult)

MEMORANDUM
  58 min BW McGraw-Hill '66
  *Best Documentary, San Francisco
Probes the phenomenon of Nazi concentration camps in flashbacks
through the mind of a survivor as he visits the "New Germany."
Produced by the National Film Board of Canada. (College-Adult)

MEMORIAL
  10 min color Mass Media '72
  *Silver Medal, Venice
  *Merit Certificate, Chicago
An elegaic film that tries to describe what it must have been like to
fight and die on the Somme in the summer and autumn of 1916 ...
a battle that exceeded the death toll and property loss even of Hiroshima. Directed by James Allen. (Senior HS-Adult)

MEN AT BAY
  26 min color BFA Educ. Media '70
  *Gold Medal, Atlanta
A world-renowned bay is drowning. Nearly half of one of America's
most beautiful landmarks has already been lost to pollution. And
cities everywhere face a similar fate. This documentary probes the
reality of the problem in an attempt to understand how and why it
could happen. San Franciscans voice their explanations or suggest
alternatives to the death of their harbor. Produced with the cooperation of Earth Science Curriculum Project and Environmental Studies
Project. (HS-Adult)

MEN'S LIVES
  43 min color New Day '74
  *Blue Ribbon, American/EFLA
This is a live-action report on masculinity in America, as interpreted

by representative citizens. The format incorporates interviews with men and boys alike, as they discuss their life and life style. Additional narration by Josh Hanig and Will Roberts. (Senior HS-Adult)

MERCHANT TO THE MILLIONS
        28 min   color   Assn.-Sterling   '69
        *Bronze Award, NY Int.
How Mr. Sears met Mr. Roebuck. The history of the world's largest distributor of general merchandise. Accompanied by an original score. Free loan. Sears, Roebuck & Co., sponsor. (HS-Adult)

METAMORPHOSES
        2 1/2 min   color   Nat. Film Bd.
        *Award Winner, Venice
Here the animation artist has created a clown so versatile in juggling that he even juggles himself. One moment the clown stands tossing balls; the next, he becomes dismembered, following the balls about, but coming together again in one piece to finish the act. The artist is Laurent Coderre. (Elem.)

METHODS OF FAMILY PLANNING
        18 min   color   Oxford Films
        *Award, NY Int.
Methods of contraception are explained and illustrated: rhythm, pills, diaphragm, intrauterine device, vaginal spermicides, and condoms. Vasectomy and tubal ligation are included. The medical pros and cons of different methods are explained in relationship to the circumstances of various couples. Produced by Moreland-Latchford, Ltd. (Senior HS-Adult)

THE METRIC SYSTEM
        13 min   color   Films Inc.   '70
        *Award Winner, Chicago
        *Winner, Int. Film & TV
Over eighty per cent of the countries of the world use the metric system, and it is necessary to be able to convert from one unit to another. Compares the advantages of "going metric" as opposed to "staying imperial." (Intermediate-HS)

A MEXICAN-AMERICAN FAMILY
        17 min   color   Atlantis   '70
        *Award, Nat. Educ. Film
        *Prize, San Francisco
        *Chris Award, Columbus
An insight into the life of a Mexican-American family: the traditions they cherish, adjustment to a new language while maintaining the unity of the family. Produced by J. Michael Hagopian. (Intermediate-Adult)

THE MEXICAN-AMERICAN: Heritage and Destiny
        29 min   color   Handel   '70
        *Chris Award, Columbus

The purpose of this film is twofold: 1) to instill cultural pride in Chicano students; and 2) to generate respect for Mexican Americans among their peers. Available in Spanish and English. Both versions are narrated by Ricardo Montalban. (HS-Adult)

MEXICAN OR AMERICAN?
    17 min color Atlantis '70
    *Chris Award, Columbus
Faces the fundamental problem of cultural conflict in the U.S. Is it possible to enjoy the freedoms and opportunities of this land without giving up the heritage of one's parents? (Junior HS-Adult)

MICROPHONE SPEAKING
    14 1/2 min color Centron '69
    *Chris Award, Columbus
    *Blue Ribbon, American/EFLA
How would Lincoln's Gettysburg address have gone over if he had been interrupted by the squealing of microphone feedback? The microphone can be a help or a hindrance, depending on how the speaker uses it. This film teaches the proper use of microphones in public-address systems and radio. (HS-Adult)

THE MIDDLE EAST
    28 min color Int. Film Foundation
    *Blue Ribbon, American/EFLA
    *Award, Scholastic Teacher
John Snyder's animation portrays 4,000 years of Middle Eastern history. The film surveys the life of nomadic tribes, peasants, and city dwellers. Touches on problems such as water and the difficulties of adjusting to the 20th century. Julien Bryan, producer. (HS-Adult)

MIGRANT
    54 min color NBC Educ. Ent. '70
    *Award, duPont-Columbia
    *Prize, Ohio Univ.
    *Award, Christopher Society
    *Winner, American/EFLA
The migrant farmworker was ignored before Edward R. Murrow's documentary, "Harvest of Shame." Today the situation is not much better. Most of the 2 1/2 million people, sometimes called rented slaves, are not covered by unemployment insurance or the minimum wage law. They earn less in real money than ten years ago. Children miss school because they are needed in the fields. No child labor laws prevent them from working. Migrants are still victims of the cost and profit squeeze between the consumer and the producer. NBC News. (College-Adult)

MIGUEL--UP FROM PUERTO RICO
    15 min color Learn. Corp. '70
    *Certificate, Columbus
How does a Puerto Rican boy adjust to a large American city?
Born in Puerto Rico but now living in N.Y., Miguel still remembers

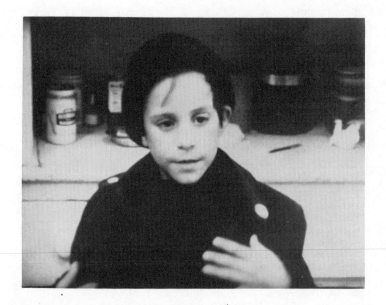

From **MIGUEL--UP FROM PUERTO RICO** (courtesy Learning Corporation of America)

his former home and how he and his father would go fishing near their house on the island. Life in their crowded apartment in the big industrial city is very different. The film portrays a close family relationship and a lesson in the advantages of biculturalism. Film-maker: Bert Salzmann. (Elem. -Junior HS)

MIGUELIN
      63 min BW & color Trans-World
      *Children's Award, Cannes
The story of an altar boy's personal war on poverty by passing the poor box among the villagers. In his dream (filmed in color), he finds the answer is selling his burro, which the villagers then recover for him in time for the annual blessing of animals. Made in Spain. Available with and without subtitles in English. (Intermediate)

MILA 23: SIMION'S WORLD
      15 min color Wombat '72
      *Bronze Plaque, Columbus
      *Best of Festival, Birmingham
      *Blue Ribbon, American/EFLA
Mila 23 is a place, a Rumanian village in the midst of mile after mile of reed-covered marshes at the mouth of the Danube--a distinctive environment, inhabited by a distinctive people. Poses questions

about intrinsically human values and life goals.   Made by Films de
L'Adagio.   (HS-Adult)

MIME OVER MATTER
         12 min   color   SIM Production   '70
         *Bronze Medal, Atlanta
Czechoslovakia's leading mime artist, Ladislav Fialka, and his company use their bodies to show the characteristics and malice of the
mechanical things people take for granted.   Shows that even the
man-about-town who surrounds himself with gadgets is vulnerable to
their malfunctions.   Non-verbal.   Produced by Kratky Film Studios,
Prague.   (HS-Adult)

MIMI
         12 min   BW   Billy Budd Films   '72
         *Documentary Prize, Cork
         *Award, San Francisco
         *Biography Prize, Atlanta
         *Award Winner, Nyon
         *Golden Eagle, CINE
A physically disabled young woman tells how she responds to people
and the world, touching on such sensitive areas as family, personal
relationships, school, career, and barriers.   Produced by Frank
Moynihan.   (HS-Adult)

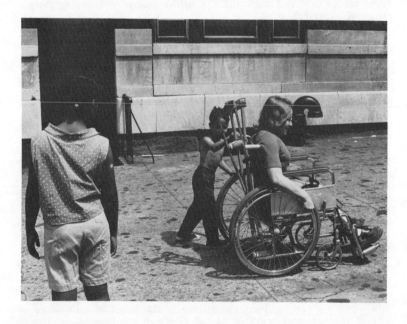

From MIMI (Billy Budd Films, Inc.)

MINERS OF BOLIVIA
15 min color Films Inc. '68
*Chris Certificate, Columbus
Focuses on a group of Indians living in the highlands of Bolivia.
They eke out their existence in the mines and along the creeks and
rivers, digging for tin ore. Family life is difficult. Almost everyone chews the coca leaf (from which cocaine is derived) to ease the
hardship of their lives. Beauty of the locale is a sharp contrast to
the squalor of their lives. Institut für Film and Bild. (Intermediate-HS)

MINER'S RIDGE
22 min color Assn.-Sterling
*Bronze Award, NY Int.
Filmed in the Glacier Peak Wilderness, adjacent to the North Cas-
cades National Park. With pictures, music, and very few words,
this film states the case for inclusion of the Glacier Peak area in
the park. (HS-Adult)

MIRROR OF AMERICA
52 min color Films Inc. '69
*Honor Medal, Freedoms Foundation
Washington, D.C. serves as backdrop for this re-creation of some
stirring moments in our nation's history. Landmarks act as a time-
machine for examining the ideals and values they represent. This
film gives perspective to today's headlines by showing that history
has always had civil protest and violence. NBC News. (College-
Adult)

MISS GOODALL AND THE WILD CHIMPANZEES
51 min color Films Inc. '65
*Award, Edinburgh
*Golden Eagle, CINE
Armed only with binoculars and an aptitude for field research, Jane
Goodall launches a five-year study of the wild chimpanzees of Tanzania's Gomb Stream Reserve. Through tenacity and dedication, Ms.
Goodall wins acceptance by the chimpanzees, and logs a unique record of their behavior. She is the first person to confirm that chimpanzees actually eat meat and that untrained chimpanzees not only
use, but make, tools. Her insights into the life patterns of the most
nearly human of animals yields more understanding of the evolution
of human behavior. Narrated by Orson Welles. National Geographic
Society. Also available a re-edited 28 minute version. (College-
Adult)

MR. EUROPE AND THE COMMON MARKET
51 min BW Carousel '62
*Blue Ribbon, American/EFLA
The revolutionary economic marriage of France, Italy, West Germany, Belgium, the Netherlands, and Luxembourg. We are taken
back through two centuries and shown how political boundaries, with
tariffs, duties, and red tape, hindered economic growth and prosperity. The possibility of a business relationship between a U.S. of

Europe and the U.S.A. is explored. Concludes with an interview with the chief architect of the Common Market, Jean Monnet. Produced by CBS News. (College-Adult)

MR. GREY
     10 min   color   ACI Films   '69
     *Golden Eagle, CINE
     *Gold Medal, Atlanta
A suburban commuter has begun to fantasize about wine, women, and pleasure. He even toys with the idea of how much better it would be if he had followed a life of crime and been punished with imprisonment. The film ends with a morning exodus of men in grey from their suburban homes, dressed not in the grey of flannel suits, but of prison uniforms. Mr. Grey turns to the camera and wails "No-o-o" ... the only word in the film. Produced by Wm. Dean and Robt. Dyke. (HS-Adult)

MR. SHEPARD AND MR. MILNE
     29 min   color   Weston Woods   '73
     *Recognition, Columbus
     *Gold Medal, Atlanta
About the collaboration of Ernest Shepard and A. A. Milne. Tells the story behind their children's books through visits to the English locales of their Pooh stories and poems. Produced in association with E. P. Dutton, publishers, by Andrew Holmes. (College-Adult)

MRS. CASE
     14 1/4 min   BW   Nat. Film Bd.
     *Prize Winner, Canada
     *Award, Conf. on Children
Represents a view of a parent attempting to bring up children in an impoverished area of a big city. She tries to cope with the problems of the single parent, deals with welfare workers, is involved in community affairs, and worries about her medical problems. (College-Adult)

MITOSIS
     24 min   color   Encyc. Brit.   '61
     *First Prize, Italian Society
On the fundamental process of cell division in plant and animal life and the importance of the mitotic process in the growth and maintenance of an organism. Photomicrography shows cell division actually taking place in a living cell. The effects of chemicals and radiation on dividing cells are demonstrated. (HS-College)

THE MOCKING BIRD
     39 min   BW   Macmillan   '62
     *Direction Prize, San Sebastian
A private in the Union Army, standing night guard, sees an indistinct figure and fires. The next day, he goes in search of his victim and finds the body of his twin brother in Confederate uniform. The shock causes the soldier to desert. Directed by Robert Enrico. Based on the short story by Ambrose Bierce. No dialog. (HS-Adult)

MOEBIUS FLIP
>   28 min   color   Pyramid   '69
>   *Golden Eagle, CINE
>   *1st Place, US Industrial
>   *First Place, Day of Visuals

A science-fiction fantasy that employs optical effects, solarized colors, and trick skiers. The world's polarity is suddenly reversed, according to the story-line of this film, and, as a result, skiers find themselves on the opposite side of normal perception. The acrobatic skiers somersault and twist in slow-motion efforts to "flip back" to reality. A Summit Films production. (HS-Adult)

MONASTERY
>   19 3/4 min   BW   Nat. Film Bd.
>   *Award Winner, India

In their monastery in Quebec, the Benedictine monks pursue their life of prayer, service, and self-discipline. In the fields they till the soil and gather the harvest. Then they turn to meditation, study, research, and the artistic work that enriches the life of their nation. (HS-Adult)

MONUMENT TO THE DREAM
>   27 min   color   ACI Films   '63
>   *Golden Eagle, CINE
>   *Blue Ribbon, American/EFLA
>   *Nomination, Academy Award

The Gateway Arch, by architect Eero Saarinen, is a product of modern engineering, erected in St. Louis as a tribute to the pioneers who passed through that city on their westward migration. This film shows how that gateway was planned and built from concepts related to the design of aircraft. Produced by Charles Guggenheim. (HS-Adult)

MOODS OF SURFING
>   15 min   color   Pyramid   '68
>   *Gold Medal, Int. of NY
>   *Silver Medal, Cortina

A sensory experience in which sea, spray, and sun provide the setting for surfers who ride the tide in California and Hawaii. With the grace of ballet dancers, they are lifted on the crests or they tunnel through great walls of water--and stay upright, too. Produced by Jim Freeman and Greg MacGillivray. (Junior HS-Adult)

MORNING ON THE LIÈVRE
>   13 min   color   Encyc. Brit.   '61
>   *Awards: Edinburgh, Boston, and Brussels (Belgium)

A pictorial interpretation, line by line, of Archibald Lampman's poem of the Lièvre River as it wends its way through the autumnal maple forests of Quebec. Produced by the National Film Board of Canada. (Intermediate-Adult)

MOSAIC
>   5 1/2 min   color   Int. Film Bur.   '65

*Awards: New York, Vancouver, Melbourne, and Buenos Aires
Being largely a play on the retina of the eye, this film might be
called an example of cinematic "op" art. It is geometric and non-
literal, making use of rapid fluctuations of matching and contrasting
colors, as well as after-image illusions. The soundtrack was made
by engraving directly on the film surface. Animator: Norman Mc-
Laren, National Film Board of Canada. (HS-College)

MOUNTAIN COMMUNITY OF THE HIMALAYAS
    11 min color Atlantis '64
    *Award, Asian Pacific
    *Honors, Edinburgh
    *Merit Prize, San Francisco
A study of the cultural contributions of the natives of that region,
with explanations of why people live in the mountains, and how they
trade with their neighbors in the lowlands. Produced by J. Michael
Hagopian. (Elem.-Junior HS)

A MOUNTAIN DAY
    9 min color Barr Films '71
    *Golden Eagle, CINE
Follows three young people on horseback as they explore and experience the beauties of their mountain environment. Non-verbal. Produced by Joern Gerdts. (Intermediate-Adult)

THE MOUNTAIN PEOPLE
    24 min color Wombat '74
    *Blue Ribbon, American/EFLA
Designed to reveal the relationship between social conditions and human values, this production documents the way of life of our Appalachian poor who are seen from a different perspective by a team of
English film-makers. They see a people made unique not only by
circumstance but also by pride and strength. Produced by Granada
International TV/United Kingdom. (HS-Adult)

MROFNOC (Conform)
    7 min BW Film Images
    *Award of Merit, Cracow
    *Merit Award, San Francisco
    *Merit Award, Edinburgh
    *1st Prize, Independent Film
An essay on the subject of conformity. A man, alone in a crowd,
finds himself doing the exact opposite of what the others consider
normal, i.e., walking backwards. Surprised and confused, he tries
to go against the crowd, only to realize it's easier to give in and to
start walking backwards himself. Non-verbal. Directed by Josef
Sedelmaier. (Intermediate-Adult)

MULTIPLE MAN
    16 min color McGraw-Hill
    *Grand Trophy, Bogotá
    *Gold Medal, Barcelona
    *Experimental Prize, Montevideo

*Blue Ribbon, American/EFLA ... and other honors
Originally produced in 70mm format for post-Expo '67 presentation,
this film employs a multi-image technique to show how people of all
races and places can stand united and live side-by-side. The titles
are displayed in seven languages. Produced by the National Film
Board of Canada. (Intermediate-Adult)

MULTIPLY AND SUBDUE
    8 min color Pyramid '70
    *Prize, Alpha Cine Lab
    *Merit Award, Bellevue (Wash.)
Designed to encourage viewers to re-evaluate attitudes toward nature.
The Biblical quote, "Be fruitful and multiply, and replenish the earth,
and subdue it," serves as the reference point for discussion on the
problems of pollution. Also of interest for its use of experimental
color techniques by producer Eric L. Hutchinson. (HS-Adult)

MUSCLE: A Study of Integration
    30 min color CRM Films '72
    *Gold Medal, Int. Film & TV
Beginning with an over-view of the three different sets of muscles
in the human body (striated, smooth, and cardiac), the film moves
into a more detailed description of the properties of each muscular
tissue. Includes animated and live-action segments where appropriate. (HS-College)

MUSEUM ... GATEWAY TO PERCEPTION
    16 min color Atlantis '64
    *Award, Edinburgh (Scotland)
A motivational film, designed to increase interest in visiting local
facilities and exploring their resources. Produced by J. Michael
Hagopian. (Elem.-Adult)

MUSIC FOR THE MOVIES
    54 min BW McGraw-Hill '70
    *Series Award, Saturday Review
From the Young People's Concert series, with Leonard Bernstein as
master of ceremonies, narrator, and conductor of the New York
Philharmonic. Produced by CBS-TV. (Intermediate-Adult)

THE MUSIC RACK
    20 min color ACI Films '68
    *Golden Eagle, CINE
The principles of designing and making a music rack, as conceived
by Wendell Castle, artist and craftsperson. His method is shown
from the initial sketch to the final sanding, coating, and polishing.
Produced by the American Crafts Council. (HS-Adult)

MUTINY ON THE BOUNTY
    42 min BW Films Inc. '35
    *Best Picture, Academy Award
A condensed version of the original feature film by MGM Studios,
with Mr. Christian played by Clark Gable, and Capt. Bligh by
Charles Laughton. (HS-Adult)

MY CHILDHOOD
    51 min BW Benchmark '72
    *Best Film, M. L. King, Jr.
    *Blue Ribbon, American/EFLA
    *Golden Eagle, CINE
A study in contrasts: on one extreme is Senator Hubert Humphrey
who enjoyed his boyhood in a South Dakota town; at the other extreme is writer James Baldwin who grew up in the poverty of Harlem. This film is available in two parts, one devoted to each subject. Originally produced for network television. (College-Adult)

MY FINANCIAL CAREER
    6 3/4 min color Sterl. Educ.
    *Award, San Francisco
    *Nomination, Academy Award
    *Award, NY Int.
An animated version of Stephen Leacock's essay on a young man's
first brush with big business. When he tries to open his first bank
account, he is so awed by the institution that nothing he says comes
out right. Produced by the National Film Board of Canada. (HS-
Adult)

MY SON, KEVIN
    24 min color Wombat '74
    *Blue Ribbon, American/EFLA
The subject of this film is one of the 400 children born handicapped
in England as a result of their mothers' use of the untested drug,
thalidomide. Implicit is the question of how government allowed
such hasty access to this "wonder drug," and whether other similar
perils await unsuspecting parents and children. (Senior HS-Adult)

MYSTERY OF TIME
    28 min color Moody Institute
    *Award, Scholastic Teacher
High-speed and time-lapse cameras help viewers to escape their
"time compartments" and to sample the elementary concepts of the
theory of relativity. As a result, yardsticks seem to shrink, clocks
and heartbeats slow down, while the laboratory itself is accelerated
almost to the speed of light. (HS-College)

MYSTERY ON BIRD ISLAND
    57 min BW Sterling Educ. '70
    *Silver Gondola, Venice
Four children organize a campaign to establish a bird-watch station
on a Channel Island wildlife sanctuary, but they meet opposition from
a band of smugglers. Still, all ends well for the forces of good.
Produced by the Children's Film Foundation, Britain. (Ages 7-12)

MYTH OF THE PHARAOHS
    13 min color ACI Films '71
    *Honors, American/EFLA
Animation based on tomb paintings is used in introducing the legend
of the ancient Egyptians. Tells of a Pharaoh's life from conception,

birth, achievements, death, and final judgment before the gods. A study-guide, identifying the gods and goddesses mentioned, is available with the film. (Intermediate-Adult)

NAHANNI
  18 1/2 min   color   McGraw-Hill   '62
  *Awards: Columbus, Berlin, Acapulco
The tale of a man too old to continue trapping, who travels hundreds of miles alone through the Canadian wilderness, searching for a lost gold mine. He fails but returns to try again. National Film Board of Canada. (Intermediate-Adult)

NAICA AND THE SQUIRRELS
  20 min   color   McGraw-Hill   '66
  *First Place, Venice (Child.)
Naica leaves his parents' farm in search of a hen-stealing fox. Armed with an old rifle, Naica heads into the forest with his friend Maricica. They come upon an abandoned hut and discover some squirrels inside. Suddenly, the very fox they wanted appears. His new-found animal friends are now in danger, Naica tries to protect them and, after a series of events blending suspense and humor, the squirrels save themselves. Without narration or dialogue. (Elem.)

THE NAKED EYE
  70 min   BW   McGraw-Hill   '65
  *Nomination, Academy Award
Traces the history of the camera and of photography from the primitive efforts of da Vinci through the pioneer work of Matthew Brady, William Jackson, and Daguerre, to Margaret Bourke-White, Alfred Eisenstadt, Weegee and Edward Weston. Producer: Louis Clyde Stowman. (College-Adult)

NAVAJO GIRL
  20 1/2 min   color   Xerox Films   '73
  *Blue Ribbon, American/EFLA
The realities of tribal life are explored in this story of Cathy Begay who, like generations before her, lives on an Arizona reservation. Her family raises sheep, and it's Cathy's job to help with the care of the young lambs. Produced by Bobwin Associates. (Elem.)

NAVAJO SILVERSMITH
  10 min   color   ACI Films   '60
  *Blue Ribbon, American/EFLA
  *Other Awards: Melbourne, Venice, Montevideo and Sydney
By focusing on a single and sensitive craftsperson this film studies the essence of the Navajo today. Here is a blending of the old with the new, the tribal with the industrial. (Intermediate-HS)

NEGRO KINGDOMS OF AFRICA'S GOLDEN AGE
  16 min   color   Atlantis   '68
  *Merit Award, Landers
  *High Honors, Edinburgh
  *Chris Award, Columbus

Reviews important contributions made by advanced African kingdoms 400 years ago. Examines how centuries of slavery robbed the world of a unique African heritage, and how in our own day Black nations and peoples are looking with pride upon the accomplishments of the past. (Elem. -Adult)

THE NEIGHBORING SHORE
        15 min color Macmillan '59
        *Grand Prize, Venice
The United States is interpreted visually through 100 woodcuts by Antonio Frasconi and selections from Walt Whitman. The result is an overview of our country and its people--with its wealth, its natural beauty, its urban and industrial complexes, and its yet-to-be realized possibilities. Produced by Meyers-Frasconi. (HS-Adult)

NEIGHBORS
        18 min color Int. Film Bur. '52
        *"Oscar," Academy Awards ... and other prizes
A Norman McLaren film employing "pixillation" in which the principles normally used to put drawings or puppets into motion are used to animate actors. The story is about two men who come to blows over a flower that grows where their properties meet. The film has neither dialogue nor narration. National Film Board of Canada. (HS-Adult)

NEW BEAM, LASER
        16 min color Macmillan '66
        *Merit Diploma, A. I. C. S.
        *Award, Montreal
Explanation of the nature and use of the laser beam, one of the most important recent innovations in physics. Produced by Mafilm, Budapest. (HS-Adult)

NEW LIFE FOR A SPANISH FARMER
        18 min color Films Inc. '68
        *Chris Certificate, Columbus
Ramon Cortes makes a difficult decision to take his family from the arid land of his ancestors to an agricultural project. By donkey cart, they travel toward their new home. Cortes' family moves into a government housing unit. He goes to classes where modern farming techniques are taught. Officials bring him a new cart and implements, and he goes to the farmland allocated to him. Cortes and his son begin clearing the land, preparing for the new life ahead. Produced by Germany's Institut für Film und Bild. (Intermediate-Adult)

N. Y. , N. Y.
        16 min color Pyramid '57
        *Honors: Cannes, London, Edinburgh and the American Film
                 Festival
New York is seen as a wondrously visual Babylon, interpreted by serial prisms, fisheye lenses, fast and slow-motion--apparently all materializing out of space. Directed by Francis Thompson. (HS-Adult)

THE NEWBORN CALF
11 min color Encyc. Brit. '70
*Chris Certificate, Columbus
Reveals the birth and early development of a calf in the most natural way possible--just as it happens. The absence of narration
encourages viewers to interpret the film more freely and to react
more personally. Teachers should preview this film to determine
if its subject matter is appropriate to their students. Showing the
film in segments is recommended for a primary audience. (Elem. -
Adult)

NIGERIA--Problems of Nation Building (Revised)
21 min color Atlantis '67
*Chris Award, Columbus
An appraisal of nationalism and tribalism in Africa, particularly in
Nigeria. Useful in understanding the underlying forces in tropical
Africa's political situation. (Junior HS-Adult)

NIGHT PEOPLE'S DAY
11 min color FilmFair '71
*Silver Medal, Atlanta
*Merit Award, Philadelphia
*Merit Award, Landers
*Golden Eagle, CINE
While most of the city sleeps, much activity continues. Among the
"night people" there is a camaraderie that grows out of an awareness that theirs is a special kind of work. This film explores the
city at night, with emphasis on people and their occupations. The
soundtrack recreates, with voices and sound effects, the myriad
noises of the city and its activities. Night people tell why they pre-
fer to work at night. Film-maker: Bob Kurtz. (Elem. -HS)

NIKO--Boy of Greece
21 min color ACI Films '68
*Blue Ribbon, American/EFLA
*Golden Eagle, CINE
*Honors, Brussels (Belgium)
*Award, Teheran (Iran)
Niko's life is simple: when he is grown, he will be a fisherman like
his father. On a feast day, however, Niko and a friend are trapped
by a sudden storm. They are rescued by fishermen and realize that
learning the dangers of the sea is an important part of growing up
on an island. With authentic music, the film provides exposure to
the architecture, topography, industries and skills of an island people. Film-maker: Stelios Roccos. (Intermediate-Adult)

1964
54 min color McGraw-Hill
*Nat. Mass Media Award, Edison
*Nat. School Bell Award, NEA
Explores the great power of the United States and her complex problems. The significance of obsolescence--human as well as mechani-
cal--is brought home in an exploration of the challenges of automation,

old age, unemployment, equal opportunity, and leisure time. Produced by ABC Television. (College-Adult)

NO EXPECTATIONS
    57 min color New Film Co. '72
    *Award, Univ. of Florida
    *Award, Atlanta
A documentary study of four heroin addicts and their struggle within
the world of hard drugs. Film-maker: Christopher Knight. (HS-
Adult)

NO HIDING PLACE
    51 min BW Carousel '63
    *Blue Ribbon, American/EFLA
From the "East Side/West Side" TV series. Drama of a Black
family that has moved into an all-White suburb, and the hostility it
engenders. A housewife, herself a White Southerner, strikes a note
of courage as she urges her husband to stand fast when some of her
neighbors are panicked into selling their homes. (With George C.
Scott.) (College-Adult)

NO LIES
    16 min color Phoenix Films '73
    *Golden Eagle, CINE
A dramatic fiction about the ordeals that a woman who has been
raped must undergo with the police, her doctor, her friends, and
her inner self. Also available in 35mm. Film-maker: Mitchell
W. Block. (College-Adult)

From NO LIES (Phoenix Films, Inc.)

NO MAN IS AN ISLAND
    11 min   color   Dana Productions   '72
    *Golden Eagle, CINE
The poem by John Donne (1571-1631) is narrated by Orson Welles,
set to music, and sung by Andrea who composed and arranged the
score.   Examines the ways man relates to man in mutual involvement and need. Film-maker: Albert Saparoff. (Elem. -Adult)

NO REASON TO STAY
    29 min   BW   Films Inc.   '66
    *Award of Merit, Landers
    *Chris Certificate, Columbus
    *Merit Diploma, Melbourne
    *Blue Ribbon, American/EFLA
High school student Christopher Wood gets good grades because, as
Chris says, "I can memorize."   But what he is forced to memorize
has no relevancy to the issues and technological changes of his day.
The mechanized teaching, rigidity of subject matter, and dullness of
presentation drive Chris to a world of daydreams.   He knows that
as a dropout he will not easily find employment--but school gives
Chris "no reason to stay." (College-Adult)

NOBODY GOES THERE: Ellis Island
    9 min   BW   ACI Films   '69
    *Award, Oberhausen (German)
A pictorial essay on the immigration station that was the gateway to
the New World for 30 million Europeans.   Still and live-action photography create a memorial to the now abandoned island in New York
Bay. Film-maker: Joan Horvath. (Intermediate-Adult)

NOBODY WAVED GOODBYE
    80 min   BW   Macmillan   '64
    *Youth Award, National Catholic
    *Selznick Medal, San Francisco
Modern youth in conflict with the standards of parents and middle
class society.   Peter and Julie, "affluent delinquents," in their first
transgressions against law and convention, are searching for direction in a world of change.   The semi-documentary technique used by
Roman Kroitor and Don Owen--location shooting, natural sound,
semi-improvised dialog--contributes to the film's sense of reality.
Directed by Don Owen, National Film Board of Canada. (HS-Adult)

NORTH WITH THE SPRING
    52 min   color   Xerox Films   '69
    *Silver Medal, Atlanta
Focuses on the 17,000 mile journey of migratory birds from the
Florida Everglades to the Canadian Arctic.   With this northward re-
turn begins their reproductive cycle, which the camera observes in
a Tennessee mountain stream.   From the series entitled "We Need
Each Other." Produced by Hobel-Leiterman, Ltd. (College-Adult)

A NORWEGIAN FJORD
    13 min   color   Films Inc.   '68
    *Chris Certificate, Columbus

Eric, a teenage Norwegian, lives at Hardanger-Fjord. High in the mountains are dairy farmers, who transport milk in cans connected to a cable. The milk is picked up by a farmers' cooperative. On the other side of the fjord is a huge power station and aluminum factory. What does the future hold for a boy living in a small community? Eric can go into farming, work in the plant or go to college. His counterparts around the world face the same problem. Produced by the Institut für Film und Bild, Germany. (Intermediate-Adult)

NOT ME
        51 min   BW   McGraw-Hill   '71
        *1st Prize, Nat. Visual
The agonizing journey of a thirteen-year-old drug addict--from the forces that compel him to "give it a try," to his ultimate addiction and fatal overdose. Shows how home, neighborhood, friends, and individual needs bring about the needless ending of a young life. Produced by Bartley and Savage. (College-Adult)

THE NOT-SO-SOLID EARTH
        30 min   color   Time-Life   '72
        *Blue Ribbon, American/EFLA
An examination of the recent discovery that continents move and oceans shift. From the "Life Around Us" series, this film shows how scientists gather and analyze supporting data for their theory. (HS-College)

NOT THE GIANT ... NOR THE DWARF
        57 min   color   Films Inc.   '71
        *Award Winner, Chicago
        *"Emmy" Award, Nat. Academy
Few people who turn to drugs know how difficult it is to turn away. Gateway House, a rehabilitation center, is a place where addicts can try. This five-month study looks at the regimen that addicts must endure while there, and their hopes for a normal life. Through positive rehabilitation, the addict becomes "neither the giant of his dreams, nor the dwarf of his fears." Produced by WMAQ-TV Chicago. (College-Adult)

NOTE FROM ABOVE
        2 min   color   Mass Media   '70
        *Award, Oberhausen (Germany)
        *Merit Certificate, Philadelphia
Ostensibly a take-off on the conventional "religious" film, this animation is a subtle dig at legalism and literalism. A Sinai cloud hovers while outstretched hands struggle to catch the notes the divine presence is dropping. Several of these notes are picked up and obeyed, including one that reads "Thou shalt kill." Shots are exchanged before the next note, which reads, "The last note should have read: 'Thou shalt not kill.' Sorry--my mistake!" But there's no one left to read it. Film-maker: Derek Phillips. (HS-Adult)

NOTES ON A TRIANGLE
     5 min   color   Int. Film Bur.   '67
     *Awards: London, Teheran, Buenos Aires, Melbourne
This animation of a single geometric form may interest the artist
and the mathemetician.   A white triangle divides into three parts
that are red, yellow and blue.   Further divisions produce many complex designs, all accompanied by appropriate music.   Finally, the
forms return to the basic triangle and the colors disappear.   Produced by R. Jodoin, National Film Board of Canada.   (HS-Adult)

NOTHING BUT A MAN
     92 min   BW   Macmillan   '64
     *Award, Council of Churches
     *Prix San Giorgio, Venice
     *City of Venice Prize, Venice
Drama of the struggle of a Southern Black and his wife in a society
hostile to them.   A railway worker gives up a good job to settle
down and marry a preacher's daughter, a schoolteacher.   His adjustment to the universal problems of supporting a family becomes
especially difficult because the place is Alabama in 1960, and the
man refuses to play the expected "Negro" role.   Ivan Dixon and
Abbey Lincoln play the leading roles.   Producer-Director: Roemer
& Young.   (HS-Adult)

NOVEMBER
     10 min   color   McGraw-Hill
     *Special Prize, Melbourne
Impressions of the month when the ripe fullness of the Canadian autumn wilts and the earth seems to settle into brooding calm.   This
is a cine-poem, reflecting the moods of November and the muted
tones of the dying season.   Produced by the National Film Board of
Canada.   (Intermediate-Adult)

NOW IS THE TIME
     36 min   BW   Carousel   '67
     *Golden Medallion, Christians & Jews
     *"Emmy," Nat. Academy
A warning that the black American is ready for first-class citizen-
ship.   The film relates his emergence from the pagan slave state of
300 years ago to the present.   Two of America's finest actors, Ruby
Dee and Ossie Davis, lend stature to the poetry of Langston Hughes
and Countee Cullee, speeches by Malcolm X and Stokely Carmichael,
and the writings of James Baldwin.   Produced by WCAU-TV, Philadelphia.   (Senior HS-Adult)

NUBIA 64 (Saving the Temples of Ancient Egypt)
     40 min   color   Roland Films
     *Grand Prix, Cannes
The amalgamation of earthly ruler and deity is nowhere more dra-
matically attempted than in the colossal statues and temples of ancient Egypt.   This film covers the story of the salvation of the
priceless monuments of Abu Simbel and other temples in danger of
being submerged by the damming of the Nile.   Director: Robert
Genot.   (College-Adult)

NAZURI: East Africa
      30 min color Pyramid '70
      *Gold Medal, Atlanta
      *Golden Eagle, CINE
      *Award, US Industrial
With only occasional narration, this film captures the moods, life
styles, and harmonies of the nations of Kenya, Uganda and Tanzania.
Shown are game parks, wood sculptors, hunting expeditions, the
White Nile, Mt. Kilimanjaro, Murchison Falls, the Wakoma Dancers,
Zanzibar, Dar es Salaam and modern Nairobi. Produced by Summit
Films. (Intermediate-Adult)

OCCURRENCE AT OWL CREEK BRIDGE
      27 min BW McGraw-Hill '56
      *Grand Prix, Cannes
      *Winner, Academy Award
This film is a visual interpretation of the Ambrose Bierce short
story of a Civil War episode and the pre-death interval of a captured
spy. Presented over national TV as part of Rod Serling's original
"Twilight Zone" series. Directed by Robert Enrico. (HS-Adult)

OCTOPUS HUNT
      17 min color Nat. Film Bd.
      *Award Winner, Rome
A voyage to the depths of the Pacific, into the domain of the deep-
sea diver and the creatures that are his quest. This film is a report of a zoological expedition to capture octopus and wolf eel for
the Vancouver aquarium. The divers themselves describe the underwater action. (HS-Adult)

OF PICKS, SHOVELS, AND WORDS
      27 1/2 min color Graph. Curric. '69
      *Chris Statuette, Columbus
Five thousand years ago, Egypt was moving millions of tons of stone
to build a pyramid for their Pharaoh. Hidden beneath history are
places, instruments, and people; the Dead Sea Scrolls, Babylon and
Persepolis; and treasures buried for centuries. This film tries to
uncover these mysteries. (Intermediate-HS)

OH, FREEDOM!
      28 min color Sterling Educ. '71
      *Gold Award, Int. Film & TV
To understand earlier Civil Rights struggles is to appreciate today's
black militancy. This film depicts the triumphs and tragedies of a
movement that shaped the struggle for black equality in America, and
that helped advance the cause for all oppressed Americans, too.
(HS-Adult)

OH! WOODSTOCK!
      26 min color Films Inc. '69
      *"Emmy," Nat. Academy
The same segment of the film of the Woodstock Rock Festival is
used twice in this piece about the generation gap. In the first seg-

ment, five youths comment on the festival; in the second, five adults pass judgment on the same event. Their combined views provide many contrasts for discussion on perception. Produced by WNBC-TV. (HS-Adult)

OIL! SPOIL!
    17 min   color   Macmillan   '70
    *Golden Eagle, CINE
Air pollution sits like a cloud over our land and, through it all, the oil pumps, crouching like giant mosquitoes on the landscape, drill away in their probe for oil. Their search is climaxed by a huge spill. Citizens try to patch up the disaster with pitifully inadequate bundles of straw. Meanwhile, in the animal world, sea birds with plumage matted horribly by oil run in panic, doomed because unable to fly. Produced for the Sierra Club. (Intermediate-Adult)

OLD FASHIONED WOMAN
    49 min   color   Films Inc.   '74
    *Blue Ribbon, American/EFLA
A portrait of the film-maker's New England grandmother, intercutting between her present attitudes and the events of her past, as recreated through her photo album. This review covers 86 years of positive living in the course of personal and social upheaval. Film-maker: Martha Coolidge. (College-Adult)

THE OLD ORDER AMISH
    32 min   color   Andy Olenyik
    *Recommended, ALA
    *Award, Oberhausen
    *Honors, Florence
A documentary on the distinctive Amish folk who have turned their backs on the material world and its "progress" and have followed instead the scriptural virtues of humility, simplicity, and hard work. Includes their Amish songs and conversational dialect. Produced by Vincent Tortora. (HS-Adult)

OMEGA
    13 min   color   Pyramid   '70
    *Silver Hugo, Chicago
    *Silver Phoenix, Atlanta
Deals with the end of man on earth and with his liberation from worldly bounds. He roams the universe at will but, unlike in 2001: A Space Odyssey, there is no extra-terrestrial intelligence to lend a hand. A conglomeration of special effects. Film-maker: Donald Fox. (HS-Adult)

ON THE BOWERY
    65 min   BW   Impact Films   '56
    *Honors, Festival dei Popoli
    *Grand Prize, Venice
    *Award, Br. Film Academy
    *Gold Medal, Univ. of Paris
    *Nomination, Academy Award ... and many other honors

The realities of New York's skid row. Men there, paralyzed by
drink and violence, subsist in a prolonged state of aimlessness.
Filmed resourcefully in a candid style, this documentary retains the
language of the street. Preview before utilizing. Produced by
Lionel Rogosin. (College-Adult)

ON THE TWELFTH DAY
    22 min   color   Films Inc.   '64
    *Award, Venice (Italy)
An enactment of the traditional English folksong in which Truelove
brings his lady an assortment of gifts on each of the 12 days of
Christmas. The ageless mood of the song is enhanced by a balloon
escape from the bedlam of lively gifts. Produced by RTV International, Inc. (Elem.-Adult)

ONCE THERE WERE BLUEBIRDS
    5 min   color   FilmFair   '71
    *Merit Award, Landers
This animation with rhymed narration begins with scenes of bluebirds, butterflies, meadows, and beaches. Then it asks, "Where
have they gone?" The answer is seen in the form of gushing oil
wells and frantic freeway traffic. Based on the book by Bill Martin,
Jr. Produced by Dick Van Benthem. (Elem.-Adult)

ONE DAY'S POISON
    29 1/2 min   BW   Nat. Film Bd.
    *Canadian Film Award
About the poison-control centers at children's hospitals. Several incidents illustrate the poisonings there and how the center deals with
them. The facts support one doctor's claim that poisoning kills
more children under six than all infectious diseases combined. (College-Adult)

ONE-EYED MEN ARE KINGS
    15 min   color   McGraw-Hill   '73
    *Blue Ribbon, American/EFLA
A Parisian, forced to walk his mother's dog, decides to have some
fun by masquerading as a blind man. This mischief sets off a series of other misadventures that he hadn't counted on. A non-verbal,
live-action production directed by Edmond Séchan. (HS-Adult)

111th STREET
    32 min   BW   Macmillan   '62
    *Golden Eagle, CINE
How does a Youth Board worker make contact with a teenage gang?
In this semidocumentary of a typical gang in New York's upper East
Side, we see the difficulties before the first small breakthrough to
communication. A presentation-guide is available. Produced by
Arnold Federbush. (HS-Adult)

ONE LITTLE INDIAN
    16 min   color   Int. Film Bur.
    *Award, Nat. Safety Council

This puppet film points out traffic safety principles through the story of an Indian boy's first visit to a big city. Only the prompt help of some friendly grown-ups keeps him from danger; from them he passes on some safety precautions to others. Produced by the National Film Board of Canada. (Elem.)

ONE MAN'S OPINION
      5 1/2 min BW Nat. Film Bd.
      *Award, Kootenay (Br. Col.)
      *Prize, Film Council of America
How one person's judgment might run counter to majority opinion. In a campaign to raise funds for a school project, one student withholds support because of high-pressure methods. The open-ended format of the production is designed to encourage discussion. (Junior-Senior HS)

ONE OF THEM IS BRETT
      30 min BW McGraw-Hill '65
      *Golden Dragon Award, Cracow
This documentary portrays the plight of a four-year-old boy born without arms, a defect traceable to the fact that his mother took Thalidomide during pregnancy. The film looks at Brett's life and his family's, and explores their chances for normality in society. Produced by Derrick Knight. (College-Adult)

OOPS, I MADE A MISTAKE!
      4 min color Encyc. Brit. '73
      *Bronze Medal, Int. Film & TV
Sure, it's disappointing to do something wrong but figure out what caused the error, forget about it for a while, then try to do better the next time. That's one of the messages for youngsters in the Most Important Person series. Produced by Sutherland Learning Associates. (Primary)

OP HOP - HOP OP
      3 1/2 min BW Nat. Film Bd.
      *Awards: Montreal and Melbourne
A handmade experiment in intermittent animation. The images are etched onto the film as a group of twenty-four visuals, all non-representational. They arrange and re-arrange themselves in diverse combinations, resulting in a varied pattern of sound and image with its own rhythm for eye and ear together. Animated by Norman McLaren for the National Film Board of Canada. (HS-College)

OPEN SPACE
      11 min color ACI Films '70
      *Chris Award, Columbus
Contrasts the beauty of nature with the squalor of man's intrusions. Shown is suburban sprawl as it reaches farther and farther into woodlands, transforming open spaces into pits of traffic, noise, and tension. Raises questions for discussion about the value of "improvements." Produced by Communico Films. (Intermediate-Adult)

OPERA CORDIS
        10 min   color   McGraw-Hill   '70
        *Romanian Award, Mamaia
        *Golden Medal, Atlanta
        *Award, Bergamo (Italy)
A man goes through a veritable ritual of antics in trying to capture,
remove, and open the throbbing heart of a woman asleep next to
him. When he finally manages to open the heart, he finds ... another man inside! Animated by Dusan Vukotic for Zagreb Film,
Yugoslavia. (College-Adult)

OPTIONS
        8 min   color   Films Inc.   '68
        *Award, San Francisco
        *Silver Certificate, Chicago
        *Award, Ann Arbor (Mich.)
On the premise that art should be an experience, the Museum of
Contemporary Art put together a show to intensify the experience of
viewing. This was attempted by displaying art that demanded some
involvement from spectators. Beyond an introductory message, no
other indication of purpose is given. Produced by Jerry Aronson
and Howard Sturges. (College-Adult)

OPUS
        29 min   color   Pyramid   '67
        *Silver Medal, Argentina
        *First Prize, United Nations
        *First Prize, Barcelona
Impressions of British art and culture in four parts. Opens with a
sculptor working on aluminum, then goes on to new architecture,
youth fashions, and an "action" painter. The second part deals with
theatre. The third starts with Francis Bacon's paintings and ends
with modern jewelry. The final segment opens with ballet and
closes with the sculptures of Henry Moore. Produced by Don Levy
for the Central Office of Information, London. (College-Adult)

OPUS OP
        20 1/2 min   color   BFA Educ. Media   '67
        *Golden Eagle, CINE
The New York Joffrey Ballet stages an experiment in interpretive
dance and rock music. This documentary captures the highlights of
their premiere performance. To a soundtrack ranging from raucous
to melodic, young dancers act out their exuberance while the camera
interlaces the stage action with audience reaction. Produced by
King Screen. (HS-Adult)

ORANGE AND BLUE
        15 min   color   McGraw-Hill   '61
        *Golden Eagle, CINE
A journey through a junk yard, made as an adventure of two bouncing balls that explore and play like children oblivious of the squalor
around them. The large balls--one orange, the other blue--are
symbolic of childhood, each expressing curiosity, adventurousness,

timidity, coyness, and joy.   Produced by Peter and Clare Chermayeff.   (Intermediate-Adult)

THE ORANGE AND THE GREEN
 21 min   color   Films Inc.   '69
 *Award, National Press
Bigotry, demagoguery, economic rivalry, and destruction are all
part of the upheaval in Ulster, the Protestant section of Northern
Ireland.   The Roman Catholic minority there accuses the other two-
thirds of discrimination, and the Catholics, in turn, have created a
separate culture for themselves.   This documentary probes the hatred between factions and provides an example of the patterns of
prejudice.   Produced by NBC News.   (HS-Adult)

THE ORIGINS OF WEATHER
 12 1/4 min   color   Encyc. Brit.   '64
 *Chris Award, Columbus
 *Award, La Plata (Argentina)
From the vantage point of outer space, this animated and live-action
film illustrates the factors that produce the climates of earth.   It
also shows the dynamic heat exchange (the effect of the sun's heat
on moving air) and the weather that results.   Made by the National
Film Board of Canada.   (Intermediate-HS)

THE OROZCO MURALS: Quetzalcoatl
 23 min   color   Macmillan   '61
 *Music Citation, Boston
These murals were painted at Dartmouth College in 1934 and are considered one of the most important frescoes in the U.S.A. because
they embody the legend and social comment characteristic of Orozco
himself.   This work is based on the Aztec myth of Quetzalcoatl, the
white messiah who supposedly bestowed his arts on civilization, and
then left when his own people failed him.   Produced by Robert Canton.   (HS-Adult)

OUR COUNTRY'S EMBLEM
 11 min   color   Coronet
 *Award, Freedoms Foundation
Children can learn from this film why our country has an emblem
and what its elements mean.   By constructing its own model of the
Great Seal, a class might discover more about each symbol and
about the design itself.   (Intermediate)

OUR LIVING DECLARATION OF INDEPENDENCE
 16 min   color   Coronet
 *Award, Freedoms Foundation
Freedom, rights, obligations, the pursuit of happiness--these terms
introduce the theme that the Declaration ought not be a dead document but an active political guide worthy of enforcement.   The story
of an immigrant family dramatizes some of the principles stated.
(Intermediate-Junior HS)

OUR POISONED WORLD: The Human Race Is Losing
    30 min   color   Time-Life   '72
    *Award, duPont-Columbia
Shows why we're losing out against pesticides, noise, and industrial
pollution of our air and water.   One example given is a stream in
Kalamazoo, Michigan.   Its upper end is clean enough for swimming
but the lower end is little more than an open sewer for a local paper company.   Produced by WOOD-TV.   (HS-Adult)

OVER THE ANDES IN ECUADOR
    18 min   color   Films Inc.   '68
    *Chris Certificate, Columbus
A journey with a crate of machine parts takes viewers from the port
of Guayaquil to the capital city of Quito, then over the mountains and
across the jungles to a village near the headwaters of the Amazon.
Modes of transport include the train and plane, the latter utilized in
returning a sick woman to the hospital in Quito.   Produced by the
Institut für Film und Bild.   (Intermediate-Adult)

OVER THERE, 1914-1918
    90 min   BW   McGraw-Hill   '63
    *Nomination, Academy Awards
An historic record of World War I, compiled from newsreels, army
films, and previously suppressed footage.   Scenes include great battles, civilian hardships, the signing of the Versailles Treaty, and
the symptoms of early Nazism.   Produced by Jean Aurel.   (College-
Adult)

OVERCOMING RESISTANCE TO CHANGE
    30 min   color   Roundtable
    *Merit Award, NAM Institute
Teaches supervisors to prevent and eliminate objections and to gain
cooperation during transitional periods.   Demonstrates how to handle
resistance by opening up the channels of communication, developing
participation, and permitting the ventilation of feeling.   (College-
Adult)

THE OWL AND THE LEMMING
    7 min   color   ACI Films   '73
    *Award, Teheran (Itan)
    *Honors, American/EFLA
An example of Eskimo art and folklore.   Sealskin puppets are used
against backgrounds also created by Eskimo artists as their own way
of retelling their ageless tale of how the clever lemming escaped the
hungry owl by flattery.   Produced by the National Film Board of
Canada.   (Elem.)

PADDINGTON LACE
    24 min   color   Australia   '71
    *Gold Camera, US Industrial
A light-hearted story about two young people living together in Paddington, Sydney's equivalent of New York's Greenwich Village.   A
dilemma of opposing moral values--with a happy ending.   Produced
by the Commonwealth Film Unit.   (College-Adult)

PADDLE TO THE SEA
28 min   color   McGraw-Hill   '66
*Winner, Salerno (Italy)
*Award, Philadelphia
*Nomination, Academy Award
A children's odyssey that follows an Indian boy's handcarved toy canoe from Canada's northern forest downstream through the Great Lakes and the St. Lawrence River to the distant ocean.   Its adventures are many along this journey: it views wildlife; it plunges from the heights of the Niagara Cataract; it witnesses the tragedy of industrial pollution; it struggles but, by luck or kindness, the toy canoe makes its way to the Atlantic.   Produced by William Mason, National Film Board of Canada.   (Intermediate)

THE PAIN OF SILENCE
13 min   color   Mod. Learning   '70
*Golden Eagle, CINE
The personal concern of a teenage girl who suspects she has contracted a venereal disease.   This film elaborates on the mental process she goes through in deciding whether to get treatment.   It does not deal with the sexual or clinical aspects of the problem.   Producer: George Oprean.   (HS-College)

PAINTING AND DRAWING WITH EXPRESSION
13 1/2 min   color   Oxford Films   '70
*Award Winner, Columbus
Basic techniques for achieving expression are demonstrated, such as the use of line, shape, color, and exaggeration to create moods and give desired impressions.   Produced by Walter Soul.   (HS-College)

PANDORA'S BOX
7 1/2 min   color   Perspective '73
*Award, Ann Arbor (Mich.)
*Animation Prize, Cannes
In animated line-drawings, a large box rotates and changes into a variety of shapes.   Suddenly a door on the box opens and reveals a speeded-up view of a highway and city streets.   Then the box becomes the center of zooming planes, TV commercial spots, snarling animals, and even silent movie scenes ... at which point the film "runs out" and goes blank.   (HS-Adult)

PAPER CONSTRUCTION
15 min   color   ACI Films   '67
*Honors, American/EFLA
Presents a variety of possibilities for working with a universally available material.   Stressing the importance of imagination, the film demonstrates basic techniques of folding, cutting, and scoring. It also shows how these can be combined to produce many different designs.   Film-maker: Stelios Roccos.   (Intermediate-Adult)

PAPIER MACHE
15 min   color   ACI Films   '67
*Award of Merit, Landers
*Golden Eagle, CINE

*Honors, American/EFLA

Demonstrates the advantages of a medium that allows students to work in three-dimensions. The film depicts each step of the process, and shows the potential of the medium. Producer: Stelios Roccos. (Intermediate-Adult)

PARIS 1900
      81 min BW Macmillan
      *Prix Louis Delluc, French Film
      *Year's 10 Best, Nat. Board

Paris from the turn of the century to the beginning of World War I, recreated from old French newsreels, theater programs, and early silent movies. Includes rare shots of Renoir, Rodin, Matisse, Tolstoy, Gide, Valéry, Sarah Bernhardt, Monet, Rostand, Melba, Caruso, Chevalier, Mary Garden, Andrew Carnegie, and Buffalo Bill (almost everyone who was anyone came to Paris!). Directed by Nicole Vedres. (College-Adult)

THE PARK
      7 min color ACI Films '70
      *Silver Medal, Int. Film & TV
      *Chris Award, Columbus

Within most cities there are islands of nature that provide a measure of the primordium not found in the urban sprawl. These islands are the parks. Visuals combine with a narrative from Thoreau for a portrait of the city man's retreat. The film's mood changes with the seasons. A Communico Film production. (Intermediate-Adult)

PARKINSON'S LAW
      7 min BW Mass Media '70
      *Merit Certificate, Philadelphia

A man working diligently at a lathe has managers, and managers managing the managers, who are surrounded by clerks, bookkeepers, statisticians, and stenographers. Through miniaturization, multiple images, and other special effects, the man at the lathe is pushed completely out of the picture frame as the organization, meant only to be an adjunct to production, becomes both the end and the means. Created by Suvisan Covjek for Zagreb Films. (HS-Adult)

PAS DE DEUX
      14 min BW Learn. Corp. '68
      *Chris Statuette, Columbus
      *Emily Award, American/EFLA
      *Merit Award, Landers
      *Nomination, Academy Award

Through optical printing and stroboscopic effects, Norman McLaren takes a simple pas de deux and enlarges it into a cinematic and dance experience. Multiple images of balletic movement suggest the mystery of man and woman reaching out to one another. The creation of Norman McLaren. Produced by the National Film Board of Canada. (HS-Adult)

PASSING DAYS
    10 min color McGraw-Hill '70
    *Grand Prize, Oberhausen
An animated film about a man prevented from leading his simple life
by the strange people and forces that enter his world. The protago-
nist's conflicts reflect the existential absurdities of our own attempts
to achieve an unfettered life style. Produced by Zagreb Films,
Yugoslavia. A Contemporary Films release. (HS-Adult)

PASSION FOR LIFE (also known as SCHOOL OF LIFE)
    85 min BW Macmillan
    *Citation, Educational Writers
    *Citation, Parents Magazine ... and many other endorsements
The hero of the film is a courageous teacher with humor and faith
who creatively guides his pupils. Through them he helps enrich the
lives of the people in the community. French dialog with English
subtitles. Director: Jean Paul LaChanois. (College-Adult)

PATRICK
    7 min color Weston Woods '72
    *Gold Medal, Atlanta
    *Bronze Plaque, Columbus
Patrick sets out for the town marketplace, searching for a fiddle.
He buys one from a junkman. With his buoyant music, the lanky
fiddler imbues every leaf and creature in the countryside with color
and movement. Animated by Quentin Blake (Walck). Adapted and
directed by Gene Deitch. (Elem.)

PATTERNS
    6 min color Walt Disney
    *Award, Salerno (Italy)
    *Amateur Medal, Cannes
    *Honors, Photo Society
    *Silver Medal, Cannes Amateur
    *Golden Eagle, CINE
There is no need for narration as the photographer captures a series of intricate reflections that present the beauty and serenity of
nature supported by a musical score. A Trend production. (Intermediate-Adult)

PAUL BUNYAN
    11 min color BFA Educ. Media
    *Chris Statuette, Columbus
The tall tales of the work giant of the timber industry. We follow
Paul's adventures from his first logging job in Maine, then on to the
Dakotas where he digs the Mississippi River as a log-run, while his
logging crew lives through the winter of the blue snow. In the North
Woods, Paul gets tired and lets his ax drag, creating the Grand
Canyon. (Intermediate-Junior HS)

PEARY AND HENSON: North to the Pole
    15 min color McGraw-Hill '69
    *Chris Statuette, Columbus

A story of two men whose determination led them to accomplish a
feat deemed impossible for three hundred years. Robert Peary and
Matthew Henson (the black man whose accomplishments have only
lately been recognized) arrived at the North Pole where no man had
stood before. (Intermediate-Adult)

PELICAN ISLAND
     28 min   color   A-V Explorations   '69
     *Golden Eagle, CINE
Reveals pelicans' physical characteristics, behavior patterns, and
methods of adapting to environment. Stresses wildlife conservation,
develops the ecological relationship of life on the island, and describes the fight for survival. Film-maker: Bob Davidson. (HS-
Adult)

PEOPLE AND PARTICLES
     28 min   BW   BFA Educ. Media
     *Golden Eagle, CINE
A cinema-verité documentary that spans the two-and-a-half-year
period during which students and faculty worked together at the Cam-
bridge (Mass.) Electron Accelerator on a frontiers problem in particle physics. Produced by Project Physics at MIT. (Senior HS-
College)

PEOPLE MIGHT LAUGH AT US
     9 min   color   Nat. Film Bd.
     *Canadian Film Award
On a reserve in Quebec, Micmac Indian children make birds and
dolls of brightly colored paper that they hang in trees. But they are
reluctant that visitors should see them, claiming, "People might
laugh at us." The film was produced without narration. Background
music supplies the mood. (Intermediate-Adult)

THE PEOPLE SHOP
     18 min   color   Aspect IV   '71
     *Golden Eagle, CINE
Using a simulated documentary style, this film covers facilities of
a hospital including Emergency, Labs, X-ray, Surgery, Baby Care,
Internship, Food Service, and Volunteer Services. A teenage girl
comes in by ambulance, has her leg x-rayed and a cast applied, and
goes home with crutches. Twelve-year-old Mike is admitted with a
stomach ache, has his appendix removed, and later leaves for home,
cheerful and healthy. Discussion guide is available. (Elem.)

THE PERCEPTION OF ORIENTATION
     37 1/4 min   color   Nat. Film Bd.
     *Canadian Film Award
A training film for personnel of the Royal Canadian Air Force, illus-
trating how senses can be affected by stimuli peculiar to flight, how
loss of orientation occurs, and how to correct for disorientation.
Produced for Department of National Defence, Canada. (College-
Adult)

THE PERILS OF PRISCILLA
    16 1/2 min color Churchill '69
    *Gold Medal, Atlanta
    *Silver Award, Venice
    *Bronze Plaque, Int. Film & TV
    *Chris Award, Columbus
From the viewpoint of a cat, getting food and finding a quiet corner
become frightening adventures under the feet of a busy family.
When "Priscilla" becomes lost in the city, viewers share her en-
counters with dogs and cars and unpredictable humans. Non-verbal.
A Dimension Film. (Elem. -Adult)

PERU: Inca Heritage
    17 min color ACI Films '70
    *Chris Award, Columbus
In the 16th century, gold-hungry Spaniards came to the Andes and
destroyed the magnificent Inca culture. Today, majestic ruins and
the Quencha Indians are all that remain. Against the rubble of the
original Inca architecture, this film explores the contemporary life
of Peruvian Indians. It shows architecture in harmony with nature.
A Hartley Productions Film. (HS-Adult)

A PHANTASY
    8 min color Int. Film Bur. '52
    *Awards: Boston, Canada, and Venice
A surrealistic abstraction of pastel drawings and cut-out animation,
with saxophone music and synthetic sound by Maurice Blackburn.
Animated by Norman McLaren, National Film Board of Canada. (HS-
Adult)

PHOEBE: Story of a Premarital Pregnancy
    28 min BW McGraw-Hill '65
    *Grand Prix, Montreal
The mental and emotional reactions of Phoebe, a teenager, on the
day she discovers she is pregnant. Reveals her apprehension, and
depicts her thoughts about telling her parents, her boy friend, and
the school authorities. Helps students to understand some of the
rational and emotional aspects of premarital pregnancy, particularly
as they affect the female. Produced by the National Film Board of
Canada. (HS-College)

THE PHYSICISTS: Playing Dice with the Universe
    22 min color Document Associates '71
    *Gold Medal, Atlanta
Leading scientists speculate about life on other planets, explain the
cyclotron, probe the nature of matter, and experiment with the control of time itself. One of a series of 25 films on the future.
(Senior HS-College)

PICASSO IS 90
    51 min color Carousel '72
    *Red Ribbon, American/EFLA
Encompasses a lifetime of work of one of the great artists of our

From PICASSO IS 90 (Carousel Films, Inc.)

time. It traces his life from childhood into old age, with a retrospective of his paintings and sculpture filmed on location at the Pushkin Museum in Moscow, the Hermitage in Leningrad, the Museum of Modern Art and the Metropolitan Museum in New York. A CBS-TV News production. (College-Adult)

PICASSO - Romancero du Picador
    13 min BW Roland
    *Grand Prix, Vancouver
    *Quality Award, French National
To Picasso, the spectacle of the bull fight is composed of many elements. In pen and wash drawings, he focused attention on the picador, whose task is to tire and bleed the bull. Having completed an essential but graceless part of the corrida, the picador must look outside the arena for his plaudits. There, for a time, he basks in the glory of the matador. Producer: Les Productions Tanit. (HS-Adult)

PICCOLO
    10 min color Cine Concepts
    *Nomination, Academy Award
Two neighbors are friends until one of them takes up an instrument and the other tries to get even by practicing on an even louder one. In the orchestrated finale, all their families and friends become ridiculously involved, too. Non-verbal. Animated by Dusan Vukotic for Zagreb Film, Yugoslavia. (Elem. -Adult)

From PICKLES (BFA Educational Media)

PICKLES
>10 3/4 min   color   BFA   '71
>*Most Entertaining, Zagreb

A series of animated vignettes commenting pointedly on the many
absurd "pickles" we humans get ourselves into. You may laugh at
this one but come away thinking. Edited for classroom use. Produced by Bruno Bozzetto of Milan, Italy. (HS-Adult)

THE PIGS VS. THE FREAKS
>12 min   color   Pyramid   '73
>*Blue Ribbon, American/EFLA

An annual football game, played for charity, pits local policemen
against longhaired students from Michigan State University in East
Lansing. A real-life example of how diverse factions can get together, respect each other, have some fun ... and help out other
people, too. Film-maker: Jack Epps, Jr. (Intermediate-Adult)

PILLAR OF WISDOM
>9 min   color   Nat. Film Bd.
>*Award, Cork (Ireland)

Records some antics on the campus of a Canadian university, in
particular the assault on a greased pole, twenty feet high, firmly
planted in mud, which freshmen try to climb. Off-screen is the
voice of the dean extolling the pursuit of knowledge. (HS-Adult)

PIONEER JOURNEY ACROSS THE APPALACHIANS
>13 1/2 min   color   Coronet
>*Chris Award, Columbus

Tracing the journey of a North Carolina family across the mountain
chain before the Revolutionary War shows the close of a period when
the Appalachians stood as a barrier to westward movement. Why
the early settlers moved west, how they traveled, and other concepts underlying this movement are retold. (Intermediate)

PIONEER LIVING: Preparing Foods
>11 min   color   Coronet
>*Chris Award, Columbus

During summer, the settlers of the early 1800s lived comfortably on
the foods of the forest and their farms. As autumn approached,
preparations for winter included smoking meat, peeling and preserving apples, churning butter, making maple sugar, and baking bread.
Produced by Moreland-Latchford, Ltd. (Intermediate)

A PLACE IN THE SUN
>7 min   color   Films Inc.   '60
>*Award, Oberhausen

Tale of two figures competing for that important "place in the sun,"
displaying human foibles as they win or lose their place. Simple
stylized animation. Ceskoslovensky Filmexport. (HS-Adult)

A PLACE OF HEARING
>10 min   color   Assn. -Sterling   '69
>*Chris Award, Columbus

*Cindy Award, Info. Film
*Gold Camera, US Industrial
A school is operated in the Northern Transvaal by the Dutch Reformed Church, devoted to deaf and blind children. It instills in them dignity, out of which arises respect by neighbors and family. Focuses on a young deaf person filled with hope by teachers who are devoting their lives to these handicapped children. Available free of charge. Information Service of South Africa is the sponsor. (College-Adult)

PLANTING AND TRANSPLANTING
21 min color CMC-Columbia '68
*Merit Award, Horticultural
*Golden Eagle, CINE
Demonstrates techniques of planting and transplanting flowers, shrubs, and trees. Root and top-pruning, potting, watering, mulching, and soil preparation are shown, as well as related techniques such as dividing iris and rooting chrysanthemums. Produced and directed by Sumner Glimcher. (College-Adult)

PLAYGROUND
7 min color ACI Films '70
*Golden Eagle, CINE
From the "Starting to Read" series, featuring subjects of natural interest to children, accompanied by a lively song. Key words are superimposed on the screen in unison with their pronunciation on the soundtrack. Musical repetition provides reinforcement. Also available without captions. Film-maker: Jim Burroughs. (Primary)

THE PLEASURE IS MUTUAL
24 min color Conn. Films '68
*Blue Ribbon, American/EFLA
Gives guidelines for selecting and presenting books for pre-schoolers, and shows how to conduct effective picture-book programs. Produced for the New York Library Association. (College-Adult)

PLISETSKAYA DANCES
70 min BW Macmillan '64
*Special Award, Bergamo
*Blue Ribbon, American/EFLA
One of the greatest dancers of our time, Maya Plisetskaya, prima ballerina of the Bolshoi Ballet, Moscow, in a program of dances from her repertoire. Plisetskaya (with soloists and the corps de ballet of the Bolshoi) gives performances in scenes from "Swan Lake," "Sleeping Beauty," "Spartacus," "Romeo and Juliet," and "Don Quixote." Directed by Vassili Katanyan. (College-Adult)

POEN [sic]
5 min BW Films Inc. '68
*Award, Balboa
*Award, Oberhausen
A prose poem read by Leonard Cohen from his novel "Beautiful Losers," with an accompaniment of photographs and drawings from

diverse sources. While the poet reads, the camera moves in and
out and about the pictures, sometimes with surrealistic effect. National Film Board of Canada. (HS-Adult)

POETRY FOR FUN: Poetry about Animals
     13 min color Centron '72
     *Certificate, US Industrial
The eight poems in this film are presented for appreciation purposes.
Each poem was selected after a testing program with intermediate
students from a variety of ethnic and economic backgrounds. Selections include: "The Camel's Lament," "A Night With a Wolf," "The
Spangled Pandemonium," "Lone Dog," and Ogden Nash's "An Introduction to Dogs." Both cartoon animation and live-action photography are used. (Intermediate)

POLICE PURSUIT
     19 min color Film Communic. '74
     *Blue Ribbon, American/EFLA
The purpose of this film is to motivate police drivers to exercise
more caution in the operation of official vehicles. Techniques covered are: Commentary Driving, Maneuvering, Stopping, Skid Control, and Cornering. Film-maker: Ray Jewell. (Adult)

THE POLITICS FILM
     27 min color Macmillan '71
     *Chris Certificate, Columbus
War, violence, pollution, inequality, poverty, compounded by the
complexities of modern life, have grown to a magnitude unprecedented
in American history. This film presents these problems in conversations by 18-year-old voters. Designed to challenge viewers to re-
think their attitudes toward the system and their place in it. Narrated by Peter Falk. Produced and directed by Max Miller, Avanti
Films. (HS-Adult)

POLLUTION IS A MATTER OF CHOICE
     53 min color Films Inc. '70
     *Award, Int. Environment
     *Award, duPont-Columbia
     *Golden Eagle, CINE
     *Award, American/EFLA
     *"Emmy," Nat. Academy
The environmental dilemma of wanting what technology creates, yet
being destroyed by its wastes, is shown in the Everglades and in
Machiasport, Maine. People want the jobs that industry creates,
but not the destruction of surroundings. Resources grow scarce,
yet no one wants to give up his affluence. What are the priorities?
An NBC News production. (College-Adult)

POMPEII: Once There Was a City
     25 min color Learn. Corp. '69
     *Chris Statuette, Columbus
By juxtaposing everyday life in ancient Pompeii with the quality of
life in modern American society, this film asks a basic question:

Does the destruction of Pompeii, after a period of unprecedented prosperity, foreshadow the manmade violence of the twentieth century? (HS-Adult)

A POND
6 min color ACI Films '73
*Golden Eagle, CINE
The life of a pond, as observed and occasionally commented upon by two children. Close-up photography and natural sounds reveal a small world in which all living things are closely connected. Ducks, insects, frogs and other creatures eat, and are eaten, in obedience to the natural laws of survival and ecological balance. An Entheos/ Northwest Film. (Intermediate-HS)

PONIES
15 min color Oxford
*Award Winner, San Francisco
Ponies frolic on hilltops, in streams, wood, and meadow. They are seen and heard eating, drinking, sleeping. A foal is born and struggles to use its wobbly legs. A pony is curried, groomed, and schooled by its young mistress, and wins a ribbon in the show ring. Mood and motion are accented by specially composed music. A Moreland-Latchford Productions, Ltd. Film. (Elem.)

POP
2 3/4 min color BFA '71
*Animation Prize, Zagreb
Remember the comforting, pulsating rhythm of a train passing over the railroad tracks? This animated film matches visual variations with many repetitions. An experiment in synesthesia. Produced by Yoji Kuri. (HS-College)

POPCORN LADY
11 min color Schloat Prod. '72
*Student Award, Columbus
A realistically nostalgic study of the changes represented by the life of Dorothy Rich, whose Model T popcorn truck, custom-built for her father in 1925, has recently given way to the wheels of "progress." Produced by Simeon Hyde III. (Elem.-Adult)

POPSICLE
11 min color American Educ. Films '70
*Golden Eagle, CINE
Excitement, determination, and even disappointment are all shown as part of the variety of experiences inherent in motorcycling. This non-narrated film is intended to motivate discussion and self-expression. (Junior HS-Adult)

THE POPULATION EXPLOSION
43 min BW Carousel '60
*Public Service Award, Sylvania
*Blue Ribbon, American/EFLA
A look at the consequences of the growth of the world's population.

India is an example of a crisis that may become the world's number one problem--an excess of population over food supply. Government and religious leaders offer their views on this question. Produced by CBS News. (College-Adult)

POPULATIONS
15 1/2 min color Centron '72
*Certificate, US Industrial
Through live-action photography and animation, this film describes populations, investigates social structures, illustrates population growth, and considers factors that cause population to grow or decline. Sequences deal with physical factors (air, water, food) that control population, natural controls (fire, flood, disease, predation, etc.), territoriality, over-crowding, introduction of alien species, and possible effects on the environment. (Junior-Senior HS)

POSTERS
15 min color ACI Films '68
*Honors, American/EFLA
Starting with the idea that a poster must communicate quickly and forcefully, the film shows how design principles can be applied in order to achieve results. Demonstrates techniques for poster-making, including cut paper, collage, tempera paint, crayon resist, and silkscreen. Film-maker: Stelios Roccos. (HS-Adult)

POW WOW
7 min BW Macmillan '60
*Honorable Mention, Flaherty Awards
*Creative Award, San Francisco
A visual record of a university band rehearsal in the rain. Result: a document of contemporary campus customs with moments of surrealism and others of Mack Sennett. Perhaps of anthropological or sociological interest but, in any case, a lighthearted experience. Film-makers: Downs and Liebling. (HS-Adult)

POWER AND WHEELS: The Automobile in Modern Life
17 min color Encyc. Brit. '72
*Golden Eagle, CINE
*Chris Statuette, Columbus
The history of the automobile and its influence on American culture, as seen through the eyes of two visitors from outer space. Sequences reveal how people feel about their cars and how the development of the automobile led to a boom in related businesses. The car is also exposed as an abusive instrument in the hands of man, as evidenced by accidents, congestion, and pollution. (HS-Adult)

PREHISTORIC IMAGES (The First Art of Man)
17 min color Macmillan '55
*Merit Diploma, Edinburgh
*Certificate of Excellence, N.Y.
An exploration of the prehistoric caves of Spain and France, and a conjecture on the character of the people who painted on cave walls in the age of the glaciers some 10,000-40,000 years ago. Film-maker: Thomas Brandon. (College-Adult)

PRE-RAPHAELITE REVOLT
  30 min color Films Inc. '71
  *Red Ribbon, American/EFLA
The Pre-Raphaelite movement was founded in 1848 by a group of
young English artists that included Ford Madox Brown, John Millais,
John Ruskin, and Dante Gabriel Rossetti. They wanted to emulate
the naturalism of the Italian Renaissance painters before Raphael.
The movement lasted only seven or eight years, but its influence endured until the end of the 19th century, affecting fashion, literature,
interior design, and even the early history of the Socialist Movement.
Produced by Arts Council of Britain. (College-Adult)

PRESIDENT OF THE U.S.: Too Much Power?
  25 min color/BW Encyc. Brit. '71
  *Chris Certificate, Columbus
Is the power of the President too great for true democracy? This
film does not attempt a yes or no answer; rather, it examines and
explains presidential power. Hubert H. Humphrey, as commentator,
explores the history of the presidency through film clips and etchings. The use of power by Lincoln, Jefferson, the Roosevelts, Tru-
man, Kennedy and other presidents is analyzed. (HS-College)

PRIME TIME
  9 1/2 min color Xerox Films
  *Golden Eagle, CINE
  *Chris Award, Columbus
An outer space fantasy introduces the concept of prime numbers.
How does a space station from earth maintain contact with intelligent
life on a newly discovered planet? A specialist in space communica-
tions helps to answer that by demonstrating a method of testing for
primeness and distinguishing between prime and composite numbers.
(Intermediate)

PRIMITIVE MAN IN A MODERN WORLD
  23 min color Moody Institute
  *Award of Merit, Landers
  *Chris Award, Columbus
Acquaints the student with the ancient Maya and Inca civilizations,
and raises questions regarding "primitive peoples." A case-study is
made of the Lacandones of Southern Mexico. It also encourages discussion as to our society and the direction toward which we may be
heading. (Junior-Senior HS)

PRINTS
  15 min color ACI Films '66
  *Honors, American/EFLA
  *Golden Eagle, CINE
Presents print-making processes that can be carried out with simple,
readily available materials. By placing emphasis on processes, the
film opens up possibilities for individual exploration and experimentation. Film-maker: Stelios Roccos. (HS-Adult)

THE PRIVATE LIFE OF THE KINGFISHER
    25 min   color   Time-Life
    *Silver Medal, Moscow
Follows a pair of kingfisher birds throughout the year--from mating
season through nesting and rearing their young. They are shown in
sunshine and in snow, above water and below. From the BBC-TV
network. (HS-Adult)

PROBLEMS OF THE MIDDLE EAST (Revised)
    22 min   color   Atlantis '67
    *Chris Award, Columbus
Disputes and problems arising out of conflicts over oil, refugees,
and boundaries are explained in relation to the basic and enduring
factors of Middle Eastern geography, anthropology, religion, history
and economics. Produced by J. Michael Hagopian. (Junior-Senior
HS)

THE PROGRESSIVE ERA: Reform Works in America
    23 min BW Encyc. Brit. '72
    *Gold Hugo, Chicago
Describes the years 1890-1915 as a period of turmoil and violence.
Bankrupt farmers, slums, appalling work conditions, child labor,
and riots prodded the nation to improve social conditions. Though
a Progressive candidate was elected in 1912, legislation was not enacted for better living standards until the depression years twenty
years later. Original film clips document the conditions explained.
(Junior-Senior HS)

PROUD YEARS
    28 min BW CMC-Columbia
    *Silver Reel Award
    *ALA Endorsement
Explores the steps that can be taken to help old people to lead useful and active lives, even when a debilitating disease has struck.
Through case studies, this film explores emotional problems that
spring from a needlessly dependent existence, and shows how old
people regain dignity and self-respect when encouraged to fight their
infirmities. Directed by George C. Stoney. (College-Adult)

PRUNING PRACTICES AT THE BROOKLYN BOTANIC GARDEN
    22 min   color CMC-Columbia '65
    *Merit Award, Horticultural
    *Trophy Award, Salerno
    *Golden Eagle, CINE
    *Blue Ribbon, American/EFLA
Shows how proper pruning practices can yield healthy plants. Photographed at the Brooklyn Botanic Garden, the film demonstrates the
three main elements of pruning trees, shrubs, and other woody plants:
the time of year, the technique, and the tools. Included are care of
deciduous and evergreen trees, various species of roses, rhododen-
drons, forsythia, lilacs, hedges, and the Japanese art of controlled
form. Produced by Sumner Glimcher. Directed by Stuart Chasmar.
(College-Adult)

PSYCHEDELIC WET
8 min color ACI Films '67
*Golden Eagle, CINE
*Honors, American/EFLA

Water--on it, in it, under it--is the setting for a film that can be used in a session on awareness. The nonverbal techniques used may interest some viewers in film production, and the visual patterns may stimulate others toward self-expression in writing or the graphic arts. Produced by Homer Groening. (HS-Adult)

PULCINELLA
11 min color Conn. Films
*Award, Italian Film Critics
*Award Winner, Moscow

Pulcinella, a lazy rascal, has a marvelous dream filled with color and excitement. To the music of Rossini, he runs, flies, and dances through imagery from the circus, theatre, and ballet--at first bright and joyful, then dark with magical woods and monsters. From a film trilogy that began with the Academy Award candidate, "The Thieving Magpie." Animated by Emanuele Luzzati and Giulio Gianini. (Elem.-Adult)

PULL THE HOUSE DOWN
38 min color or BW Carousel '67
*Golden Eagle, CINE

A reflective dialogue between two men of conviction, Harry Reasoner and his son Stuart. They talk about the antagonism the "Establishment" feels toward its young, and the hostility with which the young react. They cover such topics as drugs, promiscuity, suburbia, racism, greed, campus revolt, and Vietnam. Rock music is supplied by The Doors, The Jefferson Airplane, and John Sebastian. WCAU-TV, Philadelphia. (HS-Adult)

THE PUNISHMENT FITS THE CRIME
7 min color Schloat Productions
*First Place, US Industrial

Takes place in the land of the black rabbits and white rabbits. Three crimes are committed, and in each case a hooded judge hands down a punishment. Although the crimes are identical, the punishments vary in severity. The deciding factor seems to involve fur color. Public reaction to the sentences also varies: the white rabbits applaud harsh punishment for one defendant and light punishment for another. But when a judge applies the law without regard for fur color, the negative public reaction nearly costs him his life. Animated. Film-maker: Warren Schloat. (Intermediate-Adult)

PURITAN FAMILY OF EARLY NEW ENGLAND
11 min color Coronet
*Award, Freedoms Foundation

In this motion picture, filmed at authentic restorations, a Puritan family, in a small New England coastal village, participates in many activities and chores. The children learn from a hornbook, dig clams, and spin wool; the mother cooks cornbread, makes soap and candles; and the father hunts and dresses skins. (Intermediate)

THE PURPLE TURTLE
        14 min   color   ACI Films   '62
        *Honors, American/EFLA
        *Golden Eagle, CINE
The events of a kindergarten art period: the children's activities
and comments, their involvement, their encounters with the teacher,
and the results of their work. Demonstrates what art activities can
mean to children. Film-maker: Stelios Roccos. (College-Adult)

QUE PUERTO RICO!
        16 min   color   McGraw-Hill   '63
        *Golden Eagle, CINE
An interpretation of this island, its people, and their special way of
life. A Contemporary Films release, produced and directed by
Tibor Hirsch. (HS-Adult)

QUEBEC IN SILENCE
        9 3/4 min   color   Nat. Film Bd.
        *Award Winner, Venice
Based on the paintings of Jean-Paul Lemieux, who recorded his observations of rural Quebec in the period between the two world wars.
His pictures show close-knit families, orderly villages, and church-
centered communities. His is a peaceful world presented, for the
most part, without commentary. (HS-Adult)

QUEST
        18 min   color   Films Inc.   '71
        *Award Winner, Chicago
A folksinger outlines the elements of a quest--a goal, some long
journey, a mode of transportation, obstacles overcome, and occasional sacrifice. Examples: Columbus' theory, Admiral Byrd's expeditions, Jules Verne's hero in 20,000 Leagues Under the Sea,
Cervantes' in Don Quixote, Steinbeck's in Grapes of Wrath, and
Mark Twain's in Huckleberry Finn. Produced by the Ontario Educational Communications Association. (HS-College)

THE QUESTION
        10 min   color   McGraw-Hill   '66
        *Award, Edinburgh
        *Prize, Annecy
A man finds a question mark and presents it to representatives of
government, art, religion, and science. None of them can answer
"The Question" but, before desperation sets in, he meets a woman
who's also carrying around a question mark. Topic for discussion:
What is "The Question"? Why didn't the institutions have the an-
swer? Is there such a thing as "The Answer"? Animation by
Halas and Batchelor. (Junior HS-Adult)

A QUESTION OF ATTITUDE
        11 1/2 min   color   Australia   '70
        *Red Ribbon, American/EFLA
Many firms are reluctant to employ the handicapped. This film
shows that the handicapped can be loyal and productive workers,

capable of doing a good day's work without any special supervision or other consideration. Produced by the Commonwealth Film Unit. (College-Adult)

THE QUIET ONE
        68 min   BW   McGraw-Hill   '70
        *Top Ten, NY Times
        *Ten Best, Time Magazine
        *Critics' Award, Venice
        *1st International Award, Venice
        *Ten Best, National Board
About an unloved child who drifts into delinquency. Documentary in treatment, this film examines the causes and effects of deviant behavior in that age group, and can give an insight into parental attitudes and relationships and, most important, how understanding and patience can lead to rehabilitation. Produced by Janice Loeb and William Levitt; directed by Sidney Meyers. (College-Adult)

THE RAFT
        29 min   color   Phoenix   '73
        *Blue Ribbon, American/EFLA
        *UN Award, Cracow (Poland)
An account of the 1000 kilometer journey of a family of four on a houseboat of sorts. When they arrive at their destination, their merchandise is sold, the raft is dismantled and it, too, is sold for money to live on in the small Brazilian town of Teresina, down the river Parnaiba. Filmed by Sluizer Productions. (Senior HS-Adult)

RAIL
        13 min   color   ACI Films   '68
        *Award, British Industrial
        *Award Winner, Locarno
The motion and excitement of rail travel. Without any narration, this film creates a blend of past and present, from the nostalgic beauty of the old steam engine to the sleek efficiency of the modern, high-speed electric train. Original music by Wilfred Josephs. A British Transport Film by Geoffrey Jones. (Intermediate-Adult)

A RAINY DAY STORY
        13 min   color   Centron   '72
        *Certificate, US Industrial
        *Chris Award, Columbus
Almost a "how to do it" film, dramatizing the procedure an elementary student can use to conceive his own stories. The film illustrates how a youngster can rediscover familiar people, objects, and events and can use these elements by arousing, sustaining, and directing daydreams. As the film points out, the key words are "What it...?" A Phoenix Production. (Elem.)

THE RAVAGED EARTH
        27 min   color   Films Inc.   '69
        *Award, American/EFLA
        *Ohio St. Univ. Award

The path of mining companies across Appalachian land is marked by acidic soil, sulphuric rivers, and unhappy people. This defacement has not been stopped because it is the economic base for the region. Stewart Udall points out that, although strip mining is presently profitable, when land is permanently destroyed, it is both foolish and short-sighted. Produced by WKYC-TV. (HS-Adult)

REACH OUT
      5 min   color   FilmFair   '71
      *Merit Award, Landers
Explores the concept of opening the mind to new sights, new sounds, and new people to counteract the urge to settle for the comfort of the familiar. (Based on the book by Bill Martin, Jr.) A Ben Norman Film. (Elem.)

REACHING YOUR READER
      17 min   color   Centron   '71
      *Chris Award, Columbus
Crystal MacIntosh is convinced she has composed a brilliant article about her summer tour of Europe--but even her best friends and her faithful dog won't sit still for a reading of it! Then Crystal begins learning how to involve her readers. She discovers the power of appealing to the five senses. She learns to create dynamic rather than static descriptions, and finds that, instead of describing emotions for her readers, she can make them feel emotions. (HS)

THE REAL WEST
      54 min   BW   McGraw-Hill   '62
      *Grand Prize, Prix Italia
      *Award, American/EFLA
Re-creates the American West as it really was when pioneers moved west to fill in the last frontiers (1849-1900). Shows the trek of pioneers in every type of conveyance. The importance of cattle is depicted. Legends of famous gunfighters are placed in proper perspective, and the conquest of the proud Plains Indians in the last of the great Indian wars is brought to life. Gary Cooper narrates. (College-Adult)

THE RED BALLOON
      34 min   color   Macmillan   '55
      *Award, French Film Critics
      *Special Award, Cannes
      *Best Screenplay, Academy Awards ... many other honors
         and awards
A French boy makes friends with a balloon. It follows the boy to school, in the bus, and to church. Boy and balloon play together in the streets of Montmartre, and try to elude the urchins who want to destroy the balloon. In the end, the enemy wins and the balloon dies. Then, all of the other balloons in Paris come down to the boy and lift him up into the sky. Written and directed by Albert Lamorisse. (All Ages)

THE RED KITE
     17 min   color   Wombat   '66
     *Award, NY International
     *Chris Award, Columbus
The setting is Montreal, and the story about a kite a man buys for
his daughter.   This mildly impulsive act leads to encounters with
strangers that cause him to wonder about the purpose and meaning
of life.   National Film Board of Canada.   (Elem.-Adult)

THE REDWOODS
     20 min   color   Macmillan   '68
     *Best Short, Academy Award
The creation of America's new Redwoods National Park.   This film
was a factor in helping to build both the public and the Congressional support that made that creation possible.   A King Screen Production.   (HS-Adult)

THE REFINER'S FIRE
     6 min   color   Doubleday   '70
     *Merit Award, Philadelphia
     *Golden Eagle, CINE
     *Chris Award, Columbus
Using the interaction of bright circles and squares accompanied by
a dramatic score by Moussorgsky, Strauss, and Grieg, three high
school students have created a film depicting a situation with social
and religious implications--open to a variety of interpretations.
(Intermediate-HS)

REFLECTIONS
     14 min   color   ACI Films   '67
     *Honors, American/EFLA
     *Golden Eagle, CINE
Paul Hultberg works with sheets of copper and colored enamel to
make abstract compositions.   He explains what he is doing and why,
as the film shows him selecting the copper sheet, laying on patterns
of powdered enamel, annealing the metal, then cooling and finishing
the work.   An American Crafts Council Film.   (HS-Adult)

REFLECTIONS
     15 min   color   McGraw-Hill   '69
     *Golden Eagle, CINE
     *Merit Award, Edinburgh
     *First Prize, Locarno
A Chinese-American boy (Carl Chu) living in New York's Chinatown,
meets a charming Puerto Rican girl (Diane Cecilio).   The two get
acquainted and open a new world of fantasy.   Then the adult world
intervenes and prevails. A Contemporary Films release.   (Intermediate-HS)

REFLECTIONS IN SPACE
     27 min   color   Screenscope   '71
     *Gold Camera, US Industrial
     *Golden Eagle, CINE

Edward Villella, of the New York City Ballet, interprets the walk
on the moon's surface. Concerns the imagination of humanity, our
achievement in Apollo 11, and our possibilities in the fine arts.
The film is composed of views of the flight, photographs taken during the project, excerpts from science-fiction films, paintings, and
other materials. Closes with a poem by Archibald MacLeish, in
which the moon, so traditionally important to poets, is brought into
human scale. Produced by Harold Weiner. (HS-Adult)

REFLECTIONS ON TIME
      22 min color Encyc. Brit.   '70
      *Chris Certificate, Columbus
      *Golden Eagle, CINE
A film that helps to "experience time" in three ways: subjectively,
objectively, and geologically. The first two parts show a montage
of visual and verbal ideas. The last follows a geologist down Grand
Canyon (a "geologic calendar"), recording his interpretation of what
each rock layer signifies. Questions then encourage the students to
formulate their own definition of time. Sponsored by the American
Geological Institute. (Intermediate-Junior HS)

THE REFORMATION
      13 1/2 min color Coronet
      *Merit Certificate, Cleveland
Explains the Reformation of the Church, the cultural changes brought
about by the Renaissance, the emergence of national states, and new
interpretations of the Scriptures. Such figures as Calvin, Zwingli,
and Knox are recognized, while the film devotes special attention to
Luther and the Protestant Reformation in Germany. (Junior-Senior
HS)

REMBRANDT: Painter of Man
      18 1/2 min color Perspective   '58
      *Chris Award, Columbus
Produced in commemoration of the 350th anniversary of the artist's
birth. The camera analyzes over sixty selected canvasses from
twenty-nine museums in twelve countries. Suggested are Rembrandt's
novel use of light and shadow, and his genius for expressing human
compassion toward his subjects. Produced by Bert Haanstra for the
Netherlands Government Information Service. (HS-Adult)

REMBRANDT'S CHRIST
      40 min BW Roland
      *Chris Award, Columbus
      *Art Award, Assisi
From 1,400 Rembrandt drawings around the world, 160 were selected
for this film. The chosen drawings are in 62 collections in 12 countries. The Christ story takes place in the houses, towns, canals,
and meadows of 17th-century Holland. The painter's models were
Rembrandt's family, friends, citizens and peasants. Producer: Les
Films du Saturne. (College-Adult)

RENAISSANCE
        10 min color (with BW) Pyramid '63
        *Special Jury Prize, Tours
An explosion; the objects in a drawing room are shattered. Then
they reassemble themselves. Charred paper is transformed, leaf by
leaf, into an intact book. A clock, a faded photograph, a dented
trumpet--each stubbornly returns to its original place as though the
old human order was immutable, ordained by the laws of physics.
Then it all blows up--object animation in reverse. (HS-College)

A REPORT ON ACUPUNCTURE
        28 1/2 min color Macmillan '73
        *Silver Medal, Atlanta
Filmed in Taiwan, this report shows methods of training, practice,
and research in major Chinese hospitals there. It demonstrates the
move toward the integration of Chinese and Western medicine as exemplified in a tooth extraction that is performed quickly and painless-
ly by using acupuncture as an anesthetic. Also outlines the concept
of "Ch'i" as an energy flow within the body. Producer: Leo Seltzer.
(HS-Adult)

REPORTING AND EXPLAINING
        13 1/2 min color Centron '70
        *Chris Award, Columbus
The type of speech given most often is the speech of exposition:
giving reports, instructions, directions, or explaining processes.
Clarity and interest are of primary importance, and this film shows
how to achieve both. (HS-College)

REPTILES AND THEIR CHARACTERISTICS
        11 min color Coronet
        *Award, Scholastic Teacher
Identifies the five orders of animals that make up the reptile group
and points out their common characteristics and some of their differences. We see the snakes, lizards, turtles, crocodilians, and
the rare tuatara in their native habitats, and learn something of how
they live and reproduce, their adaptations to environments, and some
of the ways they benefit mankind. (Intermediate)

THE RESCUE SQUAD
        54 min BW Sterling Educ. '70
        *Silver Ocella, Venice
Six children lose a toy airplane in a high tower. After many attempts at recovery, they themselves become trapped until rescued
by a donkey! Produced by the Children's Film Foundation, Britain.
(Ages 7-12)

THE RETURN OF MILTON WHITTY
        17 1/2 min color Aim-Assn.
        *Bronze Plaque, Nat. Committee
        *Blue Ribbon, American/EFLA
Buster Keaton returns to the screen with a new safety problem: a
shortsighted foreman who thinks he knows all the answers. He does.

Except for one. And that is how to prevent accidents. Only when
tragedy strikes does he realize that "an ounce of prevention is worth
a pound of cure. " (Adult)

RHYTHMS OF PARIS
9 min color Encyc. Brit. '71
*Chris Certificate, Columbus
The excitement of Paris and its people. Rush-hour jams and café-
lined streets contrast with serene parks and fishing along the Seine.
Also explored are couturier shops along Place Royale, boutiques in
the Latin Quarter, historical sites, and night club life. (Also available with French narration.) (HS-Adult)

RICE FARMERS IN THAILAND
19 min color Films Inc. '68
*Chris Certificate, Columbus
Payong, a rice farmer and mayor of a village, is a step ahead of
his neighbors. He has built a water pump to flood his land so that
he can plant two successive crops, while the other villagers wait
for the rainy season. At Payong's urging, the villagers listen to a
government expert who encourages them to irrigate so that they, too,
can increase their harvest. In the capital city, the king performs
the ceremony of blessing the rice at the beginning of the planting
season. When Payong's first harvest is in, he invites the Buddhist
priests to bless his crop in an ancient ceremony. The old ways of
life contrast with the new ideas. Produced by Institut für Film und
Bild. (Intermediate-HS)

RICKY'S GREAT ADVENTURE
11 min color Atlantis '69
*Chris Award, Columbus
This story of a boy unable to see is designed to motivate students
to make better use of their sense of touch, taste, smell, and hearing. Produced by J. Michael Hagopian. (Primary)

RIGHT ON/BE FREE
15 min color FilmFair '70
*Best of Class, San Francisco
Shows the vitality and strength of the Black American artist. In
more than one art form, this film reveals the diversity of talents
expressed in music, poetry, painting, and dance. A Sargon Tamimi
Film. (Elem. -Adult)

THE RISE AND FALL OF THE GREAT LAKES
17 min color Pyramid '69
*Blue Ribbon, American/EFLA
The history and future of the Great Lakes as told through the imaginary odyssey of a canoeist who experiences it all. Begins with the
pre-ice age, and moves up over the glaciers, down to clear drinka-
ble waters, to the polluted murk that engulfs the Great Lakes today.
Tomorrow could be worse. National Film Board of Canada. (Elem. -
Adult)

RIVER BOY
        17 min color McGraw-Hill '69
        *First Prize, Venice
        *First Prize, Vancouver
        *Golden Eagle, CINE
The story of Phillip Lombas, a boy in Baratario Bayou (near New
Orleans), who finds someone more important than his dog when he
meets Chrissy Lapeyre. But early enchantment fades to disillusion
when he spends his savings on a mail-order suit, only to find that
she laughs at his ungainly appearance. Reflects the bittersweet experience of that first crush, and shows how the boy grows from his
experience. (Intermediate-Junior HS)

RIVER PEOPLE OF CHAD
        20 min color Films Inc. '69
        *Chris Certificate, Columbus
In the new African country of Chad, people in villages live as they
have for generations. The film visits the Kotoko tribe for a day
and a night, showing how they farm, fish, cook, make tools and
pots, and live by using the resources around them. In contrast is
the capital of Fort Lamy, a modern city with hotels, department
stores, and airports. The villagers bring their fish and wood here
to trade. Institut für Film und Bild. (Intermediate-HS)

RIVER: Where Do You Come From?
        10 min color Learning Corp. '69
        *Certificate Winner, Columbus
Explains the water cycle by using folk ballad as narrative. Follows
a river from its origin to its return to the sea. Shows water
threatened by pollution when man harnesses it for power in lumber
and paper mills. (Intermediate-HS)

RIVERS OF SAND
        83 min color Phoenix '74
        *Blue Ribbon, American/EFLA
A study of the Namar tribe that lives in the thorny scrublands of
Ethiopia, isolated from other tribes both by choice and conditions.
Shown are their customary activities along with the effect of sexual
inequity on mood and behavior. Producer: John Gardner. (College-
Adult)

THE RIVERS OF TIME
        26 min color McGraw-Hill '62
        *Award Winner, Venice
The contributions of Arab culture to world civilization are examined
in this documentary, an examination of museum pieces of Sumeria.
Live photography, with commentary based on contemporary texts,
provides an overview. Produced by Sinclair Road for Iraq Petroleum.
(HS-College)

THE ROAD
        28 min BW Carousel '67
        *Blue Ribbon, American/EFLA

Examined here is the day-by-day work of a group of nurses in Appalachia. Through the difficult seasons they come, by jeep and on foot, to the mountain and valley cabins. There they minister to the aged and infirm, the infant and the mother, to those who have no access to modern clinics or hospitals. (HS-Adult)

ROAD SIGNS ON A MERRY-GO-ROUND
      57 min   color   Carousel '67
      *Network Award, American Baptist
      *First Prize, Monte Carlo
Script, cinematography, and director weave together related concepts to illumine concern about our relationship to God, to nature, to humanity, and to our own destiny. The film focuses on a man and woman sensitive to each other's needs and hopes. They talk, walk through the city and the countryside, play with their children, and love each other. They are everyman and everywoman. Produced by CBS News. (College-Adult)

THE ROAD TO GETTYSBURG
      54 min   color   McGraw-Hill   '69
      *Geo. Foster Peabody Award
      Re-creates the battle that was the turning point in the Civil War, and the events that led up to it. This is the story of a war told by the men who fought it. Historic photographs and modern re-enactments combine to reproduce the impact of brother against brother in one of the bloodiest wars in history. ABC-TV Production. (College-Adult)

THE ROADBUILDERS
      20 min   color   AIM-Assn.
      *Award, US Industrial
Reveals the hazards in highway construction work, starting with the clearance of underbrush and giant trees, the spotting of potential dangers, and the precautions that must be followed in using equipment and machinery. (Adult)

ROBERT E. LEE: A Background Study
      16 min   color   Coronet
      *Merit Certificate, Columbus
Lee is studied first as a Virginian, a devout Christian who was forced to decide between his home and the Union he loved; then, as a brilliant strategist and beloved commander whose integrity of principle, even in defeat, set an example for the New South. (Junior-Senior HS)

ROBERT SCOTT AND THE RACE FOR THE SOUTH POLE
      55 min   color   McGraw-Hill   '68
      *Golden Eagle, CINE
Documents the dangers and tribulations encountered by Scott and his party in their arduous drive to the pole. Motion pictures, photographs, and personal diaries provide insights into the courage of the explorers, showing the glory and tragedy of the search. Produced by ABC-TV. (College-Adult)

THE ROBIN
 5 1/2 min   color   AV Explorations   '66
 *Honors, American/EFLA
The life cycle unfolds, from nesting until the young are independent
of their parents.   Variations in songs and calls are compared, as
well as plumage and behavior.   The protective instinct at nesting
time is illustrated as a robin defends her home from a cat.   Study-
guide available.   Non-narrated.   Photographed by Dan Gibson.
(Elem. -Adult)

ROBIN, PETER AND DARRYL: Three to the Hospital
 53 min   BW   CMC-Columbia   '68
 *Golden Eagle, CINE
The reactions of three children, aged two years and ten months, to
their hospitalization for minor surgery.   Produced to show the effect of maternal separation, this film is a potential training resource for nurses, medical students, psychologists, social workers,
and family life counselors.   A study guide accompanies the film.
(College-Adult)

ROCK-A-BYE-BABY
 30 min   color   Time-Life Films   '72
 *Blue Ribbon, American/EFLA
One of 14 films in the "Life Around Us" series.   Examines some
of the techniques that psychologists use to compare maternal practices around the world.   (College-Adult)

ROCKET TO NOWHERE (Also known as CLOWN FERDINAND AND
 THE ROCKET)
 79 min   color   Macmillan   '62
 *First Prize, Venice (Child.)
Fantasy about a clown, some children, and their kidnapping by a
robot in a rocketship.   Told with camera tricks, music, and mini-
mal dialogue.   Directed by Jindrich Polak.   (Primary-Intermediate)

RODEO
 20 min   color   McGraw-Hill   '71
 *Golden Eagle, CINE
The final event in rodeo is bull riding.   To win, the cowboy must
stay on for eight seconds.   In slow motion, the film conveys the
dangers in this confrontation of man and beast.   Directed by Carroll
Ballard.   Produced by Concepts Unlimited.   (HS-Adult)

THE ROLE OF THE CONGRESSMAN
 23 min   color   Xerox Films   '73
 *Award, Chicago
 *Chris Award, Columbus
What is the role of a member of Congress?   Congressman Richard
Bolling, D-Kansas (urban area), is sponsoring a bill concerned with
Congressional reorganization.   Who must be convinced that his bill
should pass?   And what must he do to convince them?   Will he suc-
ceed or fail ... and why?   (HS-Adult)

THE ROMANCE OF TRANSPORTATION
11 min   color   Int. Film Bur.
*Awards: Cannes, Edinburgh, et al.
While a commentator delivers the historical narrative, animated
figures independently portray stages in the development of transportation, from the first footpaths through canoe, barge, steamboat,
oxcart, railway, and automobile to the aircraft of today and tomorrow.   (Intermediate-HS)

ROMANESQUE PAINTERS (1000-1200 A. D.)
11 min   color   Roland
*Merit Award, Bergamo
*Merit of Honor, Venice
*Honorable Mention, Cannes
Using vast unbroken wall spaces of comparatively windowless build-
ings, fresco painters created scenes of heroic proportions. Bril-
liant in color, these served as illustrated Bible history lessons for
people in the late Middle Ages in France. Producer: L'Atelier du
Film. (HS-Adult)

ROOFERS' PITCH
21 1/2 min   color   AIM-Assn.
*Award of Merit, Nat. Committee
A serious accident suffered by a roofer causes everyone, from the
boss down, to take a second look at their work habits. Team effort
results in a reduction of accidents and a new pride in workmanship.
(Adult)

ROOM TO BREATHE
26 min   color   Films Inc.   '69
*Award, Int. Environment
An exploration of the human and environmental problems involved in
the redevelopment of the historic Delaware River Valley. This project has been kept on the drawing boards for 14 years because of
lack of funds. When completed, it will become a major recreation
center and source of water and electric power for northern New
Jersey and eastern Pennsylvania. Produced by WNBC-TV. (HS-
Adult)

THE ROSE AND THE MIGNONETTE
9 min   BW   Film Images
*Prize, Marianske Lazne
*Grand Prize, Venice
Illustration of the thesis that faith, regardless of individual beliefs,
can form an unbreakable bond against tyranny. Based on an actual
incident in a French village occupied by the Germans during World
War II. From a poem by Louis Aragon; English translation by
Stephen Spender. Read by Emlyn Williams. Music from a Bach
chorale. Directed by André Michel. (HS-Adult)

ROSIE'S WALK
5 min   color   Weston Woods   '70
*Golden Eagle, CINE

*Recognition, Calif. Center
*Chris Statuette, Columbus
*Blue Ribbon, American/EFLA
An animated version of the children's picture book of the same
name. Also available with captions. Produced by Mort Schindel.
(Primary)

RUBENS
    45 min BW Macmillan '50
    *Art Prize, Cleveland
    *Prize Winner, Venice
    *Prize Winner, Cannes
The nature and form of Rubens' paintings in relation to his predecessors, contemporaries, and successors. The film itself is an
early example of the liveliness and interest that can be created by
the camera from a static subject. A Paul Haesaerts and Henri
Storck Production. (College-Adult)

RUSSIA
    24 min color Int. Film Foundation
    *Award, Scholastic Magazine
This documentary on the Soviet Union is useful in understanding the
Russian people. Historical footage depicting life under the Czar is
combined with sequences of contemporary conditions in the U.S.S.R.
Among the activities described are: religious worship, collective
farms, work in a textile plant, school life, and scientific research.
Producer: Julien Bryan. (HS-Adult)

RYTHMETIC
    9 min color Int. Film Bur.
    *Awards: Br. Film Academy, Edinburgh and others
An animated film by Norman McLaren and Evelyn Lambart that en-
dows arithmetic with humor. The screen becomes a numerical free-
for-all as digits meet in playful encounter, jostling, attacking, and
eluding one another. A National Film Board of Canada production.
(Intermediate-Adult)

SABRE AND FOIL
    7 1/4 min BW Nat. Film Bd.
    *Award, Cortina d'Ampezzo
The ancient and deadly sport of fencing, demonstrated by masters.
The film is not a record of duels but it does focus the eye on every
swift maneuver and the clash of steel, the staccato of feet, and the
sculptured postures of the masked figures. (HS-College)

SAD SONG OF YELLOW SKIN
    60 min color Films Inc. '70
    *Grand Prize, American/EFLA
    *Flaherty Award, British Society
    *Best Documentary, Hollywood
    *Gold Medal, Atlanta
    *Award of Merit, Landers ... and other honors
A documentary that focuses on three young Americans in Saigon.

One lives with a group of Vietnamese child-men who work as shoe-shine boys; another, a journalist, tours a barbaric neighborhood called "The Graveyard;" and the third is John Steinbeck, Jr., who lives on an incredible island of Peace in the Mekong Delta. This film is not about death in war, but about what little life there is with war all around. Produced by the National Film Board of Canada. (College-Adult)

SAFE CLOTHING
      7 3/4 min   BW   Nat. Film Board
      *Award, Nat. Committee
Brogan thinks Foreman McCardle has gone off his rocker when Mc-Cardle has him carted away to the hospital perfectly well. When Nurse Gilfillan starts to operate--on Brogan's trailing necktie, baggy-sleeved sweater, cuffed pants, and worn-out shoes--horrid tales of workers who have worn similar clothing make everything clear. (Adult)

SAFE HOME
      13 1/2 min   color   Assn. -Sterling
      *Gold Medal, Atlanta
Using dummies in simulated accident sequences, this film shows why safety features in cars are being pressed. Are lap and shoulder belts fastened? Doors locked? Windshields clean? The importance of seatbelts, collapsing steering wheels, and other devices is shown. Also highlighted is a safer windshield that absorbs impact. Libbey-Owens-Ford Company, sponsor. Free loan. Available only to senior high school driver-training courses and adult organizations.

SAFETY AS WE PLAY
      7 min   color   ACI Films   '72
      *Honors, American/EFLA
From the "starting to Read" series, featuring subjects of natural interest to children, accompanied by a lively song. Key words are superimposed on the screen in unison, with pronunciation given on the soundtrack. Musical repetition provides subtle reinforcement. Also available without captions. (Primary)

SAFETY IN THE BALANCE
      24 min   color   AIM-Assn.   '71
      *Creative Award, US Industrial
Men and equipment in actual job situations. Scenes include near-misses and the exercise of safety rules. The camera pinpoints the teamwork required when operating near live wires, obscure lines of vision, and major hoisting problems. (Adult)

SAFETY ON THE WAY TO SCHOOL
      11 min   color   Coronet
      *Merit Award, Nat. Committee
Stresses ways of going to and from school safely. It reveals the safe way of riding in a car or bus, the skills needed to walk safely to school, and how to select the safest route. (Intermediate)

SAHARA - LA CARAVANE DU SEL
      52 min   color   Films Inc.   '69
      *Award, National Press
      *Prize, Christophers
      *Award, American/EFLA
      *"Emmy," Nat. Academy
      *Golden Eagle, CINE
The Sahara provides a setting of parched beauty for the camel cara-
vans that cross the desert in the salt trade.   This film follows a
small caravan through its four-week, 1,000-mile journey through extreme temperatures and sandstorms, with only the occasional relief
of the oasis until it reaches its destination, the marketplace at
Agades.   There, the salt will be sold to sustain the drivers until
the next caravan across the desert.   NBC-TV News.   (College-Adult)

SAM'S SECRET
      9 1/2 min   color   Perennial Education
      *Award, National Visual
      *Award, Society/Management
This sales motivation film uses cartoon animation to provide a point
of view that can help salesmen achieve a higher score in the serious
game of selling.   Produced by Portafilms.   (College-Adult)

SANDMAN
      4 min   color   Eccentric Circle   '72
      *Special Prize, Annecy (France)
This story of a man's dream is accompanied by a bluegrass banjo
soundtrack.   Included with the film are instructions on sand animation and other post-screening activities of special interest to children.   Animation by Eliot Noyes, Jr.   (Elem.)

SATAN IN THE CHURCH
      9 min   color   Mass Media   '70
      *Fipresci Award, Mamaia
      *Winner, Oberhausen
This animated film will be taken as provocative by some, as sacri-
legious by others.   His Satanic Majesty is seen disguising himself
as a worshipper and as a voluptuous woman, causing distractions
during worship.   The height of his seductive influence is the dese-
cration of Christ himself in his spiritual as well as physical form.
Produced by Ivan Ivanov.   (College-Adult)

SAUL ALINSKY WENT TO WAR
      57 min   BW   McGraw-Hill   '69
      *Chris Certificate, Columbus
      *Blue Ribbon, American/EFLA
A professional radical whose first organized protest dates back to
the 1930s, Saul Alinsky was a white man in the middle of the black
revolution.   This film explores his thinking and working philosophy,
and shows his tactics in action.   The "war" on Eastman Kodak by
the black people of Rochester, N.Y.--organized by Alinsky in 1964--
provides a study of his special form of protest.   National Film
Board of Canada, producer.   (College-Adult)

SAY GOODBYE
      50 min color Films Inc. '71
      *Golden Eagle, CINE
      *Chris Statuette, Columbus
      *Red Ribbon, American/EFLA
A dynamic filming of perhaps the last of some species of animals
that are being eliminated thoughtlessly by man in his search for
space, for pleasure, or for financial gain. An attempt is being
made to save some animals, but the effort is infinitesimal in a crisis that some ecologists believe has passed the point of no return.
David Wolper Production/Quaker Oats Company. (College-Adult)

SCAG (Heroin)
      21 min color Encyc. Brit. '71
      *Silver Medal, Venice
A black girl from the ghetto and a white boy from suburbia had different reasons for turning to scag, and experienced similar sufferings when it wouldn't let them turn away. The girl is off drugs
now and struggling to straighten out her life. The boy is still hung
up and looking for help. These stories allow viewers to examine
the physical, emotional, and social consequences of shooting heroin.
A Concept Film. (HS-College)

THE SCARECROW
      17 min color Films Inc. '73
      *Blue Ribbon, American/EFLA
Dramatization of a poor farmer and his wife who struggle for survival against the heat, plagues of rooks, and crows that ravage
their crops. Set in southern Ireland in July, 1931. Producer:
British Film Institute. (HS-Adult)

SCHOOL OF PARIS: Five Artists at Work Today
      25 min color McGraw-Hill '62
      *Special Award, Bergamo
Paris welcomes artists from every point of the earth. Its incom-
parable light and its sympathetic atmosphere have attracted artists
and sculptors from traditionalist to pop. Dewasne, Hartung, Di
Teana, Fruhtrunk, and Weisbuch demonstrate a diversity of techniques and media from steel to oils. Filmed and directed by Warren Forma. A Contemporary Films release. (College-Adult)

SCHOOL WITHOUT FAILURE
      46 min color Media Five '70
      *Chris Award, Columbus
A documentary showing "no-fail" education in a public elementary
school. Based on the theory expounded in the book of the same
name by Dr. William Glasser. (College-Adult)

THE SCIENCE OF FIRE
      20 min color Assn. -Sterling
      *Chris Award, Columbus
      *Blue Ribbon, American/EFLA
A scientific explanation of the principles of combustion and how

fires can be prevented. Sponsor: American Insurance Association. Available to groups of junior high school age level and above, from Sept. 15-Dec. 31 only. No charge.

SCRAPS
    5 1/2 min color Washburn Films '72
    *Golden Eagle, CINE
Accompanied by flute music, an Indian village woman creates a colorful toy bird out of scraps. Her work-worn fingers fashion the body from bits of paper and string. She has transformed material, discarded by society, into a delightful toy. (Elem.-Adult)

SCULPTURE 58--The Story of a Creation
    12 min color Roland
    *Commendation, German Center
    *Culture Award, German Govt.
    *Award of Honor, Cork (Ireland)
    *Honor Award, Bergamo (Italy)
In his Berlin studio, Bernhard Heiliger traces the designs for the large sculpture group that was installed outside the German Pavilion at the 1958 Brussels World Fair. We follow the development from the clay maquette to the original size plaster model. Apart from the physical handicraft involved, viewers become aware of the artist's struggle for expression. Non-verbal. Music composed by Boris Blacher. Producer: Roto Film. (College-Adult)

THE SEA HORSE (A Most Exceptional Fish)
    12 min color Macmillan '68
    *Golden Eagle, CINE
External anatomy, feeding and birth of young, time-lapse microscopic scenes of developing embryos, macroscopic scenes of newborn. Function of air bladder and graphic animation of this apparatus, and the counter-current exchange system. A Reela Film. (HS-College)

SEACOAST VILLAGES OF JAPAN
    19 min color Atlantis
    *Chris Award, Columbus
    *Prize Winner, Venice
    *Award, Asian Pacific
Seacoast village life of Japan, its seasonal changes, and Japan's dependence upon the sea. Produced by J. Michael Hagopian. (Elem.-Junior HS)

THE SEARCH FOR THE NILE: Episode 1--The Dream of the Wanderer
    52 min color Time-Life '72
    *"Emmy," Nat. Academy
The saga of world explorer Richard Burton: his voyage to Mecca disguised as a Persian Muslim; his romance with Isabel Arundel; preparation for the expedition with John Hanning Speke to find the source of the Nile River. Narrator: James Mason. Produced by BBC-TV. (College-Adult)

THE SEARCH FOR THE NILE: Episode 2--Discovery and Betrayal
        52 min   color   Time-Life   '72
        *"Emmy," Nat. Academy
Burton and Speke begin their Nile expedition.   They discover Lake
Tanganyika.   While Burton is ill, Speke alone discovers Lake Victoria and claims it to be the true source of the Nile.   Burton accuses Speke of betrayal.   Narrated by James Mason.   A BBC-TV
production.   (College-Adult)

THE SEARCH FOR THE NILE: Episode 3--The Secret Fountains
        52 min   color   Time-Life   '72
        *"Emmy," Nat. Academy
Speke is chosen by the Royal Geographic Society to return to Africa
and confirm his theory about the Nile.   At Lake Victoria, he discovers Ripon Falls, where the Nile leaves the lake.   Speke meets
two other explorers, Samuel Baker and his wife Florence.   James
Mason, narrator.   From BBC-TV.   (College-Adult)

THE SEARCH FOR THE NILE: Episode 4--The Great Debate
        52 min color   Time-Life   '72
        *"Emmy," Nat. Academy
The Bakers discover Murchison Falls and Lake Albert, both vital
links in the search for the source of the Nile.   Speke and Burton,
enemies now, are invited to a public debate.   Before the debate,
Speke is discovered shot by his own gun, a victim either of an accident or of suicide.   Narrated by James Mason.   From the BBC-TV
Network.   (College-Adult)

THE SEARCH FOR THE NILE: Episode 5--Find Livingstone
        52 min   color   Time-Life   '72
        *"Emmy," Nat. Academy
Livingstone disappears, and the New York Herald sends a reporter,
Henry Morton Stanley, to find him.   Stanley finds Livingstone in
Ujiji.   Livingstone dies while searching for the source of the Nile.
James Mason is the narrator.   From the BBC-TV series.   (College-
Adult)

THE SEARCH FOR THE NILE: Episode 6--Conquest and Death
        52 min   color   Time-Life   '72
        *"Emmy," Nat. Academy
Stanley launches the largest expedition ever.   The riddle of the Nile
is solved.   Burton dies, and his wife burns his manuscripts--one of
the great literary wastes of the 19th century.   Narration by James
Mason.   A BBC-TV production.   (College-Adult)

THE SEARCH FOR ULYSSES
        53 min   color   Carousel   '65
        *Blue Ribbon, American/EFLA
This story has its genesis in Homer's Odyssey.   For nearly 3,000
years, readers of that Greek epic poem have been asking, "Where
did Ulysses really go after Troy?"   Ernle Bradford, British sailor
and scholar whose book Ulysses Found inspired this film, goes on a
journey of discovery, and finds that Ulysses really lived, and that

his adventures took place on islands that still exist.   Produced by
CBS News.   (College-Adult)

THE SEARCHING EYE
       18 min color Pyramid '64
       *Lion of St. Mark, Venice (Child.)
       *Grand Award, Int. of N.Y.
       *Grand Award, Canada/Science
       *Golden Decade, Chicago
       *Grand Award, Cordova ... and other honors
A boy's observations as he walks along a beach, seeing, touching,
exploring, and absorbing his environment.   A guide to greater visual
awareness in relation to nature.   High speed, time-lapse, and stroboscopic photography are used.   Produced by Saul Bass for the Eastman Kodak pavilion at the N.Y. World's Fair.   (Intermediate-Adult)

THE SEASON
       15 min color McGraw-Hill '68
       *Award, San Francisco
       *Certificate, Nat. Student/UCLA
       *2nd Place, Nat. Student/N.Y.
       *First Prize, Chicago
       *Candidate, Academy Award
A cinema-verité indictment of the commercialization of Christmas.
A student film by Donald MacDonald.   Filmed by the Color Produc-
tion Company.   A Contemporary Films release.   (HS-Adult)

SEASON OF FIRE
       15 min color Macmillan '74
       *Red Ribbon, American/EFLA
This record of an erupting volcano, filmed over a seven-week period, shows how civil defense workers struggled to save the seaport
of Heimaey, Iceland.   A blizzard of tephra (volcanic ash) threatens
to bury the town completely, but a fortunate shift of wind blows the
ash out to sea.   Narrator: Robert Earle.   Produced and directed
by Hamlin/Barney.   (HS-Adult)

SECRET IN THE HIVE
       32 min color McGraw-Hill '70
       *Special Planning Prize, Japan
       *Highest Prize, Japanese Sci.
       *Silver Prize, Tokyo
       *Gold Prize, Cultural Document
An indication that complex social systems exist in all levels of the
animal kingdom.   Shows the intricate life of a honeybee colony.
Through close-up photography, the habits and duties of each member
of the colony are examined, including the worker bees and their
ritual dance.   Produced by Sakura Motion Picture Company, Ltd.
and McGraw-Hill Films.   (HS-Adult)

THE SECRET OF MICHELANGELO: Every Man's Dream
       51 min color AIM-Assn.
       *Geo. Foster Peabody Award and other critical honors

Dialogue by Christopher Plummer and Zoë Caldwell. The viewer
will see the Renaissance masterpiece of the Sistine Chapel as
Michelangelo himself saw it over 450 years ago--at arm's-brush
length. An American team performed this artistic feat by climbing
a 64-foot aluminum scaffolding, to record this spectacle: one continuous 5,599 square foot composition containing over 100 figures in
scenes from the Old Testament. Directed by Milton Fruchtman.
Produced by Capital Cities Broadcasting. (College-Adult)

THE SELLING OF THE PENTAGON
        52 min   color   Carousel   '71
        *Award, San Francisco St. College
        *Geo. Foster Peabody Award
        *TV Award, Ohio State Univ.
        *Red Ribbon, American/EFLA
This documentary (which elicited howls of protest from the military)
focuses on the Pentagon's public relations activities that annually
cost from $30 million (admitted) to $190 million (denied). Such activities include free V. I. P. junkets for industrialists to costly war
games; colonels on speaking tours to champion pro-war ideologies;
and a $6.5 million film-radio-TV budget to enlist public support.
Produced by CBS News. (College-Adult)

SENSE PERCEPTION
        28 min   color   Moody Institute
        *Chris Award, Columbus
Sight, hearing, touch, taste, and smell are examined in structure
and function. A demonstration in inverted vision is included, as
well as an experiment in which odors are made "visible." Evidence
is presented that perception takes place in the brain; that sense
organs are merely receptors. The point is made that man's feeble
senses put him in touch with only a very limited part of reality.
(HS-Adult)

SENTINEL: The West Face
        25 min   color   Pyramid   '69
        *Golden Eagle, CINE
        *Bronze Medal, Int. Film & TV
        *Honors, American/EFLA
        *First Place, Trento (Italy)
A record of two men scaling Sentinel Rock in Yosemite Park, a
vertical wall so steep that it is gradually ascended by piton and rope,
foot by foot. Techniques are explained as the men climb, along with
philosophic considerations about their purposes. The ascent becomes
not so much a physical feat as a human expression, just as individual as a name or a signature. Produced by Summit Films. (HS-
Adult)

SERENAL
        4 min   color   Int. Film Bur.
        *Awards: San Sebastian, Bilbao, and Bergamo
To the accompaniment of a string band from Trinidad, a series of
abstract designs, varying in shape, size, position, and movement

cavort in the non-verbal style of Norman McLaren who animated
this production for the National Film Board of Canada. (Intermediate-Adult)

SHADES OF PUFFING BILLY
  11 min color Australia '68
  *Blue Ribbon, American/EFLA
A family film about the miniature railway that runs through the
scenic Dandenong Ranges near Melbourne, Australia. Filmed by the
Commonwealth Film Unit. (Intermediate-Adult)

SHADOW OF AN APPLE
  10 min color New Line Cinema
  *Chris Plaque, Columbus
A subtle yet erotic barrage of animated images encompasses the
violent, anxiety-ridden history of a man. Directed by Robert Lapou-
jade. (College-Adult)

SHAMAN, A TAPESTRY FOR SORCERERS
  26 min color Impact Films '66
  *Award, San Joaquim Delta College ... and many international
    showings
Animated abstractions intended, in the words of the film-maker, "for
the magic makers of the world, those who enter the atlas of the soul
and rummage through the refuse and flowers of time to weave a
talisman for man's rebirth in his house of breath. " Produced by
Storm de Hirsch. (College-Adult)

SHANGO
  10 min color Macmillan '51
  *Award Winner, Venice
  *Prize Winner, Edinburgh
A pair of dance films featuring Geoffrey Holder and his troupe per-
forming authentic African dances that have found their way to Trinidad. A frantic voodoo dance of the Yarubas reaches its climax in
the blood sacrifice of a white chicken. Photographed and edited by
Fritz Henle. (College-Adult)

THE SHAPE OF THINGS
  10 min color Int. Film Bur.
  *Award, La Felguera (Spain)
Records the work of eleven sculptors who came from all over the
world to work in Montreal's mountain park. Varying techniques and
materials resulted in a permanent exhibit for strolling citizens. The
only sounds are the natural ones of the artists chipping, chiseling,
and hammering, blended with a musical score. National Film Board
of Canada. (Intermediate-Adult)

SHELTERED WORKSHOPS
  26 min color Australia '71
  *Gold Camera, US Industrial
The role of community organization in setting up special workshops
for the training and employment of the mentally and physically

handicapped people of Australia. Filmed by the Commonwealth Film
Unit. (College-Adult)

THE SHEPHERD
      12 min   BW   Int. Film Bur.
      *Awards: Johannesburg, Edinburgh, Ireland, and others
A day in the life of a shepherd and his two dogs is portrayed without commentary. Serenity exists in the shepherd's routine, but the
stillness is broken as he comes upon signs of a marauder and goes
in pursuit. National Film Board of Canada. (Intermediate-Adult)

THE SHIP THAT WOULDN'T DIE
      51 min   color   Films Inc.   '69
      *Gabriel Award, Cath. Broadcast.
The U.S.S. Franklin's two years of World War II service are legendary. In this film, the story of her struggle to survive a Kami-
kaze attack is told by 15 survivors. In all of U.S. naval history,
no ship ever took a worse beating and survived. With 720 killed,
nearly 300 wounded and trapped below decks, she limped home under
her own power. NBC News. (College-Adult)

THE SHOOTING GALLERY
      6 min   color   SIM Productions   '70
      *Certificate, Los Angeles
      *Merit Certificate, San Francisco
      *Red Ribbon, American/EFLA
      *Chris Statuette, Columbus
      *Citation, Atlanta
      *Silver Hugo, Chicago
An allegory about the repression of freedom and the destruction of
love. Designed for discussion in language arts, English, and social
studies, as well as public library programs. Produced by Miroslav
Stepanek. (HS-Adult)

SHORT AND SUITE
      5 min   color   Int. Film Bur.
      *Awards: Venice and Bergamo
Abstract imagery interprets jazz in this experimental film by Norman
McLaren and Evelyn Lambart. Effects are drawn directly onto the
film, resulting in a kind of "visual music." Different themes, different instruments, different movements are interpreted by line and
color variations and motion. National Film Board of Canada. (Intermediate-Adult)

A SHORT VISION
      7 min   color   Films Inc.
      *Short Subject Award, Venice
      *Experimental Prize, Cannes
Suggests the effects of a bomb exploded over a sleeping city, destroying all life there--even the animals of nearby fields and forests.
Only a flame lives for a little while. Joan and Peter Foldes are
the co-producers. (HS-Adult)

SHOSTAKOVICH'S NINTH SYMPHONY: An Analysis
    57 min BW McGraw-Hill '67
    *Series Award, Saturday Review
From the Young People's Concert series, with Leonard Bernstein as
master of ceremonies, narrator, and conductor of the N. Y. Philharmonic. A CBS-TV production. (Elem. -Adult)

THE SILENT DRUM
    23 min color Roch. Inst. of Tech. '73
    *Golden Eagle, CINE
Rod Serling explains the job-oriented programs of study at the National Technical Institute for the Deaf. Also described is the special
relationship between NTID and its sponsor, Rochester Institute of
Technology, the world's first college to educate the deaf within a
hearing environment. Produced by Raul da Silva. Sponsor: the
U. S. Dept. of Health, Education and Welfare. Available on free
loan. (College-Adult)

SIQUEIROS: "El Maestro"
    14 min color Encyc. Brit. '69
    *Golden Eagle, CINE
A documentary of the largest mural ever created, "The March of
Humanity in Latin America" by David Siqueiros in Mexico City. Focuses on the technique he employs, a combination of sculpture and
painting, called esculpto-pintura. With students, painters, welders,
architects, and artisans, the artist involves a whole community of
people. Throughout the film, Siqueiros supervises, paints, and discusses his techniques and philosophy. Available in Spanish and English. (HS-Adult)

SIRENE
    10 min color Int. Film Bur. '70
    *Silver Hugo, Chicago
This wordless story of a mermaid in the harbor of a large city is
a comment on modern life. The creature from another era is
charmed by a young man playing a flute, but the machines that surround the harbor destroy the mermaid. The investigation of her
death provides a satirical look at bureaucratic institutions. When
the chaos has ended, the young man finds the mermaid's spirit has
survived. Animation by Raoul Servais. (Intermediate-Adult)

SIXTEEN IN WEBSTER GROVES
    47 min BW Carousel '66
    *Blue Ribbon, American/EFLA
Webster Groves, Missouri, is an affluent suburb of St. Louis. A
good car, good looks, the "right family" are of primary importance.
Missing is the spirit of adventure and an awareness of racial wars
or poverty. Shows that teenagers there are motivated by pressures
to "make the grade," that children's attitudes stem from parents'
expectations and the constraining level of conformity. Produced by
CBS News. (HS-Adult)

THE SIXTIES
>15 min   color with BW   Pyramid   '70
>*Bronze Medal, Int. Film & TV
>*Special Award, Chicago
>*Ten Best, Ann Arbor
>*Gold Medal, Atlanta

The passions and polarizations of a decade are composed from miles of CBS News footage which are edited to point out parallels and contradictions. An overview of events in an era of great change. Produced by Charles Braverman. (HS-Adult)

60 CYCLES
>17 min   color   McGraw-Hill
>*Blue Ribbon, American/EFLA
>*Honors: Moscow
> London, Prague, and Cork

The 11th St. Laurent long-distance bicycle race over 1,500 miles of Quebec countryside in 12 days--the longest amateur competition in the world. The cyclists race away, a hundred strong, forcing their bright circles of steel along the black ribbon of asphalt. Produced by the National Film Board of Canada. (Intermediate-Adult)

SKATER DATER
>18 min   color   Pyramid   '65
>*Grand Prix, Cannes
>*Silver Medal, Moscow
>*Best Film, Cork
>*Silver Trophy, Cortina
>*Merit Award, Edinburgh

A boy's emergence into adolescence is the underlying theme. As some boys on skateboards are coasting down their neighborhood hill, one youth's meeting with a girl is broken off by the peer pressure of his "gang." With his loss of a contest for leadership, the youth returns to the girl. His pals seem to realize he will not come back. Film-maker: Noel Black. (Intermediate-Adult)

SKI RACER
>36 min   color   Pyramid   '70
>*1st Place, US Industrial

A documentary on the international ski racing circuit. Cinema-verité shows lockerroom preparations, casual chatter before the race, and the world's most competitive skiers talking about winning and losing. A blend of the real and the poetic, an examination of the art of skiing, and the psychology of the skier. Produced by Summit Films. (HS-Adult)

SKI THE OUTER LIMITS
>25 min   color   Pyramid
>*Grand Prize, American/EFLA
>*First Place, Trento
>*Golden Eagle, CINE
>*Honor Cup, Cortina
>*Bronze Medal, Atlanta ... and other awards

Philosophy, photography, and skiing are combined in this film.
Slow motion and natural speed photography show the style, control,
and balance required to push towards the "outer limits" of one's
ability. Downhill racing, slalom, ski dancing, and acrobatics are
some of the limit-pushing activities. Producer: Summit Films.
(HS-Adult)

SKINNY AND FATTY
    45 min BW McGraw-Hill '69
    *Grand Prize, Vancouver
Skinny and Fatty meet when Fatty arrives at a new school in the
middle of the term. Shy and unsure of himself, Fatty has a knack
of making people detest him. Skinny has no trouble making friends.
Gradually, the two become inseparable. But soon Skinny's family
must move, and Fatty is left with only memories and a primitive
toy that Skinny gave him. However, this toy prods Fatty into his
first awkward steps toward growing up. Originally shown as part
of the CBS Children's Film Festival. Produced by World Presentations, Inc. A Contemporary Films release. (Intermediate-Adult)

SKY
    10 min color McGraw-Hill '62
    *Awards: Columbus and Saskatchewan
From the height of the rim of the western plains,
this film condenses the spectacle of the sun's daily arc across the
sky. Photographed with many lenses and camera speeds, the result
is a cinematographic experience of changing appearance of the open
sky. Produced by the National Film Board of Canada. A Contemporary Films release. (Intermediate-Adult)

SKY CAPERS
    15 min color Pyramid '68
    *Prix du President, Grenoble
    *Merit Award, Columbia
This sky-diving world of free-falling bodies, somersaulting, twisting,
and group patterns in the upper air was photographed by cameras
mounted on parachutist helmets. The rock song "Fly High" is the
theme, and there are scenes of comedy and night shots. Film-
maker: Fred Hudson. (HS-Adult)

SKY OVER HOLLAND
    22 min color Warner Bros. '66
    *Gold Palm, Cannes
What such great Dutch masters as Rembrandt, Ruysdael, Van Gogh,
Mondrian put on canvas, the modern motion picture camera parallels,
as it skims over modern Holland's fields, cities, industries, trans-
portation system, waters, playgrounds and people. (Intermediate-
Adult)

THE SLAVE EXPERIENCE
    9 min color Doubleday '70
    *Merit Award, Philadelphia
The story of slavery in North America, from the arrival of the first

Africans to the eve of the Civil War, is told in the words of slaves.
Etchings, engravings and other graphics from the period, and a
musical score based on indigenous themes add to the authenticity.
This animated film is based on a concept developed by two social
studies teachers. Designed by Tee Collins, animator of Sesame
Street's alphabet. (Intermediate-Adult)

SLAVERY AND SLAVE RESISTANCE
    23 1/2 min color Perspective '71
    *Grand Award, Int. of N.Y.
    *Creative Award, US Industrial
How the black people endured and resisted slavery at the risk of
life itself. Presented are achievements of some famous runaway
slaves, including poet Phillis Wheatley; novelist and playwright William Wells Brown; and anti-slavery orator and editor Frederick
Douglass. Produced for the New York Times. (HS-Adult)

THE SLOW GUILLOTINE
    53 min color Films Inc. '69
    *"Emmy," Nat. Academy
    *Award, duPont-Columbia
If no action is taken, most of our urban centers will be uninhabita-
ble before the year 2000. It is not only the quality of life that is
in danger, but the actual existence of life. This film focuses on
Los Angeles but makes it clear that air pollution is a danger to the
whole country. Produced by KNBC-TV. (College-Adult)

THE SMILE (Le Sourire)
    18 min color McGraw-Hill '63
    *Best Short Subject, Cannes
The smile belongs to Aung, a Burmese child who is a novice in a
monastery. It is also the smile of Unarada, the Buddhist priest,
who sees the child's fervor in the depth of his meditation. Aung's
smile is the response of his heart to things and people who speak to
him as he makes his way to the Great Golden Pagoda of Rangoon,
seeking to discover the meaning hidden beneath appearances. Produced by Serge Bourguignon. A Contemporary Films release.
(Intermediate-Adult)

SNAILS
    11 min color ACI Films '70
    *Award of Merit, Landers
    *Red Ribbon, American/EFLA
Here, in close-up, are snails in their normal activities--moving,
eating, resting, and reproducing. Action has been speeded up but
not enough to destroy the distinctive quality of snail movement.
Shows shells of snails from all over the world and, in a cutaway
view, exhibits the complexity and beauty of the spiral shell. (Intermediate-HS)

SNOW
    10 min color ACI Films '69
    *Awards: Barcelona, Genoa, Oberhausen, Edinburgh, and Tours

*Nomination, Academy Award

A documentary contrasting the comfort of train passengers with the cold, hard work done to keep the tracks clear of snow. Begins with naturalistic color. Then come shots of first one rail, then the other, the snowplow, the train with its passengers--all in progressively shorter cuts. The pace then builds to a pandemonium of picture and cuts, distorted natural sounds, and jazz by Sandy Wilson. A British Transport Film by Geoffrey Jones. (Intermediate-Adult)

THE SNOWMAN
          10 min color McGraw-Hill '69
          *Honor Prize, Int. Congress
          *Silver Plaque, Int. Review
          *Silver Pelican, Int. Festival
          *Lion of St. Mark, Venice
The characters and setting for this film were created by animating wool fibre. Snowmen are usually condemned to melting in the sun, but not this one. After rescuing his friends from disaster, the snowman is saved from melting by his friends who carry him to the Arctic. Electronic music. A Contemporary Films release. (Primary-Intermediate)

SOIR DE FÊTE
          6 min color Macmillan '55
          *Prix Émile Cohl
The spirit of a celebration--fireworks, people, events--is suggested in these animated abstractions coupled with the music of Robert Monsigny. Film-maker: Albert Pierru. (Intermediate-Adult)

SOLILOQUY OF A RIVER
          19 min color A-V Explorations '68
          *Golden Eagle, CINE
Story of a river from its spring source to its struggle for life, as it lethargically moves past a city. "There is no end to a river and to its story, except as man decrees," says this film with a water pollution message, emphasizing the importance of all life in and around a stream. Filmed by Bob Davidson. (Intermediate-Adult)

SOLO
          15 min color Pyramid '72
          *Academy Award Nomination
          *Golden Eagle, CINE
          *Special Prize, Moscow
          *Grand Prize, Thessalonika
          *Red Ribbon, American/EFLA ... and many other awards
The pleasures and dangers of mountain climbing. The filmmaker non-verbally presents three aspects of climbing: the rhythm of sustained physical effort; the discovery of scenes and weather unknown to others; and the commitment to challenges that must be met alone. Produced by Mike Hoover. (Intermediate-Adult)

SOME ARE MORE EQUAL THAN OTHERS
          40 min BW Carousel '71

*Silver Gavel, American Bar Assn.
*TV Award, Christopher Movement
This segment from the "Justice in America" series scrutinizes the
legal treatment of ethnic minorities, an inequitable bail system, dis-
criminatory practices in jury selection, and, in property or creditor/
debtor civil actions, a system that works mostly against the poor.
Produced by CBS News. (College-Adult)

SOMEBODY WAITING
    24 min   color   Ext. Media Center   '71
    *Nomination, Academy Award
    *1st Prize, National Educ.
About children who live at Sonoma State Hospital. They have severe
cerebral dysfunction and are among the most physically, emotionally,
and mentally handicapped children in society. Demonstrates how
further handicapping can be prevented by therapeutic nursing and environmental stimulation. Produced by Berkeley for the School of
Nursing of the University of California at San Francisco. (College-
Adult)

SOMETHING CONCRETE
    24 min   color   AIM-Assn.
    *Bronze Plaque, Nat. Committee
Documents an authentic structural collapse and what contributed to
the weakness. This entails the stresses and strains on concrete
placement and the behavior of concrete under various conditions.
Construction techniques are coupled with safety practices. (HS-Adult)

SOMETHING TO WORK FOR
    30 min   color   Roundtable
    *Golden Eagle, CINE
Contrasts the attempts of two managers to motivate their subordinates.
One uses an overly enthusiastic technique, while the other more suc-
cessful manager sets high but attainable standards for his personnel.
As a result, employee self-esteem and performance increase. (Col-
lege-Adult)

THE SONNETS: Shakespeare's Moods of Love
    21 min   color   Learn. Corp.   '72
    *Silver Hugo, Chicago
Photographed in the English countryside, this film's visual treatment
attempts to parallel Shakespeare's language. A printed sheet containing the ten sonnets recited is provided with each print of the
film. Spoken and played by members of the Royal Shakespeare Company. (HS-College)

THE SORCERER'S APPRENTICE
    14 min   color   Weston Woods   '63
    *Chris Certificate, Columbus
A live-action interpretation of the classic fairy tale that became the
basis for musical composition of that name. Produced by Mort
Schindel. (Primary-Intermediate)

SORT OF A COMMERCIAL FOR AN ICEBAG
   16 min   color   Benchmark   '70
   *Blue Ribbon, American/EFLA
Artist Claes Oldenburg creates an outdoor sculpture for the World's
Fair in Osaka.   With wit and virtuosity, he explores familiar objects for combinations of characteristics and conditions.   This finally leads him to a giant, metal-capped, pink icebag with a motor inside.   You'll probably never see an icebag in quite the same way
again.   (College-Adult)

THE SOUND OF POETRY
   10 min   color   Doubleday   '70
   *Golden Eagle, CINE
Designed to help students explore the poetry of Wallace Stevens, and
to think about the meanings and possibilities of all poetry.   (HS)

SOUNDS OF NATURE
   26 min   color   A-V Explorations   '70
   *Best Outdoor Sound, Canadian
Illustrates the ease with which even children can record birdcalls
and other natural sounds with a cassette recorder and sound para-
bola.   Seen and heard are the western chorus frog, Canada geese,
loons, white-throated sparrow, indigo bunting, yellow warbler, yellow shafted flicker, and the chestnut-sided warbler.   Film-maker:
Dan Gibson.   (HS-Adult)

SOUTH AFRICA'S ANIMAL KINGDOM
   18 min   color   Assn.-Sterling
   *Chris Award, Columbus
This film visits South Africa's many game preserves, where animals
roam freely.   These parks and preserves offer sanctuary for an array of birds and beasts, many saved from extinction.   Rangers guide
safaris, on foot and horseback, to see these animals in their natural
surroundings on deserts, plains, and mountains--offering a variety
of opportunities for exploration.   South African Tourist Corporation,
sponsor.   Free loan.   Available to adult groups.

SOUTHERN ACCENTS, NORTHERN GHETTOS
   50 min   BW   Benchmark
   *Chris Certificate, Columbus
This case history of a black family dramatizes one of the great
problems facing our nation today: black families who flee southern
rural poverty for northern cities, only to be trapped on welfare in
black inner city ghettos.   ABC-Television (College-Adult)

SOUTHERN ASIA--Problems of Transition
   16 min   color   Barr Films   '67
   *Award Winner, Columbus
Explores some of the traditions, attitudes, and conditions that affect
the modernization of the ancient cultures of Southern Asia.   Photography: Ed Lark.   (HS-Adult)

THE SOVIET UNION: A Student's Life
      21 min   color   Encyc. Brit.   '72
      *Red Ribbon, American/EFLA
      *Golden Eagle, CINE
Introduces Nikolai Diachenko, a chemical engineering student. As
he traces his life from nursery school to the university in Moscow,
viewers see the vital part that Communist youth movements play.
Nikolai spends a summer at a work camp in Siberia, an example of
the dual emphasis on intellectual achievement and manual labor to
help develop the vast land. (HS-College)

SPAIN--Proud Past and Promising Future
      13 min   color   Neubacher-Vetter
      *Statuette Award, Columbus
Designed to enrich the student's understanding of modern Spain.
Emphasizes its geography and its contributions to world history and
culture. With new freedoms and a progressive spirit, Spain is seen
moving toward a promising future. (Junior-Senior HS)

THE SPANISH EARTH
      54 min   BW   Macmillan   '36
      *Ten Best, Nat. Board
A screen story of the issues behind the Civil War in Spain, dramatizing the effect of the Fascist uprising on the ordinary citizen. A
warning, at the time, of days to come after the destruction of the
Republic of Spain. Ernest Hemingway wrote and spoke the narration
for this film--the only one on which he ever actually worked. Directed by Joris Ivens. Script by Lillian Hellman, John Dos Passos,
and Archibald MacLeish. Music by Virgil Thompson and Marc
Blitzstein. (College-Adult)

SPIRES/BALLOTS REPORT
      15 min   color   Ext. Media Center   '70
      *Chris Award, Columbus
A non-technical description of how computers are used in controlling
the mass of library materials and the increasing costs of manual
processing systems. Outlines current research at Stanford Univ.,
with satiric reviews of man's earlier efforts at information storage.
Produced by the University of California. (College-Adult)

THE SPIRIT OF THE RENAISSANCE
      31 min   color   Encyc. Brit.   '71
      *Golden Eagle, CINE
      *Chris Statuette, Columbus
Explores the intellectual and artistic climate of Italy during the 15th
and 16th centuries, framed against scenes from the life of a contemporary Florentine. The lives of Petrarch, Alberti, and da Vinci
illustrate facets of the Renaissance that made it unique in religion,
education, science, art, literature, and politics. The invasion of
Tuscany by French armies brought the Renaissance to an end. But
the viewer is left with the question: does the spirit of an age ever
die? From the EBE Humanities Series. (HS-Adult)

SPIRIT POSSESSION OF ALEJANDRO MAMANI
    27 min   color Fieldstaff   '74
    *Blue Ribbon, American/EFLA
An old Bolivian nears the end of his days. He has property and
status but not contentment. Believing himself possessed of evil
spirits, he reveals an anguish that can bring viewers an insight into
the universal confrontation with old age and death. Produced by
Norman Miller for the American Universities Field Service. (Senior HS-Adult)

SPORTS MEDICINE
    27 1/2 min   color   Australia   '70
    *Gold Camera, US Industrial
The role of medical science in improving performance and remedy-
ing injuries. Scientific training techniques enable the competitor to
make greater demands on his stamina. Photographed by the Commonwealth Film Unit. (College-Adult)

SPOTTY: Story of a Fawn
    11 min   color   Coronet
    *Participation, Venice
Filmed in the North Woods, the adventures of Spotty, a wild fawn,
are believably presented. Participation techniques are aurally and
visually built into this material, and the narration has been keyed
to primary grade wordlists. (Elem.)

SPUD'S SUMMER: Interracial Understanding
    26 min   color   McGraw-Hill   '68
    *TV Award, San Francisco
The feelings and experiences of a six-year-old boy from Harlem,
making his first visit to the country. Spud, the lad who narrates
the film, moves--trustful and confiding--from a New York ghetto to
wholesome farm life in Chester Country, Pennsylvania. Expressing
his feelings about farm and city, Spud reveals how his world broad-
ens and his ideals change. Produced by CBS News. (College-Adult)

STALIN vs. TROTSKY
    25 min   BW   Films Inc.   '64
    *Blue Ribbon, American/EFLA
The struggle between Trotsky's genius and Stalin's ruthlessness is
illuminated in this episode tracing Stalin's brutal efforts to rule all
Russia, and Trotsky's bitter, futile fight for supremacy. The film
begins with the end of the Czarist regime. Narrator: Edmond
O'Brien. Released by David Wolper's Metromedia Producers Corporation. (HS-College)

STANDING WAVES AND THE PRINCIPLE OF SUPERIMPOSITION
    11 min   color   Encyc. Brit.   '70
    *Blue Ribbon, American/EFLA
    *Golden Eagle, CINE
    *Chris Certificate, Columbus
Explains the formation and characteristics of Standing Waves, a
physics principle that is basic to understanding the behavior of

matter. Computer animation and simple experiments demonstrate how Standing Waves are produced by the superimposition of two identical wave patterns traveling in opposite directions. The principle is then extended to an explanation of atomic structure. Collaborator: Albert V. Baez, Ph. D., Science Consultant to UNESCO. (HS-College)

THE STATUE OF LIBERTY
        14 min   color   Handel   '64
        *Freedoms Foundation Award
A visit to the Statue of Liberty by a social studies teacher and his son interprets the history and the meaning of one of the greatest monuments in the world. A close look at the famous lady in New York Harbor. Produced by the National Park Service. (Intermediate-Junior HS)

THE STEADFAST TIN SOLDIER
        14 min   color   Macmillan
        *Winner, Golden Reel Award
From the fairy tale by Hans Christian Andersen. This cartoon is the fantasy of the one-legged toy soldier who falls in love with a ballet doll. Produced by Ivo Caprino. (Preschool-Intermediate)

STICKY MY FINGERS, FLEET MY FEET
        23 min   color   Time-Life   '72
        *Red Ribbon, American/EFLA
Deflates one of the classic American myths with pathos and humor: the middle-aged male who clings to a youthful standard of physical prowess and he-man virility through "touch" football. Produced by John Hancock with aid from the American Film Institute. (College-Adult)

STITCHERY
        15 min   color   ACI Films   '69
        *Award of Merit, Landers
The techniques of embroidery, needlepoint, and appliqué. Through the use of examples, this film illustrates the wide variety of designs that can be achieved. These range from simply conceived ideas to motifs of considerable complexity. (HS-Adult)

THE STOLEN NECKLACE
        8 min   color   ACI Films   '71
        *Golden Eagle, CINE
Based on the book by Anne Rockwell, this story from India is retold in animation. A princess owns a necklace of pearls. While she is bathing in her garden, one of the monkeys there steals the necklace. The gardener thinks up a way to trick the thief. A William Claiborne Film. (Primary-Intermediate)

THE STOLEN PLANS
        57 min   BW   Sterling Educ.   '70
        *Silver Gondola, Venice
An adventure story set in London, this film deals with the successful

efforts of a boy and a girl to outwit spies who are trying to steal secret plans from an aircraft designer. Produced by the Children's Film Foundation (Britain). (Ages 7-12)

STONE SOUP
    11 min   color   Weston Woods   '55
    *Award of Merit, Columbus
An iconographic version of the children's picturebook of the same name. Also available with Spanish narration. Produced by Mort Schindel. (Elem.)

THE STONECUTTER
    6 min   color   Int. Film Foundation
    *Award of Merit, Landers
    *Golden Eagle, CINE
In this ancient Japanese tale of envy, Tasaku the stonecutter in his search for happiness is changed into a Prince, the Sun, a Cloud, and finally a Mountain ... only to realize he was happiest as himself! Animated images are combined with traditional Japanese forms, while authentic music provides the background. (Elem.)

STONES OF EDEN
    25 min   color   McGraw-Hill   '65
    *Golden Eagle, CINE
Documents a year in the life of a farmer in the mountains of central Afghanistan, showing the ancient implements he must use, and the harsh system of credit under which he must labor. His goal in life: to have his son go through school so that he can become a truckdriver. Directed and photographed by William A. Furman. A Contemporary Films release. (HS-Adult)

STOP IN THE MARSHLANDS
    30 min   BW   New Line Cinema   '72
    *Blue Ribbon, American/EFLA
A Swedish railroad brakeman quietly rejects his job for a life of reflection on the natural beauty around him. He is chastised by the station master, whose only reflection of the country is its mosquitoes. Throughout the day, the brakeman wanders and enjoys the smells of nature and the sound of a waterfall. At the end of the day, he returns to the station, and viewers are left to conclude whether he resumes his working life on the next train. Directed by Jan Troell; starring Max von Sydow. Swedish with English subtitles. (HS-Adult)

A STORM OF STRANGERS
    27 min   BW   ACI Films   '69
    *Best Film, San Francisco
    *Gold Medal, Atlanta
    *Golden Eagle, CINE
    *Chris Award, Columbus
    *Blue Ribbon, American/EFLA ... and other honors
Jewish immigration to New York's Lower East Side around 1910 is told through photographs of the period. The narrator, Herschel

Bernardi, speaks as an elderly Jew still living on Delancey Street.
The story ends as the old man looks with a sympathetic eye on the
new immigrants in his neighborhood--the Black and Puerto Rican
families who have even greater obstacles to surmount.   Produced by
the National Communications Foundation Project.   (HS-Adult)

STORM OVER THE SUPREME COURT, Part I: 1790-1932
　　　　21 min   BW   Carousel   '63
　　　　*Geo. Foster Peabody Award
Traces the development of the Court as a force in American government.   Photographs, political cartoons, and portraits bring to life
the early days with Thomas Jefferson, Andrew Jackson, and Chief
Justice John Marshall.   Also studied is Abraham Lincoln's clash
over the Dred Scott decision.   Produced by CBS News.   (HS-College)

STORM OVER THE SUPREME COURT, Part II: 1933-Present
　　　　31 min   BW   Carousel   '63
　　　　*Geo. Foster Peabody Award
FDR and his attempt to "pack" the Court, the ideological clashes be-
tween Justices Felix Frankfurter and Hugo Black are discussed by
Harvard law professor Paul Freund.   Readings by Frederic March,
Carl Sandburg, Archibald MacLeish, and Mark Van Doren.   Pro-
duced by CBS News.   (HS-College)

THE STORY ABOUT PING
　　　　10 min   color   Weston Woods   '55
　　　　*Award of Merit, Columbus
An iconographic version of the children's picturebook of the same
name.   Also available in Spanish and in Super 8 Sound.   Produced
by Mort Schindel.   (Elem.)

THE STORY OF A CRAFTSMAN
　　　　21 min   color   Malibu Films   '73
　　　　*First Prize, Marin County Fair
　　　　*Silver Cindy, Info. Film
In his home, at his own pace, in his own way, Dominic Calicchio
begins the making of his 2,135th trumpet.   His five-day week is condensed into the length of this film, reflecting one man's way of working in tempo with himself.   Produced by S. Marc Tapper and Karl
H. Dempwolf.   (HS-Adult)

THE STORY OF DR. LISTER
　　　　28 1/2 min   color   Assn. -Sterling
　　　　*Golden Eagle, CINE
Dr. Joseph Lister's discovery of an antiseptic to combat infection is
enacted in this Hollywood production.   Richard Ney as the young
surgeon who dedicated himself to ridding the world of this age-old
scourge, and Wanda Hendrix as his wife, recreate the story of how
a man's courage and convictions changed the course of modern medicine.   Free loan.   Warner-Lambert Company, sponsor.   (HS-Adult)

THE STORY OF ELECTRICITY--The Greeks to Franklin
　　　　13 1/2 min   color   Coronet   '70

*Golden Eagle, CINE

Re-enactments of advances in man's knowledge of electricity are given in the words of the discoverers, from the early Greeks' elektron (or amber) to Benjamin Franklin's single-fluid theory. The ideas, methods, and inventions of William Gilbert, Stephen Gray, Francis Hauksbee, Pieter van Musschenbroek and, finally, Franklin are illustrated. (Intermediate-Junior HS)

THE STORY OF MY LIFE: HANS CHRISTIAN ANDERSEN
27 min BW Macmillan '55
*Silver Reel Literary Award

This biography projects Andersen's own spirit, expressed in words from his diary, and shows his life in the world of 1805-1875, reconstructed by the use of documents, drawings, paintings, photos, and even his belongings. A Danish Culture Film. Written and directed by Jorgen Roos. (Elem.-Adult)

STORY OF THE BLOOD STREAM
24 min color Moody Institute
*Golden Eagle, CINE

The circulatory system supplies the human body with fuel, with oxygen to burn the fuel, and it carries off waste as well. Some of the components of this system are studied in detail: the red cell as it performs its chemical magic; the white cell in its clean-up function; capillaries so tiny the blood cells go through in single file. The familiar bi-conclave shape is confirmed as ideal for the job. Also available in Spanish. (HS)

STORY OF THE SOUTHERN CROSS
11 min color AIM-Assn.
*Chris Award, Columbus

Aboriginal legend of the story of the Southern Cross constellation. The film is endowed with colorful drawings of Australian landscapes. Authentic background music is played on the didgeridoo and the bullroarer. (Intermediate-Adult)

STRANGE PARTNERS (Symbiosis in the Sea)
12 min color Macmillan '68
*Blue Ribbon, American/EFLA
*Chris Certificate, Columbus
*Science Prize, La Plata
*Silver Anchor, Toulon
*Golden Eagle, CINE

Explanation of mutualism, commensalism, and parasitism with examples of symbiosis. Includes scenes of pearl fish entering the anal cavity of the sea cucumber, and shows the neon goby cleaning the gills and mouth of the moray eel. Demonstrates the ecological effects of "cleaning stations" upon the area. Produced by Reela Films. (HS-College)

THE STRANGE STORY OF A FROG WHO BECAME A PRINCE
11 1/2 min color Xerox Films '73
*Golden Eagle, CINE

Who wants to be a prince? Not this hapless frog who runs up
against a snap-happy witch. No amount of finger-snapping or magic
words can restore his former froghood. All ends happily, as viewers discover that being what you are is the greatest magic of all.
(Primary-Intermediate)

THE STRANGEST VOYAGE
       52 min   color   Mariner   '74
       *Statuette, Columbus
Coleridge's Rime of the Ancient Mariner is prefaced by a brief
background study of the author and how he was inspired to write
this classic poem.   The live-action scenes of his memorabilia are
coupled with original animation.   The narrative poem itself includes
the Gustave Doré engravings, with color effects added.   Narration
is provided by Sir Michael Redgrave.   Produced and directed by
Raul da Silva.   (HS-Adult)

THE STRAY
       14 min   color   TeleKETICS
       *Golden Eagle, CINE
Humorous irony is the tone of this story of 12 lovable children and
their harried chaperone on an outing to the San Diego Zoo.   In its
treatment of the familiar lost child theme, the film shows how Number Twelve strays from the group.   The ending goes beyond the
obvious "Don't stray" safety message as Number Twelve is joyously
returned to the group.   (Elem. -Adult)

STREAM
       15 min   color   ACI Films   '70
       *Golden Hugo, Chicago
       *Golden Eagle, CINE
       *Chris Statuette, Columbus
       *Honors, American/EFLA
A man finds a place where he can sail his model boat in privacy.
But he allows the boat to slip away, and its downstream journey is
marked by confrontations with pollution.   Upon recovery of his boat,
the man makes a futile attempt to cleanse it.   No longer a thing of
beauty, however, it is discarded into refuse on the bank of the
stream.   Non-narrative.   A Communico Film.   (Intermediate-Adult)

STREET MUSIQUE
       9 min   color   Learn. Corp.   '73
       *Silver Hugo, Chicago
       *Award, National Educ.
Moving from line-drawings to complex abstractions, this animation
offers a non-verbal interpretation of reactions to music played spontaneously in the open.   Produced by Ryan Larkin for the National
Film Board of Canada.   (Elem. -Adult)

STREET TO THE WORLD
       13 3/4 min   BW   Nat. Film Bd.
       *Award: Locarno (Switzerland)
A study of the Montreal dock area where a boy escapes the monotony

of his backyard to while away a few hours by exploring the wharves and watching ships passing up and down the St. Lawrence River. (Intermediate-Adult)

THE STRING BEAN (Le Haricot)
17 min BW with color McGraw-Hill '64
*Golden Palm, Cannes
An old Parisian woman cultivates a bean plant with a devotion close to love. Concerned for its future, she surreptitiously plants it in the Garden of Tuileries. The fate of her plant-friend and her act of optimism form the thread of this wordless film story. Film-maker: Edmond Séchan. (Intermediate-Adult)

THE STRONGER
17 min color Doubleday '70
*Golden Eagle, CINE
*Blue Ribbon, American/EFLA
*Chris Award, Columbus
*Silver Medal, Atlanta
Based on the one-act play by Swedish playwright August Strindberg. An actress is sitting alone in a cafe. An old acquaintance--also an actress--approaches, joins her and begins to talk. The first woman never speaks, but her wordless responses compel the other to go on talking, almost compulsively, finally expressing a long-harbored sus-picion that the silent woman has been having an affair with her hus-band. Viveca Lindfors plays both parts. (HS-Adult)

A STUDY IN WET
7 min color ACI Films '66
*Golden Eagle, CINE
*Blue Ribbon, American/EFLA
All the pictures and all the sounds originate from water. The sound-track is a musical score made by drops of water; photography is of still water, ripples, waves and great breakers. Surfers, swimmers, water skiers appear and disappear, in and out of the water, to involve the viewer in the sound and feel of water. A Homer Groenig Film. (Intermediate-Adult)

STYLE OF CHAMPIONS
18 1/2 min color Australia '70
*Best Sports Film, Yorktown
The Australian crawl is demonstrated by Olympic swimmers training in Australia. Slow-motion underwater sequences reveal some secrets of their style. Produced by the Commonwealth Film Unit. (HS-College)

SUFFER THE LITTLE CHILDREN
53 min color Films Inc. '72
*"Emmy," Nat. Academy
*Award, San Francisco St.
What are the effects of violence and suspicion on children? This examination of Northern Ireland focuses on the pervasive hatred be-tween Catholic and Protestant groups, and what that hatred is doing

to their children. It looks at life in the Catholic ghetto, the role
of the army, and the silent majority of Protestants in this breeding
ground of bigotry. An NBC News production. (College-Adult)

SUMMERHILL
    28 min color Nat. Film Bd.
    *Award, Conf. on Children
A visit to a school without rules, where pupils study what they wish,
and where students are their own masters. This coeducational English boarding school, Summerhill, was founded by Alexander Neill a
half-century ago. He explains his objectives and the activities of
the children. (College-Adult)

SUMMERPLAY
    14 min color Counterpoint '71
    *Golden Eagle, CINE
A vignette of the relationships and pressures that develop when a
day at the beach brings together two boys and their dog, a young
man and his girlfriend, and a motorcycle gang. The two boys have
their bravery measured, with some unexpected reactions from the
others. Film-maker: Tony Stefano. (Intermediate-HS)

SUMMERTHING
    22 3/4 min color Boston Film Center '70
    *"Emmy" Nomination, Nat. Academy
The story of Boston's summer festival of the arts that takes place
in fourteen neighborhoods. Depicts art programs, rock concerts,
tot lots, puppet shows, and theatrical improvisations in the streets.
Made by 18-20 year olds, with the help of WBZ-TV. (HS-College)

SUNDAY LARK
    12 min BW McGraw-Hill '66
    *Golden Eagle, CINE
    *Silver Bear, Berlin
What happens when a little girl wanders into a large office on Sunday? Six-year-old Stella, lost in Wall Street, strolls into the silent
offices of a brokerage firm. Stella builds a wall of wastepaper
baskets. She learns how to answer six telephones at once, and puts
a new listing on the stock "quote" board. And when Stella finds her
way into the IBM room, the computers go wild. Electronic music
accompanies the IBM sequence. No dialogue or narration. A Contemporary Films release. (Elem.-Adult)

SURPRISE BOOGIE
    6 min color Macmillan '57
    *Animation Prize, French Govt.
    *First Prize, Mannheim (Germany)
Animated impressions of Robert Cambier's original jazz score.
Film-maker: Albert Pierru. (HS-Adult)

SURVIVAL ON THE PRAIRIE
    54 min color Films Inc. '70
    *Award, West. Heritage

*Award, TV Newsfilm

The prairie is a vast area covered with grass. Years ago, it was a paradise for the gopher, the bison, and the elk. These creatures of the grass lived on it, and the balance of nature protected them and the land. Then came man with his plow. The land was turned over. The rich grass and humus were destroyed. Drought followed, and the air was filled with dust. Man finally realized that land has to be protected. NBC News. (College-Adult)

THE SWAN SONG
　　25 min　color　Carousel　'70
　　*Gold Medal, Atlanta
This Russian classic provides a springboard for bravura acting by Richard Kiley and Michael Dunn. Adapted from Chekhov's 1886 stage version, this film is an exercise in theater arts, showing the adaptability of the short story to an audiovisual format. Cinerep Productions. (HS-College)

SWIMMER
　　26 min　color　Australia　'71
　　*Gold Camera, US Industrial
The life of an Olympic gold medalist is seen as discipline, self-sacrifice, and interruptions in study in this portrait of two young champions from Australia. Photographed by the Commonwealth Film Unit. (HS-College)

THE SWING
　　7 min　color　Washburn Films　'73
　　*Award, Festival de Tours
　　*Golden Eagle, CINE
A non-verbal experience, this film presents a kaleidoscopic approach to circus trapeze artists, focusing on their floating, choreographic movements. With music by jazz composer Bobby Timmons, a coupling of picture and sound is achieved. Discussions might include such topics as freedom, control, self-expression, and "doing your own thing." (Junior-Senior HS)

SWISS PEASANT ARTIST: HAUSWIRTH
　　7 min　color　Macmillan　'54
　　*Award of Merit, Boston
Impressions of the work and life of 19th century Swiss artist Jean Jacques Hauswirth, whose paper cutouts are decorative peasant motifs. A Swiss-German folk song provides the musical setting. Animated. A Pinschewer Film Studio presentation. (HS-Adult)

SYDNEY OPERA HOUSE
　　8 1/2 min　color　Australia　'67
　　*Gold Camera, US Industrial
A prize-winning design by John Utzon, the Sydney Opera House has attracted worldwide acclaim and controversy. This progress report was made at an advanced stage of construction. Produced by the Commonwealth Film Unit. (College-Adult)

SYMMETRIES OF THE CUBE
   13 1/2 min   color   Int. Film Bur.   '71
   *First Prize, Venice-Padua
   *Golden Eagle, CINE
The symmetries of a square are exhibited as products of reflections.
The film then studies the octahedral group via reflections produced
by a kaleidoscope, and shows how construction of these kaleido-
scopes is related to the cube and the octahedron.   Mathematicians:
H. S. M. Coxeter and W. O. J. Moser.   (HS-College)

SYMMETRY
   10 1/2 min   color   McGraw-Hill   '67
   *First Prize, Salerno
   *Golden Eagle, CINE
   *Honors, American/EFLA
The imagery of this film has applications in art, science, and mathematics.   There is no narration on the soundtrack; only music, especially written to provide a rhythmic base for the abstract movements and synchronized arrangement of shapes.   Production was
supported by a grant from the National Science Foundation.   (HS-
College)

SYNCHROMY
   8 min   color   Learn. Corp.   '71
   *Blue Ribbon, American/EFLA
An experience that enables the viewer to "see" music.   Colors move
and pulsate as shapes stretch and collide, then vibrate and recede
in rapid succession.   What we see are not merely impressions of
sound, but the images that are actually creating the sound.   This is
music made without conventional instruments.   It is the familiar
percussive synthetic sound drawn by Norman McLaren and photographed onto his soundtrack.   Produced by the National Film Board
of Canada.   (HS-College)

SYRINX/CITYSCAPE
   4 min   BW   Learn. Corp.   '67
   *Awards: N. Y., San Francisco, Canada, Ethiopia
Two different themes--one ancient, one modern--are presented here.
In both, rapidly dissolving charcoal drawings create the effect of an
animated painting, through a blend of sound and visuals without narration.   SYRINX depicts the Greek fable of the goat-god Pan, set to
Claude Debussy's music for solo flute; the second, CITYSCAPE, is
a brief impression in which shifting images and a pulsing sound convey the agitated rhythm of modern city life.   These two short films,
SYRINX (3 minutes) and CITYSCAPE (1 minute), are mounted on one
reel.   Produced by Ryan Larkin, National Film Board of Canada.
(HS-Adult)

TAHTONKA
   30 min   color   ACI Films   '67
   *Award, San Francisco
   *Golden Eagle, CINE
   *Honors, American/EFLA

The last days of the great buffalo herds and the powerful Plains Indians are tragic episodes in the history of America. Live-action
shows the buffalo hunts, the ceremonial and economic importance of
the buffalo, the conflict with settlers, exploiters, and railroad build-
ers; and the near-extermination of the buffalo and the Indians. A
Nauman Film. (HS-Adult)

TAKE TIME TO SEE
      10 1/2 min   color   Barr Films   '72
      *Award, Nat. Educational
Contrasts the troubled thoughts of a freeway driver with the joy and
serenity of nature. A variety of people bicycle through a city park;
four young people bicycle through the fall color of mid-America;
and a family explores a rural byway. Non-verbal. A film by Joern
Gerdts. (HS-Adult)

TASSILI N'AJJER
      16 min   color   Roland
      *Quality Prize, French National
      *Bronze Medal, Bilbao
      *Gold Medal, Venice
The Tassili N'Ajjer is a group of mountains in the Eastern Sahara.
The peoples who lived there through the ages left behind rock paintings that have been preserved by the dry climate. Most of these
paintings belong to the neolithic period. The Tassili region has
preserved the oldest group, characterized by the vitality of composition and color, showing hunting scenes, war, and daily life. Human and animal forms cover the rocks, and the feeling of movement
is suggested. Music: Maurice LeRoux. Producer: Les Editions
Cinegraphiques. (College-Adult)

THE TATTOOED MAN
      35 min   color   Impact Films   '68
      *Sharits Award, Yale Univ.
      *Vanderbilt Award, St. Lawrence Univ.
"Children of the Water World drift the ocean in an empty crystal
ball, swim in beaded beds of mist, and spawn in pools of murder
to see a lantern sunk in the pit of an empty face. They knock on
wood, then come to watch the Tattooed Man, marked for life, tattooed by tears running down the womb, by thrashing crazy in the
cage, by lure of unscaled mountains dancing in the specks of space."
(Description by Storm DeHirsch.) Produced with the help of the
American Film Institute. (College-Adult)

TAXI
      2 1/2 min   color   Nat. Film Bd.
      *Award: Yorkton (Saskatchewan)
Claude Léveillée expresses the frustrations of a taxi driver steering
his vehicle through downtown traffic. Accelerated camera-action
heightens the effect. Sung in French with a brief introduction in
English. (HS-Adult)

TEEN SCENE
> 37 min   color   Warner Brothers   '72
> *Bronze Award, Int. Film
> *Chris Award, Columbus

Teenagers play themselves, speaking their minds on the subject of birth control. A documentary, made originally for Planned Parenthood. Study guide is available. Chia Productions. (Grades 9-12)

TEMPLES OF TIME
> 42 1/2 min   color   Nat. Film Bd.
> *Awards: Belgium and Canada

Filmed in the Canadian Rockies and in Garibaldi Park, this picture brings footage of mountain solitude and the wildlife found there, of natural splendor in all its changing moods. Carries the implicit warning that this may pass away if man does not preserve it. (HS-Adult)

TEMPO--Australia in the Seventies
> 23 1/2 min   color   Australia   '71
> *Golden Hugo, Chicago
> *Award, San Francisco
> *Gold Camera, US Industrial

A modern computer is used to piece together a dynamic picture of Australia in the seventies. Brisk, contemporary film technique. Photography by the Commonwealth Film Unit. (HS-Adult)

THE TENDER GAME
> 7 min   color   McGraw-Hill   '69
> *Special Award, Venice

An exercise in free association of popular music and popular images, to the tune of "Tenderly" sung by Ella Fitzgerald, accompanied by Oscar Peterson. Produced by John Hubley and Faith Elliot. (HS-Adult)

THE TEST
> 28 1/2 min   color   Nat. Film Bd.
> *Award, Yorkton (Saskatchewan)
> *Chris Award, Columbus

Does a little cheating matter? Focus of this film is a conflict in a community when an idealistic teacher chooses to resign rather than condone cheating in class. Portrays the role of the Home and School Association in providing a middle ground where parents and teachers can meet. (HS-Adult)

TEXTURE IN PAINTING
> 20 min   color   Bee Cross-Media   '63
> *Golden Eagle, CINE

Demonstrates the function of texture in painting and in everyday life. Watercolorists Phoebe Flory and Eliot O'Hara explain their use of texture, along with examples from the Ming Dynasty, through the Renaissance, to today's non-objective painters. Their ideas are conveyed musically with an original score for percussion orchestra by Donald Erb. Film-maker: Phoebe Flory. (HS-Adult)

TEXTURES
10 min   color   ACI Films   '70
*Golden Eagle, CINE
Directed toward developing a consciousness of surface, this film explores factors that influence our impression of texture: light, point of view, function. Examples range from the sculpture of Henry Moore to simple kitchen utensils. Produced by Wheaton Galentine. (Grade 8-Adult)

THAT'S ME
15 min   BW   McGraw-Hill '63
*Nomination: Academy Award
A comedy-drama about a young Puerto Rican, played by Alan Arkin, who loves to play his guitar and finds it difficult to adjust to life in New York. Trying to help him is a conscientious social worker who is made aware of some surprising gaps in his own adjustment. Produced and directed by Walker Stuart. (HS-Adult)

THEY CALLED IT FIREPROOF
28 min   color   Int. Film Bur.
*Award: Nat. Committee
It was considered a fireproof hospital, yet fire did break out. The building was modern in construction, reasonable safety precautions were observed, but this proved insufficient. This film argues for safety-consciousness and vigilance by the staff of any institutional building. (College-Adult)

THEY'VE KILLED PRESIDENT LINCOLN
52 min color   Films Inc.   '71
*Blue Ribbon, American/EFLA
*Gold Medal, Atlanta
The assassinations of the 1960s recalled Abraham Lincoln's murder a century before. Like the modern conspiracy theories, there are still unanswered questions surrounding Lincoln's death. Matthew Brady photographs are integrated with "antiqued" footage that looks similar to the daguerreotype photographs of 1865. The result is a "vintage documentary" of the events and intrigue leading to the assassination and its aftermath. Wolper Productions. (College-Adult)

THE THINKING BOOK
10 min   color   McGraw-Hill   '66
*Blue Ribbon, American/EFLA
This simple story explores some of the thoughts that can fill children's minds as they awake in the morning and prepare for the day ahead of them. Read by Sidney Poitier. (Elem.)

THIRD AVENUE EL
9 min   color   ACI Films   '55
*Award Winner, Edinburgh
*Golden Reel, American Film Assembly
*Nomination, Academy Award
Begins with morning in New York--vacant streets and buildings, the clatter of an elevated train, a sprinkling of passengers. The camera

explores the old "El" and its environment, as the train writhes through the changing colors of the city from dawn to neon-night. A Carson Davidson Film. (HS-Adult)

THIS CHILD IS RATED X
    52 min color Films Inc. '71
    *Award, Christophers
    *Sidney Hillman Award
    *Award, San Francisco
    *Award, duPont-Columbia
    *Award, American Bar
    *"Emmy," Nat. Academy
This study of the inequities of juvenile justice focuses on the child who has committed an offense such as truancy and the child who has committed serious crime. These youngsters often end up sharing the same dehumanizing facilities, with the result that many emerge as hardened criminals. Awareness of injustices under the law may lead to sensible programs for rehabilitation. NBC News. (College-Adult)

THIS IS EDWARD STEICHEN
    27 min BW Carousel '65
    *Blue Ribbon, American/EFLA
Actor David Wayne narrates this portrait of the man who elevated photoportraiture to an art. Steichen, a dynamic octogenarian, supplements his technique with an understanding and love of mankind. Also shown are some of his photographs, as well as his renowned "Family of Man" exhibit. Especially suitable for camera and graphic arts courses. Produced by WCBS-TV, N.Y. (Senior HS-Adult)

THIS IS NEW YORK
    12 min color Weston Woods '62
    *Chris Certificate, Columbus
An iconographic version of the picturebook of the same name. Produced by Mort Schindel. (Elem.)

THIS IS NO TIME FOR ROMANCE
    28 min color Perennial Educ. '70
    *Awards: Canada and France
Does a woman's dream of romance end after she marries and has a family? This film suggests that for some women the dream may not end, that it may take more urgent form as the years go by. Filmed in the Laurentian countryside north of Montreal. The family shown is French-speaking but the voices are dubbed into English. National Film Board of Canada. (Senior HS-Adult)

THIS IS THE HOME OF MRS. LEVANT GRAHAM
    15 min BW Pyramid '70
    *First Prize, Independent
    *First Prize, Ann Arbor
    *First Prize, Monterey
A portrait of an urban black mother and the life around her. The black production company that made this cinema-verité has given us

a view of real people that is specific, immediate, and individual.
The picture of crowded housing, unemployment, and other problems,
is balanced by the richness and variety of the culture of this community in the Shaw area of Washington, D. C. Directed by Eliot
Noyes, Jr. (HS-Adult)

THIS MAN IS NOT DYING OF THIRST
        22 min   color   New Line Cinema
        *Chris Plaque, Columbus
About medical research in communistic Czechoslovakia with L. S. D.
therapy, delving into what "civilized" society is all about: technology running rampant, man's alienation from self and others, and
the effect all this has on mental health. Directed by U. Hapl. (College-Adult)

THOMAS JEFFERSON
        28 min   color   Handel   '66
        *Freedoms Foundation Award
        *Award, Landers Assoc.
His involvement in the Louisiana Purchase, the Lewis and Clark Expedition, the Library of Congress, West Point, and our money system. His contribution to agriculture and science, and his talent as
an architect in the creation of Monticello. (HS-Adult)

THOROUGHBRED
        22 min   color   Pyramid   '73
        *Red Ribbon, American/EFLA
A non-narrated, live-action observation of the exuberant power and
grace of horses that were born and raised to run. Traces the life
of a colt from its birth in winter, to its auction, training, and race-
track competition. An Insight production by Pen Densham and John
Watson. (Elem.-Adult)

THREE FROM ILLINOIS
        52 min   color   Films Inc.   '69
        *Award, Nat. Assoc./TV
        *Award Winner, Atlanta
        *"Emmy," Nat. Academy
Three Illinois communities. Galena has lost its aura of glory. It
once outshone Chicago, but the frontier moved on. The scene shifts
to poet Vachel Lindsay's Springfield. His home, preserved and run
by a retired English teacher, provides a setting for his poems.
Then to the village of Bishop Hill. A Swedish religious sect migrated to the prairie town and began an experiment in Christian Com-
munalism. Restorations show what life was like in this Utopian community. Produced by WMAQ-TV. (College-Adult)

THREE LOOMS WAITING
        52 min   color   Time-Life   '72
        *Blue Ribbon, American/EFLA
A look at the goals and methods of Dorothy Heathcote, an innovative
drama teacher. Her aim: to "teach teachers to receive, to have
emotion flow from children." From BBC-TV. (College-Adult)

THE THREE ROBBERS
  6 min   color   Weston Woods   '72
  *Jack London Award, Nat. Educ.
  *Bronze Award, Int. Film & TV
  *Bronze Medal, Atlanta
  *"Emily" Award, American/EFLA
An animated version of the children's picturebook of the same name.
Also available in Super 8mm Sound.   Produced by Mort Schindel.
(Elem.)

THRESHOLD
  25 min   color   Pyramid   '70
  *Gold Medal, Atlanta
A young man runs frantically from a deputy.   He is shot.   During
the brief interval between life and death before Death pulls him
down, he is given the realization of love--the complementary fullness of the life he had never known.   Without dialogue.   By J. May-
nard Lovins.   (College-Adult)

THURSDAY'S CHILDREN
  22 min   BW   McGraw-Hill   '56
  *Award, Golden Reel
  *Winner, Academy Award
About young deaf children, photographed in one of the private houses
that make up the junior section of the Margate School for the Deaf,
in England.   It shows the methods used to open up the minds of
children who have never heard.   Traces the growth of understanding
to their later ability to lip-read simple words in order to communicate with others.   Produced by World Wide Pictures and Morse
Films.   Commentary spoken by Richard Burton.   (College-Adult)

TIBETAN TRADERS
  22 min   color   Atlantis   '68
  *Chris Award, Columbus
The daily life of a tribal family, as seen in an epic journey by semi-
nomadic Tibetans searching for trade in the heartland of Asia.   Produced by J. Michael Hagopian.   (Intermediate-Adult)

TIM DRISCOLL'S DONKEY
  57 min   BW   Sterling Educ.   '70
  *Special Mention, Uruguay
  *First Prize, Venice
A young Irish boy gets involved in many adventures as he pursues
his pet donkey that has been sold to a family in England.   Produced
by Children's Film Foundation (Britain).   (Ages 7-12)

TIME AND PLACE
  16 1/2 min   color   Australia   '71
  *Gold Camera, US Industrial
Every environment creates its own mood and atmosphere.   A simple
house in the country; the elegant Victorian town house; stark geometric high-rise: which would you choose?   Photographed by the
Commonwealth Film Unit.   (HS-Adult)

From TIME LINE (FilmFair Communications)

A TIME FOR BURNING
    58 min BW McGraw-Hill '66
    *Nomination, Academy Award
A portrait of the American conscience struggling with its racial relationships. This is an actual drama of real people: the members
of an all-white, middle-class Lutheran congregation in Omaha, Ne-
braska; the inhabitants of Omaha's Negro ghetto; and the young pas-
tor who attempted to build a bridge of understanding between the
races. Produced for Lutheran Film Associates by Quest Productions.
A Contemporary Film release. (College-Adult)

TIME LINE
    10 min color FilmFair '71
    *Chris Statuette, Columbus
A child unrolls a large roll of paper--the Time Line. Each era is
designated according to predominant life forms: Azoic, Fish, Mammals, etc. The child starts to walk through time. As he goes from
era to era, he sees the changing geological state of the earth and
its patterns of plant and animal population. The Time Line ends
with Man--Man's history, a tiny part of earth's history. A film by
Norman and Claire Gerard. (Elem. -Junior HS)

TIME OF THE LOCUST
   12 min BW Macmillan '66
   *First Prize, Florence
   *Critics' Prize, Tours
   *First Prize, Protestant
   *Second Prize, Mannheim
   *Golden Dove, Leipzig
Assembled from footage by American, Japanese, and Vietnamese
cameramen, revealing aspects of the war in South Vietnam.   The
voice of President Johnson plus a percussive soundtrack provide a
contrast to the scenes depicting troops beating and killing prisoners,
tanks roaring through rice paddies, execution in the Saigon market
place, etc.   Produced and directed by Peter Gessner, with the cooperation of the American Friends.   (HS-Adult)

TIME PIECE
   10 min color McGraw-Hill '65
   *Nomination, Academy Award
A satire on a day in the life of contemporary man as he is motivated by advertising, hypnotized by movies, and surrounded by modern sex symbols.   Produced by Muppets, Inc.   A Contemporary
Films release.   (College-Adult)

TIME TO BEGIN
   29 min color Colonial Wmsburg.   '70
   *Chris Award, Columbus
Scenes of countryside and metropolitan elegance are followed by evidence of man's neglect and indifference: beer cans and trash, polluted air and water, auto graveyards, landscapes mutilated by industrial ravage, and the bombardment of bad taste, tinsel, chrome,
and plastic.   (HS-Adult)

THE TITAN, STORY OF MICHELANGELO
   67 min BW McGraw-Hill '50
   *Best Documentary, Academy Award
One of the first full-length documentaries on art ever produced, this
in-depth study is a representation of the life of the timeless Renaissance artist.   Score: Beethoven's "Moonlight" Sonata.   Narrator:
Fredric March.   Directed by Curt Oertel.   A Contemporary Films
release.   (College-Adult)

TO BE GROWING OLDER
   13 1/2 min color Billy Budd '72
   *First Prize, Atlanta
   *Golden Eagle, CINE
Young people discuss senior citizen problems as pictured on the
screen.   From the series on important contemporary issues.   Producer: Frank Moynihan.   (HS-Adult)

TO BE SOMEBODY
   35 min color Atlantis '71
   *Honors, Calif. Personnel
   *Award, Nat. Educ. Film

From TO BE GROWING OLDER (Billy Budd Films, Inc.)

An unstaged documentary depicting the progress of a young Spanish-speaking woman searching for a job in the world of the Anglo. We witness the development of two personalities, one seeking guidance and the other giving counsel ... two persons becoming somebody, because they share a relationship of respect. Produced by J. Michael Hagopian. (HS-Adult)

TO CATCH A MEAL (Feeding in the Sea)
        12 min color Macmillan '69
        *Chris Certificate, Columbus
        *Honor Certificate, American/EFLA
The eating patterns of several species: the barnacle that snares the cilia; the angler that lures the victim; the sea horse's use of vacuum; and the man-of-war's use of venom. Others shown are the octopus and a number of predators and scavengers. Reela Films. (HS-College)

TO LOVE
        25 min color Wombat '72
        *Grand Prix, Belgrade
A leisurely, unglamorized look at the ways love can be manifested in an age-old institution, marriage. Produced by Vlatko Gilic. (College-Adult)

TO SEE OR NOT TO SEE
        15 min color Learn. Corp. '69
        *Gold Bear Statuette, Berlin
        *Film of the Year, Canada
Czech film-artist Bretislav Pojar uses animation to take a look at our inner thoughts and fears, and ways our psyche copes with them. A droll little psychiatrist has a magic cure. When a harried client puts on a special pair of glasses, everything that threatens him suddenly seems much smaller. Even his boss beats a retreat. But there are drawbacks, as this satiric ending reveals. National Film Board of Canada. (HS-Adult)

TO SEEK...TO TEACH...TO HEAL
        29 min color Assn. -Sterling
        *Bronze Medal, Atlanta
        *Award, Federal Artists
        *Red Ribbon, American/EFLA
        *Gold Medal, 1st Int.
        *Golden Eagle, CINE
Using the format of popular TV medical dramas, the film is a "suspense documentary" on medical and paramedical personnel fighting to save a three-year-old boy afflicted with a blood disease. Follows one doctor's nationwide search for diagnosis and lifesaving treatment. Free loan. Sponsor: National Institutes of Health. Available to adult groups, high schools and colleges.

TO SPEAK OR NOT TO SPEAK
        11 min color Int. Film Bur. '72
        *Special Mention, Annecy

*Best Film, Oberhausen
This animated film shows how lack of concern may endanger us all.
The question, "What's your opinion of the political situation?" evokes
evasive replies until a hippie gives a direct answer.   When a to-
talitarian power takes over, the hippie is forced to submit to a
sterile, regimented life.   One lone witness, however, finds the courage to resist.   Produced and written by Raoul Servais of Belgium.
(HS-Adult)

TO YOUR HEALTH
        10 min   color   CMC-Columbia
        *Golden Reel Award
For centuries, alcohol has been a part of social custom.   In tracing
its history, this animated film explores answers to the questions:
"What is alcohol?", "What causes drunkenness?", "Why do people
drink?" Animation by Philip Stapp.   Spanish and French versions
available.   (HS-Adult)

THE TOBACCO PROBLEM: What Do You Think?
        17 min   color   Encyc. Brit.   '71
        *Golden Eagle, CINE
Historical perspective and timely data on the smoking habit.   Footage of Congressional hearings on warning labels, with rebuttal from
tobacco companies, and debate by teenagers.   Also inquires as to
how prohibition of smoking would affect the economy.   (HS)

TOKYO OLYMPIAD
        93 min   color   Pyramid   '65
        and 32 min   color
        *Documentary Award, Cannes
One of the most ambitious projects in film history for a documentary
on an unlimited production scale, given to the Japanese director as
his own to conceive.   A film about the human figure and the human
spirit.   The initial rough-cut of the footage from 164 cameramen ran
70 hours.   Directed by Kon Ichikawa for Toho Films.   (HS-Adult)

TOKYO--THE 1ST VOLCANO
        51 min   color   Time-Life   '72
        *Blue Ribbon, American/EFLA
What happens in Tokyo may affect us all.   In cities like it, people
face stresses never before encountered.   From BBC-TV.   (College-
Adult)

TOMMY, SUZIE AND THE CARDBOARD BOX
        15 min   color   Oxford
        *Award, San Francisco
The stage of this film is an inner city street; the situation: two
children pulling a large cardboard box in a small wagon.   In one
story, Tommy and Suzie share the problems of having a snake in the
box.   In a second episode, Tommy helps Suzie bring the box and a
vase to her mother.   In the last tale, the box itself is the main
character in a series of adventures.   (Elem.)

TOMORROW'S YESTERDAY
      29 min   color   Brigham Young Univ.
      *Winner, Abe Lincoln Award
      *Runner-up, Columbus
An interpretation of American Indian culture that shows these native
citizens as they were, as they are, and as they hope to be.   (Elem. -
Adult)

TONDO: A Round About a Round
      10 min   color   BFA Educ. Media   '71
      *Golden Eagle, CINE
Between a prologue and epilogue of children playing with circular
sculpture, this film explores some of the new abstractions formed
by dancers interacting with giant hollow cylinders in settings of light
and sound unique to the film medium.   A King Screen Production.
(Intermediate-Adult)

THE TOP OF THE WORLD: Taiga, Tundra, and Ice Cap
      20 min   color   Learn. Corp.   '72
      *Statuette Winner, Columbus
Exploring the northernmost outposts of our world--the remote areas
of Canada, Siberia, and Alaska--the camera sweeps from the forests
of the taiga, to the permafrost of the tundra, to the ice and snow of
the ice cap.   We see how early Eskimos, Lapps, and Indians adapted to their environment, making few demands on natural resources
and wildlife.   Then came fur traders, timber mills, hydroelectric
power plants, and finally cities.   Stressing the delicate ecological
balance in this part of the world, the film ponders what this will
mean to the future.   Narrated by Alexander Scourby.   (HS-Adult)

TOULOUSE-LAUTREC
      22 min   color   Macmillan   '52
      *Art Film Award, Cleveland
Photographs, paintings, drawings and etchings, plus scenes from
Parisian streets and cafes, recapture Lautrec's special world.   Lau-
trec's own works are used to picture that world with his own vision
of Paris at the turn of the century.   Directed by Peter Riethof and
Carolyn Hector.   (HS-Adult)

TOUR EN L'AIR
      49 min   color   Eccentric Cir.   '74
      *Blue Ribbon, American/EFLA
Explores the lives of Canadian dancers David and Anna-Marie
Holmes who are shown in their many activities: rehearsing, per-
forming, entertaining, planning tours, and relaxing.   A final scene
shows them preparing for a role in Norman McLaren's film Ballet
Adagio.   Producer: National Film Board of Canada.   (College-
Adult)

THE TOWN MUSICIANS
      9 min   color   Macmillan
      *Winner, Silver Reel Award
From "The Bremen Town Musicians" by the Brothers Grimm, the

story about the donkey, dog, cat and rooster who set out to become musicians. Cartoon. A Piper Production. (Preschool-Intermediate)

TOYS
8 min color McGraw-Hill '66
*Silver Medal, La Plata (Argentina)
As children watch from outside, store-window playthings come to life and start to make war. Their audience remains frozen in terror, even after the toys return to normal. Discussion topic: Do our playthings shape or reflect our values? How does society perpetuate its values? A non-verbal live-action dramatization. Directed by Grant Munro for the National Film Board of Canada. (Elem.-Adult)

THE TRAINING MEMORANDUM
12 min color Nat. Educ. Media '73
*Bronze Medal, Int. Film & TV
Shows the benefits of proper employee training. Intended for food service and hotel-motel managers and supervisors. Accompanied by tests and leader's guides. (College-Adult)

TRANSPORTATION: A Ship Comes Home
16 min color Perspective
*Chris Award, Columbus
The complexity of modern ocean transportation is demonstrated as we observe the exacting maneuvers, the expert timing, and the alertness that are needed to bring the majestic liner, The United States, into port. Produced by Manfred Kirchheimer. (Intermediate-Adult)

TREEHOUSE
9 min color BFA Educ. Media '70
*Merit Award, Landers
This vignette of summertime and boyhood focuses on the conflict between progress and environment. A boy climbs to his treehouse while a friendly bulldozer driver works nearby. Behind the rumbling, a regiment of tract houses waits for the tank to move the last obstacle from the path of its advance. Almost wordlessly, this film reflects man's battle with his natural world. A King Screen Production. (Intermediate-Adult)

TRIKFILM
4 min color Eccentric Circle '73
*Winner, Independent Filmmakers
An experiment that employs one of the oldest methods of simple animation: a series of pictures in progression is drawn on the pages of a white pad. The pages are then flipped through by hand, unfolding a story in motion. Includes background on this technique. Designed by George Griffin. (Intermediate-Junior HS)

TRIP TO NOWHERE
52 min color Films Inc. '70
*Prize, Nat. Headliner

*Award, Christopher Society
Who are the kids "doing drugs?" Why do kids turn to drugs? This
is an attempt to answer these questions by focusing on a white, suburban high school boy and his parents. This boy had been on heroin
for five years without his parents' knowledge. Interviews with young
people show the attraction to drugs in a depersonalized and materi-
alistic society. Citizens, police, and Phoenix city government are
shown trying to reach the heart of the problem. NBC News. (HS-
Adult)

THE TROUBLE WITH WORDS
    15 min color Macmillan '68
    *Top Prize, Int. Labor
    *Blue Ribbon, American/EFLA
    *Winner, New York
    *Award, Columbus
    *Honors, Chicago
An effort at filling the gap of employer-employee communications.
Explores the nature of that relationship and proposes solutions to
some inherent problems. (College-Adult)

A TRUMPET FOR THE COMBO
    8 min BW Sterling Educ. '67
    *Award, N.Y. Int. Film
An "open end" film designed to encourage discussion. Presents the
case of a school combo in need of a trumpet player. Two boys try
out and, while there is no doubt that Randy is better, the director
of the music department puts pressure on the group to choose Bruce,
a Black who (he claims) needs the chance to develop. Which should
come first: the group or individual? National Film Board of Canada. (HS-Adult)

TUB FILM
    2 min BW BFA Educ. Media '71
    *Special Prize, Zagreb
An animated tale of a woman and her sweet-voiced kitten. Both are
playful and carefree, but one is in for a surprise. Edited for classroom use. A film by Mary Beams. (Elem.)

TUMBLEWEED
    14 min color ACI Films '72
    *Award Winner, Brussels
    *Golden Eagle, CINE
An original country-and-western score accompanies a tumbleweed
from its desert origins, across farmlands and plains ... until it
lodges itself in a fence. A woman takes it home and transforms it
into a Christmas decoration. Once the season ends, the tumbleweed
is tossed out, taken to a dump, and burned. We return to the desert and watch another tumbleweed begin to roll toward us. A Bill
McCusker and Jerry Clark Film. (Intermediate-Adult)

TUP TUP
    8 3/4 min color BFA Educ. Media '71

From TUP TUP (BFA Educational Media)

---

*Nomination, Academy Award
An animated man settles down for some peace and quiet, but the persistent annoyance of a "thump, thump" interrupts him. As one ploy after another fails to remedy the distress, our frenzied anti-hero acts out a fantasy of retaliation against a world that won't co-operate. Edited for classroom use. A Zagreb Film. (Elem.-Adult)

TURNER (1775-1851)
    12 min color Roland
    *Merit Certificate, Vancouver
    *Koussevitsky Award (Music)
    *Chris Award, Columbus
    *Commendation, Wiesbaden
    *Silver Cup, Salerno ... and other honors
Credited with liberating color from its role of describing the subject, William Turner evoked an intensity of feeling in his landscapes that future impressionists and abstract artists were to try to capture years later. This film is a cinematographic essay on the most important period of Turner's work, his last 25 years. The selection, made from 10,000 paintings, illustrates Turner at his creative apogee. The majority of works filmed here have never been photographed or exhibited before. Producer: Les Films de Saturne. Director: Anthony Roland. (Senior HS-Adult)

21-87
    10 min BW McGraw-Hill '63
    *Awards: Chicago, Ann Arbor, and Palo Alto
Commentary on machine-dominated man, to whom nothing matters,

who waits for his number to come up. The film is a succession of
many unrelated views of the passing crowd. Produced by the Na-
tional Film Board of Canada. Edited by Arthur Lipsett. (College)

23 SKIDOO
       8 min   BW   McGraw-Hill   '64
       *Awards: London, Cracow, and Salerno
If you erase the people of downtown America, the effect is bizarre,
not to say disturbing. That is what this film does. It shows the
familiar city scene without a soul in sight: streets empty, buildings
empty, yet everywhere evidence of recent life and activity. At the
end of the film we learn that a neutron bomb has destroyed all living cells. Produced by the National Film Board of Canada. (HS-
Adult)

TWO BALLET BIRDS
       51 min   BW   McGraw-Hill   '70
       *Series Award, Saturday Review
From the Young People's Concert series, with Leonard Bernstein as
master of ceremonies, narrator, and conductor of the N.Y. Philharmonic. Produced by CBS-TV. (Elem.-College)

THE ULTIMATE TRIP
       32 min   color   Films Inc.   '70
       *Award, American/EFLA
Turning on to God is the ultimate trip, according to the growing
number of young adults who have joined the Christian communal
movement documented in this film. Some people call them "Jesus
Freaks"; they call themselves the Children of God. Their main purpose is evangelical, seeking out especially those who are lost in
drugs, promiscuity, and despair. Their antidote is Christ. An
NBC News Production. (HS-Adult)

THE UNANSWERED QUESTION
       5 min   BW   Macmillan   '66
       *1st Prize (shared), Chicago
What is brotherhood? That question is posed in this cinema-verité
of an interview-style TV spot prepared for the National Conference
of Christians and Jews. Instead of the usual clichés on the subject,
this film consists of the "out-takes" of these street interviews, that
is, the answers that some people are unwilling or unable to give.
Perhaps a more truthful picture than the one later presented over
television. Produced by David Hoffman. (Intermediate-Adult)

UNDALA
       28 min   color   CMC-Columbia
       *Hon. Mention, Florence
       *Golden Eagle, CINE
Village life in the Thar desert in northwest India during the hot
windy months before the monsoons. Among the views of Rajasthani
life are pottery making, spinning, leather craft, ropemaking, and
the vital chore of drawing water. The film is presented without narration but has an original score in the Hindustani classical and folk
styles. Produced by Marek Jablonko. (College-Adult)

UNDER THE BLACK MASK
50 min color Macmillan
*Grand Prize, Bergamo
This examination of primitive art in the former colony of Belgian
Congo provides an introduction to Central African culture. Masks,
sculpture, and artifacts of tribes now prominent on the world stage,
reflect their early concepts of the origins of life. Available in three
separate parts upon request. Produced by Paul Haesaerts. (College-Adult)

UNDERGROUND FILM
23 min color ACI Films '70
*Golden Eagle, CINE
An insight into the work of underground cinema, with particular attention to film-maker Chick Strand, a young woman well known in
her field. Excerpts from underground productions demonstrate the
improvisational nature of this art form. Produced by Paul Marshall.
(HS-Adult)

UNDERSTANDING OUR EARTH: Soil
11 min color Coronet '57
*Recognition Award, Golden Reel
Here is an explanation of the soil profile, plus an analysis of the
elements of soil. Presents examples of the varieties of soil throughout the U.S., and mentions the importance of conservation practices.
(Intermediate-Junior HS)

THE UNEXPLAINED
52 min color Films Inc. '70
*Golden Eagle, CINE
Reveals the investigations of scientists (and amateurs) into the unex-
plored areas of knowledge: the Continental Drift theory; communication with dolphins; life in outer space; extra-sensory perception
(ESP); and "cyborgs," creatures that are part human and part mechanical. Co-produced by Encyclopaedia Britannica and Mendelsohn
Productions. (College-Adult)

THE UNITED STATES CONGRESS: Of, By, and For the People
26 min color Encyc. Brit. '73
*Golden Eagle, CINE
The development of the U.S. congressional system is surveyed from
earliest (i.e., colonial) times to the present decade. Examines the
daily work of a Representative and Senator. Produced by Concept
Films. (HS-College)

UNITED STATES EXPANSION: California
15 min color Coronet
*Chris Award, Columbus
The history of California, from its discovery by the Spanish to its
admission into the Union, is told in graphics and quotations. Includes references to the role of the conquistadores, development by
the missionaries, colonization of Mexico, and invasion by Americans. (Intermediate-HS)

UNITED STATES EXPANSION: Texas and the Far Southwest
13 1/2 min   color   Coronet
*Merit Certificate, Cleveland
The development of this vast area is traced from original Spanish
explorations through important events such as the Texas revolution,
the Mexican War, the admission of Texas as a state, and the opening of the Far Southwest to immigration and settlement.   (Intermediate-HS)

THE UNQUIET DEATH OF ETHEL AND JULIUS ROSENBERG
90 min   color   Impact   '74
*Blue Ribbon, American/EFLA
In a recreation made possible through extensive availability of news
film of that era, this production probes the questions left unanswered
by the execution of these alleged Cold War spies.   This issue is
compared with and related to the current climate engendered by the
Watergate mentality of our own era.   Directed by Alvin Goldstein.
(HS-Adult)

UP IS DOWN
6 min   color   Pyramid   '70
*Chris Statuette, Columbus
*Red Ribbon, American/EFLA
*Golden Dove, Atlanta
An animated story about a boy who walks on his hands and sees
things differently as a result.   For instance, frowns look like smiles.
But other people try to "correct" him and to make him see things
"the right way."   After a series of injections, TV commercials, and
a lobotomy, the boy finally stands on his feet--but not for long.
For, when he sees that the world looked better the other way, he
resumes walking on his hands.   Produced by Mildred Goldsholl.
(Elem.-Adult)

UPPITY AL McGUIRE
10 min   color   Learn. Corp.   '73
*Winner, US Animation
This animated story in verse mocks the vanity of social competition,
in which Uppity Albert irreverently beats out a millionaire known as
Sid.   Produced by student filmmakers Steve Adams and John Stern.
(Elem.)

UPS/DOWNS (Amphetamines and Barbiturates)
24 min   color   Encyc. Brit.   '72
*Golden Eagle, CINE
Examines the testimony of youths who tell of being trapped on
"speed," "barbs," and even diet pills.   Indicates how our society
fosters these abuses, and how severe such dependence can become.
(HS-College)

US
28 min   color   Churchill   '70
*So. Calif. Social Sci. Assn.
*Blue Ribbon, American/EFLA

With intentional irony, we are shown a group of women deploring the young drug culture while taking diet pills themselves; two business men getting drunk while criticizing drug addicts; a group of young adults smoking pot while downgrading everyone else. (HS-Adult)

VALLEY FORGE
    16 min color Handel '69
    *Chris Award, Columbus
    *Award, Landers Assoc.
    *Freedoms Foundation Award
This film utilizes the subjective "I Was There" approach, through the eyes of a Continental soldier who, with other men of the Massachusetts Brigade, waits out the severe winter, fighting against the cold, hunger, disease, and despair. (Intermediate-Junior HS)

VALLEY OF DARKNESS
    18 min color Films Inc. '70
    *Award, TV Newsfilm
The men of West Virginia have a dilemma: the state's economy is based on coal mining, but the dust causes black-lung disease. And there's also the danger of explosion or cave-in. Miners discourage their sons from this work. Doctors warn about the health hazards involved. Yet the economic and political pressures continue in favor of "business as usual." Produced by NBC News. (HS-Adult)

VALUES AND GOALS: A Way to Go
    28 1/2 min color Oxford Films
    *Award Winner, Columbus
    *Golden Eagle, CINE
    *Gold Camera, US Industrial
    *Honors, NY International
Without professional actors or fancy sets, this film communicates its message with a "cast" of young people being themselves. Its "script" is their explanation of their feelings, their position on values by today's standards, and setting goals that mean something to them, not to somebody else. A Copley Production. (HS)

VAN GOGH
    17 min BW Pictura
    *Winner, Academy Award
Ignored and misunderstood, this painter persisted without compromise. His art was a new way of seeing. This study, directed by Alain Resnais, follows Van Gogh from his years among the miners, through his Paris period, and on to his final madness and suicide. (College-Adult)

VARIATIONS ON A THEME
    11 min BW Macmillan '61
    *Prize, Hungarian Critics
A statement against the glorification of war and the complacency of society to its long-term dangers. There are three parts to this piece: "Objectively" is a view of what the last war was like;

"Shocked" is the version that fathers recite to their sons; and "Shreiking" is a vision of what could happen while people sleep (literally and figuratively). No narration or dialogue. A Bela Balazs Studio Production. (HS-Adult)

VD: A Plague On Our House
    35 min color Films Inc. '70
    *Winner, Ed Murrow Award
    *Award, Broadcast News
Gonorrhea and syphilis attack two million Americans every year. Both ignorance and shame often prevent many of them from seeking treatment. Parents and schools do not stress the danger enough, or they completely ignore the problem out of some puritanical confusion of values. Young people's attitudes toward sex are part of the problem but may eventually also prove to be the solution. Produced by WNBC-TV. (HS-Adult)

VENEREAL DISEASE: The Hidden Epidemic
    23 min color Encyc. Brit. '72
    *Red Ribbon, American/EFLA
    *Bronze Plaque, Columbus
This film's approach is organized from three perspectives: the history of venereal diseases and attitudes towards them; clinical analyses of gonorrhea and syphilis; and discussions between doctors and patients. (HS-Adult)

VENICE BE DAMNED
    52 min color Films Inc. '71
    *Award, San Francisco
    *"Emmy," Nat. Academy
Italy's Venice, a living museum of western culture, is being destroyed by age, pollution, and lack of planning. Venetians are concerned but, at the same time, are concentrating on building new industries rather than on preserving their art treasures. The problem of saving this unique city must rest with all people who value beauty, and the scope of this problem may require international cooperation. Produced by NBC News. (College-Adult)

VENUS AND THE CAT
    10 min color Film Images '71
    *Animation Prize, Belgrade
    *1st Prize, Oberhausen
    *Blue Ribbon, American/EFLA
An animation based on an Aesop fable. The soundtrack tells the story, sung in Italian to an organ accompaniment, in counterpoint to the images of a young man whose loneliness is reason enough to justify wondering if his fantasies are the problem or the solution. Preview for potentially offensive scenes. A Zagreb-Corona Production. (HS-Adult)

VERA PAINTS IBIZA IN THE SUN
    20 min color Schloat Prod. '73
    *Golden Eagle, CINE

*Knowland Award, Nat. Educ.
Ibiza is the ancient (26 centuries old) capital of the Balearic island off the east coast of Spain. Vera is a successful American fabric designer who draws much of her inspiration from that Mediterranean locale. Other scenes deal with the more practical aspects of fabric craftsmanship and manufacturing. Produced by Fred Salaff. (HS-Adult)

VERTIGE
43 min color Nat. Film Bd.
*Best Film Award, Canada
A film by a French-Canadian who is probing into the world of the unconscious: the eroticism, masochism, and self-delusions of the world. Are these the expressions of an inner search for self, or the instinctive recoil from a soul-destroying world? No narration; music and sound effects are the only non-visual components of this work. (College-Adult)

VESAK
17 min color Washburn '72
*Golden Eagle, CINE
For the Buddhists in Ceylon, Vesak is the holiest day in the year. It is the day Buddha was born, the day he attained enlightenment, and the day he reached Nirvana. This triple-blessed event is celebrated with an intensity that rivals that of Times Square. (College-Adult)

THE VICTIMS
48 min BW Anti-Defamation
*Gabriel Award, Cath. Broadcast.
*Honors, American/EFLA
*Gold Medal, Int. Film & TV
Dr. Benjamin Spock diagnoses the causes of prejudice in children, and finds it a crippling disease for those who inflict it and those who receive it. In a series of interviews, Dr. Spock shows that adults are the carriers of the sickness but that they also are the potential healers. Sponsored by B'nai Brith. (College-Adult)

VIRGINIA WOOLF: The Moment Whole
10 min color ACI Films '72
*Golden Eagle, CINE
*Honors, American/EFLA
Marian Seldes portrays the title role in this introduction to the personality and literary style of the noted 20th-century English writer. Combining stills with live-action, and scripted totally from the subject's works, the film gives an insight into her philosophy and her talent. An NET Film. (HS-Adult)

A VISIT TO PICASSO
22 min BW Macmillan
*1st Prize, Woodstock
*Grand Prize, Venice
Here are examples of the variety of skills of this great artist,

artisan, draftsman, painter, sculptor, and ceramicist. And here is
the artist himself, at work in the rustic Mediterranean cottage that
served as one of his studios. For the camera and for posterity, he
creates a series of black-and-white compositions. Produced by Paul
Haesaerts. (College-Adult)

VIVA MEXICO!
        20 min   color   Assn. -Sterling
        *Chris Award, Columbus
While such high spots as Mexico City and Acapulco are visited on
film, other off-beat retreats aren't ignored either: the daring Que-
brada cliff divers, the landscapes of the Sierra Madre Mountains,
folk artists at their trade, and traditional displays of horsemanship.
Available on free loan. Sponsor: Eastern Airlines. (HS-Adult)

VIVALDI'S VENICE
        27 min   color   Time-Life   '68
        *Silver Medal, Venice
Venice, the queen of Italian cities, is here recorded by former Life
photographer Carlo Bavagnoli. There is no spoken commentary, but
six 18th century concerti by Vivaldi sustain the action of the camera
as it reflects the city's glories and the infinite variety of moods in
its four seasons. (Intermediate-Adult)

VOICES INSIDE
        22 min   color   Films Inc.   '69
        *Gavel Award, American Bar Assn.
        *Awards, National Press Club
Told from prisoners' point of view, this film reports the miserable
conditions in America's jails. Dr. Karl Menninger, author of The
Crime of Punishment, describes the situation as "barbaric." Cutting
back and forth between Dr. Menninger and the prisoners, the point
is made that confinement leads to warped thinking, that brutality per-
petuates hatred, and that only counter-productive results can be expected from poor food, sexual deprivation, and lack of mental stimulation. Produced by NBC News. (HS-Adult)

VOLLEYBALL
        10 min   BW   Univ. Educ.   '67
        *Award Winner, Moscow
The encounter between the Russian and American volleyball teams is
presented here more as choreography than as a sports event. Various camera techniques are used in dramatizing the action, especially
stop-motion. Background music matches the mood. National Film
Board of Canada. (HS-Adult)

VOTE POWER
        18 min   color   American Educ.   '74
        *Bronze Award, Columbus
Directed toward encouraging new voters to participate at the polls,
this film records the comments of youthful office-holders, including
Julian Bond, the famous anti-war lawmaker who regained his seat in
the Georgia legislature. Narrated by Wayne (M*A*S*H) Rogers.
Produced by Tom Grubbs. (HS-College)

THE VOTER DECIDES
    15 min   color   Xerox Films   '73
    *Gold Camera, US Industrial
This film studies the pressures--social, political, and psychological
--that affect a person in a voting situation.   Of the two Missouri
gubernatorial candidates in 1972, whom should voter Bill Kuhlke
favor?   The pressure also reaches Mrs. Kuhlke who attends the
candidate's tea.   Finally the voter decides.   But exactly how?   (HS-
Adult)

THE WACKY TALE OF WILFRED WICKENBUSH
    10 min   color   Assn. -Sterling
    *Bronze Medal, Int. Film & TV
This film, narrated by Henry Morgan, presents the tale of one man's
quest to catch a cold.   Determined to get a day off from work, Wilfred reads up on the common cold.   His imagination (shown through
silent film footage) soars with the prospect of waging his private
"Cold War. "   Free loan.   Sponsored by a major pharmaceutical
firm.   (HS-Adult)

WALKING
    6 min   color   Learn. Corp.   '68
    *Awards: Chicago, Toronto, Krakov, Barcelona, LaPlata,
               Rio de Janeiro
The individuality of various styles of walking--and by extension, various styles of living--are accented by a lively rock music score, the
sole "commentary" of the film.   Animated line drawings, color
wash, and water color sketches interpret movement and personalities.
(HS-Adult)

THE WALL (ZID)
    4 min   color   McGraw-Hill   '65
    *Award, Oberhausen (Germany)
    *Golden Pelican, Mamaia
Two cartoon characters are stymied by an impassable wall.   One
figure just sits and watches, while the other almost literally kills
himself in clearing a passageway.   What's on the other side of the
wall?   Another wall!   Who'll break through it this time?   Guess!
Produced by Zagreb.   (Elem. -Adult)

WALT WHITMAN: Poet for a New Age
    29 min   color   Encyc. Brit.   '71
    *Bronze Medal, Atlanta
    *Golden Eagle, CINE
About the poet's beliefs and his conflicts with contemporaries.   Reveals the "cosmic consciousness" of Whitman, his belief in democracy, the oneness and sacredness of all living things, his distaste
for war, and his concern for the primacy of personality and love.
From the Humanities Series.   (HS-College)

THE WAR COMES HOME
    28 min   BW   New Film Co.   '72
    *Prize, Univ. of Florida

*Winner, Monterey (Calif.)
*Award, Bellevue (Wash.)
Probes the psychological results of the Vietnam war on returning
American veterans. Produced by Christopher Knight. (HS-Adult)

WAR ... MAN'S DESTINY?
    12 min   color   Bosustow Productions   '73
    *Special Jury Prize, Cannes
This animated film, set to the score of Tchaikovsky's "1812 Overture," uses classical European paintings by such artists as da Vinci
and Courbet to depict Napoleon's war against Russia.   (HS-Adult)

WASHINGTON, D.C.: Story of Our Capital
    11 min   color   Coronet
    *Merit Certificate, Cleveland
Through the words of the designer of our nation's capital, students
are given the early history of Washington, D.C., the city's development, and its significance as a center of government and culture.
(Intermediate-HS)

WASHOE
    56 min   BW   McGraw-Hill   '69
    *Chris Award, Columbus
The Washoe Indians, among this continent's earliest settlers, derived
their culture from the cycles of nature itself.   This film gives an insight into their society and philosophy, and shows the importance of
tradition within their system of values.   Highlights include the Pine
Nut Ceremony and the Girls' Puberty Rites.   Produced by Western
Artists Corporation.   (College-Adult)

WATCH OUT FOR MY PLANT
    13 1/2 min   color   Barr Films   '72
    *Award Winner, Columbus
    *Golden Eagle, CINE
    *Award Winner, Chicago
    *Award Winner, Atlanta
    *Arbor Day Award
    *Award, American/EFLA
As an inner-city boy struggles to grow a flower in the dirt between
his house and the sidewalk, we see his determination, the relationship between him and an older man, then the flowering and accidental destruction of the plant.   Suggests that everyone can do something about environment.   Non-verbal.   (Elem.-Adult)

WATER
    14 1/2 min   color   CMC-Columbia
    *Merit Diploma, Melbourne
    *Film of the Year, London
    *Silver Award, San Francisco
The theme of this film is: increasing demands and increasing pollution have brought us to the verge of a worldwide water crisis.   Animation, live-action photography, and collage underscore the fact that advanced countries face problems as serious as underdeveloped, arid lands.

Shows how the alternative to future famine and misery is cooperative planning reaching across state and national boundaries. (Intermediate-Adult)

WATER'S EDGE
    13 min   color   Films Inc.
    *Grand Prix, Venice
A camera study of natural water forms, from the quiet of a melting icicle to the pounding of the waves. Set to a musical score by Frank Lewin, this film is a blend of sight, sound, and color. (Intermediate-Adult)

WATERS OF YOSEMITE
    9 min   color   Pyramid '65
    *Merit Award, Edinburgh
Begins with commentary by Joseph Wood Krutch, then follows a stream in Yosemite National Park as it becomes a crystal clear river progressing downward from its source, building to a climax, receding, then rebuilding its force. (Intermediate-Adult)

WATERSMITH
    32 min   color   Time-Life '72
    *Blue Ribbon, American/EFLA
This swimming film merges man and water in the eye and the mind of the viewer. A portrait of man's relationship with his most valuable, indeed, indispensable element--water. (HS-Adult)

THE WAYS OF WATER
    13 min   color   Encyc. Brit.   '71
    *Merit Certificate, Chicago
    *Golden Eagle, CINE
This non-narrated film follows the water cycle in the wilderness of the Olympic Peninsula in Washington. Water from snow-capped mountains flows down to the forests and valleys in a continuous process of precipitation, runoff, and evaporation. A symphonic musical background. (Elem.-Adult)

WE CAME IN PEACE
    38 min   color   Assn.-Sterling   '70
    *Gold Award, Int. Film & TV
    *Golden Eagle, CINE
Man's dream of conquering space is developed in this documentary of space exploration, from Jules Verne to the moon landing by the Apollo 11 astronauts. Shows the triumphs and tragedies of the U.S. space program, experiments in rocketry by Robert Goddard, German V-2 rockets, and first successful space flight by a Russian. Narrated by the late Frank McGee. Free loan. Gulf Oil, sponsor. (HS-Adult)

WEAVING
    15 min   color   ACI Films '69
    *Red Ribbon, American/EFLA
After demonstrating the basic principle of interlocking fibers, a

variety of weaving methods is presented. These demonstrations encourage student experimentation, by showing the range of possibilities for innovation. (HS-Adult)

THE WEIRD NUMBER (An Arithmetic Mystery)
     12 1/2 min   color   Xerox Films
     *Chris Statuette, Columbus
     *Golden Eagle, CINE
     *Gold Medal, Atlanta
Involves the visit of a fraction to a community of whole numbers.
The "weird" number ... 2/3 ... steals a piece of cake and then
leads the townspeople on a merry chase. He escapes, and his
friend ... 1/6 ... assumes his disguise and explains the concept of
equivalent fractions. Produced by Davidson Films. (Primary-Intermediate)

WELCOME ABOARD
     21 min   color   Roundtable
     *Golden Eagle, CINE
Purpose: to demonstrate the importance of employee orientation.
This message is designed to start a program among supervisors
that will help them in getting new employees and recent transfers
off to a good start, help them achieve productivity faster, and cut
employee turnover. Combines a dream sequence of the perfect orientation, contrasted with the harsh realities of the first days on the
job of a transferred employee. (College-Adult)

WE'RE GONNA HAVE RECESS
     9 1/2 min   color   Nat. Film Bd.
     *Award, Conf. on Children
This is a view of a schoolyard during recess when, within fifteen
minutes, hearts are broken, grudges are settled, secrets told, and
where a bouncing ball or a turning rope can still tell the future with
a chanted rhyme. Filmed without commentary. (Elem. -Adult)

WEST CHICHAGOF!
     20 1/2 min   color   Assn. -Sterling
     *Silver Award, NY Int. Film
The Tongass National Forest covers most of southeastern Alaska.
A proposal has been made to "harvest" 97 per cent of the forest
acreage. With such a harvest would go the deer and bear, the
eagles' nests and the Peregrin Falcon. Suggests our civilization set
aside part of this area to become a home for creatures who share
our planet. (HS-Adult)

THE WEST OF CHARLES RUSSELL
     53 min   color   Films Inc.   '70
     *Award, American/EFLA
     *Golden Eagle, CINE
Charles Russell was a painter of an era fading into the past. He
caught and preserved the spirit of the west that really was. Often
seeing the west from the Indians' point of view, he felt as they did--
that the crush of settlers was ruining the beauty of the land where

he had chosen to make his life. As the bison and empty land disappeared, Russell felt the west was dying. But its color lives on in
his paintings. Produced by NBC Television. (College-Adult)

WESTERN GERMANY: The Land and the People
      11 min color Coronet '55
      *Merit Certificate, Cleveland
      *Award of Merit, Columbus
      *Award of Merit, Boston
The industrial, agricultural, and commercial life of Western Germany
is shown in relationship to the dense population, natural resources,
and relatively infertile soil of this area. The importance of coal,
farming, trade, and synthetic products to the development of this
country is seen against the background of its economy. (Intermediate)

WHAT COLOR IS THE WIND?
      27 min color Allan Grant '69
      *"Best," Nat. Educ. Film
      *Blue Ribbon, American/EFLA
      *Golden Eagle, CINE
      *Nomination, Emmy Awards
Courageous parents help their blind three-year-old twins share the
different worlds of darkness and light. (College-Adult)

WHAT DOES MUSIC MEAN?
      58 min BW McGraw-Hill '65
      *Series Award, Saturday Review
From the Young People's Concert series, with Leonard Bernstein as
master of ceremonies, narrator, and conductor of the New York
Philharmonic. Produced by CBS Television News. (Elem.-Adult)

WHAT DOES OUR FLAG MEAN?
      11 min color Coronet
      *Award, Freedoms Foundation
When little Susy Kim and her family become citizens, the children
of the neighborhood surprise them with a parade of homemade flags.
Through the story of the Kim family, we learn about the meaning of
our flag, how the flag changed through the years, how to display it,
and how to show our respect for it. (Primary)

WHAT IS A CAT?
      13 1/2 min color FilmFair '72
      *Golden Eagle, CINE
      *Chris Statuette, Columbus
      *Creative Award, US Industrial
This film traces the lineage of this animal from its emergence 5,000
years ago in the Nile Valley, to its heroic role against the plague of
the Middle Ages, and to its present role as household friend. An
Amital Film. (Elem.-Adult)

WHAT IS A MELODY?
      53 min BW McGraw-Hill '65

*Series Award, <u>Saturday Review</u>
From the Young People's Concert series, with Leonard Bernstein as master of ceremonies, narrator, and conductor of the New York Philharmonic. Produced by CBS. (Elem.-Adult)

WHAT IS LIFE?
    8 min   color   McGraw-Hill
    *Chris Certificate, Columbus
An animated treatment on the origins of life from the beginning of the earth to the evolution of man. Concepts include cell formation, bio-chains of protein molecules, DNA-controlled growth. Produced by the National Film Board of Canada. (HS-College)

WHAT IS NOTHING?
    9 min   color   Barr Films   '73
    *Award Winner, Atlanta
Two boys use the word "nothing" both in fun and in earnest, as they search out its meanings in the dictionary and their everyday actions. An exploration of multiple meaning and connotation in a common term. (Elem.)

WHAT MAN SHALL LIVE AND NOT SEE DEATH?
    57 min   color   Films Inc.   '71
    *Award, Council of Churches
    *"Emmy," Nat. Academy
There is a "conspiracy of silence" surrounding the subject of death. Through conversations with doctors, clergymen, terminally ill patients, and bereaved people, the silence is lifted. This study of death and how Americans deal with it provides insight into a profound and universal experience. Produced by WNBC-TV. (College-Adult)

WHAT ON EARTH?
    10 min   color   McGraw-Hill   '71
    *Winner, Trieste
    *Blue Ribbon, American/EFLA
    *Cup Award, Salerno
Shows what earthlings have feared, and what Martians could infer: that the auto has inherited the earth. This animation shows life here as being one long conga-line of cars which the Martians consider to be the true inhabitants, and we as merely parasites that infest the auto bodies. Producer: the National Film Board of Canada. (Intermediate-Adult)

WHAT WILL CHRISTY DO? (Cover Brother's Guilt)
    6 min   color   Doubleday   '68
    *Honorable Mention, San Francisco
Christy sees her brother throw a rock through the cafeteria window, and then hears him tell the principal that another boy did it. Christy knows right from wrong but family loyalty is involved. If she doesn't tell, an innocent child might suffer. What should Christy do? (Elem.)

WHAT'S IT GOING TO COST YOU?
        10 min   color   Perennial Education
        *Award, US Industrial
        *Award, Nat. Committee
        *Golden Eagle, CINE
This film punches home a message to contractors and construction
workers: "Check before you dig." Examples present the reasons
in the language of costs, as well as personal hazards and threats to
the lives of others.   (Adult)

WHERE ARE MY PEOPLE?
        28 min   color   Atlantis   '66
        *Chris Award, Columbus
World War I history, depicted in the light of genocide of the Arme-
nians.   The three-thousand-year life story of a small nation's substantial and enduring contributions to the culture of man ... Arme-
nia.   (HS-Adult)

WHERE MRS. WHALLEY LIVES
        28 min   BW   Nat. Film Bd.
        *Chris Award, Columbus
A study of the conflict between generations that can arise despite
the best efforts of everyone.   Mrs. Whalley is an aging grandmother
who lives with her son's family.   Sometimes it becomes a strain to
hide the hurt and loneliness for the sake of harmony.   (College-
Adult)

WHERE SHOULD A SQUIRREL LIVE?
        11 min   color   Barr Films   '71
        *Award, Nat. Educational
The experiences of a squirrel in two contrasting environments.   The
squirrel is raised in a human's home, and then released to find a
home in the natural world.   Non-verbal.   (Elem.)

WHERE THE PELICAN BUILDS HER NEST
        22 min   color   A-V Explor.   '67
        *International Award, Sydney
The Spectacled Pelican, Australia's only pelican, has no voice other
than a pig-like grunt, and is considered the most handsome of the
world's eight species.   Includes sequences on black swans, white
headed stilts, egrets, and Australia's only breed of cranes and storks,
the stately brolga and the jabiru.   Close-up photography and sound
provide another look at Australian wildlife.   (Intermediate-Adult)

THE WHITE HOUSE, PAST AND PRESENT
        13 1/2 min   color   Coronet   '61
        *Chris Award, Columbus
A camera tour of the Executive Mansion.   From the original plans
to remodeled and expanded building of today, this treatment traces
the history of this landmark and its presidential inhabitants up to
and including John F. Kennedy.   (Intermediate-Adult)

WHITE MANE
38 min BW Olenyik
*Grand Prize, Cannes
The story of a wild white stallion, living in freedom; of the men who
want to capture him and break his spirit; and of the boy who ultimately tames him with love. This allegorical film delineates the
character of man's relationship to the natural world. Produced by
Albert Lamorisse. (Elem. -Adult)

WHITE THROAT
10 min color A-V Explorations '65
*Award of Merit, Landers
*Golden Gate, San Francisco
*Honors, American/EFLA
The White-Throated Sparrow is your film guide to the forest. Synchronized sound allows the forest to speak for itself as White Throat
leads you to observe and listen to the birds, frogs, wolves, beaver,
loons, and ducks. Non-verbal. Available with study guides. Produced by Dan Gibson. (Intermediate-Adult)

WHO ARE THE PEOPLE OF AMERICA?
11 min color Coronet '53
*Award, Freedoms Foundation
Explains where Americans came from, how they fought together, how
they plowed the land, built their cities, and how they are still building to create a finer America. "The people of America are the people of the world, " is the film's theme. (Intermediate)

WHO KILLED LAKE ERIE?
51 min color Films Inc. '69
*Golden Eagle, CINE
*Geo. Peabody Award
Shows how the muck, oil, and debris that cover much of this "Great
Lake" originate from industrial wastes that are carelessly and ille-
gally dumped into this public resource--while government looks the
other way. Produced by NBC Television News. (College-Adult)

WHO KILLED THE SALE?
21 min color Roundtable
*Silver Award, British Industrial
*Golden Camera, US Industrial
*Chris Award, Columbus
This film is a case-study showing how a company that seems to be
in a strong position to win a large sale fails to do so. In this film,
the work and attitudes of employees are seen--showing that all were
partially responsible for the lost sale. The film draws no conclusions, but is open-ended for discussion purposes. Produced by Rank
AV Ltd. (College-Adult)

WHO STOLE THE QUIET DAY?
15 1/2 min color Higgins '74
*Bronze Plaque, Columbus
*Silver Award, Info. Film

*Golden Eagle, CINE

An outline of examples of the contamination caused by loud noises and high frequencies that destroy our nerve cells. Suggests how we can protect ourselves so as to continue to enjoy one of our precious senses. (HS-Adult)

WHO'S RUNNING THINGS?
    5 3/4 min BW Nat. Film Bd.
    *Award, Scholastic Teacher

After a leader is elected, can his supporters override his authority? That is the question a high school gym class tries to answer when their captain penalizes them for breaking regulations. How do you feel about his position? (HS)

WHY DO YOU BUY?
    9 1/2 min color Journal Films '71
    *Blue Ribbon, American/EFLA
    *Chris Bronze Plaque, Columbus

Meet Frank Frontlash and Mildred Maximum. Frank and Mildred are modern consumers. In addition to material needs--food, clothing, shelter--they have psychic needs they try to satisfy. Frank buys love in a tube of toothpaste. The film, through this fictionalized approach, focuses on the emotional elements that enter into buying, and shows how advertising utilizes emotional appeals. Produced by Gilbert Altschul. (Junior-Senior HS)

WHY DO YOU SMILE, MONA LISA?
    14 min color Macmillan '62
    *First Prize, Bergamo

This Czechoslovakian cartoon depicts Leonardo as one of those attic painters who makes his living knocking out portraits and turning out a few tunes and inventions on the side. One of his customers is a husband who would like a picture of his rather dumpy wife, but not with the scowl she usually displays. Leonardo, his assistant, and the husband try to get some reaction from the stubborn woman. Meanwhile, she has her eye on Leonardo's assistant, and has her own idea of what's worth a smile. Produced by Fleetwood Films. (HS-Adult)

WHY MAN CREATES
    25 min color Pyramid '68
    *Oscar, Academy Award
    *Grand Award, Moscow
    *Golden Gate, San Francisco
    *Best Script, Vancouver
    *Grand Award, Berlin ... and many, many other awards

This film is an inquiry into the sources of creativity by the graphics designer Saul Bass. It is a series of explorations, episodes, and comments, including an animated history of the world; illustrations of how ideas begin in the creative mind; a close-up of the process by which scientists develop ideas; and the interplay between the artist and the temper of the times. (HS-Adult)

WHY NOT BE BEAUTIFUL?
>20 min   color   Handel   '69
>*Award, American/EFLA

"Beauty is more than a pretty face--it's a way of life." This is the leitmotiv of this film. Interest in life and the arts, the community, and people are shown as essential elements of a healthy mind. Produced by Leo Handel. (HS-Adult)

WHY THE SUN AND THE MOON LIVE IN THE SKY
>11 min   color   ACI Films   '71
>*Golden Eagle, CINE
>*Honors, American/EFLA

Based on the book by Elphinstone Dayrell, with illustrations by Blair Lent. A legend of eastern Nigeria is brought to life by collage animation and a specially composed score. The story, like most nature myths, has implications beyond the obvious plot. (Primary-Intermediate)

WILD FIRE!
>50 min   color   Films Inc.   '71
>*Golden Eagle, CINE

The saga of the Wenatchee forest fire, one of history's worst, is documented. For 16 days, 8,500 fire fighters face flames, smoke, hot ash, and the fire storm that generates temperatures up to 2500°. Bulldozers batter out fire lines; airplanes and helicopters drop water and chemical retardants; and an army of fire fighters set backfires. Hundreds of years of growth are seen destroyed in a few minutes of film time. An MGM Documentary. (College-Adult)

WILD WATER
>20 min   color   Schloat Prod.   '73
>*Golden Eagle, CINE

Kayak racing is gaining sports interest in the United States. The U.S. Kayak and Canoe Team captured a Bronze Medal at the 1972 Olympics. That team is the subject of this film, from tryouts on New Hampshire's Mascoma River to the World Championship in Italy's scenic resort town, Merano. The viewer is placed at a "kayak's-eye view" of the treacherous course filled with rocks, swirls, and a fifteen-foot drop. Producer: Jon Fauer. (Intermediate-Adult)

WILD WINGS
>35 min   color   Int. Film Bur.   '66
>*Best Short, Academy Award

The Wildfowl Trust at Slimbridge, England, where 122 of the 147 species of ducks, geese, and other wildfowl have been identified. Included are activities such as using blinds to observe feeding, taking eggs of rare species, and using rocket-propelled nets to capture geese for banding. Many species of wildfowl have been photographed, especially in the "mating display" where the male fowl perform. Produced by British Transport Films. (HS-Adult)

THE WILL TO WIN
15 min   color   Pyramid   '70
*First Place, Hollywood
Features scenes of car racing, skiing, rodeo, football, and sky-
diving.   Longer sequences of other action sports include ice hockey,
bullfighting, surfing, motorboat racing, karate, and motorcycling.
The   commentator discusses the motivations of people who engage in
high-risk sports, and asks: Why does man have a will to win?
Also available in a 25-minute version.   Film-maker: Peter Brown.
(HS-Adult)

WIND
8 min   color   ACI Films   '71
*Golden Eagle, CINE
From the "Starting to Read" series, featuring subjects of natural interest to children, accompanied by a lively song.   Key words are
superimposed on the screen, with pronunciation on the soundtrack.
Musical repetition provides reinforcement.   Also available without
captions.   (Primary)

WIND
9 min   color   Learn. Corp.   '73
*Grand Prize, US Animation
With neither narration nor dialogue, this animated film gives a simulation of the sight, sound, and feel of the air in motion ... as experienced by a carefree child.   Produced by Ron Tunis.   (Elem.)

WINDOWS
11 min   color   ACI Films   '70
*Award Winner, Adelaide
*Golden Eagle, CINE
The creation of a modern stained glass window.   There is no narra-
tion.   The photography not only shows the process in detail, but
also conveys the artist's feeling for his craft.   Produced by Yehuda
Yaniv.   (HS-Adult)

THE WINDS OF FOGO
20 1/2 min   color   Nat. Film Bd.
*Award, London(England)
Fogo is an island off the coast of Newfoundland where the inhabitants
for generations have lived by, on, and from the sea.   William Wells,
fisherman, and his two sons take a day off from the nets for a journey to the gannet colony, fifty miles out to sea.   There are close-
up views of enormous flocks of seabirds swarming the cliffs and sky.
(Intermediate-Adult)

THE WINGED WORLD
52 min   color   Films Inc.   '67
*Golden Eagle, CINE
Nature's most eloquent expression--the flight and song of the world's
100 billion birds.   Each of the 8,600 species adds its own nuance to
the language--in courtship, plumage, and migration.   For members
of the winged world, however, the emphasis today is on survival.

While birds have adapted to alterations in living conditions for 150 million years, they cannot change rapidly enough to combat man's assault on the environment. Over 200 species face extinction--an indication of the importance of preserving their natural habitats. Narrated by Alexander Scourby. Also available in 25-minute version. Produced by the National Geographic Society. (College-Adult)

WINKIE, THE MERRY-GO-ROUND HORSE
 11 min color Coronet
 *Merit Certificate, Cleveland
When a merry-go-round horse winks at him, Danny knows that he and "Winkie" are going to be special friends. Off they go into the wonderful world of make-believe, where a cowboy, Indians, and a stagecoach are part of an adventure in which Danny rides the pony express. (Kindergarten-Primary)

WINTER GEYSER
 7 min color Pyramid '66
 *Golden Eagle, CINE
The beauty of Yellowstone Park and its geysers. As autumn ends, leaves swirl and snow begins to fall, elks feed among the snow-laden trees. A fox finds it hard going in the deepening snow. Huge icicles drip in the rays of the rising sun, and the fury of the geysers steaming in the snow creates striking visual contrasts. Filmmaker: Fred Hudson. (Intermediate-Adult)

WINTER OF THE WITCH
 22 min color Learn. Corp. '68
 *First Prize (Children), Chicago
 *Honors, American/EFLA
 *Certificate, Columbus
 *Silver Medal, Venice
 *Golden Eagle, CINE
This story, starring Hermione Gingold as "The Witch," and narrated by Burgess Meredith, shows what happens when Nicky and his mother get acquainted with a not-so-wicked witch, and learn about her recipe for "happiness pancakes." The film offers observations on people and the world, and stimulates children to think about basic values. Based on the book "Old Black Witch" by Harry and Wende Devlin. Produced by Parents Magazine. (Grades K-6)

WINTER ON AN INDIAN RESERVATION
 11 min color Atlantis '73
 *Golden Eagle, CINE
 *Bronze Chris, Columbus
A non-narrative film about children on a forest reservation. Using documentary style, the film shows the rhythm of life and the dependence on and harmony with the environment. Original and ethnic music. (Elem.)

WITCH DOCTOR
 9 min BW Macmillan '52
 *Award Winner, Edinburgh

*Prize Winner, Venice
A dance stylization of a voodoo rite performed by a Haitian witch
doctor, with Jean Léon Destiné dancing the title role. Produced by
Ritter-Young-Lerner Associates. (HS-Adult)

THE WITCHES OF SALEM: The Horror and the Hope
    35 min color Learn. Corp. '72
    *Silver Hugo, Chicago
Exposes the poisonous atmosphere of Puritanic Salem in 1692, when
twenty residents are condemned and hanged for witchcraft. Has man
changed in the intervening centuries or can extremism still panic us
to mindless action? Film-maker: Dennis Azzarella. (HS-College)

WOLVES AND THE WOLF MEN
    52 min   color Films Inc. '71
    *Statuette, Salerno
    *Merit Diploma, Melbourne
    *Golden Eagle, CINE
    *Blue Ribbon, American/EFLA
Legends and superstitions portray wolves as vicious creatures. This
misconception has led to their virtual extinction in the U.S., except
in Minnesota where 300 survive, and in Alaska where a population of
5,000 is quickly diminishing. Actually, wolves never attack humans;
are essential in maintaining healthy deer, moose, and elk populations;
and make friendly, loyal pets. Only a handful of dedicated people,
known as wolf men, are active in the fight to save wolves from wanton destruction by uninformed hunters. It is a race against time,
for before man learns the truth about wolves, he may condemn them
to death. An MGM Documentary (College-Adult)

A WOMAN'S PLACE
    52 min   color Xerox Films '74
    *Golden Eagle, CINE
The traditional role of women and how it is changing in American
society: this is the subject examined in interviews with a cross-
section of individuals and narrator Bess Myerson. Produced by ABC
News. (College-Adult)

WOMEN ON THE MARCH: The Struggle for Equal Rights
    60 min   BW   McGraw-Hill
    *Award, Cannes
    *Honors, New York
Documents the struggle for female suffrage with historical photos of
Emmeline Parkhurst and other radicals who faced prison and humiliation for the sake of their beliefs. From that perspective, the rest
of the film goes on to analyze the current status of women's rights
and achievements. Produced by the National Film Board of Canada.
(College-Adult)

WOO WHO? MAY WILSON
    33 min   color New Day '69
    *Golden Eagle, CINE
When her husband informed her that his plans no longer included her,

318 / Superfilms

May Wilson, a 60-year-old wife-mother-housekeeper-cook-and-grand-
mother, moved to New York City and began the painful process of
working out a new life. In New York she became successful with
her junk assemblage sculpture. She is called the Grandma Moses
of the Underground by the young artists who are her friends. Produced by Amalie Rothschild. (College-Adult)

WOODBLOCK PRINTER
        16 min   color   ACI Films   '68
        *Chris Award, Columbus
Lowell Naeve is shown making a color woodblock print, as the film
follows each state of the process from original design to completed
edition. Mr. Naeve, as the narrator, explains his approach to art,
and describes the procedures as they are demonstrated. Film-
maker: Carson Davidson. (HS-Adult)

THE WOODPECKER GETS READY FOR WINTER
        9 min   color   Moody Institute
        *Award, Scholastic Teacher
Reveals the special manner in which "El Carpentero" woodpecker
stores acorns for winter. As a destroyer of harmful tree insects,
this "carpenter of the forest" is a valuable friend of man. (Elem.)

WOOF WOOF
        10 min   color   McGraw-Hill   '64
        *Scenario Award, Belgrade
        *Animation Award, Belgrade
        *Special Prize, Oberhausen
A bully of a dog is stalemated by a hard-to-bully cat. Both of them
decide to settle matters by enlisting their litters in the fray. But
the young ones are too smart for that and, instead of fighting together, they just play! Animated by Zagreb. (Elem.)

WORDS AND MUSIC
        54 min   BW   McGraw-Hill   '71
        *Series Award, Saturday Review
From the Young People's Concert series, with Leonard Bernstein as
narrator, master of ceremonies, and conductor of the New York
Philharmonic Orchestra. Produced by CBS Television. (Elem.-
Adult)

THE WORLD OF CARL SANDBURG
        59 min   BW   McGraw-Hill   '68
        *TV Award, Edison Foundation
Biographer of Lincoln, poet of Americana, singer of folk music ...
these are some of the facets of the subject. This film is a tribute
to his many contributions to history and the arts. Produced by NET.
A Contemporary Films release. (College-Adult)

THE WORLD OF ENRICO FERMI
        48 min   BW   BFA Educ. Media
        *Chris Award, Columbus
        *Golden Eagle, CINE

*Golden Rocket, CINE
The life and contributions of the scientist who helped transform not
only physics and the style of research, but also the course of history itself.   In following Fermi's work--from the discovery of slow
neutron-induced radioactivity to the nuclear reactor and the A-bomb
--questions are raised about the relationship shared by physics,
technology, and social concerns. Sponsor: Project Physics. (College-Adult)

THE WORLD OF THE BEAVER
        32 min color BFA Educ. Media
        *Golden Rocket, CINE
        *Chris Award, Columbus
Narration by Henry Fonda provides background for this film that follows the beaver from birth through life with its mate. Emphasizes
the ecological role of the beaver and the example it presents to
mankind. Underwater footage shows this champion swimmer in an
environment to which it is superbly suited. Also available in 50-
minute version exploring the behavior and life cycles of the many
animals that share the beaver's habitat. Produced by CBS. (Intermediate-Adult)

WRESTLING
        28 min BW McGraw-Hill '61
        *Prize, Cortina d'Ampezzo
        *Robert J. Flaherty Award
        *Award, American/EFLA
A candid view of professional bouts and backstreet parlors where
the paid gladiators of modern times practice their craft, an unusual
mixture of athletic skill and just plain showmanship. Produced by
the National Film Board of Canada. A Contemporary Films release.
(HS-Adult)

YANKEE CRAFTSMAN
        18 min color Journal '72
        *Golden Eagle, CINE
This film is about a New England cabinetmaker with a trained eye
and an instinct for quality. It is about the way furniture is made,
with older techniques contrasted to the production line. Producer:
Wendy Wood. (HS-Adult)

THE YANKS ARE COMING
        50 min BW Films Inc. '62
        *Academy Award Honors
        *Golden Eagle, CINE
        *Golden Nymph, Monte Carlo
On-the-spot footage shows how the U.S. mobilized its resources in
1917, formed an army (with the help of the draft), and joined its
allies for the offensive climax to World War I. The nation then reflected and counted up the cost of war and its aftermath. Narrator:
Richard Basehart. Made by Metromedia Producers Corp. (College-
Adult)

YEAST DOUGH SHAPING MADE EASY
    14 1/2 min   color   Assn. -Sterling
    *Blue Ribbon, American/EFLA
Shows techniques for making dinner rolls, cinnamon buns, coffee
cake, and foreign specialties ... all from two basic doughs.   Free
loan.   Sponsor: Fleischman's Yeast.   (HS-Adult)

YOU AND OFFICE SAFETY
    8 1/2 min   color   Xerox Films   '68
    *Chris Statuette, Columbus
    *Golden Eagle, CINE
    *Golden Decade, US Industrial ... and many other honors
This film makes its point by using visual hyperbole and sight gags.
It treats the opening and closing of doors, for example, with out-
right slapstick.   Then it warns of the typewriter that is improperly
lifted, the file drawer left open, or the match carelessly tossed into
a waste basket.   Probably the most "decorated" safety film ever
made.   Released by Holland-Wegman Productions.   (HS-Adult)

YOU SEE, I'VE HAD A LIFE
    32 min   BW   Eccentric Circle   '72
    *Academy Award (Student Film)
Documentary of a family realistically facing the imminent death of
a 13-year-old boy.   Raises issues on how family members and medical personnel can relate to such situations.   Producer: Ben Levin.
(HS-Adult)

YUDIE
    20 min   BW   Bank   '74
    *Blue Ribbon, American/EFLA
An elderly woman talks freely about her past and her present.   With
humor and wisdom, she conveys the impression that she knows who
she is, and seems to be trying to help the viewer to achieve this
same awareness.   Written and edited by Mirra Bank.   (HS-Adult)

ZEBRAS
    10 min   color   Texture   '74
    *Finalist, Teheran (Iran)
This is a non-verbal story, with musical effects of how two male
and female animals find each other and then resolve a near tragedy
through the power of love and cooperation.   Animated by John Hagel-
back for G-K Studios of Stockholm, Sweden.   A Choice Films import.
(Elem.)

PART IV

FILM FESTIVALS AND COMPETITIONS

Underlined portions of names represent the partial or abbreviated form given within individual film descriptions

Academy Awards:
Academy of Motion Picture Arts
  & Sciences
Hollywood, California

Acapulco
Film Festival, Mexico

ACT:
Action for Children's Television

Adelaide:
Auckland International Film
  Festival
Australia

AIA:
American Institute of Architects
Washington, D.C.

AICS Congress

American Baptist
Annual Radio-Television Convention

American Bar Association

American/EFLA:
American Film Festival
Education Film Library Associa-
tion
New York

American Personnel and Guidance
  Association Film Festival

Ann Arbor Film Festival
Michigan

Annecy:
International Festival of Ani-
  mated Films
France

Antwerp
International Labor and Indus-
  trial Film Triennial
Belgium

Anvers:
National Festival of Belgian
  Films

APGA:
American Personnel & Guidance
  Association Film Festival
Washington, D.C.

Argentina:
Festival of the Arts

Arnheim Film Festival
Holland

Asian Pacific Film Festival

ASIF-East:
Chapter of the International Animated Film Association

Aspen Design Conference
Aspen, Colorado

Assisi Film Festival
Italy

Associated Press:
Best Local Documentary

321

Atlanta International Film Festival
Georgia

Barcelona
International Week of Color
Films
Spain

Belgian National Film Festival

Belgium:
International Week of Films on
Tourism & Folklore

Belgrade:
Yugoslavian Festival of Short
Films

Bellevue:
International Film Festival
Washington State

Benelux:
Belgium, Netherlands
Luxembourg Film Festival

Bergamo:
International Art Film Festival
Italy

Berlin International Film Festival
Germany

Bilbao Film Festival
Spain

Birmingham Educational Film
Festival
Alabama

Bogotá:
Annual Festival of Short Films
Colombia

Bordighera Film Festival
Italy

Boston:
Film Council of Greater Boston
Massachusetts

British Film Academy

British Film Institute

British Industrial and Scientific
Film Festival

British Society of Film & Arts
(Television)

Broadcast News Magazine

Brussels:
Belgian International Week of
Educational and Teaching
Films

Buenos Aires Film Festival
Argentina

California Center of Films for
Children

California Personnel and Guidance Association

Calvin Workshops:
Calvin Communications Co.
Kansas City, Mo.

Canada Science:
Canadian International Festival
of Films on Science

Canadian Film Award

Cannes Amateur:
International Festival of Amateur
Films
France

Cannes International Film Festival
France

Catholic Broadcasters:
The Gabriel Award

Catholic Film Office (OCIC)

Chevalier de la Barre
Paris

Chicago International Film Festival

Christians and Jews
(National Conference of)

Christopher Movement
Father Keller, Director
New York

CINE:
Council on International Nonthe-
atrical Events
Washington, D. C.

Cinestud:
Student Animation Festival
Amsterdam, Holland

Città di Trento:
City of Trent Film Festival
Italy

Cleveland Annual Film Festival

Colombo Film Festival
Ceylon

Columbia International Film
Festival

Columbus:
Film Council of Greater Colum-
bus
Ohio

Comité International du Cinema
d'Enseignement et de la Culture

Conference on Children
Washington, D. C.

Congress of International Asso-
ciations of Cinematographic
Techniques
Turin, Italy

Cordova International Film Festival

Cortina d'Ampezzo Sports Film
Festival
Italy

Council of Churches of the City
of New York
("Family of Man" Awards)

Council on Drug Abuse Education & Information

Cork International Film Festival
Ireland

Cracow (Krakow)
National Festival of Short Films
Poland

Cultural Documentary
Films on Japan

du-Pont-Columbia University
TV-Journalism Award

Edinburgh International Film
Festival
Scotland

Edison (Thomas Alva) Foundation

Educational Writers Association

Edward R. Murrow
Documentary Award

Federal Artists and Designers
Society
Washington, D. C.

Festival dei Popoli
Festival of the People
Florence, Italy

Filmcentron Foundation & the
Netherlands Film Institute

First International Festival of
Medical Films
West Germany

Flaherty (Robert) Award

Florence
Festival dei Popoli
Festival of the People
Italy

324 / Superfilms

Freedoms Foundation
Valley Forge, Pennsylvania

French Film Critics

French National Film Center

Gabriel Award
Catholic Broadcasters

German Center for Film Classi-
    fication
Wiesbaden

Gijon
Children's Film Festival
Spain

Golden Reel Award
American Film Assembly

Gottwaldov
International Children's Film
    Festival
Czechoslovakia

Grenoble
International Festival of Sports
    Films

Guadalajara Film Festival
Mexico

Hemisfilm
World's Fair International Film
    Festival
San Antonio, Texas

Hollywood
Festival of World Television

Horticultural
American Horticultural Society
International Film Festival

Human Environment
International Film Festival
Montreal (Canada)

Hungarian Critics Award

Independent Film Makers Festival
Foothill College
Los Altos, California

Independent Motion Picture Dis-
    tributors and Exhibitors So-
    ciety

Industrial Photography Magazine
N.Y.C.

Information Film Producers As-
    sociation

International Animated Film
    Festival

International Animation Tournée

International Congress: UNIATEC

International Environmental Film
    Festival

International Federation of Film
    Societies

International Festival of Ani-
    mated Films
Mamaia, Romania

International Film & TV Festi-
    val of New York

International Industrial Film
    Festival
Belgium

International Labor Organization
    Festival, Geneva

International Management Festi-
    val
Society for the Advance of Man-
    agement

International Review of Short
    Films
La Felguera (Spain) & Milan
    (Italy)

International Scientific Film
    Festival
Rio de Janeiro, Brazil

International Security Conference

Italian Film Critics

Italian Society for the Progress
of Science

Japanese Educational Film Festival

Japanese Scientific & Technical
Film Festival

Kennedy (Robert F.)
Journalism Award

King (Martin Luther) Film Festival
Hoboken, New Jersey

Koussevitsky Award for Contemporary Music; U.S.A.

Krakovy Film Festival
Czechoslovakia

Krakow (Cracow)
National Festival of Short
Films
Poland

LaFelguera
International Review of Short
Films
Spain

Landers Associates: (Bertha)
Landers
Film Reviews
Los Angeles, California

LaPlata
International Festival of Films
for Children
Argentina

Leipzig
International Documentary Film
Festival
East Germany

Locarno International Film Festival
Switzerland

London Film Festival
England

Los Angeles International Tournée of Animation

Malta International Film Festival

Mamaia
International Festival of Animated Films, Romania

Mannheim Film Festival
West Germany

Marianske Lazne Film Festival

Martin Luther King, Jr. Film
Festival
M.L.K. Foundation, New York

Melbourne Film Festival
Australia

Mental Health, National Association of

Michigan State University Student Film Festival
East Lansing

Midwest Film Festival
East Lansing, Michigan

Milan International Film Festival
Italy

Monte Carlo
International Catholic Association for Radio and Television

Monterey
Independent Film Makers Festi-
val
California

Montevideo
International Festival of Docu-
mentary and Experimental
Films
Uruguay

Montreal
Canadian Film Festival

Moscow
International Film Festival
USSR

N. A. M. National Association of
Manufacturers
Institute on Industrial Relations

National Academy of TV Arts &
Sciences
U. S. A.

National Agricultural Advertising
& Marketing Association

National Association of TV
Program Executives

National Board of Review
U. S. A.

National Catholic
Office for Motion Pictures
Chicago

National Center of Cinematography

National Committee on Films for
Safety

National Conference of Christians
& Jews

National Council on Family Relations

National Educational Film Festival
Oakland, California

National Film Institute
Argentina

National Headliner Achievement

National Press Photographers

National Safety Council
Chicago

National Student Awards Convention

Lincoln Center, New York

National Visual Presentation Association

NEA
National Education Association
Washington, D. C.

Necochea Film Festival
Argentina

New York International Film &
TV Festival

Newton College of the Sacred
Heart
Massachusetts

Novi Sad
Instructional Festival on Hunting
& Fishing
Yugoslavia

Nyon International Festival
Switzerland

Oberhausen Short Films Festival
West Germany

Ohio State University Film Festival
Columbus

Padua Film Festival
Italy

Paris Biennale des Arts

Peabody (George Foster) Award
for TV Programming Excel-
lence

Philadelphia
International Festival of Short
Films

Photographic Society of America
International Film Festival

Prades Film Festival

Prague Film Festival
Czechoslovakia

Prix du Conseil de l'Europe

Protestant Film Jury

Radio-TV
Council of Greater Cleveland

Red Cross
International Red Cross &
  Health Film Festival
Varna, Bulgaria

Rehabilitation International Congress
Sydney, Australia

Religious Public Relations Council

Rhode Island School of Design
Providence

Rio de Janeiro Film Festival
Brazil

Robert F. Kennedy Journalism
  Award

Rochester (N. Y.) International
  Film Festival

Rome International Exhibition of
  Specialized Cinema (Italy)

Salerno
Short Films International Festival
Italy

St. Lawrence University
Independent Film Makers Compe-
  tition
Canton, New York

San Francisco International Film
  Festival

San Francisco Museum of Art

San Francisco State College
Broadcast Media Awards

San Sebastian Film Festival

Saskatchewan
Swift Current Film Festival
Canada

Saturday Review
Magazine Award for Distin-
  guished TV Programming

Scholastic Teacher Magazine

Seattle (Wash.) Film Seminar/
  Festival

Silver Reel Award
American Film Assembly

Sinking Creek Film Celebration
Greenville, Tenn.

Society for the Advancement of
  Management

Southern California
Social Studies Association

Stamford (Conn.) Annual Film
  Festival

Stratford (Ontario) Film Festival
Canada

Sydney
International Film Festival
Australia

Tehran/Teheran
Festival for Children & Young
  Adults
Iran

Tokyo
Municipal Educational Film Con-
  test
Japan

Toronto Film Festival
Canada

Toulon
International Festival of Marine
  Exploration
France

Tourfilm
Annual Festival
Spindleruv Mlyh, Czechoslovakia

Tours
International Federation of Cine
France

Trento (Trent)
International Festival for Mountain & Exploration Films
Italy

Trieste
Films of Science Fiction
Italy

Trieste International Film Festival

Turin International Film Festival (Italy)

TV Newsfilm Annual Awards

University of Illinois Festival of Contemporary Arts

Vancouver
International Film Festival
Canada

Varna Film Festival

Venice Film Festival
Italy

Venice (Children)
Biennial Exhibition of Films for Children
Italy

Venice (Documentary)
Exhibition of Documentary Films
Italy

Venice (Industrial)
Festival of Commerce, Industry & Agriculture
Italy

Vienna Film Festival
Austria

West German International Short Film Festival

Western Heritage Center

White House Conference on Children, Washington, D.C.

White House News Photographers
Washington, D.C.

Wiesbaden
Center for Film Classification
West Germany

Woodstock
Art Film Festival

Yale University Film Festival
New Haven, Connecticut

Yorkton (Ontario)
Canadian International Documentary Film Festival

Zagreb
International Animated Film Festival
Yugoslavia

PART V

COMPANY-TITLE INDEX

ACI FILMS [ACI Media]

The Art of Age
At Your Fingertips: Boxes
At Your Fingertips: Grasses
Baggage
Bali Today
Barrier Beach
Batik
Being
The Birch Canoe Builder
Brake Free
Career and Costume Circus
Cats and Dogs
Children of the Kibbutz
City Tree
Crayon
Cry of the Marsh
Darwin's Galapagos Today
A Drop of Water
Ducks
The Empty Hand
Exchanges
Fall River Legend
Feather
Figures From a Fable
Flurina
The Flutterbye
Forest Fisherman: Story of an
  Otter
Garden Party
Good Morning, Freedom
The Greater Community Animal
Hopi Kachinas
How Beaver Stole Fire
The Hunter
Imagery in Space
India: Crafts & the Craftsman
Jazzoo
Joanjo: A Portuguese Tale
The Jogger
Junkdump

The Kingfisher
A Little Girl and a Gunny Wolf
Macramé
Maple Sugar Farmer
Masuo Ikeda: Printmaker
Monument to the Dream
Mr. Grey
The Music Rack
Myth of the Pharaohs
Navajo Silversmith
Niko: Boy of Greece
Nobody Goes There: Ellis Island
Open Space
The Owl and the Lemming
Paper Construction
Papier Maché
The Park
Peru: Inca Heritage
Playground
Posters
A Pond
Prints
Psychedelic Wet
The Purple Turtle
Rail
Reflections
Safety As We Play
Snails
Snow
Stitchery
Stolen Necklace
A Storm of Strangers
Stream
Study In Wet
Tahtonka
Textures
Third Avenue El
Tumbleweed
Underground Film
Virginia Woolf: The Moment
  Whole
Weaving

Why the Sun and the Moon Live
  in the Sky
Wind
Windows
Woodblock Printer

AIMS

African Elephant
Freighter
How's School, Enrique?
Information Explosion
Machine in Between

AMERICAN EDUCATIONAL FILMS

Anti-Matter
Caterpillar and the Wild Animals
Continents Adrift
Forest: Trees and Logs
Popsicle
Vote Power

AMERICAN FILM PRODUCTIONS

Drownproofing

ANTI-DEFAMATION LEAGUE

Can We Immunize Against
  Prejudice?
The Victims

ASPECT IV

The People Shop

ASSOCIATION INSTRUCTIONAL MATERIALS and ASSOCIATION-STERLING now ASSOCIATION FILMS

America Goes Camping
Art Is ...
Assignment: Children
Aurum
Carbon
Celebration of Winter
Changing View of Change of Life
Child of Darkness
Cycles
Dangerous Playground
Deep Sea Drilling Project
The Eurail Story

First Aid Now
First Five Minutes
Food, The Color of Life
Glory of Their Times
Golden Transvaal
High in the Himalayas
Inner Mind of Milton Whitty
It Starts at the Top
Just Once
Kids and Cookies
Lake Wilderness
Maine's Harvesters of the Sea
Merchant to the Millions
Miner's Ridge
Monument to the Dream
Place of Hearing
The Redwoods
Return of Milton Whitty
Roadbuilders
Roofer's Pitch
Safe Home
Safety in the Balance
Science of Fire
Secret of Michelangelo
Something Concrete
South Africa's Animal Kingdom
Story of Dr. Lister
Story of the Southern Cross
To Seek, To Teach, To Heal
Viva Mexico!
Wacky Tale of Wilfred Wicken-
  bush
We Came in Peace
West Chicagof!
Yeast Dough Shaping Made Easy

ATLANTIS PRODUCTIONS

Africa Is My Home
African Girl ... Malobi
Ali & His Baby Camel
Ancient Phoenicia
Apryl and Her Baby Lamb
As Long as the Grass Is Green
Asian Earth
Henry ... Boy of the Barrio
Himalaya ... Life on the Roof
  of the World
Hindu Village Boy
History of Southern California
  (Part I) (Part II)
How Vast Is Space?
If Kangaroos Jump, Why Can't
  You?

India and Her Food Problem
Israel ... Nation of Destiny
Jerusalem & Its Contributions
Jerusalem ... Center of Many
   Worlds
Mexican-American Family
Mexican or American?
Mountain Community of the
   Himalayas
Museum ... Gateway to Percep-
   tion
Negro Heroes From American
   History
Negro Kingdoms of Africa's Gold-
   en Age
Nigeria ... Problems of Nation
   Building
Problems of the Middle East
Ricky's Great Adventure
Seacoast Villages of Japan
Tibetan Traders
To Be Somebody
Where Are My People?
Winter On an Indian Reservation

ATTICA FILMS

Attica

AUSTRALIAN INFORMATION SERVICE

Bullocky
Country Jazz
Desert People
Eighteen Footer
Everything Under the Sun
Forest Without Spears
Gallery Down Under
I'm Going to School Today
Kangaroos - Part I
Kangaroos - Part II
The Line Across Australia
Paddington Lace
A Question of Attitude
Shades of Puffing Billy
Sheltered Workshops
Sports Medicine
Style of Champions
Swimmer
Syndey Opera House
Tempo--Australia in the Seventies
Time and Place

A-V EXPLORATIONS

Canada Goose
The Choice ... Is Yours
Great White Pelican
Land of the Loon
Pelican Island
The Robin
Soliloquy of a River
Sounds of Nature
Where the Pelican Builds Her
   Nest
White Throat

(MIRRA) BANK

Yudie

(ARTHUR) BARR FILMS

Ark
By the Sea
Drop of Water
Farm Boy of Hungary
Greenhouse
King of the Hill
Lost Pigeon
Master Kiteman
Mountain Day
Southern Asia
Take Time to See
Watch Out for My Plant
What is Nothing?
Where Should a Squirrel Live?

BEE CROSS-MEDIA

Bayanihan
Texture in Painting

BENCHMARK FILMS

Beginnings of Life
Child Behavior = You
Drugs Are Like That
Grooving
The Hoarder
How to Kill
Southern Accents, Northern
   Ghettos
My Childhood

BFA EDUCATIONAL MEDIA

Aggregation of Dissociated
  Sponge Cells & Species-
  Specific Sorting
The Day Grandpa Died
11:59 Last Minute to Choose
From the Face of the Earth
Harmony of Nature and Man
Jump!
Keep Cool
La Linea
Life Cycle of a Parasitic Flat-
  worm
Men at Bay
Opus Op
Paul Bunyan
People and Particles
Pickles
Pop
Tondo: A Round About a Round
Treehouse
Tub Film
Tup Tup
The World of Enrico Fermi
World of the Beaver

BILLY BUDD FILMS

Mimi
To Be Growing Older

(ROBT.) BLOOMBERG

Animation Pie

BLUE RIDGE FILMS

Basket Builder

BOSTON FILM CENTER

Summerthing

(STEPHEN) BOSUSTOW PRODUC-
TIONS

Is It Always Right To Be Right?

BRIGHAM YOUNG UNIVERSITY

Cipher in the Snow
Love Is for the Byrds
Tomorrow's Yesterday

(WILLIAM) BROSE PRODUC-
TIONS

Bomb Threat! Plan, Don't
  Panic
The Bunco Boys--And How to
  Beat Them!

CANADIAN TRAVEL BUREAU

Island Eden

CAROUSEL FILMS

Ain't Gonna Eat My Mind
Battle of East St. Louis
Bulldozed America
But What If the Dream Comes
  True?
The Cabinet
Case History of a Rumor
Christmas in Appalachia
City of Necessity
Conformity
Golden Age of Comedy
Hunger in America
Inside Red China
"J. T."
The Japanese
Ku Klux Klan
Manhattan Street Band
Mr. Europe & the Common
  Market
No Hiding Place
Now Is the Time
Picasso Is 90
Population Explosion
Pull the House Down
The Road
Road Signs on a Merry-Go-
  Round
The Search for Ulysses
Selling of the Pentagon
Sixteen in Webster Groves
Some Are More Equal than
  Others
Storm Over the Supreme Court
  Part I: 1790-1932
Storm Over the Supreme Court
  Part II: 1933-Present
Swan Song
This Is Edward Steichen

CENTER FOR MASS COMMUNI-
CATIONS (Columbia University)

Alberto Giacometti
All My Babies
Antonio Gaudi
Genesis
Hiroshima-Nagasaki (Aug. 1945)
The Invader
Ladies & Gentlemen, Mr.
  Leonard Cohen
Little Man, Big City
Memento
Planting & Transplanting
Proud Years
Pruning Practices at the Brook-
  lyn Botanic Garden
Robin, Peter and Darryl
To Your Health
Undala
Water

CENTRON EDUCATIONAL FILMS

Age of Exploration & Expansion
Cave Ecology
The Crusades (1095-1291)
The Day that Sang & Cried
Goodbye Lynn
Grassland Ecology
Handling Dangerous Chemicals:
  Acids
The Heritage
Lakes--Aging & Pollution
Leo Beuerman
Maria of the Pueblos
Microphone Speaking
Poetry for Fun: Poems About
  Animals
Populations
Rainy Day Story
Reaching Your Reader
Reporting and Explaining

CHURCHILL FILMS

Eat, Drink and Be Wary
Ivan and His Father
Perils of Priscilla
Us

CINEMA CONCEPTS

Piccolo

COLONIAL WILLIAMSBURG

Time to Begin

CONNECTICUT FILMS

Frederick
The Pleasure Is Mutual

CORONET INSTRUCTIONAL
MEDIA

Abraham Lincoln
Adaptations of Plants & Animals
Alexander Learns Good Health
American Revolution: Back-
  ground Period
American Revolution: Postwar
  Period
American Revolution: War
  Years
Aristotle & the Scientific
  Method
Beethoven & His Music
Beginning Responsibility: Books
  and Their Care
Birds of Our Storybooks
Blow, Wind, Blow!
Boy of Mexico: Juan & His
  Donkey
Boyhood of Abraham Lincoln
Boyhood of George Washington
Boyhood of Thomas Edison
Christmas on Grandfather's
  Farm
Civil War: Background Issues
Colonial Expansion of European
  Nations
Colonial Life in New England
Colonial Life in the Middle Colo-
  nies
Colonial Life in the South
Colorado River (2nd Edition)
Darwin & the Theory of Natural
  Selection
Dawn of the American Revolution
Democracy: Your Voice Can Be
  Heard
Development of the Chick Em-
  bryo
Easter Season
Edgar Allan Poe
Farm Village of India
Farmyard Babies

Federal Taxation (2nd Edition)
Five Colorful Birds (3rd Edition)
Folksongs of the Western Move-
ment
Folksongs of the Western Settle-
ment
Forms of Music: Instrumental
Galileo
Golden Rule: A Lesson for Be-
ginners
Goldilocks & the Three Bears
Harmony in Music
The Holy Land
Honeybee: Social Insect
Human Body: Circulatory System
Human Body: Reproductive Sys-
tem
The Incas
Instruments of the Band and
Orchestra: Introduction
Instruments of the Band and
Orchestra: The Brasses
Jamestown Colony
Japan: Land and People
Johnny Appleseed: Legend of
Frontier Life
Life in Ancient Rome: The
Family
Life of a Philippine Family
Life of Christ in Art
Little Red Hen
Littlest Angel
Liverwort: Alternation of Genera-
tions
Lonnie's Day
Matter and Energy (2nd Edition)
Maurits Escher
Meaning of Patriotism
Our Country's Emblem
Our Living Declaration of Inde-
pendence
Pioneer Journey Across the Ap-
palachians
Pioneer Living: Preparing Foods
Puritan Family of Early New
England
Reformation
Reptiles & Their Characteristics
Robert E. Lee
Safety on the Way to School
Spotty: Story of a Fawn
Story of Electricity
Understanding Our Earth: Soil

U.S. Expansion: California
U.S. Expansion: Texas & the
Southwest
Washington, D.C.
Western Germany: Land & Peo-
ple
What Does Our Flag Mean?
White House: Past & Present
Who Are the People of America?
Winkie, Merry-Go-Round Horse

COUNTERPOINT FILMS

The Audition
Summerplay

CRM EDUCATIONAL FILMS
now McGraw-Hill

Alcoholism: A Model of Drug
Dependency
Cell: Functioning Structure
Emotional Development: Aggres-
sion
Evolution & Origin of Life
Fifth Street
Muscle: Study of Integration
The Heart: Attack

DANA PRODUCTIONS

No Man Is An Island

(RAUL) DA SILVA & OTHER
FILM MAKERS

Chronology

DATAFILMS

Bob & Caren & Ted & Janice

(TOM) DAVENPORT

It Ain't City Music

(WALT) DISNEY EDUCATIONAL
MATERIALS CO.

Patterns

DOCUMENT ASSOCIATES

Fashion

Genetics
The Physicists

DOUBLEDAY MULTI MEDIA

An Actor Works
Age of Exploration
The Bird Room
Careers: Communications
Careers: Health Services
Careers: Leisure Industries
China: The East Is Red
Founding of the American Colonies
The Jewish Wife
Lines, Spines & Porcupines
The Refiner's Fire
The Slave Experience
The Sound of Poetry
The Stronger
What Will Christy Do?

ECCENTRIC CIRCLE CINEMA WORKSHOP

Harold and Cynthia
How Could I Not Be Among You?
Sandman
Tour en l'Air
Trikfilm
You See, I've Had a Life

EDUC. DEVELOPMENT CTR.

Girls at 12

ENCYCLOPAEDIA BRITANNICA EDUC. CORP.

Acid (LSD)
Aging of Lakes
Bird of Prey
Bird Who is a Clown
Blue Dashiki
Boy Creates
Buffalo: Ecological Success Story
Canada Goose Adventure
Casals Conducts: 1964
Cheetah
Country Vet
Crosstown Adventure
Ecology of a Hot Spring

Essay on War
Fantasy of Feet
Fire in the Sea
Fire Mountain
Fish Embryo
Fog
Follow Mr. Willoughby
Frog Prince
Galapagos: Darwin's World
Ganges: Sacred River
Geyser Valley
Haunted House
Heartbeat of a Volcano
High Arctic Biome
Intern: A Long Year
Introduction to Holography
James Dickey: Poet
Lady or the Tiger?
Legend of the Magic Knives
Lemonade Stand
Little Mariner
Making Haiku
Mayfly: Ecology of an Aquatic Insect
Mitosis
Morning on the Lièvre
Newborn Calf
Oops, I Made a Mistake!
Origins of Weather
Power and Wheels
President of the U.S.
Progressive Era
Reflections on Time
Rhythms of Paris
Siqueiros: El Maestro
Soviet Union: Student's Life
Spirit of the Renaissance
Standing Waves & the Principle of Superposition
Tobacco Problem
U.S. Congress (2nd Edition)
Ups/Downs
Venereal Disease
Walt Whitman
Ways of Water

EXTENSION MEDIA CENTER see University of California

FIELDSTAFF FILMS

Spirit Possession of Alejandro Mamani

FILM COMMUNICATORS

Another Man's Family
Fire in My Kitchen
Have a Wonderful Evening
In a Fire ... Seconds Count
Police Pursuit

FILM IMAGES/RADIM

Animated Cartoons: The Toy
  That Grew Up
Artist in Manhattan: Jerome
  Myers
Balzac
Because, That's Why
Biography of the Motion Picture
  Camera
Daguerre: Birth of Photography
Don Quixote (vs. The System)
Emerging Woman
Goya: Disasters of War
Great Jewel Robbery
Grey Metropolis
Highway
Images Medievales
MROFNOC
The Rose & the Mignonette
Venus & the Cat

FILMFAIR COMMUNICATIONS

Acupuncture: An Exploration
America, I Know You
Creative Hands
Fire
Forces Make Forms
Hand and Clay: A Celebration
Horses
How Do You Feel?
I Am Freedom's Child
Making It In the World of Work
Night People's Day
Once There Were Bluebirds
Reach Out
Right On/Be Free
Time Line
What Is a Cat?

FILMS FOR THE HUMANITIES

e. e. cummings: The Making of
  a Poet

FILMS INC.

Alaska!
And Who Shall Feed This World?
Atonement
Bedouins of Arabia
Capitol: Chronicle of Freedom
Childhood: The Enchanted Years
Danny & Nicky
David
The Day Manolete Was Killed
Deep Sea Trawler
The Desert
Dr. Leakey & the Dawn of Man
Dot & the Line
The Empty Quarter
Espolio
Ethiopia: Hidden Empire
Everglades
Flower Lovers
Flowers On a One Way Street
Future for the Past
Great Mojave Desert
Grizzly!
Grizzly Bear
Hello Mustache
Hidden World
Highland Indians of Peru
Industrial Region in Sweden
Japanese Farmers
Journey of Robert F. Kennedy
Kennedy: What Is Remembered
  Is Never Lost
Kifaru: Black Rhinoceros
Let My People Go
The Making of a President, 1960
The Making of a President, 1964
The Making of a President, 1968
Man Hunters
Miners of Bolivia
Miss Goodall & the Wild Chim-
  panzees
Mutiny on the Bounty
New Life for a Spanish Farmer
No Reason to Stay
Norwegian Fjord
Old Fashioned Woman
On the Twelfth Day
Options
Over the Andes in Ecuador
Place in the Sun
Poen
Pre-Raphaelite Revolt

Rice Farmers in Thailand
River People of Chad
Sad Song of Yellow Skin
Say Goodbye
Scarecrow
A Short Vision
Stalin vs. Trotsky
They've Killed President Lincoln
The Unexplained
Water's Edge
Who Killed Lake Erie?
Wild Fire
Winged World
Wolves & Wolf Men
Yanks Are Coming

(ALLAN) GRANT PRODUCTIONS

What Color is the Wind?

GRAPHIC CURRICULUM

El Greco
Of Picks, Shovels & Words

HANDEL FILM CORPORATION

The American Indian
America's Foundations of Liberty
Benjamin Franklin
The Chinese-American: Early
  Immigrants
The Chinese-American: The
  Twentieth Century
George Washington
George Washington's Inauguration
James Monroe
The Japanese-American
The Laser Beam
The Mexican-American
Statue of Liberty
Thomas Jefferson
Valley Forge
Why Not Be Beautiful?

HARTLEY PRODUCTIONS

Evolution of a Yogi

(ALFRED) HIGGINS PRODUCTIONS

Who Stole the Quiet Day?
Ghost Towns of the Westward
  March

IMPACT FILMS

Black Roots
China!
Color of Ritual, Color of
  Thought
Come Back, Africa
Good Times, Wonderful Times
Inside North Vietnam
On the Bowery
The Tattooed Man

INDIANA UNIVERSITY

The Great Gamble: Cyrus W.
  Field
Holidays ... Hollow Days

INTERNATIONAL ASSN. OF
CHIEFS OF POLICE

Management of Conflict

INTERNATIONAL FILM BUREAU

Angotee
Begone Dull Care
Bellota
Birth of the Red Kangaroo
Blades and Brass
Blinkity Blank
Canon
Central Similarities
Chairmaker & the Boys
Chairy Tale
Corral
Dance Squared
Dots
Eternal Children
Eyes
False Note
Fiddle De Dee
Fire in Town
Flight
Happy Anniversary
Hen Hop
I Know an Old Lady Who Swal-
  lowed a Fly
Isometries
Kaleidoscope Orissa
Land of the Long Day, Part II
Le Merle
Lines--Vertical & Horizontal
Long Way Back

Loops
Mosaic
Neighbors
Notes on a Triangle
One Little Indian
Phantasy
Railroaders
Romance of Transportation
Rythmetic
Serenal
Shape of Things
The Shepherd
Short and Suite
Sirene
Symmetries of the Cube
To Speak or Not to Speak
The Unquiet Death of Ethel and
  Julius Rosenberg
Wild Wings

INTERNATIONAL FILM FOUNDATION

American Super 8 Revolution
Ancient Egyptian
Ancient Peruvian
Israel
Japan
The Middle East
Russia
The Stonecutter

JOURNAL FILMS

Why Do You Buy?
Yankee Craftsman

LAWREN PRODUCTIONS

Birth Day

LEARNING CORPORATION OF AMERICA

Boomsville
Bronze
Brown Wolf
Canada: Take It From the Top
Caterpillar
The Changing World of Charles
  Dickens
Christ Is Born
Citizen Harold

The Critic
Denmark 43
Doodle Film
The End of One
Evolution
Fable of He and She
Freud: The Hidden Nature of
  Man
Galileo: Challenge of Reason
Geronimo Jones
Hello, Up There
Hunger (La Faim)
The Interview
Juggernaut: A Film of India
Magic Machines
Me and You, Kangaroo
Medieval England: Peasants'
  Revolt
Miguel--Up From Puerto Rico
Pas de Deux
Pompeii: Once There Was a City
River: Where Do You Come
  From?
Sonnets: Shakespeare's Moods
  of Love
Street Musique
Synchromy
Syrinx/Cityscape
Top of the World
To See Or Not to See
Uppity Al McGuire
Walking
Wind
Winter of the Witch
Witches of Salem

LOUISIANA STATE SCHOOL FOR THE DEAF

Breakthrough to Language

McGRAW-HILL FILMS
see also CRM

A Valparaiso
Adventures of *
America & the Americans
Animal Farm
Anatomy of an Orchestra
Animal Movie
Animation Goes to School
Archaeology
Archangel Gabriel and Mother

Goose
Babel
Ballad of Crowfoot
Beethoven: Ordeal & Triumph
Berlioz Takes a Trip
Bethune
Bighorn
Blake
Blind Bird
Blood & Fire
Cages
Cajititlan
The Cars in Your Life
Chaim Soutine
Chickamauga
The Chicken
Christmas Cracker
Cortez and the Legend
Cosmic Zoom
Cosmopolis/Big City 2000 A. D.
D. H. Lawrence in Taos
Day
Days of Dylan Thomas
Desert People
Desert Victory
Dom
Dream of the Wild Horses
Dulle Griet
The Egg
Ersatz
Eskimo Artist Kenojuak
Family of the Island
Family of the River
Fidelio
Fireman Is Sad & Cries
Five British Sculptors Work &
  Talk
Flatland
Folk Music in Concert Hall
Forever Beethoven
1492
Frederick Douglass
Free Fall
Freedom's Finest Hour
Geneviève
Geology of Yellowstone Park
The Gift
Glass
The Goal
Good Night, Socrates
Great Toy Robbery
Half-Masted Schooner
The Hand

The Hangman
The Hat
Helen Keller
Hobby
The Hole
The House
How Death Came to Earth
Huelga!
Humor in Music
I, Leonardo da Vinci
I'm a Man
In India the Sun Rises in the
  East
Indian Summer
International Atom
Interregnum
Interviews with My Lai Veterans
Jail Keys Made Here
Jazz in the Concert Hall
Journey into Spring
Journey to Chinale
Kienholz on Exhibit
La Joconde
Les Escargots
Little Island
Little Joys, Little Sorrows
Little Spoon
London of Wm. Hogarth
Lonely Boy
Mammals
Man Without a Country
Masque of the Red Death
Mark Twain's America
Martin and Gaston
Matrioska
Matter of Survival
Meet Comrade Student
Memorandum
Multiple Man
Music for the Movies
Nahanni
Naica and the Squirrels
Naked Eye
1964
Not Me
November
Occurrence at Owl Creek Bridge
One-Eyed Men Are Kings
One of Them is Brett
Opera Cordis
Orange and Blue
Over There, 1914-1918
Paddle to the Sea

Passing Days
Perry & Henson
Phoebe
Que Puerto Rico!
The Question
The Quiet One
The Real West
Reflections
River Boy
Rivers of Time
Road to Gettysburg
Robert Scott & the Race for the
  South Pole
Rodeo
Saul Alinsky Went to War
School of Paris
The Season
Secret in the Hive
Shostakovich's 9th Symphony
60 Cycles
Skinny and Fatty
Sky
The Smile
Snowman
Spud's Summer
Stones of Eden
String Bean
Sunday Lark
Symmetry
Tender Game
That's Me
The Thinking Book
Thursday's Children
Time for Burning
Time Piece
Titan: Story of Michelangelo
Toys
21-87
23 Skidoo
Two Ballet Birds
The Wall
Washoe
What Does Music Mean?
What Is a Melody?
What Is Life?
What On Earth?
Women on the March
Woof Woof
Words and Music
World of Carl Sandburg
Wrestling

MACMILLAN FILMS

Adolescence
American Girl
Ares Contre Atlas
Arthur Penn
Assembly Line
Ballet Girl
Bicyclist
Boring Afternoon
The Box
Cassandra Cat
Changing of the Guard
Children Who Draw
Daisy
Day of the Painter
Day with Timmy Page
Double Portrait
Dreamer that Remains
Egg Into Animal
Eleanor Roosevelt Story
Endless Sea
Ephesus
The Face
Fish: Master of Movement
Genesis
Geometry Lesson
Gospel According to St. Matthew
Great Rights
High Lonesome Sound
I Miss You So
Instincts of an Insect
It Starts at the Top
Ivanhoe Donaldson
I've Got This Problem
Japanese Calligraphy
Jealousy
Joachim's Dictionary
Just Sign Here
Krakatoa
Lecture on Man
Legend of Jimmy Blue Eyes
Life Cycle of the Wasp
Mockingbird
Neighboring Shore
New Beam, Laser
Nobody Waved Goodbye
Nothing But a Man
Oil! Spoil!
111th Street
Orozco Murals: Quetzalcoatl
Painting with Tempera
Paris 1900

NATIONAL EDUCATIONAL MEDIA

Courtesy: Inside Story
Decision at Delano
Dining Room Safety
Discipline: A Matter of Judgment
Eye of the Supervisor
Hamburger Sandwich
Kitchen Safety: Preventing Fires
The Training Memorandum

NATIONAL FILM BOARD OF CANADA

Age of the Beaver
Alphabet
Are You Safe at Home?
Around Perception
Ballerina
Best Damn Fiddler from Cala-
   bogie to Kaladar
Bing, Bang, Boom
Caroline
City Out of Time
Cross-Country Skiing
Death of a Legend
Devil's Toy
Dimensions
Early Handling of Special Injuries
Fabienne
Fields of Sacrifice
Figure Skating
First Aid for Air Crew
Flight in White
Four-Line Conics
Ghosts of a River
Go to Blazes
Gold
Here's Hockey
The Hoarder
Hot Stuff
The Hutterites
In One Day
In Search of Innocence
In Search of the Bowhead Whale
Island Observed
Jacky Visits the Zoo
Joy of Winter
LaCrosse
Laurette
Les Fleurs de Macadam
Longhouse People
Magic Molecule

Majority Vote
Manhattan Odyssey
Manouane River Lumberjacks
Mathematics at Your Fingertips
Matter of Fat
Metamorphoses
Mrs. Case
Monastery
Octopus Hunt
One Day's Poison
One Man's Opinion
Op Hop - Hop Op
Paddle to the Sea
People Might Laugh at Us
Perception of Orientation
Pillar of Wisdom
Quebec in Silence
Red Kite
Sabre and Foil
Safe Clothing
Street to the World
Summerhill
Taxi
Temples of Time
The Test
They Called It Fireproof
Vertige
We're Gonna Have Recess
Where Mrs. Whalley Lives
Who's Running Things
Winds of Fogo

NAT. GEOGRAPHIC SOCIETY

Carnivorous Plants
Journey to the Outer Limits

NBC EDUCATIONAL ENTER-PRISES

Alone in the Midst of the Land
Angry Prophet: Frederick
   Douglass
Bank Called Freedom
Beautiful River
Besieged Majority
Between Two Rivers
The Blue Collar Trap
CBW: Secrets of Secrecy
Circus Town
Cities Have No Limits
Cloistered Nun
Cry Help!
Dark Corner of Justice

Down to the Sea in Ships
Drownproofing
Everglades
Fabulous Country
The First Flickers
Footnotes on the Atomic Age
For the Love of Fred
From Yellowstone to Tomorrow
Giants and the Common Men
Give Us the Children
Great Barrier Reef
The Great War--Fifty Years After
Guadalcanal--Island of Death
Hero
Home Country, U. S. A.
How to Make a Dirty River
I'll Never Get Her Back
The Insiders
It Couldn't Be Done
Jefferson's Monticello
Meet George Washington
Metric System
Migrant
Mirror of America
Not the Giant ... Nor the Dwarf
Oh! Woodstock!
Orange and the Green
Pollution Is a Matter of Choice
Quest
Ravaged Earth
Richard II
Room to Breathe
Sahara
Ship that Wouldn't Die
Slow Guillotine
Suffer the Little Children
Survival on the Prairie
This Child Is Rated X
Three from Illinois
Trip to Nowhere
The Ultimate Trip
Valley of Darkness
VD: A Plague on Our House
Venice Be Damned
Voices Inside
The West of Charles Russell
What Man Shall Live and Not
  See Death?

NEUBACHER-VETTER PRODUC-
TIONS

How Do We Know?
Land of the Swiss

Spain--Proud Past & Promising
  Future

NEW DAY FILMS

Anything You Want to Be
Betty Tells Her Story
Men's Lives
Woo Who? Mary Wilson

THE NEW FILM COMPANY

No Expectations
The War Comes Home

NEW LINE CINEMA

The Father
Shadow of an Apple
Stop in the Marshlands
This Man Is Not Dying of Thirst

OPEN CIRCLE CINEMA

I. F. Stone's Weekly

OXFORD FILMS
[Paramount-Oxford]

Annabel Lee
Audition
Big Red Barn
Busted
Cheating
Children in the City
Conrad, Josie and the Zoomerang
The Creation
Cry for Help
Dead Bird
Francine, George and the Ferry-
  boat
Friends & Aliens
Haiku
Henry
James Weldon Johnson
The Matter with Me
Methods of Family Planning
Painting & Drawing with Ex-
  pression
Ponies
Summerplay
Tommy, Suzy and the Cardboard
  Box
Values & Goals: A Way to Go

PACIFIC ST. FILM COLLECTIVE

Frame-up!

PARAMOUNT-OXFORD
see Oxford Films

PERENNIAL EDUCATION

Berfunkle
Electric Safety ... From A to Zap
Like Other People
Sam's Secret
What's It Going to Cost You?

PERSPECTIVE FILMS

Kinetic Sculpture of Howard
 Barlow
Pandora's Box
Rembrandt: Painter of Man
Slavery & Slave Resistance
Transportation: A Ship Comes
 Home

PHOENIX FILMS

Abyss
Antonia
Close-up on Fire
Dorothy and the Pop Singer
Katutura
Land Divers of Melanesia
No Lies
The Raft
Rivers of Sand

PICTURA FILMS DISTRIBUTION
CORP.

The Charm of Life
Leonardo da Vinci: Man of
 Mystery
Van Gogh

PRENTICE-HALL MEDIA
see Schloat Prod.

PYRAMID FILMS

American Time Capsule
Americans on Everest
Arena
Autumn: Frost Country

Balloon Tree
Bolero
Brazil: I Love You
Capt. Arbanos Marko
Catch the Joy
Claude
Claw
Closed Mondays
Cockaboody
Concert of M. Kabal
Concrete Poetry
Dancing Prophet
Dunes
Energy
Experiments in Motion Graphics
Frank Film
From Here to There
Gate 73
Hang Ten
Have a Heart
Homage to Rodin
Icarus Montgolfier Wright
Iran
Life Times Nine
Lover's Quarrel with the World
Machine
Moebius Flip
Moods of Surfing
Multiply & Subdue
New York, New York
Nzuri: East Africa
Omega
Opus
The Pigs vs. the Freaks
Renaissance
Rise & Fall of the Great Lakes
Searching Eye
Sentinel: West Face
The Sixties
Skater Dater
Ski Racer
Ski the Outer Limits
Sky Capers
Solo
This Is the Home of Mrs. Levant
 Graham
Thoroughbred
Threshold
Tokyo
Up Is Down
Waters of Yosemite
Why Man Creates
The Will to Win
Winter Geyser

TEXTURE FILMS

Dogs, Cats and Rabbits
Zebras

TIME-LIFE MULTIMEDIA

America--Gone West
Christians at War
City That Waits to Die
Communicating Successfully
Eyes of a Child
Gale Is Dead
Golda Meir
Imogen Cunningham, Photographer
Jesus Trip
Koestler on Creativity
Not-So-Solid Earth
Our Poisoned World
Private Life of the Kingfisher
Rock-A-Bye-Baby
Search for the Nile Part 1
Search for the Nile Part 2
Search for the Nile Part 3
Search for the Nile Part 4
Search for the Nile Part 5
Search for the Nile Part 6
Sticky My Fingers, Fleet My
  Feet
Three Looms Waiting
Tokyo--51st Volcano
Vivaldi's Venice
Watersmith

TRANS-WORLD FILMS

Miguelin

UNIVERSAL EDUCATION & VISUAL ARTS

Embryonic Development of the
  Chick
Embryonic Development of the
  Fish

UNIV. OF ALASKA

At the Time of Whaling

UNIV. OF CALIFORNIA
  (Extension Media Center)

Deaf Child Speaks

VOCATIONAL FILMS

After High School--What?

VORPAL GALLERIES

Inside the World of Jesse Allen

WARD'S NATURAL SCIENCE see Modern Learning Aids

WARNER BROTHERS

Sky Over Holland
Teen Scene

WASHBURN FILMS

Scraps
The Swing
Vesak

WESTON WOODS STUDIO

Alexander & the Car with the
  Missing Headlight
All Gold Canyon
Andy and the Lion
Changes, Changes
Drummer Hoff
The Foolish Frog
The Fox Went Out on a Chilly
  Night
The Happy Owls
Lentil
Leopold, the See-Through Crumb-
  picker
Little Red Lighthouse
Lively Art of Picture Books
Mr. Shephard & Mr. Milne
Patrick
Rosie's Walk
Sorcerer's Apprentice
Stone Soup
The Story about Ping
This Is New York
The Three Robbers

WOMBAT PRODUCTIONS

Almost Everyone Does
I Think
Joseph Schultz
A Journey

Mila 23
Mountain People
My Son, Kevin
To Love

XEROX FILMS

Crash, Bang, Boom
Danze Cromatiche
DDT--Knowing It Survives Us
Fable
Firefly Named Torchy
The Guitar
I Got Six
If You Hear the Explosion, the
  Danger Has Passed
Industrial Hygiene
Journey Into Summer
Navajo Girl
North With the Spring
Prime Time
Role of the Congressman
Strange Story of a Frog Who
  Became a Prince
The Voter Decides
Weird Number
A Woman's Place
You and Office Safety

ZIPPORAH FILMS

Hospital
Law and Order

PART VI

FILM COMPANIES:
Addresses and Abbreviations

ACI MEDIA
35 West 45th Street
New York, New York 10036

AIMS
AIMS Instructional Media
P. O. Box 1010
Hollywood, California 90028

AMERICAN EDUC.
American Educational Films
331 North Maple Drive
Beverly Hills, California 90210

AMERICAN FILM PRODUCTIONS
1540 Broadway
New York, New York 10036

ADL
Anti-Defamation League
of B'nai Brith
315 Lexington Avenue
New York, New York 10016

ASPECT IV
Educational Films
21 Charles Street
Westport, Connecticut 06880

ASSN. FILMS
Association Films
866 Third Avenue
New York, New York 10022

ASSOC. INTERNATIONAL
MATERIALS and ASSOCIATION
STERLING see Assoc. Films

ATLANTIS
Atlantis Productions
1252 La Granada Drive

Thousand Oaks, California
91360

ATTICA
Attica Films, Inc.
789 West End Avenue
New York, New York 10025

AUSTRALIAN INFO.
Australian Information Service
636 Fifth Avenue
New York, New York 10020

A-V EXPLOR.
A-V Explorations
505 Delaware Avenue
Buffalo, New York 14202

BANK
Mirra Bank
347 West Broadway
New York, New York 10012

BARR FILMS
(Arthur) Barr Productions
P. O. Box 7-C
Pasadena, California 91104

BEE CROSS-MEDIA
36 Dogwood Glen
Rochester, New York 14625

BENCHMARK
Benchmark Films
145 Scarborough Road
Briarcliff Manor, New York
10510

BFA EDUC. MEDIA
BFA Educational Media
2211 Michigan Avenue

Santa Monica, California 90404

BILLY BUDD FILMS
235 East 57th Street
New York, New York 10022

BLOOMBERG
Robert Bloomberg
5857 Skyline
Oakland, California 94611

BLUE RIDGE FILMS
9003 Glenbrook Road
Fairfax, Virginia 22030

BOSTON FILM CENTER
25 Church Street
Boston, Massachusetts 02116

BOSUSTOW
(Stephen) Bosustow Productions
1649 Eleventh Street
Santa Monica, California 90404

BRIGHAM YOUNG UNIV.
Motion Picture Department
Provo, Utah 84602

BROSE PROD.
(Wm.) Brose Productions
3168 Oakshire Drive
Hollywood, California 90068

CANADIAN TRAVEL BUREAU
1251 Ave. of the Americas
New York, New York 10020

CAROUSEL FILMS
1501 Broadway
New York, New York 10036

CENTRON EDUC. FILMS
1621 West Ninth Street
Lawrence, Kansas 66044

CHURCHILL FILMS
622 North Robertson Blvd.
Los Angeles, California 90069

CINE CONCEPTS
Cinema Concepts
Chester, Connecticut 06412

CMC /COLUMBIA
Center for Mass Communication
Columbia University Press
136 South Broadway
Irvington, New York 10533

COLONIAL WILLIAMSBURG
AV Distribution Center
Williamsburg, Virginia 23185

CORONET
Coronet Instructional Media
65 East South Water Street
Chicago, Illinois 60601

CONN. FILMS
Connecticut Films
6 Cobble Hill Road
Westport, Connecticut 06880

COUNTERPOINT FILMS
Counterpoint Films
5823 Santa Monica Boulevard
Hollywood, California 90038

CRM EDUCATIONAL FILMS
see McGraw-Hill

DANA PRODUCTIONS
Div. of Saparoff Films
6249 Babcock Avenue
North Hollywood, California
91606

DASILVA
Raul da Silva & Other Film
Makers
1400 East Avenue
Rochester, New York 14610

DATAFILMS
2625 Temple Street
Los Angeles, California 90026

DAVENPORT
(Tom) Davenport Films
Pearlstone, Dept. DM
Delaplane, Va.   22025

DISNEY
(Walt) Disney Educational
Materials Company

800 Sonora Avenue
Glendale, California 91201

DOCUMENT ASSOC.
Document Associates
573 Church Street
Toronto 285, Ontario

DOUBLEDAY MULTIMEDIA
1371 Reynolds Avenue
Santa Ana, California 92705

ECCENTRIC CIRCLE
Cinema Workshop
Box 1481
Evanston, Illinois 60204

ED. DEVEL. CTR.
Educational Development Center
39 Chapel Street
Newton, Massachusetts 02160

ENCYC. BRIT.
Encyclopaedia Britannica
Educational Corporation
425 North Michigan Avenue
Chicago, Illinois 60611

EXTENSION MEDIA CENTER
see University of California

FIELDSTAFF FILMS
American Universities Field Staff
3 Lebanon Street
Hanover, New Hampshire 03755

FILM COMMUNICATORS
11136 Weddington St.
North Hollywood, Calif. 91601

FILM IMAGES
Film Images/Radim
17 West 60th Street
New York, New York 10023

FILMFAIR COMMUNICATIONS
10900 Ventura Blvd.
Studio City, California 91604

FILMS, INC.
Films, Incorporated
1144 Wilmette Avenue
Wilmette, Illinois 60091

FILMS/HUMANITIES
Films for the Humanities
P.O. Box 378
Princeton, New Jersey 08540

GRANT PROD.
(Allan) Grant Productions
808 Lockearn Street
Los Angeles, California 90049

GRAPHIC CURRICULUM
P.O. Box 565, Lenox Hill
New York, New York 10021

HANDEL FILM CORPORATION
8730 Sunset Boulevard
West Hollywood, California
90069

HARTLEY PRODUCTIONS
Cat Rock Road
Cos Cob, Connecticut 06807

HIGGINS PROD.
(Alfred) Higgins Productions
9100 Sunset Boulevard
Los Angeles, California 90069

INT. FILM FOUND.
International Film Foundation
475 Fifth Avenue, Suite 916
New York, New York 10017

IMPACT FILMS
144 Bleecker Street
New York, New York 10012

INDIANA UNIVERSITY
A-V Film Sales
Bloomington, Indiana 47401

INT. ASSN./POLICE
International Assn. of Chiefs of
Police
11 Firstfield Road
Gaithersburg, Maryland 20760

INT. FILM BUR.
International Film Bureau
332 South Michigan Avenue
Chicago, Illinois 60604

JOURNAL FILMS

Journal Films
909 Diversey Parkway
Chicago, Illinois 60614

LAWREN PRODUCTIONS
1881 Rollins Rd. -Suite C
Burlingame, California 94010

LEARN. CORP.
Learning Corp. of America
1350 Ave. of the Americas
New York, New York 10019

LOUISIANA STATE SCHOOL
FOR THE DEAF
800 St. Ferdinand Street
Baton Rouge, Louisiana 70821

McGRAW-HILL FILMS
1221 Avenue of the Americas
New York, New York 10020

MACMILLAN FILMS
866 Third Avenue
New York, New York 10022

MALIBU FILMS
P.O. Box 428
Malibu, California 90265

MARINER
Mariner Productions
16 East Main Street
Rochester, New York 14614

MASS MEDIA ASSOCIATES
2116 North Charles Street
Baltimore, Maryland 21218

MEDIA FIVE FILM DISTRIBUTORS
1011 North Cole Avenue, Suite 9
Hollywood, California 90038

MIC/FP
MIC/FP Project
377 Broadway
New York, New York 10013

M. L. KING
Martin Luther King Foundation
309 East 90th Street
New York, New York 10028

MODERN LEARNING AIDS see
Ward's Natural Science

MOODY
Moody Institute of Science
12000 E. Washington Blvd.
Whittier, California 90606

NAT'L AV CTR.
National Audio-Visual Center
National Archives (GSA)
Washington, D.C. 20409

NAT. EDUC. MEDIA
National Educational Media
15250 Ventura Blvd.
Sherman Oaks, California
91403

NAT. FILM BD.
National Film Board of Canada
1251 Avenue of the Americas
New York, New York 10020

NAT. GEO.
National Geographic Society
17th and M Street NW
Washington, D.C. 20036

NBC EDUC.
NBC Educational Enterprises
c/o Films, Incorporated
1144 Wilmette Avenue
Wilmette, Ill. 60091

NEUBACHER-VETTER
Film Productions
1750 Westwood Boulevard
Los Angeles, California 90024

NEW DAY FILMS
P.O. Box 315
Franklin Lakes, New Jersey
07417

THE NEW FILM COMPANY
331 Newbury Street
Boston, Massachusetts 02115

NEW LINE
New Line Cinema
121 University Place
New York, New York 10003

OLENYIK
(Andy) Olenyik Films
10927 Carroll Wood Way
St. Louis, Missouri 63128

OPEN CIRCLE CINEMA
P.O. Box 315
Franklin Lakes, New Jersey
07417

OXFORD see PARAMOUNT
OXFORD

PACIFIC ST.
Pacific Street Film Collective
280 Clinton Street
Brooklyn, New York 11201

PARAMOUNT-OXFORD FILMS
1136 North Las Palmas Avenue
Los Angeles, California 90038

PERENNIAL ED.
Perennial Education
1825 Willow Road
Northfield, Illinois 60093

PERSPECTIVE
Perspective Films
369 West Erie Street
Chicago, Illinois 60610

PHOENIX FILMS, INC.
470 Park Avenue South
New York, New York 10016

PICTURA FILMS
43 West 16th Street
New York, New York 10011

PRENTICE-HALL MEDIA
150 White Plains Road
Tarrytown, New York 10591

PYRAMID FILMS
P.O. Box 1048
Santa Monica, California 90406

RED CROSS
American National Red Cross
Public Relations Office
18th and E Street NW
Washington, D.C. 20006

ROCHESTER INSTITUTE OF
TECHNOLOGY
Rochester, New York 14623

ROLAND
The Roland Collection
1825 Willow Road
Northfield, Illinois 60093

ROUNDTABLE FILMS
113 North San Vicente Blvd.
Beverly Hills, California 90211

SCHLOAT see PRENTICE-HALL
MEDIA

SCREENSCOPE, INC.
1022 Wilson Boulevard
Arlington, Virginia 22209

SIM PRODUCTIONS
Weston Woods Studio
Weston, Connecticut 06880

STANFIELD HOUSE
900 Euclid Avenue
Santa Monica, California 90403

STANTON FILMS
7934 Santa Monica Blvd.
Los Angeles, California 90046

STERLING EDUC.
Sterling Educational Films
241 East 34th Street
New York, New York 10016

STOUFFER PRODUCTIONS
P.O. Box 15057
Aspen, Colorado 81611

TeleKETICS
Franciscan Communications Ctr.
1229 South Santee Street
Los Angeles, Calif. 90015

TEXTURE FILMS
1600 Broadway
New York, New York 10019

TIME-LIFE MULTIMEDIA
43 West 16th Street
New York, New York 10011

354 / Superfilms

Trans-World Films
332 South Michigan Avenue
Chicago, Illinois 60604

UNIVERSAL EDUC.
Universal Education & Visual Arts
445 Park Avenue
New York, New York 10022

U. OF ALASKA
University of Alaska
Native Heritage Film Project
Fairbanks, Alaska 99701

UNIV. OF CALIFORNIA
Extension Media Center
Berkeley, California 94720

VOCATIONAL FILMS
111 Euclid Ave.
Park Ridge, Illinois 60068

Vorpal Galleries
1168 Battery Street
San Francisco, California 94111

WARD'S NATURAL SCIENCE
Modern Learning Aids Division
P.O. Box 1712
Rochester, New York 14603

WARNER BROS.
Non-Theatrical Division
4000 Warner Blvd.
Burbank, California 91522

WASHBURN FILMS
9 East 32nd Street
New York, New York 10016

Weston Woods Studio
Weston, Connecticut 06880

Wombat Productions
87 Main Street
Hastings-on-Hudson, New York
10706

XEROX FILMS
245 Long Hill Road
Middletown, Connecticut 06457

ZIPPORAH
Zipporah Films
54 Lewis Wharf
Boston, Massachusetts 02110

DATE LOANED

OCT 14 1989			
GAYLORD 3563			PRINTED IN U.S.A.